Johnny Cash FAQ

Johnny Cash FAQ

All That's Left to Know About the Man in Black

C. Eric Banister

An Imprint of Hal Leonard Corporation

Published in 2014 by Backbeat Books
An Imprint of Hal Leonard Corporation
7777 West Bluemound Road
Milwaukee, WI 53213

Trade Book Division Editorial Offices
33 Plymouth St., Montclair, NJ 07042

The FAQ series was conceived by Robert Rodriguez and developed with Stuart Shea.

Kevin Sport's interview with Larry Butler used by permission.
Gun World magazine cover used by permission.

Printed in the United States of America

Book design by Snow Creative Services

Library of Congress Cataloging-in-Publication Data

Banister, C. Eric.
Johnny Cash FAQ : all that's left to know about the man in black / C. Eric Banister.
pages cm
Includes bibliographical references and index.
ISBN 978-1-4803-8540-5
1. Cash, Johnny. 2. Country musicians—United States—Biography. 3. Cash, Johnny—Miscellanea. I. Title. II. Title: Johnny Cash frequently asked questions.
ML420.C265B36 2014
782.421642092—dc23
[B]

2014012206

www.backbeatbooks.com

To Brittany, Porter, and Claire

Contents

Foreword

Johnny Cash. The name resonates. Everywhere. With everyone; young, old, without regard to gender, race, or creed.

I knew Johnny Cash on a personal level for some forty years. As a child, he was my favorite singer and my hero. Later in life, he became my friend, a man who was humble, sincere, compassionate, complicated, and conflicted. Throughout the forty years I knew and observed him, he never fell off the pedestal I had placed him on when I was nine years old. Despite the recurring bouts with drug dependency, the career ups and downs, and the triumphs and tragedies he experienced throughout our friendship, he always remained the same human being. The fabric of the man may have unraveled at times, but his heart, soul, and integrity always endured.

During those four decades, Johnny and I spent a lot of time together, and I never ceased being his greatest fan. I launched his official website in 1996, well before more than a handful of celebrities even knew what a website was (and Johnny didn't!). In fact, to put things into perspective, JohnnyCash.Com launched within six months of the Microsoft website.

As you will read in C. Eric Banister's fine book, there were several Johnny Cashes in various carnations through his amazing fifty-plus-year career. Cash was many things to many people—a humble farm boy who sang of his childhood experiences back in Dyess, Arkansas, the young troubadour who drove to hundreds of concert dates a year, fueled by raw ambition and a determination to give the folks a show, the edgy rebel who knocked out every footlight on the stage of the Grand Ole Opry, the man who nearly killed himself with amphetamines and barbiturates, all the while scoring millions selling records, the guy who took a recording crew into one of California's most dangerous penitentiaries to record one of his best known albums, the entertainer who hosted a groundbreaking variety show on primetime television, the redeemed follower of Christ who threw himself into making a feature film on his savior, the superstar whose career skidded to a near halt in the 1980s after he was unceremoniously dropped from the record label he sold millions and millions of records on, and, finally, the aged-yet-hip icon who reinvigorated himself and his career after pairing with hip hop record producer Rick Rubin for a series of stark and brilliant records, which would expose him to an entirely new generation of fans.

This past year, I opened the Johnny Cash Museum in Nashville, Tennessee. I felt that it was akin to a crime for Johnny Cash to not have a major presence in the very town he nearly single-handedly put on the map by virtue of spending the majority of his life and career based in the city. Yet, despite his impact on the town, it had almost been denuded of any fingerprints he might have left behind. Other than a few T-shirts and souvenirs bearing his image, the downtown area visited by millions of tourists from around the world was nearly devoid of anything Cash. Today, we offer visitors an intimate and comprehensive exhibit chronicling the man's personal and professional life in a setting that has received accolades and awards from the most prestigious critics and publications in the world. Johnny Cash is back in Nashville, and he's here to stay.

What C. Eric Banister has accomplished on the pages that follow is something of a historical museum archive in words. Every day, visitors from around the world cause our museum team to dig into the Johnny Cash FAQ bag. "Was he in prison?" "Why did he wear black?" "Did he and June really love each other as portrayed in the movie?" These and many other questions arise daily. They never cease as Johnny's impact, presence, and popularity increase every day, despite the fact that he passed over a decade ago.

Dig into this amazing collection of facts. Learn things you didn't know about Johnny Cash's career. The records, the influences, those he influenced, and much more. There are things I didn't know, which I found on these pages. It's a great reference and a great read. I know it will be placed among the books I reach for when I want to know more about my late, great friend.

Bill Miller
Founder of the Johnny Cash Museum

Acknowledgments

Thanks to the many writers I've read who have helped me gain insight and knowledge on this thing I love—music.

Thanks to the writers who've given me time to talk and who continue to produce great work that inspires me: David Cantwell, Don Cusic, Barry Mazor, Alanna Nash, and John Rumple.

Thanks to Dale Sherman, my fellow FAQ'er, who took a chance and recommended me to his editor. Thanks to Robert Rodriguez, that editor who took a chance and recommended me to Hal Leonard Performing Arts Publishing Group. Thanks to Backbeat Books editor Bernadette Malavarca for her immense patience and her guiding hand, and to publisher John Cerullo for running such a fine operation. Thanks to copyeditor Tom Seabrook for making my work presentable.

Thanks to the great Cash historians: Peter Lewry—your work and research is a fantastic resource and an honor to Cash's enduring legacy; Mark Steipler—thank you for answering my questions and helping point me in interesting directions; and to the late John L. Smith, who did more Cash research than anyone and to whom this work is indebted. Bill Miller—you've made Nashville into the Mecca for Cash fans with the Johnny Cash Museum! The work and research you've put in is astounding and serves as an example of following one's passion and honoring a friend's legacy.

Thanks to my family: my Mom for always encouraging me to do what I love; my Dad for being a music fan; my Aunt Kathy for leaving behind some great records when she moved out of my Grandma's; my Uncle Randy, who is still just as enthusiastic about a new music find as he was when I was in single digits thumbing through his record collection; Aaron, Joy, Aiden, Maggie, and Aubrie, thanks for the encouragement and laughs.

My greatest thanks go to the three who have to put up with me the most: my wife, Brittany, who put up with my weird moods, stacks of books, records, and CDs, and allowed me to pursue this. I adore you, and I love you more every day. Porter, a Cash fan since birth: thanks for letting Daddy miss a few things in order to write. Claire, my silly sweetie: I can come out of the laundry room now.

Introduction

I guess I have Dick Clark to thank for introducing me to Johnny Cash. Though I'm sure I had heard his music in the background of life, one moment at around age six stands out the most. My grandma lived just down the road from us when I was growing up, and we used to spend a lot of time at her house. My uncle and aunt had left behind records when they moved out, so I spent a lot of time listening through the stacks of 45s and LPs. One of them was a double album called *Dick Clark: Twenty Years of Rock N' Roll,* and there, placed between Carl Perkins' rockabilly rave-up "Blue Suede Shoes" and Fats Domino's bouncy "I'm Walkin'," I found "I Walk the Line." The song stuck out—even to a six-year-old. It seemed darker than any of the other songs on the album. There was something about the singer that drew me in, made me listen.

This scenario isn't unique to me. Countless people share—and probably will continue to share—the same story of the first time they heard Johnny Cash. His music was his own—incomparable to anyone else's—and from the beginning, his unique talent captured listeners of all ages. In the early part of his career, he was claimed by country-music fans and young rockabillies alike, and by the end of his life, he had been inducted into the Country Music Hall of Fame, the Rock and Roll Hall of Fame, the Gospel Music Hall of Fame, and the Songwriters Hall of Fame.

Despite these accolades, it seems to me that his music has always been pushed into the background of any story told about him. Drug addiction became the central point of many of the stories written about him—even ones that he himself told. And after the drug addiction, the second headline is always the fairytale love story of Johnny and June Carter. That story often intermingles with the drug story, making June the savior that rescued him from certain doom.

Sure, Cash's life had all of the makings of a Hollywood blockbuster, what with the girls and the money and the fame and the pain—and indeed it eventually became one, in the form of 2006's *Walk the Line.* And sure, his life story tells a fascinating tale of caution and redemption, but what gets left behind is the music—the thing that everyone loves the most about him. Of all of the books written about him, none is fully focused on the music. And yet Cash left a legacy of recorded music that spanned forty-seven years. It is a legacy filled with incredible music, all of it worth examining.

Cash's time at Sun Records may have been brief in the context of his whole career, but it produced some of his best-known and most definitive songs. The music he recorded at 706 Union Avenue laid the foundation for the sound he would carry through his whole career.

In the 1960s, Cash worked hard to grow as an artist, releasing concept albums on topics that interested him, from the history of the True West to the plight of the Native American. His career dipped through the mid-'60s, as addiction took hold, but even then he continued to produce hit records that endure to this day.

By the end of the decade, Cash had come into the light. He was now one of the biggest names in music. With a weekly television show and a string of #1 albums, he was an American icon as the 1970s dawned. He continued to grow as an artist, releasing vital music that is often overlooked today—in large part because it doesn't fit in with the dark image of Cash the rebel—including a string of gospel recordings, into which he poured more time and energy than any of his other projects.

Those gospel recordings were Cash's lifeline as he transitioned into the 1980s. His mainstream work often paled in comparison. The decade also brought the supergroup of the Highwaymen: Cash, Willie Nelson, Waylon Jennings, and Kris Kristofferson. The group went to the top of the charts, but Cash could no longer reach it as a solo artist. By the midpoint of the decade, Columbia Records, his label of over thirty years, had released him. He landed next at Mercury, where he made a series of albums that are largely overlooked.

In the early 1990s, Cash was a man adrift, releasing only a new gospel project and a Christmas album. And then he hooked up with Rick Rubin, for the *American Recordings* series. Those recordings found Cash a new audience, solidifying his reputation as a musical icon to fans of all ages.

The aim of this book is to expand on some of the music you might know about, and to introduce you to some of the music you might not have heard. To do that, we will be looking at some of the stories behind the songs and albums. We'll put much of it in context, in terms both of Cash's life and also whatever else was going on in the world of music at the time. And although it is true that chart success doesn't always mean artistic success, we'll examine Cash's chart runs as a gauge of how the public, radio, and the industry accepted or rejected him at various points during his career.

C. Eric Banister
Scottsburg, IN
February 2014

Johnny Cash FAQ

1

Where Did All of the Old Songs Go?

The Roots of Johnny Cash

"You wouldn't believe how many different kinds of things he listened to," Marshall Grant told writer Hank Davis in 2006. "He just absorbed everything he heard." On *Personal File*, also released in 2006, Cash himself can be heard, in a recording from 1973, introducing a song by recalling, "Some of those old songs that I used to sing when I was a kid, I still remember every word to 'em."

J. R. Cash grew up in Depression-era Arkansas, and music became an escape for him—as it did for many people, young and old, right across the country. In 1935, when Cash was three, his family was selected to move from Kingsland, Arkansas, to a new home in the town of Dyess, a community that had sprang up under the New Deal to help farmers who needed a fresh start. The program was run by the Federal Emergency Relief Administration, with each family chosen receiving twenty acres of land, a house, a barn, a mule, a cow, and the first year of groceries, all to be repaid once crops started coming up. The crop in that rich soil was cotton, but before it could be planted, the family would have to clear the land.

Johnny wasn't the only member of the Cash family for whom music became a lifeline. In 1939, his eldest brother, Roy, began playing with a local group called the Delta Rhythm Ramblers. After a short stint on a radio show and victory in a local talent contest, Roy was drafted into the army, and was soon out of Dyess, leaving behind younger sister Louise, brothers Jack and J. R., and baby sister Reba.

Johnny continued to listen intently to the radio, dreaming of one day becoming one of the voices being broadcast. It was at this time that he first began to absorb the songs, learning as many as he could listen to. In introducing the song "There's a Mother Always Waiting at Home" on *Personal File*, he says:

> I learned a lot of them from the radio—I learned a lot of them from the boys that lived across the road, the Williams boys. There was Guy and Otis Williams, Jack Williams. They didn't play the guitar or anything, but they sang a little bit, and they had a Victrola that they played those old

> records on. There was Cowboy Slim Rinehart, there was the Carter Family, and there was Jimmie Rodgers, and there was Clayton McMichen. There was the Georgia Crackers. There was Arthur Smith. There was Vernon Dalhart, songs like "The Death of Floyd Collins." There was a song about "Mother" that I remember especially well. I believe Bradley Kincaid might have sung this song—I'm not sure. I remember a lot of his songs—I used to sing a lot of them.

In fact, this particular song was done not by Bradley Kincaid but by Goebel Reeves. In any case, these names—Dalhart, Carter, Rodgers—had a special importance in the formation of Cash as an artist.

The Original
CARTER
FAMILY
CARTER FAMILY
CPM1-2763
Wildwood Flower
Keep On The Sunny Side
Diamonds In The Rough
INCLUDES BOOK
WRITTEN BY
JOHNNY CASH

Before and after marrying June, Cash was one of the Carter Family's biggest cheerleaders.
Author's collection

Vernon Dalhart

Taking his name from two Texas towns located near to where he grew up, Marion Try Slaughter became Vernon Dalhart when he moved to New York to begin a music career. Though he was a classically trained singer, he didn't hit pay dirt until he affected a Southern drawl in an audition for Thomas Alva Edison, who was looking for artists for his new label. Dalhart's biggest success came with the recording of "Wreck of the Old 97" b/w "The Prisoner's Song." The pairing proved to be a tremendous hit and became the first million-selling country record. It was released on at least forty-nine other labels under different names, and Dalhart became a star.

Cash first recorded a version of "The Wreck of the Old 97" in 1957 and included it on his debut album, *Johnny Cash with His Hot and Blue Guitar.* It also became a staple of his live performances.

The Carter Family and Jimmie Rodgers

Both of these artists were present at what has been termed the "Big Bang" of country music—when record man Ralph Peer made his way to Bristol, Tennessee, in 1927 to record new acts. Here, the solo act of Jimmie Rodgers and the family band of the Carter Family—husband and wife Sara and A. P. Carter plus Maybelle, who was Sara's cousin and A. P.'s sister-in-law—made their legendary first recordings and launched careers that would influences scores of performers, including Johnny Cash.

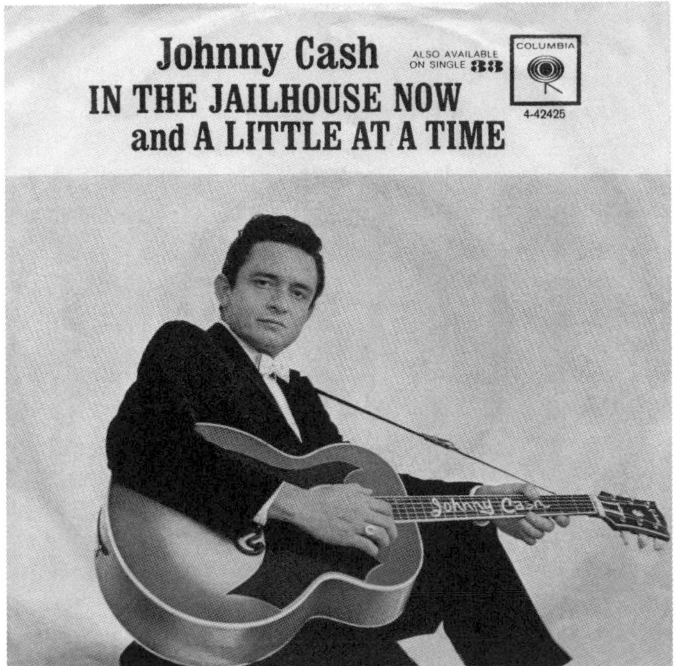

In 1962, Cash released his version of Jimmie Rodgers' "In the Jailhouse Now." *Private collection*

Cash drew from each of these pioneering acts throughout his career. He recorded ten songs closely associated with the original Carter Family trio, beginning in 1962 with "I'll Be All Smiles Tonight." At his first Newport Folk Festival appearance in 1964, he made a point of ending his set with "Keep on the Sunnyside," and throughout his touring career he often ended his shows with "Will the Circle Be Unbroken." He continued to honor the memory of the family in any way that he could.

Although Cash's respect and admiration for Rodgers was deep, he only dipped into his catalogue five times, and only three of those recordings would be released on albums during his lifetime. One of them, "Brakeman's Blues," wasn't even a complete take: though it dates back to a Sun recording session in 1956, it first saw the light of day on the 1990 import collection *The Man in Black: 1954–1958.*

In 1962, Cash took a swing at "In the Jailhouse Now" and connected with a hit. Webb Pierce's version of the song had spent thirty-seven weeks on the *Billboard* charts in 1955, twenty-one of them at #1. Cash's version spent only ten weeks on the chart, peaking at #8. He included it on *The Sound of Johnny Cash,* which also featured a version of "I'm Free from the Chain Gang Now," a song made popular by Rodgers.

The following year, 1963, Cash cut "Waiting for a Train" for his album *Blood, Sweat and Tears.* In 1969, he and Bob Dylan would ramble through something resembling "T for Texas" during their only session together. It remains unreleased. Finally, during the last act of his career, Cash recorded Rodgers' 1937 song "The One Rose" (written by Lani McIntire) for his second American release, *Unchained.* He also returned to "I'm Free from the Chain Gang Now" during his later years, including it as the closing track on *American V: A Hundred Highways.*

Beyond the music, Cash sought various ways to honor the memory of Rodgers. Early in his career, he appeared—alongside two other heroes of his, Hank Snow and Ernest Tubb—at the 1957 Jimmie Rodgers Memorial Day, an annual event held in Meridian, Mississippi. Just after the release of his "In the Jailhouse Now" in 1962, he began to collect Rodgers memorabilia and the singer's personal effects. That same year, he scheduled a concert at Carnegie Hall, a tribute to country, where his love for Rodgers was literally center stage, as Cash was wearing one of Rodgers' "Singing Brakeman" outfits, on loan from the singer's widow, Carrie. Cash had also began to tell reporters that he would be producing a movie based on the life of Jimmie Rodgers, with himself in the lead role.

The Louvin Brothers

The Louvin Brothers, Ira and Charlie, had a radio show with Smilin' Eddie Hill at noon on WMPS, and Cash and the men he worked the fields with would listen to it during their lunch break. The Louvins and Hill then became the Lonesome Valley Trio and performed gospel songs. "Mr. Cash donated about two pages, maybe three pages [in his first autobiography, *Man in Black*], to telling when he first saw the Louvin Brothers," Charlie Louvin said in 2007. "In fact, he said he got fired. He said he was the water boy, and he got in somebody's truck and listened to our one o'clock gospel show on WMPS and he had to get out and carry water real quick and he forgot to turn the man's radio off and it ran his battery down and he said he got fired for that."

The Louvins and Hill also toured churches and schools throughout the region, including one in Dyess:

> Right about 1947, we played Dyess, Arkansas. My brother and I was working with Smilin' Eddie Hill, and this little boy was standing out—John's about five years younger than me, maybe six—and he was standing outside the door. It was my job to sell the tickets and when I got done selling tickets I was about to die for a bathroom and I said to him, "Son, do you all have a bathroom?" and he practically led me to the outhouse. And when I got through, when I came out, he was outside. When I came out I reached into my shirt pocket and got two soda crackers. And I was eating those soda crackers on the way back to the school building, and he said, "Why are you eating those soda crackers?" And I guess I gave him a

> smart-aleck answer—I said, "To keep from starving to death." In his book he said for the next three or four years—right after he got into the business—the first three or four years he would always eat two soda crackers before he went on the stage. Which would have been the worst thing that you could do, [to] get those dry crackers in your throat, you know?

Brother Jack

A few years before Cash was introduced to the music of the Louvin Brothers, two events occurred in 1944 that would come to define his life. That year, as he turned twelve, he went forward during a service at the Baptist church his family attended to make a public profession of his faith. There is no doubt that the influence of his older brother Jack, to whom he looked up, had led J. R. forward in his decision. Jack, now aged fifteen, had committed himself to his calling to become a preacher. But he would never fulfill that call.

On a Saturday in May, J. R. decided it would be a good day for fishing, and asked his brother to come along. Jack declined, since he had the opportunity to earn $3 by going to the agriculture building of the high school to cut some wood slabs—$3 that the family could use. Jack and J. R. walked along the road together and then split up, J. R. heading for the fishing hole while Jack went to work. But J. R.'s fishing excursion was cut short by the sound of a car skidding to a halt on the dirt road behind him. It was his father, who yelled for him to immediately get into the car. There he found out that Jack had been seriously injured when a saw blade jumped out of place and cut through his abdomen. Jack lingered between life and death for a few days before seeming to come alive in new spirit. But then, with the family surrounding his bedside, he asked his mother if she could hear the angels singing. He told them he was looking forward, and it was beautiful. With that, on May 20, 1944, he slipped from this life to the next.

It was a devastating blow to young J. R. Just months earlier, he had pledged his loyalty to God, and he could tell how proud his mother and Jack were of that decision. He was God's child now. Wouldn't everything be perfect from now on? And yet here he stood, on a Sunday, the Lord's day, watching the person to whom he looked up to the most—the one who had so encouraged him on his path—leave him forever.

Jack's death was something Cash never really got over. In *Man in Black*, he writes, "The memory of Jack's death, his vision of heaven, the effect his life had on the lives of others, and the image of Christ he projected have been more of an inspiration to me, I suppose, than anything else that has ever come to me through any man." In his second book, *Cash: The Autobiography*, he adds, "[Jack's] been showing up in my dreams every couple of months or so, sometimes more often, ever since he died. . . . He's a preacher, just as he intended to be, a good man and a figure of high repute."

J. R.'s sister Reba noted a change in him following Jack's death, telling biographer Christopher Wren, "He thought more and talked even less." The event led J. R. inward, and he began to express himself with stories and poems. Jack hadn't only been his brother but also his best friend. Without him, the loneliness grew.

Ernest Tubb

In time, J. R. found other friends, and one in particular who shared his interest in music. Jesse Barnhill (or Pete, as he is referred to in some texts) lived just a few houses down from Cash and owned a guitar. "Pete was crazy about music the way I was," Cash writes in *Cash.* "He was the first person I knew who was that way." Barnhill shared J. R.'s love of the radio, and the two spent time listening to and imitating what they could. Barnhill had caught polio as a child, and his right hand and foot were withered, affecting how he walked but not how he played guitar. He could form chords with his left hand and beat out a rhythm with his right. He and J. R. spent hours singing the songs of their heroes, particularly those of Ernest Tubb and Hank Snow.

Ernest Tubb was born in 1914 in Crisp, Texas. At age thirteen, he was captivated by a Jimmie Rodgers record, and later, after a few years of recording,

Cash recorded two songs in 1979, including this one, with his hero Ernest Tubb. *Private collection*

playing shows, and doing radio, he found his own voice. He hit with "Walking the Floor Over You" in 1941 and became one of the biggest stars of country music and the *Grand Ole Opry*.

Cash and Tubb crossed paths several times, starting early in Cash's career. They first met in Meridian, Mississippi, for the Jimmie Rodgers Memorial, and not long after that Tubb recorded Cash's "My Treasure." Cash returned the favor on his 1960 album *Now There Was a Song*, for which he recorded "I Will Miss You When You Go," a 1953 album track for Tubb. In 1977, producer Pete Drake put together *Ernest Tubb: The Legend and the Legacy*, which paired Tubb with popular country artists of the time as a tribute to his influence. Among those included on the album, singing with Tubb on some of his best known songs, were Merle Haggard, Willie Nelson, Waylon Jennings, George Jones, Conway Twitty, and Johnny Paycheck. Cash appears on two songs, "Jealous Loving Heart" and "Soldier's Last Letter."

Hank Snow

As Ernest Tubb drew on one of Cash's inspirations, Jimmie Rodgers, so Hank Snow drew on another: Vernon Dalhart. Born Clarence Eugene Snow in Brooklyn, Nova Scotia, Canada, on May 9, 1914, Snow discovered Dalhart's records at a very early age and listened to them every chance he got. He learned the words to songs like "The Prisoner's Song" and "The Wreck of the Old 97," and entertained workers in nearby logging camps, accompanying himself on harmonica. Like Tubb, he discovered Jimmie Rodgers in his early teens, and he soon began to tread a similar path. "After hearing the first record by him, nothing would hold me," he told historian Charles Wolfe. He received a guitar and began to copy as much Rodgers material as he could.

After initially finding success in his native Canada, Snow made his way to the States to begin playing WWVA's *Wheeling Jamboree* and the *Louisiana Hayride*. On July 1, 1950, he released "I'm Movin' On," the song that made his career. It spent forty-four weeks on the *Billboard* charts, twenty-one of them at #1. A few further hits followed, including the 1962 tongue-twisting traveling song "I've Been Everywhere."

Snow and Tubb were artists whose music Cash would continually return to, from his early days in Dyess with Jesse "Pete" Barnhill to sitting around at the Air Force barracks in Landsberg, Germany. As he was fond of saying in concert, Cash "spent twenty years in the Air Force between 1950 and 1954." When his tour of duty ended, he made plans to move to Memphis, where his brother Roy worked for a car dealership. Roy had told him about a couple of guitar-playing mechanics he worked with, and Roy told the two mechanics, Marshall Grant and Luther Perkins, that his brother sang just like Hank Snow.

After first recording "Two Timin' Woman," Cash would return to Snow's catalogue for his 1968 Folsom Prison set list with "I'm Just Here to Get My Baby Out of Jail," a song written by Karl & Harty that Snow recorded and performed often.

Cash pulled out "I've Been Everywhere" for his 1996 album *Unchained*, and it has since been featured in several television commercials. He also recorded "I'm Movin' On" during those sessions, though it wouldn't be released until after his death.

Sister Rosetta Tharpe

In the excellent *Good Rockin' Tonight: Sun Records and the Birth of Rock 'n' Roll*, authors Colin Escott and Martin Hawkins note, "Unlike almost all of his Sun colleagues, Cash grew up without the influence of black music." This was due not to prejudice but to circumstance. The government program that created Dyess wasn't open to blacks, so there were no African Americans for him to learn from, as Hank Williams did from Tee-Tot Payne, or Bill Monroe from Arnold Schultz. Not until he moved to Memphis after being discharged from the Air Force in 1954 would he actively seek out the sounds of black music.

"I heard a lot of blues," Cash told Escott and Hawkins. One day, on a sales trip for the Home Equipment Company, for whom he sold appliances door to door, he happened upon a gentleman playing the banjo on a front porch in one of Memphis' African American neighborhoods. The man turned out to be performer and songwriter Gus Cannon, who had written "Walk Right In" and recorded it with his group, Cannon's Jug Stompers, in 1929.

"My favorite music is people like Pink Anderson, Robert Johnson, king of the Delta blues singers, Howlin' Wolf, Muddy Waters, Papa John Creach, Sister Rosetta Tharpe!" Cash told Bill Flanagan in 1988. "I love her! I've recorded some of her songs."

Sister Rosetta Tharpe was a groundbreaking gospel performer who utilized her guitar playing as much as she did her voice. Born in 1915 in Cotton Plant, Arkansas, Tharpe began performing at the age of three. By age five, she and her mother had moved to Chicago in search of better opportunities. She began to perform at churches and religious events in the early 1930s, making a name for herself in gospel music circles, but in 1938 she took a hard left and moved to New York, where she began a career singing secular music at the Cotton Club. After recording a series of records with Lucky Millender and his big band, she began to tire of the club scene, and in 1944 she made a triumphant return to gospel music. Her big hit came that same year with "Strange Things Happening Every Day," which spent eleven weeks on the charts, peaking at #2. Her slashing guitar rhythm and the boogie-woogie piano backup laid a foundation for the rock 'n' roll to come.

The song received a second life when disc jockey Dewey Phillips began to spin it on his Memphis radio show *Red, Hot & Blue*. By now, there were people hanging around Memphis who had loved her music for years and were now incorporating it into their new recording careers—people like Elvis Presley, Carl Perkins, Jerry Lee Lewis, and Johnny Cash. In *Man in Black*, Cash recalls how, during his time in the Air Force, his friend C. V. White—the same man who later inspired "Blue Suede Shoes"—had a Sister Rosetta album that included "Strange Things." "C.V. would let me borrow that record album about once a week, and I'd listen to her sing that song over and over again," Cash writes. Many years would pass before Cash covered any Tharpe songs, but he would eventually include three on his 1979 album *A Believer Sings the Truth*: "There Are Strange Things Happening Every Day," "Don't Take Everybody to Be Your Friend," and "This Train Is Bound for Glory."

Blues in the Mississippi Night and Leadbelly

"*Blues in the Mississippi Night* is my all-time favorite album," Cash told Bill Flanagan in 1988. The album, originally released in 1947, consists of folklorist Alan Lomax's recordings of three then-unidentified blues musicians—later revealed to be Big Bill Broonzy, Memphis Slim, and Sonny Boy Williamson—as they take turns singing songs and discussing the issues of racism in the South and their personal experiences dealing with it.

The work of John Lomax and his son Alan fascinated Cash, who listened intently to the field recordings they captured, including those John did at Louisiana State Penitentiary in Angola, Louisiana, in 1934. It was there that Lomax was presented to inmate LSP #19469, a prisoner named Huddie Ledbetter. Ledbetter, better known as Leadbelly, had spent time in various prisons around Texas, off and on, since 1918. When Lomax brought his equipment to Angola in 1933, Ledbetter was able to reel off seven songs, including "Frankie and Albert" (his version of "Frankie and Johnny") and an original entitled "Irene." Lomax returned in 1934 to record fourteen songs, including new takes of several of the songs he got the year before.

On his release from prison, Ledbetter went to work for Lomax, accompanying him on a song-collecting trip through Arkansas. To help ease the nerves of the people they found to record, Ledbetter would be recorded singing a song as an example of the types of songs Lomax desired, and to show how recording worked. They made a few more trips in the area before heading north. There, Ledbetter became not a man Friday but an entertainer, presented by Lomax in a concert setting. One of his most popular songs was his 1933 original "Irene," which he now called "Goodnight, Irene." He continued recording and performing until December 6, 1949, when he passed away from a bone infection.

Cash picked up records like these at the Home of the Blues, his local record shop in Memphis. Of all the black artists Cash heard, it was Leadbelly's songs that cropped up the most in his early repertoire. On *Johnny Cash with His Hot and Blue Guitar*, he included his version of "Rock Island Line," a song that Leadbelly had turned from a prison work song to a train song. On November 12, 1957, Cash recorded "Goodnight, Irene," although it wouldn't see release until 1964. Another prison work song—one that was worked over a bit by Cash—was

"I Got Stripes," which Leadbelly often performed as "On a Monday." Cash's version spent twenty weeks on the charts, peaking at #4, and became a crowd favorite after a live recording of it appeared on *At Folsom Prison.* He returned to Ledbetter's catalogue in 1962, recording "In Them Old Cotton Fields Back Home" for *The Sound of Johnny Cash* and a version of the work song "Pick a Bale O' Cotton" as the B-side to the single "Bonanza."

2

We Were Just a Plain Ol' Hillbilly Band

The Tennessee Two (and Three)

Marshall Grant says that the sound of Johnny Cash and the Tennessee Two was born in the first eight bars of the first song they played, and that after that they spent a long time trying to lose it. Luckily, they didn't.

The boom-chicka-boom sound is as instantly recognizable as the voice that follows it. Author Bill Friskics-Warren has called it "a sound as enduring as Bo Diddley's hambone beat, Ray Price's 4/4 shuffle, or the one-chord funk vamps of James Brown & the JBs." Throughout his career, Cash would add to that basic template, expanding his band to an eight-piece at times, but he always returned to his most distinctive sound—a sound that rose from Memphis, and the hands of two mechanics and an appliance salesman.

The Tennessee Two: Marshall Grant (Bass, 1954–80) and Luther Perkins (Guitar, 1954–68)

You won't find Flatts, North Carolina, the birthplace of Marshall Grant, on a map. "It's not a town," he told Christopher S. Wren in 1970. "It's not a community. It was twenty-one people when I lived there. And as far as I know, it's still twenty-one people." The population may have increased since then, or it might have died out; the location itself was nestled in the Smokey Mountains, where the Grant family—mom, dad, and twelve brothers and sisters—owned twenty acres. The family retained the land, but around 1940, when Marshall was twelve, they moved closer to a larger city—Bessemer City, twenty-five miles west of Charlotte—where they became cotton sharecroppers.

At age eighteen, Grant decided to follow a brother who had moved to Memphis to become a jeweler. Being mechanically inclined, Grant began to train to be a watchmaker. In 1946, after marrying his girlfriend, Etta, he decided that a career change was in order, and found a job running parts for mechanics at C. M. Booth Motor Company. His employers soon noticed his aptitude for things mechanical, and six months later, Grant was offered a job as a mechanic.

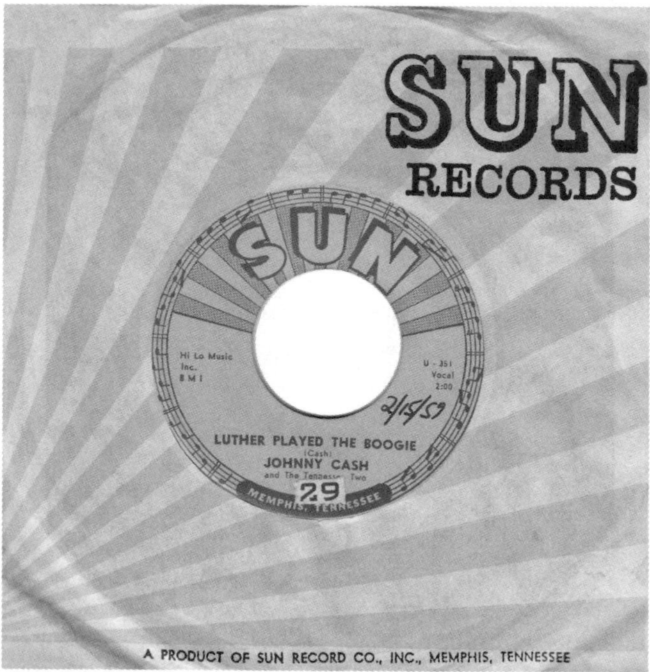

Luther Perkins had as much to do with Cash's sound as Cash himself did. Cash's 1959 single was a tongue-in-cheek tribute to his stone-faced guitarist. *Private collection*

In the garage, Grant met a fellow country-music fan named A. W. "Red" Kernodle, who played some steel guitar. At the time, Kernodle didn't have his own instrument, so Grant bought one his new friend could use. Kernodle would come over and play, and sometimes they would invite a few other pickers to join them. The duo would play country and gospel favorites while Etta spent time with Kernodle's wife and three daughters.

With his family growing, Kernodle was on the lookout for a higher-paying job, and he soon found one as a salesman at Automobile Sales, a large DeSoto-Plymouth dealership a few blocks down the street. In 1951, Kernodle told Grant that Automobile Sales was looking for a new mechanic, and, as it happened, C. W. Booth was closing its doors, so Grant went to talk to the service manager. A week later, Grant started his new job, where he was introduced to the mechanic who worked in the spot next to him: an Arkansas native named Roy Cash.

Two years later, a tall, lanky, black-haired man started work a couple of bays over from Grant. When they finally got around to meeting, Grant learned that the new mechanic was also a musician, so one evening Grant invited him to come out and join him, Kernodle, and a few other picking buddies. "As it turned out," Grant later recalled of the man, "he was probably the best musician of us all."

Luther Perkins was born in Memphis, the son of a Baptist minister, but the family soon relocated to Como, Mississippi. As a preacher's son, he was probably well aware of the many biblical stories about the power of dreams. One morning, when he was nine years old, Perkins awoke with vivid memories of that night's dream, in which he had journeyed to a rainbow's end and found a pot of gold. The dream was so vivid that he knew exactly where it was. He and his brother found the spot and started to dig, and they soon discovered what was left of an old house. Ingeniously, Luther decided to dig up the individual bricks and take them to a local construction company, which bought them from him for two cents apiece. In the end, Perkins brought along enough bricks to earn himself $9, which he used to buy his first guitar.

In 1942, the Perkins family moved back to Memphis, where Luther finished school and worked a series of odd jobs. Along the way he picked up skills in electronics, earning himself a good reputation as the go-to guy for radio installation or other automobile electronics. That reputation was enough to get him hired at Automobile Sales.

Soon, Perkins and Grant were bringing their guitars to work and killing time playing in the back room when they didn't have cars to work on. A crowd would often gather, and occasionally other musicians would join in, including a guitarist named Scotty Moore, who had just begun playing with a local singer named Elvis Presley. Roy Cash would drop in and listen to them play, telling them about his brother John, who was in the Air Force and sang just like Hank Snow. Roy told them his brother had ambitions to be a professional singer, and that he was soon to be discharged. Perkins and Grant listened to Roy but weren't too excited about the prospect.

In mid-July 1954, Roy took a break from work and went to the bus station to pick up his brother. Later that afternoon, Grant saw them enter the other end of the garage.

"It was a moment I couldn't forget if I tried, for a funny feeling—kind of a tingling—came over me, and it grew stronger as they got closer," Grant writes in his autobiography. "By the time they'd crossed the shop, the tingling had crawled up my spine, and it felt like the hair on the back of my neck was sticking straight out." He and Cash hit it off immediately, and started quickly into a conversation about music. After a few minutes, Grant took him over to meet Perkins.

Cash was only in town for a short while, passing through on his way to see his parents in Dyess, and then on to San Antonio to marry his sweetheart, Vivian Liberto. A few weeks later, he returned to Memphis with his new bride and found a one-room apartment. With plans to go into radio, and then the music business, he took whatever work he could find to pay the bills, and for now that meant a job as an appliance salesman for the Home Equipment Company. It didn't pay the bills, though, because Cash wasn't a very good salesman. Sometimes he would even tell his customers that they shouldn't pay the advertised prices. His mind was on other things, including the jam sessions with

Perkins and Grant (and sometimes Kernodle) that now took place most nights. The group played every country and gospel song they knew, and the wives often gathered to play cards or other games.

After months of playing together, the foursome decided it would be fun to make a record. They knew they couldn't sound like a real band with three acoustic guitars, though, so it was agreed that Perkins would play an electric guitar and Grant a bass. For Perkins, the switch from acoustic to electric was as simple as just picking up another guitar, but Grant's switch to bass proved a bit more of a problem. For one thing, none of them had any idea how to tune it. After being given a sketched-out diagram by a co-worker, Grant and Perkins realized it was the same as tuning the bottom four strings of a guitar. The next problem came from the instrument itself, because stand-up basses don't have frets like a standard guitar. Painstakingly, Perkins played through each note as Grant marked the fret positions on the neck with masking tape. Finally, with all of their instruments—and notes—accounted for, the musicians were ready to pursue their dream.

That process of getting a chance to record is detailed in chapter 3, so we'll fast-forward the story a bit. With singles racing up the charts, Cash and the group were performing nearly anywhere they could, zipping from Dallas to Shreveport on two-lane roads, with occasional shots up to Nashville and all points in between. They were a sight to see. Cash would be dressed in some sort of light-colored sports coat and slacks, standing center stage, guitar in hand, only his head moving as he sang. To his right, Grant was slapping his bass, bopping up, down, and side-to-side while animatedly chewing gum in time. To his left stood Perkins, arrow-straight and somewhat stone-faced. Often, the two would be in matching outfits.

Grant's animated movements were more in line with those of a rockabilly musician than the group's country counterparts, who were often planted on their spots on the stage. But Perkins was more than planted. He held his spot like he owned it, rarely giving any expression. Part of it was nerves, no doubt, especially in the beginning, but part of it was to play the straight man to Cash, who would sometimes poke fun at Perkins' stiffness. Sometimes he would stand watching Perkins play a solo while Perkins, facing straight away, no more than moved his eyes to the side to look at Cash.

Perkins would rarely say a word onstage, and that became something else Cash would use as comedy relief. For example, he would announce that Perkins was going to sing a song later in the show, and then name a song with a silly title. Perkins was certainly in on the joke. There is a fantastic clip, easily accessible online, of Perkins and June Carter singing the Carter Family's "I'll Be All Smiles Tonight." The trio's bond was the music, and it showed beautifully onstage.

Offstage, the bond was just as tight. The trio became major pranksters on the road. Long before Led Zeppelin or the Rolling Stones ever thought to throw a television out of a window, Cash's reputation for destroying hotels was legendary. Country artist and TV star Jimmy Dean once told the story of coming off the road in Calgary, Canada, to a hotel where he had a reservation, only to be turned away in the middle of the night because Cash and crew had stayed there the week before and caused such destruction that the hotel had decided not to allow entertainers anymore. Leaving dead mice on hot radiators, blowing things up with a cannon in the hotel yard, and moving furniture into elevators were just a few examples of the antics the group would take part in—often with their Sun labelmates Jerry Lee Lewis, Roy Orbison, and for a time, Elvis in tow.

The Two Record

In 1959, with Cash now recording for Columbia, the Tennessee Two signed a deal to produce some singles. Their first effort was "Bandana" b/w "Wabash Blues." The band, which included Cash on acoustic guitar, was augmented by session drummer Michael Kazak on both cuts, plus Harold Bradley on piano and Cash's nephew Roy Jr. on acoustic guitar on "Bandana." The single was credited to the Tennessee Two & Friend.

Their next single was released at the end of 1960, coupling "Blues for Two" and "Jeri and Nina's Melody." In "Blues for Two," Perkins builds the song around a variation of the opening figure of his "Folsom Prison Blues" solo, while Floyd Cramer shares the spotlight with a solo of his own. The flip side, "Jeri and Nina's Melody," was composed by Cash as a tribute to Johnny Horton's children, Jeri, Nina, and Melody. Horton had been killed in an automobile accident on November 5, 1960. The group entered the studio on November 26th to record their tribute, and the single was released on December 31st. Both sides of the single received favorable reviews from *Billboard*, showing the group could hold their own without Cash's vocals.

The three continued to share a bond, both onstage and off, for fourteen years. In that time, Luther Perkins set the standard not just for Cash's music but also for minimalist country guitar players for years to come. His guitar work on those Johnny Cash and the Tennessee Two records, from "Hey Porter" to "Come to the Wailing Wall" (his last recording with the band for *The Holy Land*) set the tone for all Cash players to follow.

Losing Luther

On August 3, 1968, after a hard day's labor around his home in Hendersonville, Tennessee, Perkins fell asleep with a lit cigarette dangling from his fingers. The room soon smoldered, and heavy smoke filled the area. Perkins was found unconscious near a sliding glass door, just feet from escape. On August 4th, Cash and his band were scheduled to play a show at Sangamon Park in Monticello, Illinois, and the decision was made to keep the date. In a letter to *Country Song Roundup*, a concert attendee named Barbara McClellend relates:

> I am writing to you mainly because I would like to commend Johnny Cash, June Carter, Carl Perkins, and all the other members of their show,

The original Tennessee Three of Perkins, Grant, and Holland released their version of "Cattle Call" in 1967. Eddy Arnold had taken the vocal version to #1 for two weeks in 1955. *Private collection*

> which I had the distinct pleasure of seeing on Aug. 4th. Unfortunately, this was the day after Luther Perkins had been so seriously burned. All of us here in Central Illinois had waited anxiously for the day Johnny Cash would appear at Sangamon Park here.
>
> We were told early in the day. However, we were not told of the seriousness of the burns until the end of the first show. When the second show began and we knew the strain the entire troup [sic] was under, it made us much more appreciative of the saying "the show must go on." Here stood a group of people, putting on a show, singing their hearts out, and not knowing if one of their own would live or die.

On August 5th, Perkins passed away in the hospital, leaving behind a guitar legacy that endures to this day.

Another Era Ends

Marshall Grant continued as Cash's bass player until 1980, when Cash, in a drug-related stupor, fired him on the spot after twenty-six years together. Grant had been one of Cash's original collaborators—as well as the man who helped June get rid of the drugs that were killing Cash—and he had been Cash's road manager for most of those years, keeping the operation running smoothly while they were on tour. Now it was all over. The last of the original Tennessee Two was sent packing. In his 1997 autobiography, Cash claims to have been held back at times by Grant and Perkins' limited musical abilities, although at the same time he admits that he could have changed things at any time. Grant's firing did signal a musical shift, but more than that, it marked the end of a brotherhood that had started in a garage bay on Union Avenue.

Rumors purported to have originated with Cash began to circulate, suggesting that Grant had been embezzling money. Grant fought back. At the same time, Perkins' children were also engaged in a lawsuit against Cash and Grant to recoup royalties they believed were owed to them. When the trio started in 1955, they formed a partnership, split 40/30/30. Now, Grant claimed that once the drugs got out of hand in the late 1950s, the money was never divided in the proper way. After nine years, both suits were finally settled out of court. But it wasn't until 1997 that Grant and Cash saw each other again. By that time, Cash had more or less kicked his drug habit and was eager to bury the hatchet. The two once again became close, and in 1999 they appeared together onstage at a concert in tribute to Cash, making music together one last time.

W. S. "Fluke" Holland (Drums, 1960–97)

As Cash gained more success in the late 1950s, he began to perform in more varied venues, including places country music didn't often frequent. In 1960, a short tour was booked that would take the band to Syracuse, New York, then down to Atlantic City. The Syracuse stop was at the Three Rivers Club, a nightclub that hosted weeklong engagements by Nat "King" Cole, Paul Anka, and Guy Mitchell. Cash decided that it was time to change things up a bit, so he added a drummer for the dates. At first, they considered asking Perkins' friend Robert "Tarp" Tarrant, who had been playing with Jerry Lee Lewis, before deciding that his style wouldn't fit with the group. Instead, they opted for another drummer they all knew from Sun Studio, W. S. "Fluke" Holland.

Holland grew up near Jackson, Tennessee, not far from a trio of boys named Perkins, and got his drum-playing start on bass. The Perkins brothers—Jay B., Carl, and Clayton—had been playing music together for a while, and they were starting to play some local shows. At one show, while Carl was singing and playing, he thought he heard drums, but the group had no drummer. He turned around to see Holland slapping out the tempo on the side of the bass. When he saw Perkins staring at him, Holland thought he was in trouble, but then Carl yelled to him, "Keep it up and play louder!"

After the show, Carl told Holland that he and the brothers (along with a few other musicians) were going to Memphis to make a record, and he should get some drums and come with them. Holland borrowed a kit, but, not knowing how to set it up, he placed the snare to his left and the hi-hat to his right—the opposite of how most drummers play. The setup worked for him, though, so he kept it for the rest of his career.

In 1954, the group packed up in Holland's big Cadillac—another key reason he got the gig, Carl later told him—and headed for Memphis to audition for Sam Phillips. The band recorded several songs over the next few years, including such classics as "Matchbox," "Honey Don't," and "Blue Suede Shoes." Holland continued to record and tour with Perkins until 1959, when Perkins' career was starting to cool a bit, and the death of Jay B. had tempered his desire to tour.

Deciding to try his hand at another part of the business, Holland discovered a singing teenager from his hometown named Carl Mann and became his manager. It proved to be a short-lived venture, though, as Mann began to develop a drinking problem. Having previously seen how alcohol had affected the Perkins brothers, Holland decided it was time to leave the music business and head back home to the job he'd left behind at a heating and cooling company.

Just before the job was to start, however, Holland received a call from Marshall Grant, asking if he could put off his departure for another week and do the New England dates with Cash and the Two. Holland agreed and joined the band for the small tour, using only a snare to help fill out the sound. Cash and the Two were pleased with how things worked out, and on the car ride back to Memphis they made the decision to permanently add Holland to the show. He would remain with Cash for nearly forty years.

The Tennessee Two duly became the Tennessee Three, but the name change took a while to settle in. A 1962 *Billboard* news clip refers to the band as the Tennessee Two Plus One, although aside from Cash occasionally introducing them from the stage in that way, this seems to be the only print reference to them by that name, and in fact the same magazine had referred to them as the Tennessee Three in 1960.

Bob Wootton (Guitar, 1969–89 and 1992–97)

Losing Luther Perkins was devastating to Cash on a number of levels. As one of the original Tennessee Two, Perkins had a highly distinctive guitar style that fans had come to expect. Cash worried that he wouldn't be able to replace him, and might now be at risk of losing his sound.

Just a month after losing Perkins, the group—now being assisted on guitar duties by the unrelated Carl Perkins—was scheduled to play a show in Fayetteville, Arkansas. Just hours before show time, word reached Cash that the flight Grant and Perkins had planned to be on had been canceled due to fog. The pair tried to charter a private plane, but even that wouldn't get them there in time for the show. This meant that the show would consist only of Cash, June, and Holland, who now began preparing to improvise a new set.

Although Grant and Perkins were absent, their gear was already with the crew, since they had been out on the road since early September. And when word spread through the crowd that the two musicians wouldn't be able to make it to the show, a young girl in the audience had an idea—her friend should

The final version of the Tennessee Three (Grant, Holland, and Wootton) recorded one full-length album for Columbia. The album was made up of instrumental versions of familiar Cash songs. *Author's collection*

get up onstage and play with the group. To the friend, Bob Wootton, the idea sounded farfetched—and perfect.

Wootton was born in 1942, on an unproductive cotton farm in a small Arkansas town. After trying his luck in the coal mines, his father decided to move the family to California, where he soon found work in the oil fields. To pass the time, Bob's father played fiddle, mandolin, and guitar, often in their local church. When Bob turned eleven, his father began to teach him chords on the guitar so that he could accompany him at these gatherings.

After graduating high school in 1960, Bob joined the army, and became a gunner in Korea. He bought a new guitar for $25 and put together a loose band called Johnny & the Ramrods, with whom he played on the base and in the NCO club.

With three years' service under his cap, Wootton returned to the States and settled near Tulsa, Oklahoma, where he soon married. Making music continued to be a way of life for him, though. He soon formed a new group, the Commancheros, and began playing the local bar scene. That meant pumping out covers of the national hits of the time, including songs by Johnny Cash. Wootton was a huge Cash fan, and he finally got to see him play live in 1966. He even met his hero backstage, along with Luther Perkins—another hero, and a major influence on his guitar style.

Fast-forward two years, and now Wootton was sitting in an audience with 7,000 other fans waiting to see if the show would go on. "I happened to be in the audience," he recalled, in an interview with Peter Lewry of the *Man in Black* fanzine, "and the girl I was with went up to June and said, 'Would Johnny like to have somebody play with him? I know a guy who knows all your songs.'" June reported back to Cash, who decided to take a chance on the young player. He summoned Wootton to the backstage area and asked him, "Do you play like Luther?"

"No one can do that," Wootton answered. "But I'll try if you want me to." Cash pointed to Carl Perkins' guitar case and told Wootton to get onstage and plug in.

In *Man in Black*, Cash tells the story of kicking off a song and—trying to be helpful—telling Wootton it is in the key of C, to which Wootton replies, "You recorded it in D." This confidence quickly won over Cash; Wootton reminded him of a younger version of himself. Indeed, the two had more in common than Cash knew at the time. They had both picked cotton, joined the military to escape, married and divorced young, and shared an ambition to make it in music.

After the show, Cash took Wootton's number. He cautioned that he wasn't really looking for another guitarist, but said that he would give Wootton a call if he was in the area and needed him. After they set off, Cash sought the opinions of June and Holland, who both thought Wootton had done a fantastic job. A few days later, Cash called to ask if Wootton was interested in joining the band for a six-month run, which Wootton eagerly accepted. A few months after that, Cash made the offer a permanent one.

Wootton's style was fully immersed in Perkins' playing, but he added his own twist, albeit a small one. *Bootleg Volume III: Live Around the World* contains selections from a show the group did at an NCO club in Long Binh, Vietnam, in January 1968, just a couple of months after Wootton joined. You can hear an extra little bounce in Wootton's boom-chicka-boom at the start of "Big River," but not so much as to immediately tip you off to the change. His solo on "Tennessee Flat Top Box" is a bit simpler than the acoustic-guitar break on the original recording, but again the difference is not too pronounced. After that, Carl Perkins joins the band—as he would for years to come—and the addition of another guitarist to the stage, especially one as influential as Perkins, pushes Wootton along. On "Ring of Fire," Wootton doubles Carl's leads, duplicating the distinctive horn line using the lower-register strings.

Wootton made his studio debut with the Cash band on "Southwind," the opening track from 1970's *Hello, I'm Johnny Cash*. Once again, the change of guitarist may not be immediately noticeable to the general fan, but Wootton does play with that added bounce.

The Tennessee Three signed an album deal with Columbia, and in 1971 they released *The Sound Behind Johnny Cash*. The album was dedicated to Luther, "who started the 'sound' as part of the Tennessee Two." All eleven tracks on the album are Cash songs (with occasional Dobro, played by Norman Blake, taking the vocal melody line), and they hew closely to versions that had been previously recorded with Cash on vocals. The exception is the lead track, "A Boy Named Sue." After the Tennessee Three introduce themselves individually, the Dobro takes over, but rather than mimic Cash's vocal, it instead takes the melody elsewhere, while the backing track sounds slightly different from the one they normally played.

In 1974, Wootton became Cash's brother-in-law when he married June's sister Anita. He continued to perform with Cash until 1989, and then resumed his spot behind him in 1992, holding it until Cash retired from the road in 1997.

3

I Never Did Play Much Rock 'n' Roll

The Sun Years

Number 706 Union Avenue in Memphis, Tennessee, is one of the most famous addresses in music history. Some call it the birthplace of rockabilly, others the birthplace of rock 'n' roll. It was unquestionably the launching pad for the careers not only of Elvis Presley and Johnny Cash but also of Carl Perkins, Jerry Lee Lewis, Roy Orbison, and Charlie Rich. And it was here that Cash and the Tennessee Two would lay the foundation for a career that lasted nearly fifty years.

A Brief History of Sun Records' Early Years

At this address, in a nondescript brick building, a local disc jockey named Sam Phillips opened the Memphis Recording Service in January 1950. The music scene in Memphis was varied and vibrant, but no one was operating a recording business, leaving the field wide open for Phillips' venture. Others tried to dissuade him from opening the studio, as a similar venture had been attempted before, in 1948, by a company called Royal Recording, but it was gone by the time Phillips opened his doors.

As confident as Phillips was in the business—he printed business cards that proclaimed, "We record anything—anywhere—anytime"—he maintained his day job at radio station WREC, viewing the new studio as a way to supplement his income and exercise some creative freedom outside of the confines of radio. His goal was to give a voice to the artists he was hearing—be they blues, gospel, or country—and help them reach a broader audience.

One way to do this was to record the acts and then lease the recordings to a record label for distribution. His first foray into that endeavor was with 4 Star Records, to whom he sent recordings of a local boogie pianist named "Lost" John Hunter. He also began to work with the West Coast label Modern Records, sending them recordings of artists like B. B. King and Joe Hill Louis. The relationship with Modern began to sour, however, when Phillips started sending recordings to a competitor in Chicago, Chess Records. Naiveté played a role in that decision, as well as the fact that the studio was barely earning enough to

Sun Records' simplistic sunrays became as iconic as the music included on the records. *Private collection*

keep the rent paid. But Phillips' prospects began to improve when Ike Turner and his band came to town to record on March 5, 1951. The group, fronted by singer Jackie Brenston, cut an ode to a hot rod, "Rocket 88," that many point to as the first rock 'n' roll song. (Its carefree and rough sound certainly became a blueprint of sorts, although there were many similar-sounding songs before it.) Phillips sold the single to Chess, and its success enabled him to quit his radio work to concentrate more on the studio.

Phillips' next stroke of luck was finding Howlin' Wolf, whose inimitable singing style—gruff, powerful, and commanding attention—was just the kind of thing Phillips kept an ear out for. Phillips sent the recording to both Modern and Chess in error, causing hard feelings all around. Wolf ended up with Chess, but Phillips smoothed things over by sending another of his finds, Roscoe Gordon, to Modern, as a peace offering of sorts.

Phillips' true love lay in the creative aspects of the business, however, and this episode proved to him that the business negotiations and hard feelings weren't worth the money. Instead, he decided to open his own label, and so, with financial backing from several partners—including fellow disk jockey Dewey Phillips (no relation)—he started the Sun Records label. Sticking initially to a policy of only recording local acts, Phillips began building a strong catalogue of artists, including Little Walter, Little Milton, and James Cotton. He had also signed a deal with Nashville studio owner Jim Bulleit, whom he brought in as a partner, which placed the Prisonaires—a close-harmony group made up of current inmates—under a Sun contract. The music was unlike anything else on Sun, but the novelty of it was enough to keep Phillips interested. It was also enough to get a curious public to purchase over 50,000 copies of the group's single, "Just Walkin' in the Rain."

Sam's brother Jud Phillips came in to help with promotion in 1953, and he subsequently became a partner after the brothers bought out Bulleits' share. By now, the hits had grown scarce, but the Phillips brothers pressed on, and in the summer of 1953 their fortunes changed when a young man named Elvis Presley came in to record a vanity record.

Johnny Cash and the Tennessee Two

In late July 1954, Cash and his musician friends Marshall Grant, Luther Perkins, and Red Kernodle began to hear Elvis' first record, "That's All Right," in heavy rotation on local stations, and started toying around with the idea of recording their own material. While they enjoyed country music—encompassing both the contemporary hits of the day and traditional standards—they liked playing the gospel songs they'd arranged even more. One of their favorites, "I Was There When It Happened," was written by country singer and Louisiana governor Jimmie Davis; their version featured harmony singing by Grant and Perkins.

Knowing that Presley recorded at Sun Studios, Cash called Moore in late 1954 and asked how he could get an audition with Phillips. Moore more than likely recommended a direct approach, and since he passed Sun on his daily commute, Cash began stopping by and asking receptionist Marion Keisker if Phillips was available. Cash was repeatedly turned away, but he was persistent. He eventually reached Phillips on the phone and introduced himself as a gospel singer, but again Phillips turned him away. A few days later, Cash spoke to Phillips on the phone for a second time, but was once again told that Phillips was too busy to listen to any new singers.

Cash's lucky break came when he decided to wait on the steps one morning and caught Phillips as he came into the studio. He introduced himself and told Phillips that he wanted to audition to be recorded by the label. Catching Phillips in a charitable mood, Cash was invited in to sing a few songs. "I sang two or three hours for him," Cash told Escott and Hawkins. "Everything I knew—Hank Snow, Ernest Tubb, Flatt & Scruggs . . . I even sang 'I'll Take You Home Again Kathleen.'" In the end, Phillips liked what he heard. He told Cash to come back with his band to record an audition.

Before that, though, Cash came in alone to record at least four original songs, accompanying himself on guitar. The first was "Wide Open Road," a song he and the Tennessee Two would return to several times in the studio. He followed it with "You're My Baby," a rockabilly jumper that Roy Orbison recorded and released as the B-side to his single "Rockhouse" in the summer of 1956. "My Treasure" was a slow love song featuring an echoing vocal that is credited by some to Sam Phillips and by others to Marshall Grant. The fourth song noted in the recording logs, "Show Me the Green," has yet to be recovered.

Cash returned to Sun Studios a few days later for a full-band audition, bringing with him Grant, Perkins, and Kernodle. He apologized for his rough crew, but the band nevertheless set up and gave it their best, performing the Davis number they loved so much. Afterward, Phillips told them that while he thought there was something special about them, he just couldn't sell gospel records. He wanted to give a platform to good local musicians, but he also had to keep the lights on. He advised them to go home and come back with an original song. Disappointed but not dejected, the quartet went home to do just that.

Cash had already performed one original for Phillips, but "Wide Open Road" apparently hadn't made an impression. The next time the four men got together, Cash brought along a poem he had written in Germany called "Hey Porter," which had previously been published in the armed-forces magazine *Stars & Stripes*. It was a story of a Southern man so excited to be returning to his homeland that he continually shouts instructions to the porter, telling him what to do when they arrive at their destination. Though none of them were really songwriters, the four musicians began shaping the poem into a number that could be performed by the group. Cash also worked up another song, "Folsom Prison Blues" (covered in more detail in chapter 18), and the group made plans to continue practicing and return to Sun in the following spring.

On March 22, 1955, the group returned to Sun for their first attempt at recording a debut single. Kernodle was visibly shaken: he played on one song—another attempt at "Wide Open Road"—but, as Grant writes in his autobiography, "He was so nervous and shaking so badly that he couldn't turn the tuning pegs accurately, and kept going a little above, then a little below the correct pitch, back and forth. Finally, he stood up and laid the steel guitar on his chair, turned to me, and said, 'Grant, I can't do anything but hold y'all back. I'm going back down to the shop and go back to work.'"

Years later, Kernodle told Cash biographers Escott and Hawkins that he quit "because there wasn't any money in it, and there was getting to be too much staying up late at night and running around." While Cash was an appliance salesman and Grant and Perkins were mechanics, Kernodle was a car salesman, and he probably did have more money coming in than he might have assumed the music would pay. But as far as his nervousness was concerned, he had little to worry about, considering the company he was keeping. Grant would later say that "inability" would become the group's defining sound; he himself only just started to play the bass months before.

Cash, Grant, and Perkins opened the session with their two new original songs. They recorded two takes of "Hey Porter," the first of which is marked by Perkins' nervous fumbling of the guitar solo. Even so, the fundamentals of what became the trademark Johnny Cash sound are evident from the opening notes. "Folsom Prison Blues" follows, although inexplicably Cash sings it with a heavily affected, higher-pitched voice and uses his normal singing voice only on occasional phrases like "down to San Antone." They also recorded a full-band version of "Wide Open Road." One take includes steel guitar, although Cash discographer John L. Smith notes that it may have been overdubbed onto the master take later, since Cash had told him that Kernodle never played on a track (which goes along with Grant's telling). Their final song was a cover of "My Two Timin' Woman," written and recorded by one of Cash's defining influences, "Yodeling Ranger" Hank Snow.

The full-band arrangement of "Wide Open Road" didn't impress Phillips any more than the demo Cash had cut earlier. Perhaps it was the steel guitar that caused him to overlook the song, because while it didn't fundamentally change the sound of the group, it did give them a more traditional sound, and one that was closer to the country music coming out of Nashville. "Folsom Prison Blues" would go on to become one of Cash's signature songs, but Phillips passed over it, too—perhaps because of the level of the performance given at this session—singling out "Hey Porter" as a potential single instead. He told the group to go home and come up with another song for the flip side. Phillips had developed a structure for Sun singles of pairing an upbeat number on one side with a ballad or slow blues on the other, and he made no exception with this new group, telling them to bring back a "weeper."

One of the most popular disc jockeys in Memphis was Eddie Hill on WMPS, with whom Cash had been very familiar as far back as his Dyess days. "When we worked in the fields in the summertime," he writes in *Man in Black*, "we usually took an hour off for lunch from noon till 1:00. We ate at 12:00, then from 12:30 to 1:00 we listened to the 'High Noon Roundup' over WMPS, Memphis, featuring Smilin' Eddie Hill and Ira and Charlie Louvin, the Louvin Brothers." From 1:00 until 1:15, the three musicians performed gospel songs as the Lonesome Valley Trio, and Cash listened every chance he could.

By 1955, Hill was well known in music circles—particularly country music circles—as he had made several appearances on the *Grand Ole Opry* and written songs for hit artists like Bill Monroe. One night, Cash was listening to Hill's show when he heard the DJ announce, "We've got some good songs, love songs, sweet songs, happy songs, and sad songs that'll make you cry, cry, cry." The phrase stuck with Cash, although he later told biographer Christopher S. Wren that he had also heard Hill say, "We're going to squaw and bawl and climb the walls," and was considering calling the song that instead. He worked on the song's lyrics over the next few weeks. If Phillips wanted a "weeper," Cash was going to give him one.

Budding Radio Stars

In the meantime, Cash and the Tennessee Two figured there was more than one way to get heard over the airwaves. In addition to working for the Home

Equipment Company, Cash was also utilizing the GI Bill to take two classes per week at Keegan's School of Broadcasting in the hope of getting into radio—a proven stepping-stone to the music industry at the time. Although by all accounts Cash wasn't much of a salesman, his boss, George Bates, liked him, and could see the potential in the young man. Cash wanted more than anything to be heard on the radio, and since his group's single wasn't quite ready, he approached Bates about sponsoring them on the local station, KWEM. Like many local stations at the time, KWEM supplemented the playing of records with short performances by live acts—if they brought a sponsor along with them. Bates bankrolled the $15 per week needed to get the trio a fifteen-minute spot on Saturday afternoons. (Wren reports it as being from 2:00 to 2:15 p.m.; author Ashley Kahn, in his liner notes to *Bootleg Volume II: From Memphis to Hollywood*, and Grant, in his autobiography, state 4:00 p.m.)

On a recording of the show from May 21, 1955, Cash sounds nervous—especially for a broadcast student—as he introduces the Tennessee Two and announces that this is their first radio appearance. They go on to perform three songs. The first is their tried and tested "Wide Open Road," followed by the Bob Nolan–penned "One More Ride," a song made popular by the Sons of the Pioneers, and one that Cash would return to throughout his career. The final song is another original, a gospel song called "Belshazzar"—possibly one they had shown Phillips at their group audition. Interestingly, the group's set didn't include the recently recorded "Hey Porter," or the song they had recorded even more recently that would become the flip side of their first single.

Just prior to their radio debut, the group had returned to Sun Studio with a new song, based on the words Cash had heard Eddie Hill say on the radio that night: "Cry, Cry, Cry." Cash later told Christopher Wren that they tried the song thirty-five times before getting it right, mainly due to Perkins not catching on. Thirty-five is an exaggeration, though, as Cash had written his old army buddy Ted Freeman after the recording session to say that they had spent two and a half hours in the studio working on the song, while the Sun records show that they recorded only four takes. The first take has Perkins taking a lead break after each verse, but the subsequent takes have only one break and an outro.

After completing the exhausting session, Phillips and the group went their separate ways for the evening. A few days later, Phillips called Cash with the news that he would be issuing "Hey Porter" b/w "Cry, Cry, Cry" as Sun 221. Finally, Cash was a professional musician, and the group was paid an advance of $3.30.

The group continued their Saturday radio performances and began picking up as many shows as they could in preparation for the single's release. The trio returned to the studio around the release of the single, which was scheduled for June 21st, bringing one new original and two cover songs. The covers were "New Mexico," sometimes listed as "Trail to Mexico," and recorded in 1958 by Cash's future friend Johnny Horton as "Out in New Mexico"; and "I Couldn't Keep from Crying," written by Marty Robbins, who had had a Top 5 national hit with the song in 1953. They also made another run at "Wide Open Road," this time sans steel guitar, although that didn't help its chances for release. The second original was "Port of Lonely Hearts," which offered an early glimpse at Cash's willingness to experiment with his sound by overdubbing a second vocal line, providing harmony as well as a call-and-response part. "Port of Lonely Hearts," like several other songs from early sessions, would later be released after Cash had made his move to Columbia.

With nothing fruitful coming from that session, but "Cry, Cry, Cry" on the way to becoming a regional success, Phillips brought the guys back in to record a few more tracks on July 30, 1955. This time, all four songs were Cash originals, three of which they hadn't attempted recording before. The first was a return to "Folsom Prison Blues," with Cash now singing in his regular voice. The other three were "So Doggone Lonesome," "Mean Eyed Cat," and "Luther Played the Boogie," a tribute to Perkins. Shortly after this recording date, "Cry, Cry, Cry" passed the 100,000 sales mark, placing it at the top of the regional country charts. Hoping the slow burn would continue, Phillips held off on releasing another single, and by late November "Cry, Cry, Cry" had reached #14 on the *Billboard* Country Best Sellers chart.

In December, Phillips released the second single by Cash and the Tennessee Two, "So Doggone Lonesome" b/w "Folsom Prison Blues." From 1948 to 1957, *Billboard* published multiple Country music charts, each focusing on a different segment of the music industry. The Juke Box Folk Records (which became the Most Played C&W in Juke Boxes in 1956) focused on jukebox plays, Best Selling Retail Folk Records (which became C&W Best Sellers in Stores) focused on retail sales, and Most Played by Folk Disk Jockeys (which became Most Played C&W by Jockeys) focused on radio airplay. Both sides of Sun 232 peaked at #4 in February 1956: "So Doggone Lonesome" on the Juke Box chart and "Folsom Prison Blues" on the Disk Jockey chart. Phillips was flush with talent at the time: "Blue Suede Shoes" by Carl Perkins, another fresh face recording at Sun, sat at #1 for three weeks just after Cash's breakthrough success.

Returning to the studio in April 1956, Cash brought with him three original songs: "I Walk the Line," "Get Rhythm," and "Train of Love." "I Walk the Line" (discussed in more depth in chapter 9) became the signature song for Johnny Cash and the Tennessee Two, and was released as Sun 241, with "Get Rhythm" on the flip side. It would spend forty-three weeks on the *Billboard* chart, six of them at #1. The song was a runaway smash, even reaching #88 on the Pop chart. It ended the year at #3, by which time Phillips had released "There You Go" b/w "Train of Love" as Sun 258. It was another double-sided hit, with the two songs hitting #1 and #7, respectively, as the year closed out.

The band paid a couple of unproductive visits to the studio between live engagements as they raced into 1957. Cash's next single, the plaintive ballad "Next in Line" b/w "Don't Make Me Go" (Sun 266), was released on April 21, 1957, and proved to be the most disappointing of his short career at Sun Records—or at least as disappointing as a Top 10 single can be—reaching only

#9 on the chart. As is the case today, the record-buying public is fickle, and too much of something—even something as strong and original as the sound created by Cash, Grant, and Perkins—can sometimes be too easily dismissed.

The Cowboy Rides In

To help cut off any downward slide before it could actually happen, Phillips began ceding a degree of control in the studio to his new engineer, "Cowboy" Jack Clement. On July 1, 1957, the trio recorded two originals, "Home of the Blues" and "Give My Love to Rose," with Clement. Released as Sun 279, they would help create a new pattern for Cash singles: a sweetened song on one side, and the bareness of the Tennessee Two on the flip. Clement overdubbed a male chorus, drums, and piano onto "Home of the Blues," while "Give My Love to Rose" is adorned only with the stark guitar and bass of the Tennessee Two. "Home of the Blues" reached #3 on the charts, while "Give My Love to Rose" peaked at #13. The latter song also marks the first appearance on record of two of Cash's favorite themes: the Old West and prisoners.

While Cash and the boys continued recording throughout 1957, they did not release another single until after their session on November 12th, which yielded the Clement-penned "Ballad of a Teenage Queen" and Cash's "Big River." Released as Sun 283, the single was a study in contrasts. "Ballad of a Teenage Queen" was the first single not to include Perkins. Clement played acoustic guitar alongside Cash and Grant and then returned to the recording a little over a week later to add a choral opening, while also providing lush background vocals and a piercing soprano throughout. The musical sweetening of "Home of the Blues" is cranked up a few notches for "Teenage Queen," while "Big River" is quintessential Cash, with Perkins' unique picking serving up the intro before Cash's acoustic guitar propels them forward. "Teenage Queen" was Cash's most pop-inflected single yet, and it placed him back at the top of the charts. It spent ten weeks at #1 on the Country charts and peaked at #16 on the Pop chart, while "Big River" climbed to #4 on the Country charts.

Early Live Appearances

Not long after their first recording sessions, Cash and the Tennessee Two started playing local gigs, including churches and bars. As the popularity of their records grew, so too did the distance they had to travel to perform. They were now routinely making appearances in Tennessee, Arkansas, Louisiana, and Texas, in venues ranging from small schoolhouses and taverns to the big stages of the *Big D Jamboree* in Dallas, the *Louisiana Hayride* in Shreveport, and the *Grand Ole Opry* in Nashville. Over the course of his career, Cash played on a lot of big stages, from the *Opry* to Carnegie Hall, but right here is a good place to mention the earliest live recordings of Cash and company that showcase the early development of their touring act.

Louisiana Hayride

Cash's first appearance on the *Louisiana Hayride* was on November 12, 1955. Recordings released in 2003 have him and the Tennessee Two performing their most current single, "Hey Porter," followed by "Luther Played the Boogie." These recordings are an excellent glimpse at the developing act. Perkins is rock-steady but still tentative in his playing, while Cash sounds like he is running out of air as he repeats the title phrase on the latter. Nonetheless, the crowd is receptive and vocal.

Johnny Cash: Live Recordings from the Louisiana Hayride—now out of print but occasionally popping up on eBay—features one selection apiece from two 1956 appearances. The first, from May 12th, is a spirited version of "So Doggone Lonesome," and it is readily evident that the group's ever-increasing live work is paying off in terms of sharpening their act. The second performance, of "I Walk the Line," is from June 23rd, just weeks after the song had started its climb up the charts (on that particular date, it sat at #4 on *Billboard*'s C&W Best Sellers list and #5 on the C&W Disk Jockey's chart). The announcer introduces Cash and "that unusual song that he wrote," as cheers rise from the audience. "We'd like to do one side of our current Sun release," Cash adds in his own introduction to the song. "It's the one we're the proudest of. It seems to be doing more for us, and we hope you like it."

Country Style USA

Throughout the 1950s, *Country Style USA*, presented by the United States Army, offered a fifteen-minute selection of "America's top country and folk artists" to regional stations that would donate the time for the program to air. It was hosted by Charlie Applewhite, a singer who had been featured regularly on *The Milton Berle Show* before being drafted in the mid-1950s. Each show followed the same basic format, although there were variations. The early shows were syndicated only to radio (on vinyl), but some of the later shows, which ran through 1960, were filmed and broadcast on television as well.

Johnny Cash and the Tennessee Two made three appearances on the show. Although their best-known appearance is dated July 1, 1957, the first two came a bit earlier, and are among the group's earliest live recordings. The first was syndicated around November 12, 1956, while the second probably aired in early 1957. For the first, they open the show with "Hey Porter," following it with "I Walk the Line," which Cash introduces as being one side of "their last Sun record" and mentions it being "one of the bestsellers in the country these days." Applewhite and Cash then do a promotion for the US Army Reserves before Cash introduces "Rock Island Line," noting that while there are a lot of versions out there, they haven't done one yet (although they would cut one the following summer). The set ends with "So Doggone Lonesome," which Cash says is on "one side of their next-to-last Sun record."

The second appearance kicks off with "Folsom Prison Blues" followed by "Cry, Cry, Cry," before Applewhite and Cash promote the US Army Youth Reserves. Even though Phillips wouldn't allow the band to record any gospel material at this point, they would still include it in their live shows, and here they present "I Was There When It Happened." Only Cash's voice is heard, with Grant or Perkins not yet contributing background vocals, as they would when the group eventually recorded the song, on August 4, 1957 (and in later live performances). They close the set with "one side of our latest release on Sun," "Get Rhythm." Based on Cash's intros, it can be deduced that both shows were probably recorded at the same time, in late 1956.

The band's final appearance on *Country Style USA* was filmed for release and illustrates a few changes to the format. In the vinyl transcriptions, the show opens with a recorded clip of the Bob Wills song "Stay All Night, Stay a Little Longer," as performed by an unknown vocalist and band. In the televised edition of the show, the guest performed the clip to open and close the show, and there was often a performance by a second guest in the middle of the episode. In this 1957 episode, which has been released by Bear Family on the *Country Style USA Season 2* DVD and the *Unseen Cash* CD, Cash and the Tennessee Two perform "There You Go," "Give My Love to Rose," and "Home of the Blues." The special guest, singing "White Silver Sands," is Carolee Cooper, the daughter of country stars Wilma Lee and Stoney Cooper, and a talented vocalist who went

After Cash left Sun, the company continued to release singles that performed well on the charts. The familiar yellow and black label was turned black and white for DJ copies. *Private collection*

on to lead the Carolee Singers and provide background vocals for performers on the *Grand Ole Opry*.

These performances give an interesting glimpse into the group's stage show during their still-formative years. In the filmed episode, we see Cash in his pre–Man in Black days, dressed in the same floral blue-gray shirt he would wear on the cover of his 1959 Columbia release *Songs of Our Soil*. The Tennessee Two wear casual, non-matching bowling-type shirts. Contrasting these performances with the 1955 KWEM recording shows the immense growth in confidence and charisma among Cash, Grant, and Perkins.

Parting Ways

The funny thing about the music business—now and then—is that a small independent record label can work tirelessly at bringing a successful artist to the forefront, only to have that success kill the very thing that created it. For every single sent out, the company had to pay for the pressing of the record, as well as ship it out to both retailers and radio stations. Radio airplay would help sell the single, driving more people to buy it, but the retailers wouldn't always pay for the records before they were sold, and would often return them if they remained unsold after a period of time. Add to that the artist and songwriter royalties and staff salaries to be paid, and you get a sense of the intense financial strain on independent labels, which were often bootstrapped operations to begin with. This was certainly true of Sun Records, and by 1956, Phillips was in financial trouble. From the start, the studio had never been flush with money, to the point where Marion Keisker would put her own money in the petty cash box so that Phillips, who suffered from depression and anxiety over the studio's intermittent lack of success, wouldn't know the real state of affairs.

By now, Phillips had bought out his partners, and as the sole owner of Sun, he was facing the possibility of bankruptcy. In such a case, as with any business, the only thing to do is to try to sell off some assets. In Phillips' case, his biggest asset at the time was the contract of Elvis Presley, whom RCA Victor was interested in acquiring. With little choice, Phillips authorized Presley's manager, Colonel Tom Parker, to enter negotiations with the label. In the end, Phillips received $35,000 from RCA, plus an additional $5,000 to cover royalties he owed to Elvis. With the deal closed, Phillips poured his interest into radio (opening a new all-female station called WHER) and the other acts at Sun, including Cash, Perkins, and one of his newest signings, Jerry Lee Lewis.

While Clement was working to add flourish to Cash's recordings, Lewis was hitting the #1 spot in 1957 with his singles "Whole Lotta Shakin' Going On" and "Great Balls of Fire." Phillips was spending more time with his new charge, and that may have piqued a little professional jealously on the part of Cash, who in the wake of Presley's departure from the label had at one time been Phillips' main concern. Cash then began to enquire about the royalty rates both he and Lewis were receiving, and when it came time to renegotiate his contract, he requested 2 percent more than he was currently earning. Phillips balked, partly out of pride and partly because he just could not afford the increase. During this time, Cash had also been lobbying to do a gospel album, but Phillips denied him the opportunity, continuing to stand by his claim that he couldn't sell gospel records.

In August of 1957, while playing the Town Hall Party in California, Cash and Carl Perkins, who was also on the bill, were approached by A&R man Don Law, who asked if they would be interested in moving to Columbia Records. Perkins still had six months on his contract, Cash a year, but both men said they would be receptive to further discussions. In his 1997 autobiography, Cash noted that the money wasn't important to him. He simply had one question: "How much freedom will I have to make whatever music I want?" As the talks progressed, Cash asked Law about the possibility of recording a gospel album. "No problem," Law told him. What about a concept album? "I'm open to hearing about it," Law replied. With those assurances, Cash signed the option to move to Columbia when his Sun contract expired.

It didn't take long for rumors about the move to spread, and when Phillips heard them, he wanted either a confirmation or a denial, direct from the source. Cash recalled that Phillips called him, while Phillips said he drove out to Cash's house to find out. Regardless, the result was the same. Phillips revealed that he had heard Cash had signed an option with Columbia, and said he wanted Cash to look him in the eye and tell him the truth. Cash replied that he had not. It was, Phillips later told Colin Escott and Martin Hawkins, in *Good Rockin' Tonight*, "The only lie Johnny Cash ever told me, that I'm aware of."

Phillips knew he was being lied to. He threatened to sue Columbia and demanded that Cash return to the studio. Cash was incensed. He told Phillips that the money he was owed by Sun would make up for any lost sessions. When he was threatened with breach of contract, Cash decided to return to the studio, but he wasn't bringing any of his compositions with him. Out of twenty-four songs recorded, only one, "Come In Stranger," was a Cash original. Three others bore his stamp as co-writer—"You're the Nearest Thing to Heaven," "Life Goes On," and "Katy Too"—the latter pair written with Clement.

The first song Cash recorded when he returned to the studio was Clement's "Guess Things Happen That Way," released on Sun 295, backed with "Come In Stranger." Once again, the sweetened Clement/Cash song went to #1, where it remained for eight weeks. The follow-up, "The Ways of a Woman in Love," written by Charlie Rich and Bill Justis and backed with "You're the Nearest Thing to Heaven," was released as Sun 302 and spent four weeks at #2.

With that, Cash was poised to leave Sun on top, but Phillips didn't want to make it that easy. When Cash left for Columbia in July 1958, Phillips placed the following ad in the trade magazines:

> Johnny Cash began his musical career three years ago with Sun Records. In a comparatively short time, he has become a unique and distinctive artist occupying the #1 spot in his field . . .

When Shelby Singleton bought Sun Records in 1969, the company became Sun International and continued to release singles and albums from the Sun catalog through the 1980s.

Private collection

However, Johnny Cash signed with Columbia Records as of August 1, 1958. Upon learning that he was anticipating this move, we spent the next five months producing some of the finest sides for future Sun releases on Cash that we have ever had the pleasure of cutting.

Please believe us when we say you are in for some tremendous releases on Cash on Sun for at least the next two years.

Our thanks to Johnny for being a wonderful person to work with during our association. We are going to miss him to no end around 706 Union, but our aim is to keep him "hot" on Sun "If the Good Lord's Willing and the Creek Don't Rise."

Appreciatively,
Sam C. Phillips, President
Sun Record Co.

Sun Never Sets

Phillips wasn't just blowing smoke. When Cash released his second Columbia single, "Don't Take Your Guns to Town," Sun released "It's Just About Time." (While "Don't Take Your Guns to Town" reached #1, "It's Just About Time" barely touched the chart, spending only one week at #30.) This pattern continued for years—Columbia would release a single, and Sun would answer with a Cash single of its own.

Aside from the singles, Phillips also began issuing albums of Cash's work. Released in October 1957, *Johnny Cash with His Hot and Blue Guitar* had been Sun's first LP, and consisted mainly of Cash's hit singles to that point. As Cash was leaving for Columbia, Phillips got in one last jab, titling Cash's second album *Sings the Songs That Made Him Famous.* It was again filled predominately with past hits alongside a selection of unreleased songs from the last series of recording sessions.

In 1959, Sun released *Greatest!*, which oddly doesn't include any of Cash's hits but rather previously unreleased songs from past sessions. *Sings Hank Williams*, released in 1960, utilized four Williams songs—"You Win Again," "I Could Never Be Ashamed of You," and "Hey Good Lookin'," all of which were available on *Greatest!*, plus "I Can't Help It (if I'm Still in Love with You)"—recorded at one of Cash's final Sun sessions, on May 15, 1958. The cover featured a model who vaguely resembled Cash, holding a guitar, leaning against a fence, and staring off into the horizon.

The remainder of Cash's Sun recordings were released, bundled up with his hits, on *Now Here's Johnny Cash* (1961); *All Aboard the Blue Train* (1963), which attempted to replicate the feel of the concept albums Cash was producing at Columbia; and *Original Sun Sound of Johnny Cash* (1964). Phillips even reached all the way back to Cash's first solo demo sessions, to which he now added overdubs. "My Treasure" was released as a single and included on the album *Now Here's Johnny Cash*, and "Wide Open Road" was featured on *Original Sun Sound.*

In the early 1960s, after years in the business, Phillips began looking for an exit, but the right opportunity wouldn't come until 1969, when Shelby Singleton bought Sun Records and its back catalogue for an undisclosed amount, rechristening it Sun International Corporation. Singleton had gotten his start in the music industry in the late 1950s, and by 1960 was working for Mercury Records. In 1966, he decided to strike out on his own and formed a series of small labels. He finally struck gold in 1968 when his Plantation Records artist Jeannie C. Riley hit #1 on both the Country and Hot 100 charts with her recording of Tom T. Hall's "Harper Valley, PTA." Riley was the first woman ever to achieve such a feat, and the only one until Dolly Parton repeated it a decade later.

Phillips had stretched his "two years" worth of unreleased Cash material to five years, but Singleton would continue to stretch it for years to come, releasing repackaged Cash recordings until 1982. On the one hand he was keeping interest in the older recordings alive, but on the other hand he was pushing into the market product that often directly competed with Cash's current output. It was at times a blessing and a curse. In the early 1960s, when Cash was releasing his concept albums and not having much action on the singles charts with his Columbia recordings, the Sun releases buoyed his chart life. But at times—such as from February through July of 1960—Cash's Columbia sides were competing directly with his Sun singles. In June and July of that year, Cash had four songs—two from Columbia and two from Sun—on the various charts, all competing for listeners'—and buyers'—attention. It was testament to Cash's popularity that the amount of available material strengthened rather than smothered his career.

4

Country Boy, Ain't Got No Blues

Sun LPs and EPs

Through the 1950s and into the 1960s, 45 rpm singles were the dominant medium in the music business, but that was being challenged by the growing popularity of the long-playing album (LP). Even though LPs allowed labels to include more than two songs per release, there was a fear within the industry over the lack of control they would have over what a DJ might play from an LP. But that was the way the industry was headed, and Sun Records followed suit, first with LPs, then with EPs—extended-play singles that featured four instead of two songs and brought the price point to a middle ground between the 45 and LP, making them more enticing to consumers.

Johnny Cash with His Hot and Blue Guitar (1957)

Sun Records chose Johnny Cash to lead their charge into the LP market with his (and its) first LP, *Johnny Cash with His Hot and Blue Guitar.* Released in September 1957 and packed with twelve songs—four previously released and eight new ones—it offers an overview of many of the themes Cash would continue to cover during his career.

The album opens with his version of Leadbelly's "Rock Island Line" (by way of Lonnie Donegan), with Cash and the Tennessee Two starting slow and folky but quickly ramping up the rhythm to a rockabilly tilt. "I Heard That Lonesome Whistle," taken from the Hank Williams catalogue that Cash would continue to draw on, has him singing lonesome blues as if he wrote them himself. What he did write was the ragged "Country Boy," on which he extols the virtues of country living before sliding into the next song, "If the Good Lord's Willing," a Jerry Reed–penned ditty about a country boy off to find his love.

The first previously released hit, 1955's "Cry, Cry, Cry," comes nearly halfway into the album, although here "hit" might be a tad generous. The single had been only a moderate regional success, although it did reach #14 on the national sales chart. Next, reaching back to 1950, Cash brings out "Remember Me," a song about a man letting the object of his affection know that he will always be there for her, which Stuart Hamblen had taken to #2, followed by the flip side of that coin, "So Doggone Lonesome"—one side of a two-sided hit for Cash in February of 1956.

On this, Cash's debut album, Sam Phillips grants Cash his long-held wish to record a gospel song. Cash opts for "I Was There When It Happened," the Jimmie Davis song that was a staple of the Johnny Cash and the Tennessee Two live show. Cash's biggest single to that date, "I Walk the Line," starts the wind-down, leading into an inspired sequencing trifecta of "The Wreck of the Old 97," "Folsom Prison Blues," and "Doin' My Time." "The Wreck of the Old 97" had long been a favorite of Cash's and would be included in the group's live act for many years to come. This true train story set to music serves as one bookend for "Folsom Prison Blues," the 1956 #4 hit, while Jimmie Skinner's "Doin' My Time" serves as the other bookend. These last five songs serve as a fairly good summation of the themes that would permeate Cash's repertoire right up to his last recordings: God, love, trains, folk songs, and prison.

Johnny Cash Sings Hank Williams (EP, 1958)

Featuring a photo of Cash, dressed in white, performing live on the cover, *Johnny Cash Sings Hank Williams* consists of new recordings of four Williams classics: "I Can't Help It (if I'm Still in Love with You)," "Hey Good Lookin'," "You Win Again," and "I Could Never Be Ashamed of You." All four tracks were recorded at Sun Studios on May 15, 1958. On May 27, with "Ballad of a Teenage Queen" falling from the charts, the Gene Lowery Singers—the voices featured on that hit—were brought in to overdub their "ohhs" and "ahhs" over the top of some very fine recordings. The sound may have fit in with songs of the times (think "Oh Lonesome Me" by Don Gibson, which knocked "Teenage Queen" from the top spot), but they date the tracks in the worst possible way. Another song recorded at the same session was "Cold, Cold Heart," though it would not be released until 1970, when Sun Internationals included it on *The Rough Cut King of Country Music.* Superior versions—stripped of the over-the-top chorus—have been released since, and are well worth giving a listen.

Sings the Songs That Made Him Famous (1958)

Shortly after Cash left for Columbia in 1958, Sun released what amounted to a greatest-hits compilation, with a title designed to make sure that everyone knew who put Cash on the map. Eight of the album's twelve tracks had already been released as singles and had some action on the charts: "Ballad of a Teenage Queen," "There You Go," "I Walk the Line" (also included on *Johnny Cash with His Hot and Blue Guitar*), "Guess Things Happen That Way," "Train of Love," "Next in Line," "Home of the Blues," and "Big River." Two further tracks, while not singles, had also been previously released: "Don't Make Me Go," the B-side to "Next in Line," and "I Can't Help It (if I'm Still in Love with You)," from *Johnny Cash Sings Hank Williams.* The only new tracks—"Ways of a Woman in

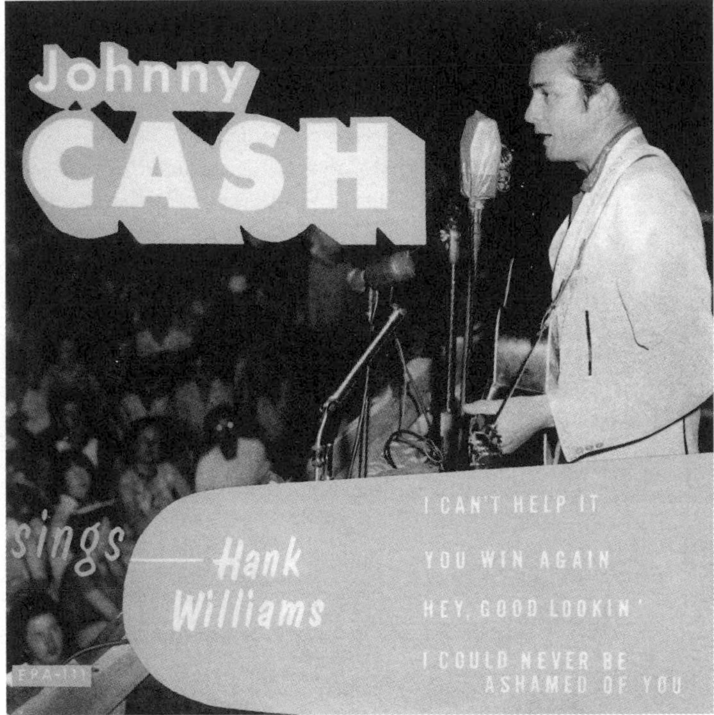

On the heels of Cash's first full-length LP, Sun issued an EP consisting of four Hank Williams–penned tunes. *Private collection*

Love" and "You're the Nearest Thing to Heaven"—were also released on a single, with the former spending four weeks at #2 and the latter peaking at #5. Overall, though, this was not a bad collection of early hits.

Johnny Cash: Country Boy (EP, 1958)

To end 1958, Sun issued *Country Boy* as a stopgap between LPs. There's nothing new here, though, as the EP merely contains the first four songs from *Johnny Cash with His Hot and Blue Guitar.*

Greatest! (1959)

While *Songs That Made Him Famous* contained predominately previously released material, *Greatest!* is made up of mostly new songs. The album was released around the same time as Cash's Columbia debut album, and Phillips did his best to match Columbia single for single in chart competition. His first release of 1959 was "It's Just About Time" (backed with "It's Just I Thought You'd Like to Know"), which hit the Country chart at #30 before falling off the next week.

It was Sun's lowest-charting Johnny Cash single to date (his second Columbia single, "Don't Take Your Guns to Town," was at #1 at the time).

The second single released from the album, "Luther Played the Boogie," fared much better, peaking at #8 and spending thirteen weeks on the chart, while the B-side, the Charlie Rich–penned "Thanks a Lot," peaked at #12. The A-side demonstrated on record a playfulness that had previously only been shown during live shows, turning the spotlight on Luther Perkins and his unique style.

"Katy Too"—an up-tempo story of a ladies' man making his way around town but always thinking about his other girl, Katy—peaked at #11. The B-side was a version of the 1956 Elvis Presley #1 hit "I Forgot to Remember to Forget." Wrapping up 1959 was the fourth single from the album, the forlorn "Goodbye, Little Darlin'" (backed with "You Tell Me"), which peaked at #22. The remaining four songs on the album included three from the *Johnny Cash Sings Hank Williams* EP—"You Win Again," "Hey Good Lookin'," and "I Could Never Be Ashamed of You"—and the 1956 B-side "Get Rhythm."

I Walk the Line (EP, 1959)

The first in a series of four EPs closing 1959 and opening 1960, *I Walk the Line* recycles the final four songs from *Johnny Cash with His Hot and Blue Guitar.*

Johnny Cash with the Tennessee Two: His Top Hits (EP, 1959)

The last Sun Cash EP of '59, *His Top Hits* consists of four previous singles that had already been included on *Sings the Songs That Made Him Famous.*

Home of the Blues (EP, 1960)

Sun began 1960 with the third EP in the series, which continues where *His Top Hits* left off and is made up of four more songs from *Sings Songs That Made Him Famous.*

So Doggone Lonesome (EP, 1960)

The final Johnny Cash Sun EP reaches back to his first LP and includes the final four songs that hadn't yet been reissued on EP.

Johnny Cash Sings Hank Williams (1960)

While Columbia released two Cash albums in 1960, Sun dashed off an expanded version of the *Johnny Cash Sings Hank Williams* EP. The cover featured a lanky, dark-haired fellow holding a guitar, standing by a fence, staring off into the distance—obviously not who he was supposed to be. The most unfortunate part of the disc is the presence of the syrupy background singers from the *Hank Williams* EP, here spilled over to other songs that had previously been hits without their help. Getting the Gene Lowery Singers treatment here are "Next in Line," "Folsom Prison Blues," and "I Walk the Line." While they don't offer a welcome change to any of those songs, their contributions aren't as grating as the high-pitched caterwauling on "I Love You Because," one side of the single released from the album ("Straight A's in Love" being the other side). The album closer, "Mean Eyed Cat," returns Cash to a stripped-down sound, and he would later return to the song itself during his American years.

Now Here's Johnny Cash (1961)

In his first two years at Columbia, Cash released five albums and one EP. The label then took a bit of a break from albums in 1961, releasing only an appearance by Cash on the classical music piece *Lure of the Grand Canyon.* Through the spring and summer of 1960 into the beginning of 1961, both Sun and Columbia were pumping out singles, most of which did not rise above the #10 spot on the Hot Country Singles chart, although there were several that danced with the Hot 100, the chart that ranked the biggest pop tunes of the day. Cash's failure to climb any higher on the charts wasn't for lack of trying. At one point, in July of 1960, there were up to five Cash singles (released either by Sun or Columbia)

In 1970, Sun International took advantage of Cash's high profile to release this "collector's edition" EP containing six of Cash's Sun-era songs. *Private collection*

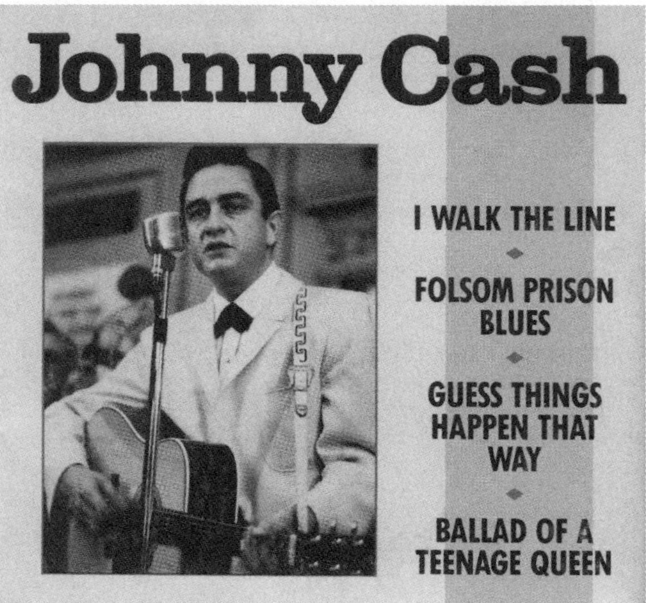

Rhino Records released a series of 3-inch CDs in 1988 entitled Lil' Bit of Gold. Other artists in the series include Eddie Cochran, the Beach Boys, Carl Perkins, and Ray Charles. *Private collection*

on the two charts. But making so many choices available at once might have diluted the sales potential of some of the singles.

The Sun singles that came out during this time were all drawn from the only Cash album released in 1961, *Now Here's Johnny Cash*. Five tracks from the album were released as singles, the first being the pairing of "Down the Street to 301" and "Story of a Broken Heart." Neither song touched the Country chart, but both flirted heavily with the Hot 100 on the "Bubbling Under" chart. The second single paired "Port of Lonely Hearts" with "Mean Eyed Cat" from Cash's previous Sun album. "Mean Eyed Cat" spent one week at #30 before falling off the charts. The final single coupled "Oh Lonesome Me" with "Life Goes On." Don Gibson, with whom Cash had toured around the same time, had spent eight weeks at #1 with "Oh Lonesome Me" in 1958. Cash's version of the song, which featured the Gene Lowery Singers, peaked at #13. This was Cash's final charting Sun Records single (two others would chart, much later, on Sun International). The rest of the album was made up of songs that had previously been issued as singles or featured on other Sun albums and EPs.

All Aboard the Blue Train (1962)

Following the path of Columbia's *Ride This Train* and Cash's other concept albums of the time, Sun pulled together *All Aboard the Blue Train* in December

1962. The single from the album was "Blue Train," a catchy tune that deserved more recognition than it got but didn't chart at all. As the title suggests, most of the songs on the album were train-related—"Blue Train," "Train of Love," "I Heard That Lonesome Whistle," "Rock Island Line," "Hey Porter," "Folsom Prison Blues," and "Wreck of the Old 97"—but a few were only peripherally train-themed ("There You Go," "Come In Stranger," and "So Doggone Lonesome" among them). The album was well received by critics, but perhaps unsurprisingly, given that it was filled with songs that could be found elsewhere, it failed to gain much traction.

Original Sun Sound of Johnny Cash (1964)

Original Sun Sound of Johnny Cash wasn't just another clever jab in the vein of *Sings the Songs That Made Him Famous.* Even in 1964—almost ten years after Cash began his career, and five years after he left Memphis—articles were still talking about "that Memphis Sound" in reference to Cash, Carl Perkins, Elvis Presley, and Jerry Lee Lewis. By 1964, none of those artists remained on Sun, but their current works were still often compared with the work they did with Sam Phillips.

This album is split fairly evenly between previously released singles like "Country Boy," "Thanks a Lot," and "Big River" and new (old) material. The only single released from the album reaches right back to Cash's earliest Sun sessions: "Wide Open Road," which was recorded in 1955 and was one of the songs that the group used in their initial audition. For the B-side, Phillips selected Cash's original gospel song "Belshazzar," which the group had been playing live since 1955 but didn't get to record until 1957.

Original Sun Sound pretty much cleared out the Cash vault at Sun, pulling together the remaining songs left over from Cash's last sessions at the studio. Two of them come from the catalogue of '40s Texas music star turned music publisher Ted Daffan, "Always Alone" and "Born to Lose." Two more draw from two of Cash's primary influences, in the form of Hank Snow's "Two Timin' Woman" and Leadbelly's "Goodnight, Irene."

5

He Changed His Clothes and Shined His Boots

Columbia 1959

Whether it was a disagreement over royalty rates, or a feeling that Sam Phillips was spending too much time grooming Jerry Lee Lewis to assume the throne vacated by Elvis' sale to RCA, Cash was ready for a change. "There were so many things I wanted to do," he told Peter Guralnick, for a 1980 *Country Music* article. "I had all these ideas about special projects, different album ventures like *Ride This Train, From Sea to Shining Sea,* the Indian album, but I felt like at Sun I would be limited in what I could do, where with a major company I could do all that and reach more people with my music. I think I was right, too. Sam couldn't understand it back then, we had a little misunderstanding at the time, he couldn't see me wanting to go to another record company—but I could."

Don Law

That major company turned out to be Columbia Records, and it was A&R man Don Law who made the offer. Born in London, England, in 1902, Law made his way to America in the mid-1920s, landing in Texas, where he married and began to look for a job. While settling in at a boardinghouse, he was told of a bookkeeping job at the Brunswick-Balke-Collender Company, which owned the small record label Brunswick. Although he tried to get a job in sales, Law's English accent kept him out of the position, so he became a record and order clerk. "It was my job to maintain the perpetual inventory, watch the movement of records, place orders on the factories, keep the records in a spot that they needed them, and not have them when they didn't need them, which is quite a trick," he told Douglas B. Green, in an interview for the Country Music Hall of Fame Oral History.

In 1931, soon after Law started at the company, Brunswick was taken over by American Record Corporation, which added it to a stable of labels that included Oriole, Perfect, and Domino, among others. Another Englishman, Art Satherley, had joined ARC in 1929, and was in charge of acquiring Southern acts for the labels—mainly western and country acts like Gene Autry and Patsy Montana. After ARC bought Brunswick, Law became Satherley's assistant, and would accompany him on his trips to make field recordings and find new talent.

In 1934, ARC purchased Columbia for $70,000, deepening its catalogue with artists like Cab Calloway and Duke Ellington. Under Satherley's tutelage, Law began to venture into A&R. "Of course, I cleared it with Art, because it was his budget I was working with," he recalled. "But in the meantime, Art and I had become very close friends, and he trusted my judgment pretty well, and if they weren't too expensive, he'd say, 'Well, go ahead. If that's what you want, we'll do it.'"

Law's most famous signing came in 1936, after he had become a regional manager. One of his salesmen, Ernie Oertle, brought to his attention a young blues singer, and Law suggested he bring the young man to a recording session in San Antonio, where Law would be recording other little-known and now forgotten acts. When it came time for the session, Law was informed that the young blues singer had been jailed for vagrancy. After convincing the local police to release the man into his custody, Law rescheduled the session for the next day.

That evening, Law received a call while he was out at a restaurant with his wife and another salesman. It was the bluesman, and he needed a bit of money. It seems he had gotten lonely, waiting around in a new town, and acquired some company, but had then come up short when it came time to pay up. "So I underwrote that piece of tail for him," Law said. It was worth it, though, because when Law finally got him in front of the microphone, the bluesman, Robert Johnson, recorded some of the most enduring songs on wax.

Soon, Law had a budget of his own, and the country territory was split between him and Satherley. "Arthur wasn't doing anything, and so they finally asked for his resignation, and gave me the whole thing," he said. "I was lucky, because right off the bat I got Lefty Frizzell, I got Carl Smith, I got Ray Price, and our sales just went up."

By the late '50s, Law had racked up several country hits from that stable, but he continued to keep an eye out for promising talent that he could bring into the fold. Cash fit the bill perfectly. For Cash, it wasn't a simple case of the grass being greener on the other side of the fence—he could see the success Presley was having on a major label, and he felt slighted by Phillips' focus on Jerry Lee Lewis. So when a respected producer and A&R man from a respected major label came calling, there wasn't much of a decision to be made, other than the particulars of the deal and the wait for his Sun contract to expire. For Law, snagging Cash eight months before the contract ended meant that he had avoided any potential bidding wars with other the majors.

The Fabulous Johnny Cash (1959)

Columbia wasted no time in getting Cash into the studio to begin cutting new material as soon as his contract allowed. He had his final Sun session on July 17, 1958, and seven days later he was in Nashville, recording songs that would show up on his first three Columbia albums. His first single for his new label was released in October of 1958, with the A-side, "All Over Again," peaking at #4 and the B-side, "What Do I Care," peaking at #7. The double-sided hit first appeared on the Pop chart, and when it entered the market it was competing with three Cash songs released by Sun, two of which contained heavy choral overdubs and a mix that sent Luther Perkins to the back and pushed Cash's acoustic guitar forward.

"All Over Again" retains both of those elements—the chorus and Perkins—but they were rightly reversed in importance. Perkins' guitar is prominent, and the chorus does its thing softly in the background. "What Do I Care" does away with the chorus completely, and sounds closer to the raw sound Cash had made famous. The pairing foretold what was to be expected on his coming Columbia debut album, although those songs would not be included on it.

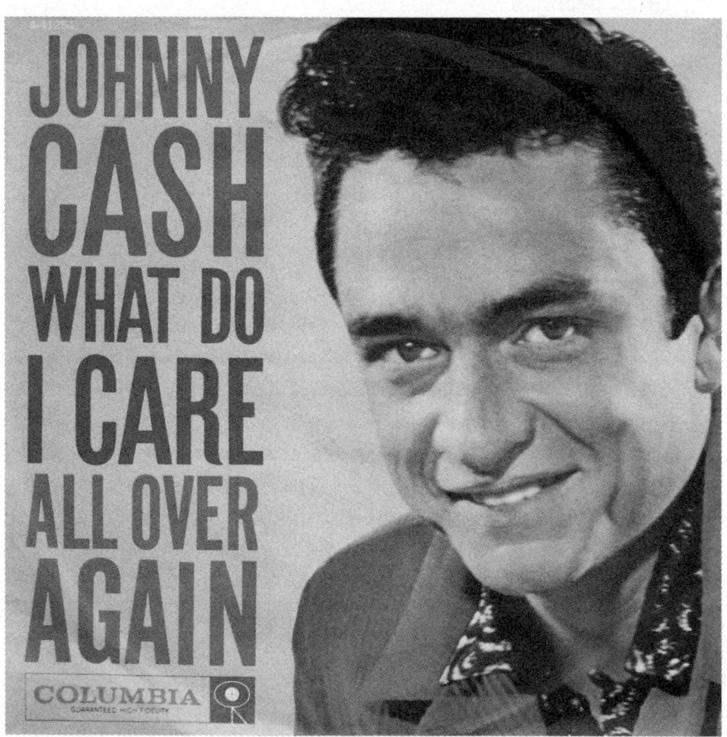

Cash's first single for Columbia was the double-sided charter "What Do I Care" b/w "All Over Again," released in October 1958. *Private collection*

The first single from the album was "Don't Take Your Guns to Town," a cautionary tale about listening to your mother's advice that spent six weeks at #1 and peaked at #32 on the Pop chart. The flip side was a masterpiece in its own right, but "I Still Miss Someone" made no waves on any chart.

A pattern had begun to form with these two 45s, with one side featuring the stripped-down sound of Cash and the Tennessee Two while the other side added sometimes a piano and drums alongside a lush chorus arrangement. The Sun releases of late were made up of Cash doing other writers' songs, but these two releases contained songs written by him (or, in the case of "I Miss Someone," co-written with nephew Roy Cash Jr.), showing that he hadn't lost any of his songwriting chops, and that he had more than likely been storing them up during those last few months at Sun.

The Fabulous Johnny Cash was released in late January 1959 and reached #24 on the Best Selling LPs chart, which included both pop and country albums. Beyond its first single, the album featured three other songs written or adapted by Cash, including the opener, "Run Softly, Blue River." The song begins with the Jordanaires—the vocal group who often recorded with Elvis Presley—singing softly as they implore the river to quietly run its course, before Cash takes center stage, echoing their request that his girl rest before they marry the next

Alongside the LP, Columbia released three EPs featuring the songs that made up Cash's debut. Each EP features four songs. *Private collection*

day and the river's "cool and deep" course soothe his nerves so that he can also sleep. It's a sweet song that probably appealed to the teenybopper, boy-crazy girls in the audience, its subject matter a light fantasy for them as they awaited their prince charmings. The Jordanaires softly and consistently flow behind the band as the river in the background.

Following the pattern established on his recent singles, the next song is Cash's contrasting "Frankie's Man, Johnny," a stark arrangement he adapted from other sources and then added his name to as writer. In it, the narrator tells us of the singer, Johnny, with his "wicked wandering eye," who was the sweetheart of Frankie "most all of the time." While Johnny is out playing a gig, Frankie sits at home thinking. Johnny then spies a redhead as she enters the club and sits close to the stage. At a break, Johnny decides to make his move, since Frankie is far away, and "what Frankie didn't know wouldn't hurt her none"—only to find out, after having his face slapped, that the redhead is Frankie's sister, come to check up on the scoundrel.

And so it goes with the subject matter of the album. At one turn there are songs for the young lovelorn, such as "That's All Over," "I'd Rather Die Young," and "Shepherd of My Heart." "That's All Over" and "I'd Rather Die Young" are two sides of the same coin. In "That's All Over," Cash tells his lost love that when they meet again, he'll be with someone new and won't give her a second thought, and on "I'd Rather Die Young" he begs her to stay, saying he would "rather die young than grow old" without her. "The Troubadour" stands with them, but comes from a more objective place, with Cash telling of the young singer who sings his hit for the crowd while his heart is breaking. The song was written by Cindy Walker, so it wasn't autobiographical, but it could have been. Cash had recently moved his family to California, but he was returning often to Nashville to record. In the meantime, he had been introduced to the amphetamines that would create a greater distance between him and his family than the miles did.

Cash revisits the past on the album in a couple of ways, first by recording the Sons of the Pioneers' "One More Ride," a song he and the Tennessee Two had attempted to record in 1956 but never finished. Here, backed by the Jordanaires, he sounds like he is back in Dyess at a singing-cowboy picture show, and loving every minute of it. The final Cash-penned song on the album, "Pickin' Time," has him remembering what it was like to grow up dependent on the harvest.

Cash also revisits his past desire to record gospel music on two of the twelve songs that make up the album. The first comes at the halfway mark in the form of the Dorothy Love Coates song "That's Enough." Coates had been a gospel singer and songwriter through the 1940s and '50s before turning her attention to the burgeoning civil rights movement right around the time this album was released. Cash, again backed by the Jordanaires, sounds confident and jubilant as he proclaims, "I've got Jesus, and that's enough!" He then closes the album with Ira Stanphill's Southern gospel classic "Suppertime," which features a recitation by Cash and the haunting steel guitar of ex–Drifting Cowboy Don Helms.

Songs of Our Soil (1959)

At those first sessions for Columbia, in 1958, Cash recorded material for three LPs: his debut album for the label, *The Fabulous Johnny Cash*; his second, the gospel record he had longed to make, *Hymns by Johnny Cash*; and *Songs of Our Soil*. The lead single from the latter album was the two-sided hit of "I Got Stripes" b/w "Five Feet High and Rising." Though "Five Feet High and Rising" has become the better known of the two, "I Got Stripes" was the more popular at the time of release, peaking at #4 on the Country charts, as opposed to #14 for the flip side. (Both also touched the Pop charts, with "I Got Stripes" spending eleven weeks there and peaking at #43, while "Five Feet High and Rising" lasted only three weeks, peaking at #76). "I Got Stripes" is another early entry in Cash's prison repertoire, and is taken from Leadbelly's "On a Monday," but with Cash and co-writer Charlie Williams claiming the copyright credit. "Five Feet High and Rising" tells a more personal story, that of the 1937 flood that drove the Cash family from their Dyess home as the water rose up over the steps on their front porch.

Before the LP format took hold, "albums" were collections of two-sided 78s. Then, when the LP format, pioneered by Columbia, began to gain prominence, they would generally be made up of a few singles plus some filler tunes. But a few artists caught the vision and potential of the LP early on and started to use the longer form to create a more cohesive whole, unifying the songs into a single theme. These albums would take one of two forms: song cycles and concept records.

Although most of the former are often lumped in with the latter, there are differences. A song cycle ties the songs on the album together under a common theme, while a concept album tells a story through the songs, from beginning to end. There are collections of songs that could be considered as song cycles on 78 albums going back as far as Woody Guthrie's *Dust Bowl Ballads*, from 1940, while Peggy Lee experimented with the conceit in 1953, with her 78 album *Black Coffee*. But it was Frank Sinatra who would truly harness the idea, starting in 1954 with *Swing Easy!* and continuing with nine other albums through 1959, each one consisting of songs that are thematically linked rather than intended to tell a story.

Released the same year as the seminal *Gunfighter Ballads and Trail Songs*, a song cycle of Old West tales by Marty Robbins, *Songs of Our Soil* was Cash's first such effort, bringing together twelve songs that are centered around the themes of the workingman and living off the earth. The star of the show is "Five Feet High and Rising," the album's one and only single, but most of the others measure up to that standard. Cash penned nine of the twelve tracks, marking a major shift from his Columbia debut. For the album opener, "Drink to Me," he

Even early in his career, Cash was a superstar with international appeal.
Private collection

wanders back into his earliest memories for inspiration, as he did with "Five Feet High and Rising." On *Personal File*, he recalls singing "Drink to Me Only with Thine Eyes" at a school performance during his junior year of high school. "I guess this is when I was looking for myself," he says, "but I never forgot that because it was one of my first public singing occasions and I've sung this song, mainly to myself, ever since I was seventeen years old, because of those memories. I suppose this song is Elizabethan. The words sound like the King James version of the Bible." Stripping away the Old English, jaunting up the melody a bit, and reframing it with a little more of the teen love song, Cash brings back the chorus of background singers for a refashioning of a song he'd had bouncing in his head for all those years.

Cash stays planted in his past for "The Man on the Hill," singing of the life of a sharecropping family and wondering who will grant them their everyday comforts as the perspective shifts from the boss man to God. Echoing in part the style of the Sons of the Pioneers' "Cool Water," the next track, "Hank and Joe and Me," is the tale of three buddies in search of gold who instead find death in the hot desert sun.

Two covers follow—Billy Mize's "Clementine" and the country-gospel standard "The Great Speckled Bird"—before Cash moves into "I Want to Go Home,"

B 2155
JOHNNY CASH
Sings THE REBEL – JOHNNY YUMA
From the ABC-TV Production "The Rebel"
with
Remember the Alamo
The Ballad of Boot Hill
Lorena
COLUMBIA
EXTENDED PLAY

One of Cash's first pursuits in Hollywood was to provide theme music for a Western called *The Rebel Johnny Yuma.* Cash moved to California in the hopes of following Elvis' silver-screen success. *Private collection*

which he based heavily on an old Jamaican song, "The John B. Sails," first publicized in the US in a magazine article around 1916. Alan Lomax recorded the song in the Bahamas in 1935 and included it on an album of field recordings, calling it "Histe Up the John B. Sails." The Weavers—containing Cash favorite Pete Seeger—then recorded it as "The Wreck of the John B." in 1950. "Blind" Blake Higgs, a Bahamian singer who recorded several albums of traditional Bahamian and Calypso songs, recorded a version he titled "Sloop John B." in 1952, and Cisco Houston followed in 1954. The Kingston Trio released another pop-folk version in 1958, a year before Cash's version. (Yet more versions would soon follow, the most famous of them being the Beach Boys' single of 1966.)

According to Colin Escott, the next track, "The Caretaker," "seemed to owe a greater debt to Cash's spiritualist leanings and a dash of chemicals." It was written from the perspective of a cemetery caretaker named John, who wonders aloud, "Who's gonna cry when old John dies?" Cash was twenty-seven when he sang the song, but he would return to it at age sixty-one in Rick Rubin's living room of as they worked on songs for Cash's American Recordings debut. ("I just remember saying that we needed some serious, heavy songs, and this is what he played, in my living room," Rubin told Sylvie Simmons for the liner notes for the boxed set *Unearthed*, where the second recording of the song would finally see release.)

The first glimpse of Cash's interest in the plight of the Native American came on this album, with "Old Apache Squaw," a song he had written two years earlier after conversations with his friend and fellow performer Johnny Horton, who was also interested in the subject. At the time, Native Americans were predominately viewed through the Hollywood lens simply as foes for cowboys, but Cash attempts here to show them in another light. "Don't Step on Mother's Roses" is a more traditional country heart song in which the singer's father asks visitors not to step on his former wife's roses as she is no longer around to tend them. "My Grandfather's Clock" is a wistfully nostalgic look at a family heirloom, featuring the tinkling piano of Marvin Hughes. Vic McAlpin, who co-wrote "Home of the Blues" with Cash, returns here with "It Could Be You (Instead of Him)," a song that exhorts the listeners to help their fellow man, because it could easily be them in a position of need instead.

Songs of Our Soil didn't make much noise on the chart or with the larger record-buying public, but it was a solid effort that kept Cash in good standing with Columbia. The year of its release, 1959, saw big changes for Cash and crew as he pulled up stakes and moved his family to California in search of bigger opportunities than Memphis could provide. Having previously played a few bit parts on television westerns like *Wagon Train* and *Shotgun Slade*, he now had his eyes on the big screen, and scripts were beginning to come in. The move also had a downside, although that's probably an understatement. After a brief time in California, Luther Perkins and Marshall Grant decided they (and their families) would rather stay in Memphis. This pulled Cash away from his support system, which meant that when he was introduced to pep pills by fiddle player Gordon Terry, he had few allies around to keep him straight.

The Rebel—Johnny Yuma (1959)

To strengthen his ties to Hollywood, Cash recorded the theme song to an ABC television western called *The Rebel*, about a former confederate soldier who traveled through the West, helping others. The song was released on an EP containing three other songs: "Remember the Alamo," "The Ballad of Boot Hill," and "Lorena." Cash also appeared on the show in a guest-starring role in January 1960.

6

One Day on the Hit Parade

The 1950s #1s

"I Walk the Line" b/w "Get Rhythm" (1956)

Knocked out "Heartbreak Hotel," Elvis Presley; knocked out by "Crazy Arms," Ray Price

The origins of "I Walk the Line" have become a bit convoluted over the years. Cash has claimed that the distinctive dark, droning mood came about after someone borrowed his tape recorder in Germany and put the tape back in the wrong way around, while Marshall Grant has claimed that he came up with the trademark "walking" riff while practicing scales on the bass at a rehearsal, and that Cash overheard it and asked him to keep playing it while he fit the lyrics to the tune. Either way, what is clear is that Cash wrote the song about dedication, both to his then-wife Vivian and to God.

When Cash played the song to Sam Phillips, Phillips knew it could be a hit but thought it was too slow. Cash insisted it was a ballad but acquiesced to Phillips' request to try a take at a slightly quicker tempo. Much to Cash's surprise, it was the fast version he heard coming over the radio speakers one night on the drive home from a show. He requested Phillips pull the single and replace it with the ballad, but Phillips had no real intention of doing that. The song's quick rise up the charts tempered the blow, and Cash soon dropped his request. The fast version would go on to sell two million copies.

Released as Cash's third Sun single, "I Walk the Line" proved to be his most successful yet, not only reaching #1 on the Country charts but also hitting the Pop charts, where it peaked at #11. Its success must have left Phillips feeling some vindication against any Nashville types who had brushed off what he had to offer. For the first half of the year, all three of *Billboard*'s Country charts (Most Played C&W in Juke Boxes, C&W Best Sellers in Stores, and Most Played C&W by Jockeys) were dominated by Sun product, with Elvis Presley, Carl Perkins, and Cash all orbiting the #1 spot and jostling around in the top three or four positions. There was but one artist who stood between them all, symbolically holding high the banner of the Nashville fiddle-and-steel sound. At the end of May, Ray Price entered the Jockeys chart with "Crazy Arms," his eighth and most successful single.

There was real concern in Nashville that rock 'n' roll—and specifically the supercharged hillbillies of rockabilly, exemplified by these Memphis boys—would crush country music. Once Price entered the charts, he spent the next several months trading the #1 spot on all three Country charts with Presley and then Cash. In time, and in turn, Cash claimed the #1 spot on the Jockey and Juke Box charts and #2 on the Best Sellers chart. After that, he and Price were bumped down by Marty Robbins' "Singing the Blues."

"I Walk the Line" also rose to #19 on the Pop charts, and was strong enough to draw the attention of other artists looking for a potential hit. In September, as the song was falling down the Country charts but slowly ascending the Pop chart, Hoagy Carmichael, writer of classics like "Stardust" and "Georgia on my Mind," released a version of the song. The following month, twenty-year-old Carole Bennett released her version on Capitol records. Bennett had made a name for herself by winning the talent show *Chance of a Lifetime* for seven consecutive weeks in 1955 before moving on to win *Arthur Godfrey's Talent Scouts.* Neither record made the charts.

Cash's Sun records were distributed in the UK on the London label.
Private collection

"There You Go" b/w "Train of Love" (1957)

Knocked out "Young Love," Sonny James; knocked out by "Gone," Ferlin Husky

Cash's follow up to "I Walk the Line" was "Train of Love," another original, but although it did modestly well, peaking at #7, DJs were more interested in the flip side, "There You Go."

While "There You Go" was a good song, it was lyrically a bit more generic than Cash's previous singles. But it obviously satisfied the listener's desire for more Cash as it spent five weeks at #1.

Although the song isn't as well remembered as other Cash hits, it serves as an interesting hinge between Sonny James' "Young Love," the million-selling single that spent nine weeks at the top before it, and Ferlin Husky's "Gone," which spent ten weeks at #1 and has gone down in history as the song that kicked off the "Nashville sound" that would dominate the 1960s.

"Ballad of a Teenage Queen" b/w "Big River" (1958)

Knocked out "Story of My Life," Marty Robbins (Jockey chart) and "Great Balls of Fire," Jerry Lee Lewis (Best Sellers chart); knocked out by "Oh Lonesome Me," Don Gibson

Barreling into 1957, Cash was on a roll, and both he and Phillips were eager to keep it going. Phillips placed a quarter-page ad in *Billboard* for his new single, "Next in Line" b/w "Don't Make Me Go," proudly announcing, "Johnny Cash just doesn't miss!" The next week, in a "Pop Records Review Spotlight," *Billboard* called "Next in Line" a "worthy successor to 'I Walk the Line.'" But it wasn't, exactly: it barely cracked the Top 10, scraping in for one week at #9.

Undeterred, Sun released a new single, "Home of the Blues" b/w "Give My Love to Rose," a few months later. Phillips' new production assistant, Jack Clement, had helped with the recording of the single, and Phillips gave him a little freedom to embellish the songs, which he did sparingly, adding only a male chorus and piano to "Home of the Blues." *Billboard* reported just after the record's release that it was selling well in all of the top markets, and soon "Home of the Blues" was on its way to its perch at #3, followed by "Give My Love to Rose" at #13. That was nothing to shrug at, but Cash hadn't had any action on the Pop chart since "I Walk the Line," and as important as the Country chart was, the Pop chart was where the big money was.

"The first thing I ever did with Johnny Cash was a thing called 'Home of the Blues,'" Clement told interviewers Bob Webster and John A. Lomax III in 1977, "and it was a fair hit but it wasn't a powerhouse. The first time I really worked with Johnny Cash was on 'Ballad of a Teenage Queen.'"

Clement had come to Sun Studios with hopes of becoming an artist, and "Ballad of a Teenage Queen" was a song he had written and thought he might be able to turn into a hit of his own. "I'd been trying to cut that myself," he continued, "and I'd made a tape and he [Cash] liked the sound of it and he wanted ME to play the guitar with him." Continuing the story years later, in an interview with Michael Streissguth, he added, "When Cash said he wanted to cut it, I started hearing numbers chinging in my head: 'Hey, I could make ten thousand dollars or something off that.'"

With Sam Phillips at the board and Clement joining the band on acoustic guitar, Cash cut "Teenage Queen" and its flip side, "Big River," in November 1957. *Billboard* alerted the industry to Cash's new single with a "Pop Record Spotlight" notice that read, "This is the most poppish try for Cash in a while. 'Teenage Queen' tells a cute story that can appeal to teens, and the artist's approach is highly attractive. Flip, 'Big River,' has more of a traditional c&w flavor, but the rhythmic presentation can also appeal in pop marts. A dual-market contender."

In January 1958, the single made its debut on the charts, first hitting #5 on the Jockey chart. Within two weeks, it was at #1, knocking the equally "poppish" "Story of My Life" by Marty Robbins from the top spot and beginning a ten-week run there. The next week, it debuted at #3 on the Best Sellers list, jumping to #1 the following week and taking the place of labelmate Jerry Lee Lewis' "Great Balls of Fire." As an added bonus, the song also rose to #14 on the Pop charts.

The song also went over huge in Canada. Sam Phillips had originally projected that Sun might sell between twelve and fifteen thousand copies of the single in Canada through its Canadian licensee Quality Records. In a 1980 piece for *Cashbox* magazine, Cash recounts the story of a fifteen-day Canadian tour around the release of the song in early 1958:

> We filled every hall, but more than that, we sold over 100,000 singles. Dan Bass, the promo man for Quality Records ... set up a Teenage Queen contest in every city. I flew into a new city each morning and did radio and television interviews. Then in the afternoon I signed records at record shops. My last promo appearance of the day, before the arrival of the Teenage Queen contestants, was to draw a name out of a box at a large department store's record counter and name the Teenage Queen and the runner up. One requirement to enter the contest was to prove the purchase of the record. I autographed hundreds and sometimes thousands of copies of that record in every city. During my concert that evening I crowned the queen and announced the first runner up.

The B-side, "Big River," was a modest hit in its own right, peaking at #4 on the Jockey chart and staying on the chart for fourteen weeks. "Big River" had the Sun sound that everyone, then and now, is familiar with, and has remained one of Cash's best-loved and most easily identifiable songs. "Ballad of a Teenage Queen," on the other hand, was a definite change of pace for Cash. Lyrically, it was a bit lighter than what listeners had grown accustomed to, and sonically there were differences, too, most notably the pronounced background chorus. It wasn't a song Cash performed often, but he did pull it out for a group performance with Rosanne Cash and the Everly Brothers on his 1988 Mercury album *Waters from the Wells of Home.*

"Guess Things Happen That Way" b/w "Come In Stranger" (1958)

Knocked out "Oh Lonesome Me," Don Gibson; knocked out by "Alone with You," Faron Young (Jockey chart) and "Blue Blue Day" Don Gibson (Best Sellers chart)

Following the success of "Ballad of a Teenage Queen," Phillips and Cash decided to try their luck again with another song from the pen of "Cowboy" Jack Clement. ("I had a hot streak going," Clement told Lola Scobey.) They returned to the studio on April 9, 1958, to record "Guess Things Happen That Way" and its flip side, Cash's "Come In Stranger," and, while they were at it, they also laid down a couple of takes on Don Gibson's "Oh Lonesome Me," Gibson's version of which was patiently waiting in the #2 spot behind "Teenage Queen" at the time they went in to the studio. (Sun released Cash's version in 1961, and it peaked at #13).

While the song was lyrically more in line with what fans had come to expect from Cash, the music was closer to "Teenage Queen." Clement overdubbed the same type of piano and vocal chorus to the song before it was released, and it proved to be what the public wanted. The song entered the charts in late May and started a slow and halting month-long climb to the top, first reaching # 1 in late June on the Jockey chart (taking the spot back from Don Gibson). A week later, it overtook "Oh Lonesome Me" on the Best Sellers chart, but gave up the spot to Gibson on the Jockey chart. In early July, it hit #1 on both charts, and it remained there for three weeks on the Jockey chart and for two more on the Best Sellers chart. It even did better than its predecessor on the Pop chart, hitting #11. And as with Cash's previous single, the B-side also became a modest hit in its own right, reaching #6 on the Jockey chart.

"Guess Things Happen That Way" gives a small insight into the complex nature of Cash's thinking. The song sports the same male chorus (the Gene Lowery Singers) as "Teenage Queen," yet Cash claimed to have hated what Clement had done to "Guess."

"I *hated* that sound!" he told Bill Flanagan in 1988. "Except for 'Teenage Queen,' which needed the singers, it called for it. After I recorded 'I Guess Things Happen That Way' they overdubbed that 'ba dum ba doom,' overdubbed all that junk on it. That ruined it for me. I never saw the singing group. They overdubbed it after I thought the song was finished."

Listening to the un-dubbed masters available on *The Man in Black: 1954–58*, the vocal chorus does seem unnecessary, but adding it brought the record's sound closer to what was coming out of Nashville. Interestingly, when Cash re-cut the song in Nashville for the album *Happiness Is You* (an album assembled piecemeal, due to his overwhelming drug problem at the time, from whatever he had in the can), he not only left the "ba dum ba doom" in, but even sang it himself to open the song.

"Don't Take Your Guns to Town" b/w "I Still Miss Someone" (1959)

Knocked out "Billy Bayou," Jim Reeves; knocked out by "When It's Springtime in Alaska," Johnny Horton

"Don't Take Your Guns to Town" was Cash's second single for Columbia, following the lackluster performance of his first single, "All Over Again" b/w "What Do I Care." Lackluster might seem an odd choice of word, considering both sides reached the Top 10 on the Hot C&W Sides chart (*Billboard* had done away with the Juke Box chart in 1957, and consolidated the Jockey and Best Sellers charts in October 1958), but Columbia was getting an artist coming off of two consecutive #1s, and had hoped to replicate that performance with a new single. They didn't get it the first time out, but they did the second.

"All Over Again" continued the path marked by Cash's last two #1s, adding a vocal chorus to fill out the sound, but "Don't Take Your Guns to Town" was a return to form, putting Luther Perkins' guitar back out front and foregrounding the sound of the Tennessee Two and Cash's acoustic guitar.

Country music songwriter Mitchell Torok recorded the earliest Cash parody in 1959. Under the name the Great Pretender, he recorded "All Over Again, Again." The parody was written by his wife under the pseudonym Ramona Redd. *Private collection*

The idea of the Old West—or at least a commercialized version of it—was thriving in popularity in the late 1950s, with numerous television shows and movies telling the thrilling tales of adventure. Cash took a different point of view on this song, telling the story of a young man, Billy Joe, who's hungry to get out into the larger world but a bit too confident in his own abilities. Rather than finding a life of adventure, he is shot down by a more experienced cowpoke he can't outdraw.

"Don't Take Your Guns to Town" entered the charts in mid-January and began a slow climb upward, eventually knocking another Billy off the top—"Billy Bayou," the Roger Miller–written hit for Jim Reeves—and staking claim on #1 for six weeks. One of Cash's best friends then bumped him from the top spot as Johnny Horton scored his first #1 with "When It's Springtime in Alaska." Horton followed up that song later in 1959 with his biggest hit, "The Battle of New Orleans," which spent ten weeks as a Country #1 and six weeks as a Pop #1, selling one million copies in the process. Meanwhile, "Don't Take Your Guns to Town" climbed to #32 on the Pop chart before sliding back down. It was the last time Cash would see any action on the Pop charts for more than four years.

7

When Papa Played the Dobro This A-Way

Columbia 1960–62

The 1960s were an interesting time for Johnny Cash. On the one hand, they were a very prolific period, both creatively and commercially. He released nineteen albums (as well as guesting heavily on two others) and thirty-six singles. On the other hand, he was deeply enslaved to drug addiction throughout most of the decade, which often left his career at the precipice.

As 1959 drew to an end, Cash jettisoned manager Bob Neal, who had been with him since his early days in Memphis. Less than a month later, he moved his booking agent, Stew Carnall, into the role. Carnall had often accompanied Cash and the band out on the road, and he knew full well the increasing severity of Cash's substance abuse. Even so, he was game for the change, and business progressed briskly.

Now There Was a Song! (1960)

After spending the bulk of January on the road, Cash returned to Nashville on February 15, 1960. He spent two days laying down tracks for the *Ride This Train* album, adding them to songs he had recorded in December 1959. Then, on the 17th, the entire three-hour session was dedicated to the recording of *Now There Was a Song!*

The first songs from the sessions to be released were "Seasons of My Heart" and "Smiling Bill McCall." "Seasons of My Heart" was written by Darrell Edwards and Cash's sometime co-headliner George Jones, who had recorded it in 1958. While Cash's version lacked some of the emotion—and the swelling tone of Jones' voice—he managed to take the song to #10 on the Country chart. The flip side also made its way to the chart, peaking at #13. "Smiling Bill McCall" marked Cash's first attempt at a novelty song, taking aim at a Southern DJ who believed himself a bigger star than any of the artists who came through town. To avoid trouble, Cash changed some of the details, making McCall a record man rather than a DJ.

When the album was released, in May 1960, it showcased in full the sound previewed on "Seasons of My Heart." Augmenting the Tennessee Two were session drummer Buddy Harman and pianist Floyd Cramer—members of Nashville's A-Team—plus Cash buddy Gordon Terry on fiddle, and Don Helms, formerly of Hank Williams' Drifting Cowboys, on steel guitar.

The change in personnel was necessitated mainly by the material Cash chose for the album. He had recorded covers before, of course, but never to the extent that he did for this album. Alongside Jones' song, he dipped into the catalogues of both influences and contemporaries. "I Feel Better All Over" had been a #6 hit in 1958 for Ferlin Husky, and Marty Robbins had taken his "I Couldn't Keep from Crying" to #5 in 1953, two years before Cash first attempted the song at Sun in 1955. Reaching back again, he pulled out "Time Changes Everything" and "My Shoes Keep Walking Back to You," the latter recorded by Bob Wills & his Texas Playboys in 1956 and then taken to #1 by Ray Price in 1957.

Unlike most of the other tracks, "I'd Just Be Fool Enough (to Fall)" wasn't a hit prior to Cash's recording of it. The songwriter, Melvin Endsley, had made a name for himself with "Singing the Blues," which became Marty Robbins' second #1 and the biggest hit of his career. "Transfusion Blues," meanwhile, had only been a minor hit for writer Roy Hogshead in 1948, and it wouldn't catch on with Cash audiences until he performed it at Folsom Prison as "Cocaine Blues."

Returning to his influences, Cash recorded songs by three of his favorite writers: "Why Do You Punish Me" by Hank Snow, "I Will Miss You When You Go," by Ernest Tubb, and Hank Williams' "I'm So Lonesome I Could Cry." He also dipped into the George Jones songbook once more for "Just One More," a #3 hit for Jones in 1956.

The album closer, Hank Thompson's "Honky Tonk Girl," was chosen as the final single. Thompson had taken the song to #9 in 1954, but the Cash version failed to chart at all—a first in his Columbia career. The flip side, a song Cash had recorded at the end of 1959 called "Second Honeymoon," peaked at #15 in June.

Five Minutes to Live

Cash might not have noticed the chart action for "Honky Tonk Girl" as he was getting started shooting his first feature film for Flower Film Productions—one of the last things brokered by ex-manager Neal before his firing, and one of the reasons Cash had moved to California. The movie was fraught with delays, and Cash ended up pouring $20,000 of his own money into it just so it could limp to the finish. Co-starring Vic Tayback as the heavy, Ron Howard as the kid who gets stuck in the middle, and Merle Travis as Cash's buddy, the movie made no impact at theaters. As Johnny Cabot, Cash is essentially playing himself, but with a much darker side.

Cash had recorded a theme song for the movie in November, but it was dropped when the project was subsequently renamed *Door-to-Door Maniac,* although in subsequent releases the title (and theme song) was restored. After the movie flopped, Cash began to concentrate more on television, where his time commitment—and presumably his financial commitment—would not be so large, although he hadn't shut the door on movies altogether.

Saul Holiff

Once again, changes were afoot on the business side, and for one reason or another, Stew Carnall was replaced as Cash's manager by Saul Holiff. Holiff was based in London, Ontario, Canada, and had booked Cash for a series of shows in the later 1950s. With the exception of Cash himself, Holiff had the biggest hand in crafting the persona the world came to know as the Man in Black.

Although he booked country-music acts like Marty Robbins for his shows, Holiff wasn't particularly a country fan—he booked them because that was what the audience wanted to hear. When he came on board with Cash—with only a handshake to seal the deal, and no contract—he brought with him a different perspective. In 1967, Holiff told country artist/journalist Blake Emmons what it was like to manage Johnny Cash: "Well, it takes a great deal of tact and diplomacy. You have to be on your toes and have to make sure you know what you're talking about. You have to take infinite care of detail, you have to cope with him and earn his respect. You see, Johnny is an extremely intelligent person and you more or less have to compete and come out on top. If not he will lose interest in you as a manager. It is a constant battle of wits."

This competitive thinking led him to take Cash out of some of the country-music concert arenas and into venues such as the Hollywood Bowl and Carnegie Hall—places country performers hadn't previously frequented. But Cash and Holiff remained attuned to their audience, and worked hard to avoid any talk of Cash leaving behind country fans, disc jockeys, or promoters. Early in 1961, Cash found a way to gain additional publicity while on the road by instituting the "Johnny Cash Award of Merit." According to a *Billboard* magazine article, "The award will be made in the various States to the deejay or promoter 'who has done the most to intelligently and honestly present country and western talent in a manner calculated to upgrade such presentations.'" The award continued annually (and sometimes biannually) through 1965.

The Lure of the Grand Canyon (1961)

Above all, the fall 1961 release of *Ride This Train* (discussed in further detail in chapter 12) showed that Cash's acting abilities might be better left to radio and sound recordings. A year earlier, in late 1960, he had recorded a near-eleven-minute narration for inclusion on this album by conductor Andre Kostelanetz. According to the liner notes, "Cash's magnificent talents as an interpreter of Americana are especially suited to the narration of this recording," adding, "*Ride This Train* is a stirring combination of song and narrative, unique in its feeling for the American scene." *The Lure of the Grand Canyon* features "actual sounds

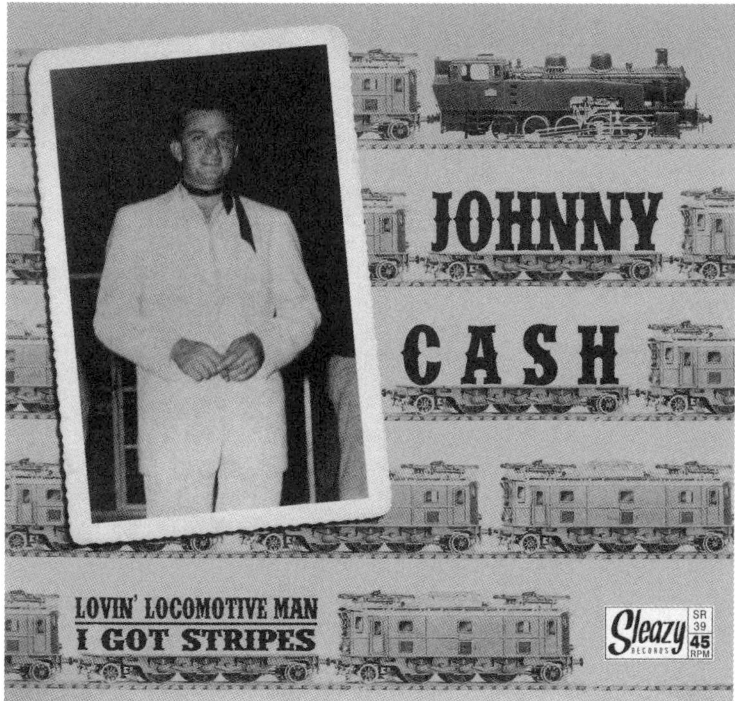

The Spanish label Sleazy Records released this single as a part of their Original Rockin' series. The two tracks come from an earlier Bear Family Records set. *Private collection*

recorded in the Grand Canyon," and Cash's narration serves as a behind-the-scenes look at how they were captured.

The Death of Johnny Horton

In November 1961 came the annual Disc Jockey convention in Nashville, where DJs from across the country would converge on the fledging Music City to be wooed—or wined, dined, and bribed—by record labels keen to secure airplay for their newest stars. Those new stars (and many of the old stars) would be on hand to entertain and grant interviews.

On November 5th, one of those stars fell when Johnny Horton was killed by a drunk driver. Cash and Horton had become close friends, and the news hit Cash hard, although he was oddly dismissive of it when he spoke to biographer Christopher Wren in 1970. "I acted like it upset me," he said, "but it didn't really. I acted weird about his death, but it was the pills I was on that made me weird about it."

In her book *I Walked the Line*, Vivian Cash confirms that the death did indeed affect both of them. "Johnny sat up in bed, put his head in his hands, and let out the most agonizing moan I've ever heard," she writes. "Without a doubt,

Johnny Horton's death had a profound impact on Johnny, and on me, too. . . . For the first time as adults, we realized how fragile this life is and how much we took for granted."

A couple of weeks after Horton's death, Cash and crew recorded "Girl in Saskatoon," a song co-written by Cash and Horton. Both that song and another recorded at the session, "Locomotive Man," were released as singles. Although promoted heavily by Columbia, neither entered the charts, but songs from his Sun days continued to do so.

While no album was on the horizon, Columbia and Cash continued to release singles. "The Rebel—Johnny Yuma" was pulled out again and backed with a new recording, "Forty Shades of Green," inspired by a trip to Ireland. "The Rebel—Johnny Yuma" charted briefly, peaking at #24 in its two-week run on the charts, but "Forty Shades of Green" remained largely unheard. Undeterred by the lack of chart action, Cash returned to the studio in April to record his second gospel album, *Hymns from the Heart* (detailed in chapter 47).

Cash paused his touring efforts for a day's session in Hollywood, continuing work on what would become *The Sound of Johnny Cash*, to be released the following year. One song from the session was chosen as a single to close out 1961. "Tennessee Flat Top Box" told the story of a young boy who "hypnotized and fascinated" the females of his audience with his dazzling fretwork until one day he disappeared only to show up on the hit parade. The part of the "little dark-haired boy," was played—on guitar, at least—by one of Merle Haggard's future Strangers, Roy Nichols, who at the time was bumping around the studios of California as well as the bandstands. The single fared better than Cash's last release, spending fourteen weeks on the chart, but fell just short of the Top 10, peaking at #11. (Rosanne Cash took her father's song—which she mistakenly thought was in the public domain—to #1 in 1987.) Cash had recorded the flip side of the single, "Tall Man," back in February. It kicks off with some grating *Chipmunks*-esque vocals provided by the B. J. Baker Group, whose voices in the chorus dominate even Cash's.

Cash and Columbia were unable to sustain their flirtation with the top of the charts through the next single, released in March of 1962. "The Big Battle" was a Civil War tale, but Cash said it was more about the battle within those who had survived the war. The charts at the time were ruled with tales of woe by Porter Wagoner and Patsy Cline, along with the comedy of Sheb Wooley, and Cash's old war tale stalled at #24 before dropping from the charts after only three weeks. The flip side, "When I've Learned," was taken from Cash's new gospel project, *Hymns from the Heart.*

Columbia wasted no time in trying again, following up weeks later with a new single drawn from Cash's soon to-be-released new album. This time, Cash went back to one of his formative inspirations for the A-side, "In the Jailhouse Now." Webb Pierce had spent twenty-one weeks at #1 with his version of the song in 1955, so it seemed like a hedged bet for Cash to record it—and, indeed, the song returned him to the Top 10, landing at #8. The song had originated with one of Cash's major heroes, Jimmie Rodgers, in 1928, and just as his version was being released, Cash was scheduled to record a live album at Carnegie Hall in New York City—one of the prestigious places Holiff had targeted to raise the profile of his client. Unfortunately, Cash was deep into his drug addiction by then, and he could barely croak a tune, so Don Law never even rolled the tape. The affair would kill Cash's chances of making a live album for many years to come.

The Sound of Johnny Cash (1962)

Cash and Law made a conscious effort to return to the stripped-down sound of his Sun recordings on *The Sound of Johnny Cash*, but they never quite hit the mark. It wasn't that the songs were bad—"In the Jailhouse Now" was included among them—but the album lacked the fire of the early recordings.

The opener, "Lost in the Desert," is a western tale co-written by Buddy Mize and Dallas Frazier, veteran writers who penned many hits, together and separately, for a number of artists. Cash then dips into the George Jones catalogue again for "Accidentally on Purpose," which Jones had taken to #16 in 1960.

Another source Cash drew upon for the album was the Glaser Brothers. Jim, Chuck, and Tompall Glaser had been signed to Marty Robbins' label and released their first single, "Five Penny Nickel," in 1958. The following year, Robbins took them on the road as both a support act and his own backing vocal group. Shortly after that, the group paused their activity while Chuck served in the army. When they resumed in 1961, Cash hired them as a supporting act for a few tours and became familiar with their songwriting. For this album, he recorded three of the brothers' compositions: "Mr. Lonesome" (written by Tompall), "You Won't Have Far to Go" (written by Chuck), and "Let Me down Easy" (co-written by Tompall and Jim). The Glaser Brothers would go on to record on their own as well as opening one of the first songwriter-focused publishing houses in Nashville.

Cash returns again to his influences with the Leadbelly song "Cotton Song," here titled "In Them Old Cotton Fields Back Home." He was probably familiar with the Leadbelly version, but most of America would be more familiar with the version the pop-folk group the Highwaymen took to #13 on the Pop charts as "Cotton Fields." The song would later be recorded by a wide range of artists, from sax man Boots Randolph to Creedence Clearwater Revival, Buckwheat Zydeco, and the Beach Boys. Here, Cash's performance borders on monotone, showing little conviction or interest.

"Delia's Gone," a murder ballad based on real-life events recorded a few days before "Cotton Fields," would become one of Cash's most famous songs—but not for another forty years. He seems more engaged here, and the song obviously holds his interest much better. Up next is "I Forgot More Than You'll Ever Know About Her," a #1 hit for eight weeks in 1953 for the Davis Sisters, Skeeter and Betty Jack, shortly after the tragic death of Betty Jack.

Nine songs in comes the first Cash-penned song, "You Remembered Me," about a woman remembering her man in faithfulness while the man, regretfully, forgets. "I'm Free from the Chain Gang Now"—another song Cash would return to during his American phase—shows him in fine form.

Cash's second original song on the album is the closer, "Sing It Pretty, Sue," the story of a young man who watches as his girlfriend gives up her love in pursuit of fame. With the strife in Cash's personal life at the time, it could easily be seen as gender-flipped autobiography. Cash would later say that it was one of his absolute favorite songs.

Rather than release another single from the album, Columbia chose to issue "Bonanza," the theme to the hit television show, with lyrics rewritten by Cash and Johnny Western. The song briefly touched the Pop chart at #94 before dropping off, and did not hit the Country charts at all. The B-side was another Leadbelly adaptation, "Pick a Bale o' Cotton," that also failed to attract much attention.

Nearing the Christmas season, Columbia opted to release a gospel-themed single, "(There'll Be) Peace in the Valley (for Me)" b/w "Were You There (When They Crucified My Lord)." "Peace in the Valley," a favorite of Cash's, was written by Thomas A. Dorsey, and had been a million-selling single for Red Foley, who took it to #5 on the Country charts in 1951. Elvis Presley's 1957 version made it to #25 on the Pop chart. Unfortunately for Cash, he was unable to produce the same chart-topping results.

8

You're the One I Need

June Carter Cash

In 2008, country artist Heidi Newfield released the song "Johnny and June," in which she runs down a number of things she would like in a relationship, all based on the union of Cash and Carter. The chorus proclaims that she wants a love like Johnny and June. It was a love that has been molded into legend as much as Cash has himself. But June Carter's story started well before her famous marriage.

Maces Spring

On June 23, 1929, two years after the sessions in Bristol, Tennessee, that have come to be known as the Big Bang of country music, Valerie June Carter was born into country music's first family, the second daughter of Maybelle and Ezra (Eck). Growing up in Maces Springs, Virginia, cradled in the rolling Clinch Mountains, June was a tomboy who liked to do whatever her father was into at the time, including riding motorcycles with him at age five. While the Carter Family traveled, June, older sister Helen, and younger sister Anita stayed with Eck and other family members including Jeanette and Joe, the children of the Carter Family's Sara and A. P.

Border Radio

The largest radio stations in the US were broadcast at 50,000 watts, including Nashville's WSM, home of the *Grand Ole Opry*, and Cincinnati's WLW, home of the *Renfro Valley Barn Dance*—two increasingly important venues for the spread of country music. Another key station, XERA, broadcast from just across the Texas border in Mexico, but with its towers aimed directly at the States, much of its programming could be heard all over the country, and even into Canada.

Although located in Mexico, the "X-stations" (of which there were three others, besides XERA) were operated by American businessmen who would procure sponsorship deals with other American companies. It was a deal like this—made with the Chicago-based Consolidated Royal Chemical Corporation—that brought the Carter Family to Texas in 1938. Broadcasting to a rural audience, the station pulled together a number of hillbilly acts, including the Carter

Family, for a show titled *Good Neighbor Get-Together*, which aired for four hours each night and again the next morning.

By February of 1939, the Carter Family was in disarray. Sara and A. P. had separated in 1932, following Sara's affair with A. P.'s cousin, Coy Bays. The couple divorced in 1939, and Sara married Bays. It was a crushing blow to A. P., who couldn't rekindle the love he had once had for music and performing. He became so distraught that he was sent home to Maces Spring, leaving Sara and Maybelle to finish out their contract with XERA. Then, with their contractual obligations completed, Sara went with Bays to California, while Maybelle returned to Maces Springs. Before she left, however, Maybelle had negotiated a contract with the show's sponsors to return to the station with a new show by the Carter Sisters.

Maybelle had begun to groom her girls to follow in their famous family footsteps. While June soon found that her sisters had perfect pitch, she herself struggled. She was able to pick up the Autoharp, but her singing voice was never strong. Early recordings of a ten-year-old June bear that out, although her performances were buoyed by a natural charisma and enthusiasm.

The reunited Carter Family returned to XERA in September of 1939, with Sara still sporting a newlywed glow and A. P. having recovered his enthusiasm for the music. This time, the show was rounded out by the younger sisters. The family began to make transcriptions of their shows that were then sent to any other station that requested them, causing the popularity of the group to spread even farther.

The Barn Dance and Midday Show Circuit

At the end of the 1939–40 season, the Bays made their way back to California and the Carters to Virginia, before reconvening in Texas in late 1940. In the interim, June began to take stock in her abilities, singing not being the strongest of them. What was among the strongest was comedy—a talent that would become an integral part of her—and the family's—act. With the Carter Family firmly back in the public eye (a *Life* magazine cover story had been readied and planned, but it was bumped by Pearl Harbor) and their records once again selling, they did two more seasons at XERA. But by 1942, the US government had begun to move against the border stations, putting the Carter Family out of a steady place to perform. Their resurgence in popularity—not to mention the sales the sponsor garnered because of their strong relationship—helped them land a morning show on WBT in Charlotte, North Carolina. But when that contract ended in March of 1943, the original Carter Family officially disbanded.

The Carter Sisters and Mother Maybelle soon made their way to Richmond, Virginia, and a spot on a small station called WRNL. Although the sisters had been playing with the family for several years in some form or other, being the headliners—the ones who were depended on to carry the show—was new to them. But WRNL was strictly a small-time operation. The family had gone from broadcasting right across the country on 500,000 watts to broadcasting solely within the Richmond area at 5,000 watts.

Keen to expand their audience, the group began to travel anywhere they could get back from in time to do their daily morning show. It was here that June began to enjoy the spotlight. Her comedy was becoming more popular with the listening audiences, and she was becoming much savvier about getting new sponsors for their shows. More than the others, she knew that this was what she wanted to do with her life. The others may have possessed perfect pitch and golden voices, but she had the ambition, and her sights were set on the *Grand Ole Opry*—the most popular of the radio barn dances, and the one that could make or break a career.

One didn't simply jump from a smalltime radio gig to the biggest stage in country music, however, regardless of one's heritage. So, in 1946, the group moved on to the *Old Dominion Barn Dance* on Richmond's WRVA, a weekly Saturday-night competitor. From there they made their way to WNOX in Knoxville, Tennessee, in 1947 to perform daily on the *Midday Merry-Go-Round.* In Knoxville, they added a second guitarist to the group, a young man who had been a fan of the original lineup, having listened back then to their border-radio broadcasts. That man, Chet Atkins, would go on to become one of the biggest stars and power-players in country music, and that potential would nearly keep the Carters from reaching their *Opry* dream. In 1949, the group, including Atkins, moved to Springfield, Missouri, to do a show on KWTO. It was there that June, in character as Little Junie Carter, began to become the jewel in the show's crown.

Grand Ole Opry

Now, just as they once had done for Consolidated Royal, Mother Maybelle & the Carter Sisters with Chet Atkins and His Famous Guitar were making good money for their sponsor, Red Star Flour. The company saw the success of the group and decided that even more success would be even better, so they started the gears going to bring them to the stage of the *Opry*. The call came in to Eck that the *Opry* wanted the family to appear every Saturday night on a segment sponsored by Red Star. But there was one thing—they couldn't bring Atkins. Some excuse or other was given about the amount of guitarists already in Nashville, and how any new musician had to be sponsored by a member of the local musicians' union. Eck listened patiently, and then declined the invitation.

The suggestion that they exclude Atkins offended Eck as much as it would have had he been asked to leave out any other member of the family. Eck knew that some of the show's other musicians were scared by Atkins' potential, and that this was why they didn't want him to come along. The *Opry* called again, and again Eck refused. This courtship lasted for six months, and with each call the offer grew sweeter, but as long as Atkins wasn't welcome, the group wouldn't be appearing. Finally, *Opry* management got the hint that this wasn't about the money. Steel guitarist Don Davis, who had gotten to know Atkins and the Carters while recording transcriptions with George Morgan at KWTO (and who would eventually marry Anita), signed on as Atkins' sponsor, and the group made plans to appear on the show.

On May 29, 1950, Mother Maybelle & the Carter Sisters, along with Atkins, played their first *Opry* appearance. In the audience was an eighteen-year-old J. R. Cash, attending the *Opry* as part of a high-school field trip to Nashville. This was a few years before rock 'n' roll exploded onto the scene, and country music was high on a wave of commercial success, with artists like Red Foley and Patti Page topping the Pop charts. Maybelle and the sisters' initial appearance was a success, and the group began to perform weekly. The *Opry* was (and still is) divided into thirty-minute segments, each hosted by a different star. When it was time for the Carter Sisters, June would do a bit with the host, and then the group would launch into a show, much like what they had been recording in Missouri for RadiOzark. During this time they also began to record, first for RCA Victor and then for Columbia, cutting eighteen singles over the next four years.

Hank Williams and Carl Smith

The Carters had moved to Nashville and become entrenched in the burgeoning country-music industry. The family befriended a rising yet troubled star named Hank Williams and his wife Audrey. Hank would often come off the road angry with Audrey, accusing her of cheating on him or making some other slight, and violence was not uncommon. He battled the bottle—both the pill and drink varieties—but the Carters did their best to help him, hopeful that they could point him down the road to recovery. Addictions such as Hank's were still foreign to the Carters, but that would all change for June in due course.

It was during this time that June found herself with a superstar suitor: singer Carl Smith. Smith had joined the *Opry* the same year the Carter Sisters made their debut, and was a smart and successful up-and-comer, riding high on a series of #1 singles like "Let Old Mother Nature Have Her Way" and "Are You Teasing Me?" He and June were married in 1952. In 1955, their daughter Rebecca Carlene was born, but within a year the couple had divorced. They were two rising stars headed in different directions, and both spent a lot of time on the road. At one point, Smith accused June of having an affair with Elvis Presley, with whom the Carter Sisters had toured. Presley actually had eyes for Anita, but Smith's remarks put into words the lack of trust between the two.

Smith soon left the Opry to join the nationally touring *Phillip Morris Country Music Show*. That same year, on July 7th, Johnny Cash and the Tennessee Two made their *Opry* debut, and Cash knocked out the crowd with his performance. After the show, while his wife Vivian waited outside, Cash ran into June backstage and told her that someday he was going to marry her.

"Is that so?" she replied, surprised.

"Yes, that's what I'm going to do," came his reply.

"Good! I can't wait," she said, walking away.

Career Choices

With her marriage to Smith over, June began to contemplate a career change. She had been recording singles without her sisters since 1949 and a novelty parody of "Baby, It's Cold Outside" with hillbilly jazz pioneers Homer & Jethro. The song reached the Top 10 on the Country charts and was featured in the Esther Williams movie *Neptune's Daughter*. But none of her other singles (all of which were novelty records) had touched the charts. She was also growing unhappy with her role in the Carter Sisters shows, where she was constantly being reminded to move farther away from the microphone. But she still enjoyed the comedy, and thought maybe that was a direction to head in.

One day, June's friend Harry Kalcheim of the William Morris Agency sent her a telegram, informing her that someone was coming into town that might be able to help with her acting ambitions. On the night of the meeting, June was performing on the *Opry*, and she spotted a man close to the stage continuously taking pictures of her. When her act was over, he asked her if she would like to go for dinner, and the two went to grab a bite. She soon found out that this was the man Kalcheim had told her about: Elia Kazan, the famed director of *East of Eden*, *On the Waterfront*, and *A Streetcar Named Desire*.

Kazan recommended June take acting lessons with his friend Sandy Meisner of the Neighborhood Playhouse. From there she went on to bit parts in several television westerns and performances on variety shows like *The Jackie Gleason Show*, *The Garry Moore Show*, and *The Jack Paar Show*. But after an incident with a director who wanted her to audition for the part of a prostitute, late at night, with no one else in the building, and then encouraged her to go off script, June decided that acting might not be the best way for her to earn a living. She didn't give up on the dream entirely, though. In 1958, she appeared in the film *Country Music Holiday* with singer Ferlin Husky and Zsa Zsa Gabor.

Edwin "Rip" Nix

Returning to Nashville and the *Grand Ole Opry*, June found herself in a relationship with stock-car driver Edwin "Rip" Nix. They were married in 1957, and had a daughter, Rozanna Lea, in 1958. But this marriage, too, was ill fated. Nix and June came from two totally different worlds, and she from one that constantly took her out of town. She had been making regular appearances on both the *Opry* and the *Louisiana Hayride*, starting in June of 1960, as well as occasional shows elsewhere.

In an attempt to salvage the marriage, June sat down and figured out how many dates, and at what price, she would have to play per month to bring in the wage she wanted to help support the family. She arrived at ten, which would allow her much more time at home with her husband and two daughters.

The Johnny Cash Show

In late 1961, a call came in from Saul Holiff, manager of Johnny Cash, asking June to appear on the *Big D Jamboree* on December 9 in Dallas. Almost two weeks after the show, on Christmas morning, Holiff wrote to June with an offer for her to join the Johnny Cash Show on a regular basis, buying up all ten of her available dates per month. By this time, Cash's career had steadied off a bit compared with his meteoric start, but June knew that by joining the show she was guaranteed to be playing in front of packed houses. And she knew that the star of the show had—at the very least—a little crush on her.

Cash made no attempts to hide it, either. In his book *I Was There When It Happened: My Life with Johnny Cash*, Marshall Grant recounts how, when June joined the tour, she was instructed to come to him to make travel arrangements to the next show. Grant told her they already had six people in their car, so he would have to ask Cash. June replied that she was used to traveling in crowded cars and would sit on someone's lap if she needed to. Grant reported this to Cash, who immediately answered, "She can sit on mine."

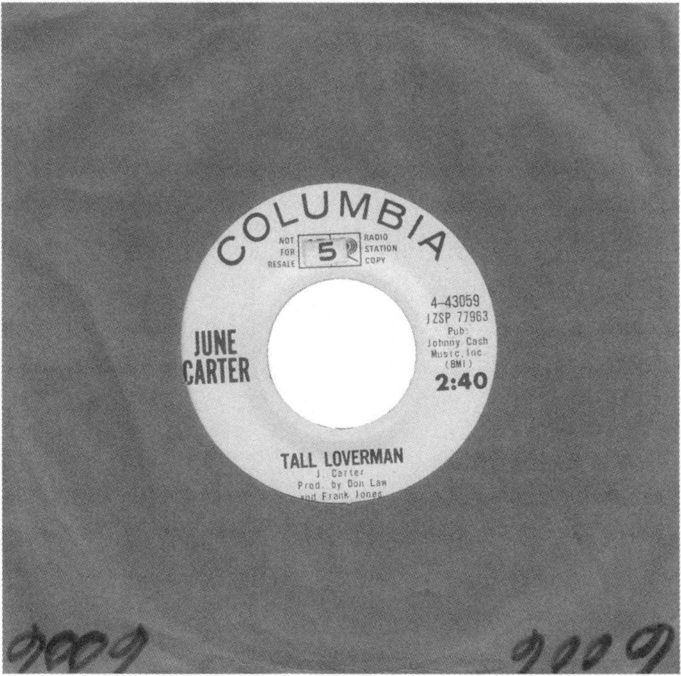

Though her career as a solo artist never took off, June recorded several solo singles throughout the years, including this mid-1960s one. *Private collection*

Cash made no attempt to hide his affection for June, even though he was still married to Vivian. The two women had first met in 1958, at an industry function, and Vivian's initial impression was not favorable. Now, with their marriage in trouble and Johnny always traveling—with June—she knew she was losing her husband, even though June was also still married at the time.

"Ring of Fire" and Courtship

June began to develop feelings for Johnny while they toured together, and they tormented her. She was married for the second time, and he was married, too, so she simply could not give in to the desire. So she channeled it into a song, setting down to write with her friend Merle Kilgore. The result was "(Love's) Ring of Fire." It was recorded first by her sister Anita, but it didn't make even a small dent in the charts. But Cash heard a hit and told them he was going to record it himself, which he did, with a new arrangement and title, taking it to #1 in June of 1963. It stayed at the top of the charts for seven weeks.

Johnny and June spent an increasing amount of time together on the road, and as their feelings grew stronger, their attempts to hide them from the rest of the band and crew crumbled away. June had divorced Edwin in 1963, but Johnny was still married to Vivian, who had been brought up a strict Catholic and refused him a divorce as a matter of principle. After years of living alone in California with their four daughters, however, her resolve began to weaken. At one point, she called June to confront her about the rumors, but June evaded the questions and provided no information. Their final confrontation would come backstage at one of Johnny's concerts, with June resolutely declaring, "Vivian, he *will* be mine."

Drugs

Aside from his marriage, there was one more obstacle in the way of Johnny's union with June: his drug use. In 1963, she discovered that he was using pills after he dropped a few in front of her. Even though she had seen how addiction had affected the lives of her friends Hank and Audrey, her feelings for Johnny remained unchanged. She felt she could help him end his addiction, and found an ally in Marshall Grant as they each took turns finding and disposing of the pills to keep them out of Cash's reach. It was a scene that would repeat itself many times over the years. But Cash's will to continue his drug use was stronger than the efforts of his two closest friends, and the amphetamine use continued. (According to Vivian, June wasn't as innocent as everyone assumes, but her claims about June's drug use at this time have not been publicly corroborated by any other sources.)

In the Hollywood version of the story, June tells Johnny that she won't marry him while he's using, so he quits, and they live happily ever after. In reality, the first part is correct, the second part waivers, and the third part falls apart. June did indeed tell him there wouldn't be a chance at marriage as long as pills were such a powerful part of his life, and she even went as far as telling him in November 1967 that the current set of tour dates were the last she was willing to work with him while he refused to clean up his act.

Proposal

In January 1968, after fourteen years of marriage, Vivian Liberto returned the divorce papers, ending her marriage with Cash. Just days later, he and June entered Folsom Prison to record one of the most important albums of his career. A year earlier, he had begun to regain some of his commercial success, in part thanks to "Jackson," a duet with June that went to #2 on the Country charts, and its follow-up, "Long-Legged Guitar Pickin' Man," also featuring June, which went to #6. Both songs appeared on the album *Carryin' On with Johnny Cash and June Carter.*

"Among my klediments are loved ones and loved things, hard times and good times..."
"A kledíment is mountain talk for treasured persons and things," begins June Carter Cash. And she has many of them to share — from her earliest childhood memories with the famed Carter Family to life with husband Johnny Cash and their seven children.
Warm, witty, intensely honest, June Carter Cash is just about everything you'd look for in a good friend. Now, in her autobiography, she sits back and talks freely, openly, almost as if from across the kitchen table.
Sharing personal stories and lessons, treasured photographs, and a generous helping of original poetry, the author not only takes you behind the scenes, but into her thoughts and prayers.
Get to know the woman behind the name. Among My Klediments by June Carter Cash. Now at bookstores in Cloth, $6.95.
Among My KLEDIMENTS
June Carter Cash
Country music's daughter and Johnny Cash's wife tells her own story
JUNE CARTER CASH/ZONDERVAN
ZONDERVAN PUBLISHING HOUSE
GRAND RAPIDS, MICHIGAN 49506

The Christian market publisher Zondervan, which had released Cash's first autobiography, *Man in Black*, in 1975, released June's story in 1979.
Author's collection

"Jackson" had become one of the highlights of their live show, too, as the two bantered back and forth, egged on by the fans' reactions. It was during a performance of this song at the Gardens in London, Ontario, on February 22, 1968, that Cash stopped singing and proposed to June in front of the whole crowd, as well as Mother Maybelle and her sisters, who had joined the Johnny Cash Show the year before. June tried to play it off, but he persisted, and she said yes. The couple had planned to wait a few months to be married, but they were encouraged by June's daughters Rosey and Carlene not to wait. So on March 1st, in Franklin, Kentucky, the two exchanged vows and became Mr. and Mrs. Johnny Cash.

John Carter Cash and the Return of the Addiction

Cash continued to struggle with his addiction, but he was making headway, with more clean days than wasted ones. When his son John Carter was born, on March 3, 1970, he resolved to completely finish with the pills. For the first time in his marriage to June, he was completely straight, and the drugs, it seemed, were behind them. Then, in 1974, June was involved in a skiing accident. She underwent a series of operations, and was prescribed pain pills in her recovery, but she continued to take them long after her injuries had healed, thus setting a pattern that would last the rest of their lives. When one was clean—or semi-clean—the other was hooked.

By the end of the 1970s, Cash was once again falling into addiction, and with that came the behaviors of an addict—aloofness, erratic behavior, and infidelity. He instructed Marshall Grant, who acted as the group's road manager, to put the couple in separate rooms, with a living area between them. In her second autobiography, *From the Heart*, June claims that her only reason for using drugs was to hide the pain. She had been publicly lauded for years as the woman who saved Johnny Cash, and now her marriage was seemingly heading for divorce.

On tour in 1979, Cash sought advice from singer Jan Howard, who had joined the roadshow and was one of June's best friends. When he called Jan in the wee hours of the morning, June overheard their conversation and concluded that they must be having an affair. The next morning, having packed her bags, she gave Johnny an ultimatum: either you send Jan home, or I'm taking John Carter and leaving—and not just the tour. This time, the crisis was averted, and Howard left the tour.

Johnny and June would continue to stay in separate hotel rooms into the 1980s, until an intervention was staged, and he accepted treatment at the Betty Ford Center. After shaking their respective addictions, Johnny and June settled into a life of travel and touring, playing dates in Australia and spending time at Cinnamon Hill, their home in Jamaica. Drugs would never be too far out of the picture, but they learned to cope with each other's addictions. They became a functioning couple again, and resumed living the life they once had.

The Johnny Cash Fan Club newsletter, *Our Kinda Cash*, often included photos like this one from the early 1990s.
Author's collection

Press On

The mid-1990s brought with them Cash's final career comeback, but by the end of the decade his health was deteriorating, and he had retired from touring. That freed up some of June's time, and she decided to resume her own career. Throughout the '80s and early '90s, she had appeared in various made-for-TV movies, mostly with Johnny, and in 1997 she appeared in the feature film *The Apostle* with Robert Duvall, whom she had gotten to know back at the Neighborhood Playhouse. Then, in 1998, she made a move back toward music.

June had made her first solo album, *Appalachian Pride,* in 1975. Released by Columbia and produced by Cash, it included a few Carter Family gems, as well as songs by other Appalachian artists, such as Jean Ritchie, and one co-written with her daughter Carlene. The follow-up eventually came twenty-three years later. *Press On,* produced by John Carter Cash, surrounds June with top-notch acoustic musicians and includes some of the banter between them. It features rerecorded versions of a few of the songs originally included on her debut, some Carter Family favorites, and a few originals. The album was met with praise from critics and fans alike, and won a Grammy for Best Traditional Folk Album in 2000. June toured in support of the album throughout 1999, and for the first time in her life—at age seventy—she was the headliner. Johnny accompanied her to many shows, appearing onstage for duets of a handful of their most famous songs.

Last Song of the Wildwood Flower

Encouraged by the success of *Press On,* June decided to return to recording a few years later. For her next album, appropriately titled *Wildwood Flower,* she would lean heavily on the catalogue of the Carter Family, with only two originals included among the thirteen tracks. In line with the content, the recording of the album took place in Maces Spring, in the home where June had been raised, and included cousins Joe and Jeanette Carter, as well as Cash.

What nobody knew during the recording sessions, however, was that June's health was slowly deteriorating. Some had noticed she had become forgetful of things she once knew by heart, and at other times she struggled to make sense when she spoke. Those around her either ignored it or simply assumed she had started to use pills again. But that wasn't the case. In late April, just a month after wrapping up the recording of the album, she was rushed to the hospital by ambulance. Her heart was failing, and there was oxygen in her blood. She suffered a major cardiac arrest after surgery and was placed on a respirator, but her brain activity had stopped. On May 12, 2003, Johnny allowed the respirator to be removed, and three days later, June passed from this earth.

Wildwood Flower was released in September, four months after June's death, and just days before Johnny's. Although her vocals had suffered with her health, the album served as an important sendoff for an artist with a direct link to two of the biggest legacies in music. As with *Press On,* the album was praised by the critics, and in 2004 June was posthumously awarded Grammys for Best Traditional Folk Album and Best Female Country Vocal Performance for the song "Keep on the Sunny Side." It was a fitting honor for a woman who had put her career on hold in order to be the best helpmate she could be to the man she deeply loved.

Johnny and June had their ups and downs, just like any other couple, although some were higher, some deeper, and others under much more public scrutiny. The start of their relationship wasn't ideal—what with both of them being married to other people—and that fact weighed heavily on both of them, coming as they did from deeply religious backgrounds. Today, we live in a time when celebrity infidelity is treated as a way to sell magazines and television ads, and it is easy to forget that when their relationship began these things weren't brushed away so flippantly. Back then, many weren't so shy with their judgment. But Johnny and June persevered, and they built a life together that has become the envy of many—a relationship built on love and passion that didn't seem to dim as the light in their eyes did. In Cash's 2002 video for "Hurt," the expression on his wife's face—a mixture of admiration, concern, and unending love—serves as the perfect summation of their relationship.

I Hate to Beg like a Dog for a Bone

Columbia 1963

As 1962 ended, Cash was slipping down the charts, but he was still popular enough to sell out venues like the Hollywood Bowl. Though he had begun to focus less on singles and more on albums, the label wanted more hits. Cash's escalating addiction to pills proved an obstacle in achieving that, but he still managed to pull out some great performances despite his problems.

Blood, Sweat and Tears (1963)

Cash's next album was a song cycle, like *Songs of Our Soil*, that put the focus on the workingman. As Bob Allen writes in the liner notes to the Bear Family collection *Johnny Cash: Come Along and Ride This Train*, "These, for the most part, are not the legends, the heroes, the icons, of American history that Cash sings about on these songs. Rather these are, more often than not, the disenfranchised and disempowered—those at or near the bottom of the economic and social heap but who nonetheless maintain a fierce sense of pride and stoic resignation about their lot in life."

The tone is set by "The Legend of John Henry's Hammer," Cash's dramatic retelling of the old folk tale. The song clocks in at eight-and-a-half minutes, making it clear that Cash isn't aiming for radio airplay. Its extended form affords him the liberty of doing a little acting as he performs, while hitting two steel bars to mimic the sound of the hammer on the railroad spikes.

"John wasn't in very good shape when we recorded 'John Henry's Hammer,'" Marshall Grant writes in his autobiography. "And I can still see him getting down on his hands and knees on the floor with his microphone, clanging those two pieces of steel together as he growled out the lyrics to the song. The record didn't get a lot of airplay, but when we played it onstage, John would give an absolutely marvelous performance."

"Tell Him I'm Gone," propelled by Bob Johnson's acoustic guitar work, is the story of a man who's had enough and walks off the work line. Johnson, who knew June Carter through playing around the Knoxville area, had come into the studio fold earlier in the year, adding twelve-string acoustic guitar, mandolin, and lute to various songs. None of those musical touches adorned the haunting "Another Man Done Gone," however. The story of an African American man who is taken from the chain gang and hung in front of his own family, the song was originally performed by Vera Hall Ward and recorded in the field by Alan Lomax in the 1940s. It was one of the few times Cash touched on racial issues in song. It's a sparse and stirring performance, with Anita Carter's angelic voice seconding Cash's.

The mood is lightened slightly by "Busted," Harlan Howard's tale of a workingman's plight, complete with a list of things that won't go right for him. "Casey Jones" is a redo of an old folk song that tells much the same story as one of Cash's old favorites, "Wreck of the Old 97." Another old folk song, "Nine Pound Hammer," came from an album that heavily inspired Cash's concept-album work, Merle Travis' 1947 set *Folk Song of the Hills.* Cash rounds out the collection with Harlan Howard's "Chain Gang," Jimmie Rodgers' "Waiting for a Train," and "Roughneck," written by Sheb Wooley, who had spent six weeks in 1958 at #1 with his song "The Purple People Eater."

There was no country album chart until 1964, but *Blood, Sweat and Tears* did make the Pop charts, albeit climbing no higher than #80. No singles were selected from the album, which perhaps signaled Columbia's declining faith in their one-time hit machine. But they didn't need to wait long.

Ring of Fire: The Best of Johnny Cash (1963)

By June 1963, Cash's career was on a commercial upswing, set in motion by the success of "Ring of Fire." His personal life was another story. His affair with June Carter was heating up, while things were rapidly deteriorating at home with Vivian. He had become an absentee father to his four girls, even when he was off the road. His pill use was escalating at an alarming rate, and that—coupled with his constant smoking—caused him to frequently lose his voice, either completely or partially, making it hard to schedule recording sessions.

Columbia was keen to release an album to capitalize on his recent chart run, but with his voice shaky and studio appearances sporadic, the label knew that getting a full album of new material out of him would be out of the question. So, for Cash's tenth Columbia album, the label decided to issue a collection of songs from the past few years instead. All of the twelve songs included on the album had been released as singles, dating from 1959 to the current hit, "Ring of Fire."

By the early 1960s, the audience for albums was beginning to change. In the late '50s, the younger crowd was buying 45s while their parents were buying albums. But then the Beatles and other youth-oriented groups appeared, changing the way teens looked at albums. In 1963, that transition was just beginning, and Columbia saw both audience groups buying the album. *Ring of Fire* entered the Pop Albums chart in July and spent twenty-six weeks there into 1964. January

1964 marked the inauguration of the new Hot Country Albums chart—which became the Hot Country LPs chart in 1968, and since late 1984 has been known as Top Country Albums—and it debuted with *Ring of Fire* at #1. The album would go on to sell 500,000 copies, earning Cash his first gold record.

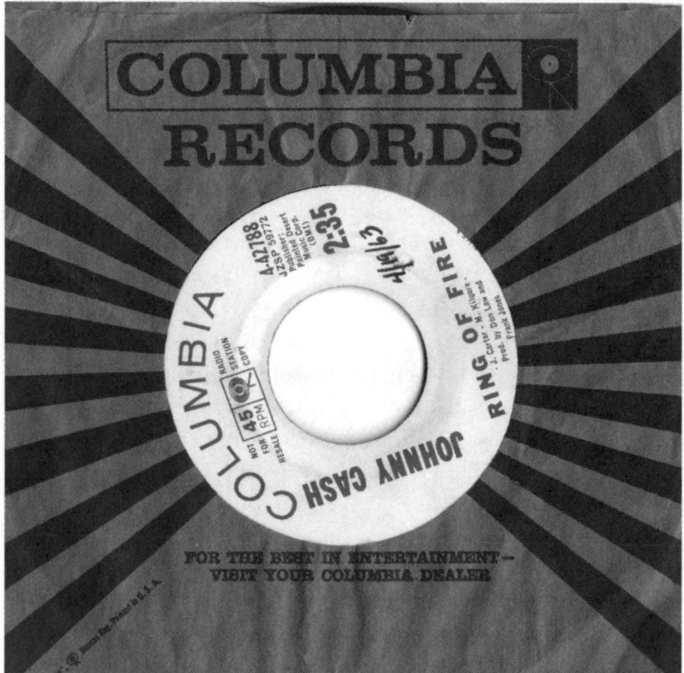

The song that returned Cash to the top of the charts was written by the woman of his affection about her feelings on loving a married man.

Private collection

10

As Long as the Moon Shall Rise

Columbia 1964

At the dawn of 1964, with the Beatles just beginning to come ashore, Cash was basking in the success of "Ring of Fire" and the new, lucrative contract with Columbia the song's success had stimulated. That year, he also released two albums: a controversial concept album, *Bitter Tears: Ballads of the American Indian* (discussed in chapter 13), and *I Walk the Line*, a haphazard collection put together in the hope of landing a hit single or two.

This was also the year that Cash made the move toward being a folksinger—or at least that's the way it seemed to many country fans and industry figures. He had always had a foot in the folk world, but in 1964 he put it all in, buddying up with Bob Dylan and performing at the Newport Folk Festival (as covered in the next chapter).

By now, Cash's drug use was becoming more widely known and was beginning to take its toll. His health, his marriage, and his relationship with his young daughters were all suffering. His voice bore the strain, too. And yet he still found the time—and the stamina—to get into the studio and record new work.

Keep on the Sunnyside with the Carter Family (1964)

Cash found his way into the studio a few times in 1963 to record a song or two. On one occasion—maybe as a way of saying thanks for the support of Maybelle Carter, and to honor the legacy of the group—he convened with the Carter Family, taking the A. P. background role alongside Mother Maybelle and daughters Helen, Anita, and June for a recording of twelve of the group's best-loved songs. The resulting *Keep on the Sunnyside* was released not long after Cash's first full Christmas album, *The Christmas Spirit*. It didn't have any impact commercially, but still offers an excellent take on the old numbers.

I Walk the Line (1964)

The year 1964 started off strongly for Cash, with *Ring of Fire* atop the new Hot Country Albums chart in January, and his new single, the Dylan-inspired

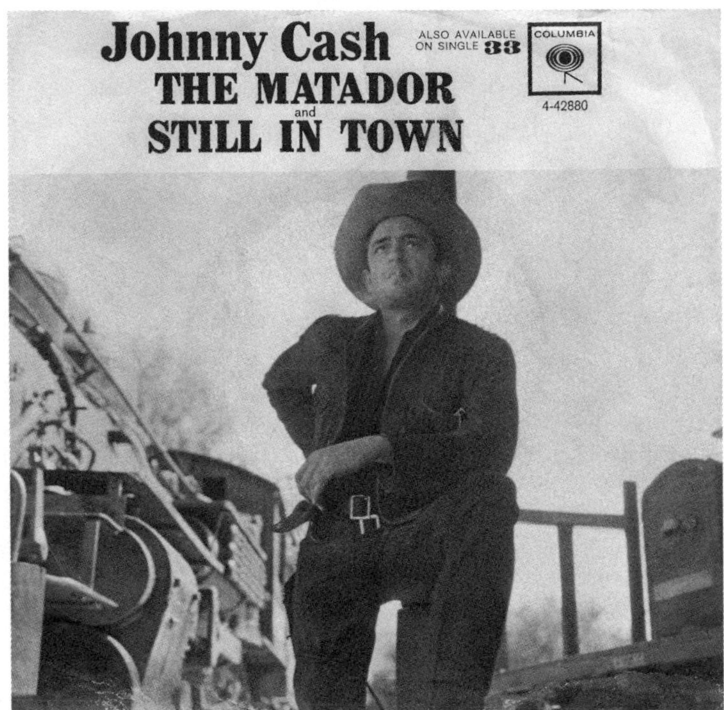

The follow-up to "Ring of Fire" was another song co-written by June Carter (this time with Cash), and featured the Tex-Mex horns. The song missed the top spot, stopping short at #2. *Private collection*

"Understand Your Man," ascending the Pop and Country charts in February. Columbia had been asking for a new album since the fall of 1963, and now wanted to release a new album to take advantage of the #1 hit. Sessions for a new album had begun in September 1963, but Cash had been on the road solidly and hadn't written anything new, aside from the single. An idea for another concept album was growing inside his mind, but it wasn't something he wanted to rush out. Instead, it was decided that he would rerecord some of his early Sun hits and throw in a few other songs.

At those fall sessions Cash brought in Bob Johnson to add some acoustic flourishes to the music, and Johnson in turn brought along Norman Blake. Cash asked Blake to add some of his own touches to the music, starting with the Dobro on what would become the follow-up single to "Understand Your Man," "Bad News."

"Bad News," one of three new songs on the album, had been recorded earlier in 1963 by its writer, John D. Loudermilk, a cousin of Charlie and Ira Loudermilk—or, as they were better known, the Louvin Brothers. Loudermilk's recording went to #23 on the Country charts but stalled out after that. Blake's

Dobro adds some added swagger to Cash's version, while the singer's rumbling laugh and raspy voice brings a menacing quality.

Of the other new songs, "Still in Town," by the powerhouse writing combo of Hank Cochran and Harlan Howard, stays closer to a contemporary country sound, with the tinkling piano of A-Team member Floyd Cramer and the steel guitar of Don Helms at the forefront. "Troublesome Waters," which closes the album with a stronger gospel feel, came from Mother Maybelle and Carter family friend and writer Dixie Deen (who went on to marry Tom T. Hall).

The remainder of the album is made up of new versions of Cash's Sun hits: "I Walk the Line," "Folsom Prison Blues," "Give My Love to Rose," "Hey Porter," "Wreck of the Old 97," "Big River," and "Goodbye, Little Darlin', Goodbye." Cash also includes a remake of one of his early Columbia hits, "I Still Miss Someone." None of the new versions stand up to the previous versions, but they do provide a glimpse at how they were performed by the band after they had lived with them, in most cases, for over five years.

In the final session for the album, on April 21, 1964, Cash wanted to record a song he had found that was the seed of the new concept album he was working on. "The Ballad of Ira Hayes" was picked to be one side of Cash's new single, the other side being "Bad News." "Bad News" reached the Top 10, resting for two weeks at #8 on the Country charts. The album itself spent four weeks at #1 on the Hot Country Albums chart, but reached only #53 on the Pop chart.

My Best Unbeaten Brother

Cash and Dylan

One of the most interesting and important friendships Cash ever had was with Bob Dylan. On paper, it would seem as though they came from drastically different worlds: Cash the country superstar from the right end of the spectrum, Dylan the protest singer from the left. But each was searching for something in the early 1960s, and in each other they found a kindred spirit and a friendship that would have a marked impact on them both, personally and professionally.

The Freewheelin' Bob Dylan

Raised in Hibbing, Minnesota, where he soaked up the sounds of country, folk, and rock 'n' roll, Dylan made his way to Greenwich Village to join the burgeoning folk movement in early 1961. He quickly made friends with other performers, one of them being a young singer named Carolyn Hester, who had recently signed to Columbia. Hester was assembling a band to record her debut album, and invited Dylan to play harmonica on it. At a rehearsal, famed A&R man John Hammond came by to check on his new signee and hear the band. He came away impressed with the young harmonica player who also strummed guitar on some songs, shyly peeking out from under his hat. Hammond invited Dylan to stop by his office for an audition, and duly signed him to a contract after one song ("Talkin' New York"). Less than a year after coming to town, Dylan was now on Columbia, home of his friend and idol Pete Seeger.

Shortly after that, Dylan was ushered into the studio, guitar and harmonica in hand, to record his first album. The album contained only two original songs, and did very little business, selling approximately 5,000 copies in its first year (enough at least to recoup the $402 Columbia spent on producing it), but after its release, Dylan returned to Hammond with his new manager Albert Grossman and successfully renegotiated his contract, gaining a higher royalty percentage on future recordings. Around the office, Dylan became known as "Hammond's

Folly." But Hammond's vindication came quickly when one of Dylan's songs, "Blowin' in the Wind," became a hit for Peter, Paul & Mary.

Dylan returned to the studio, and in April 1963 he released *The Freewheelin' Bob Dylan.* The ratio of covers to originals had flipped, with two covers to eleven Dylan originals. And what originals they were: "Blowin' in the Wind," "Masters of War," "A Hard Rain's A-Gonna Fall," and "Don't Think Twice, It's All Right," to name but a few. The album showcased what Hammond had the foresight to see: that Dylan was in a class of his own as a songwriter, and in a position to continue to grow even further.

It is estimated that *Freewheelin'* sold 10,000 copies per month for the remainder of the year. One of those copies went to Johnny Cash, who had noticed Dylan's debut and kept an eye on his progress. When *Freewheelin'* came out, he was mesmerized, taking a portable record player on tour with him so he could listen to the album as often as possible. He became so enamored with the album that he decided to write Dylan a letter to tell him he was "the best country singer I've heard in years." Thus began a series of correspondence that continued until the pair met in person. Dylan's influence on Cash is evident in the November 1963 recording of "Understand Your Man," a thinly veiled take, both melodically and thematically, on "Don't Think Twice, It's All Right." Released in 1964, the song would become Cash's ninth #1 hit.

Dylan's Defender

At the same time some at Columbia were having doubts about Dylan, they were having similar doubts about Cash. He had arrived at the label amid great fanfare and expectation in 1958, but his last #1 hit for the company had come in 1959 ("Don't Take Your Guns to Town"). But nothing silences the internal critics like success, which came with "Ring of Fire," released the same month as Dylan's *Freewheelin'*. The single rose quickly to #1 on the Country Singles chart, where it stayed for seven weeks, and entered the Pop Top 20.

Cash had regained his clout at Columbia, and he placed it squarely behind Bob Dylan. "Cash was behind Dylan every which way," Hammond noted, in an interview with Anthony Scudato, as quoted in Dustan Prial's *The Producer*, "everybody in the company knew it. Cash made it known he thought Dylan was a giant. There's no higher recommendation possible."

It wasn't just at Columbia that Dylan was placed in the crosshairs. *Freewheelin'* contained a few songs that veered from the topical protest songs that were so popular within the circles in which he ran, and his upcoming album was rumored to have even more. Fans and fellow artists who had suddenly adopted Dylan as their voice began to grouse about his choices. In early 1964, Dylan wrote a six-page essay by way of a letter to the editor of *Broadside* magazine, detailing, with great honesty and vulnerability, his struggle to adhere to increasing fan demand while at the same time exercising creative freedom. Recognizing this as a situation he had found himself in once or twice before, Cash fired off a letter of his own, defending Dylan's right to choose. In the letter, published in the magazine's March 10th issue, Cash echoed the poetic style Dylan used and sang the praises of the poet troubadour, ending with the words, "SHUT UP! . . . AND LET HIM SING!"

Two Legends Meet

When and where these two legends finally met is a little murky. In his foreword to Steve Turner's book *The Man Called Cash*, Kris Kristofferson recalls being told that the two first met backstage at the 1964 Newport Folk Festival. He was told that when Dylan first saw Cash, he made his way to him and began to circle him as one would something in a museum—with a wide smile and a sense of awe. That, Kristofferson said, is the way most people feel meeting Cash for the first time.

This is the most widely heard version of their meeting, but Dylan himself would later recall that he and Cash met face-to-face for the first time at the Gaslight, a New York club popular with members of the folk movement. Cash had played at Carnegie Hall on May 10, 1962, the night of his ill-fated attempt at a live recording. After the show, he and folksinger Ed McCurdy made their way to the Gaslight to see Peter LaFarge, a protest singer signed to Columbia by John Hammond in 1960. Dylan claimed to have met Cash backstage that night. The problem with this story is that Dylan told Cash biographer Christopher S. Wren that he and Cash had been exchanging letters prior to the meeting. According to Cash, those letters didn't start until after the release of *Freewheelin'* in 1963.

Cash himself further confuses the matter by having two recollections of their first meeting. In his second autobiography, written with Patrick Carr and released in 1997, he says that their correspondence ended when they finally met at Newport in 1964. But this contradicts what he told journalist Robert Hilburn in 1973, when he recalled that he was in New York shortly after the letter exchanges began and received a call from Hammond to let him know Dylan would be coming by the office. They met there, Cash added, and spent a few hours talking about music and swapping songs. This version of the story has been corroborated by Hammond, who recalled that Dylan and Cash spent time hanging around the office and studio prior to Newport 1964.

Newport Folk Festival, July 25, 1964

Regardless of when that first face-to-face meeting took place, all are agreed that Dylan and Cash got together in Newport. The Newport Folk Festival was established in Newport, Rhode Island, in 1959 by George Wein, who had previously founded the Newport Jazz Festival in 1954. In 1963, the Folk Festival was still focused on folk and blues musicians, including Mississippi John Hurt, Joan

Baez, and as her guest, Bob Dylan. By 1964, the Festival had expanded its scope, and Johnny Cash was invited to perform.

In recordings of the show, Cash is introduced to the crowd by Pete Seeger, who explains that he had been scheduled to appear the night before but had problems getting in from Nevada. Cash and the Tennessee Two then perform "Big River," "Folsom Prison Blues," "I Still Miss Someone," "Rock Island Line," "Don't Think Twice, It's All Right," "I Walk the Line," "The Ballad of Ira Hayes," and "Keep on the Sunnyside." Cash introduces "Don't Think Twice," from Dylan's *Freewheelin'*, by saying that they had been performing it live for the past few months, and that he is doing it tonight at the request of Dylan himself. Throughout the performance, Cash proves himself to be at home in front of a folk audience, showing his humorous side with a joke about getting a drink of water that he would repeat a few years later on *At Folsom Prison.*

After the show, Cash and June Carter went with Dylan and Baez to a hotel room, where they sat and swapped songs. Dylan suggested Cash record two of his songs, "It Ain't Me, Babe" and "Mama You've Been on My Mind," even though he was planning to record "It Ain't Me, Babe" himself for an album to be titled *Another Side of Bob Dylan.* In a show of respect, Cash gave Dylan one of the guitars he had with him.

Cash Covers Dylan

Cash took Dylan up on his offer, and would go on to record seven of his songs during his career.

"Mama You've Been on My Mind"

Recorded July 27 and 28, 1964, and December 17, 1964

Cash entered Columbia's Nashville recording studio to record this song just two days after Dylan first played it to him. This version features trumpets in a "Ring of Fire" vein and acoustic guitar breaks throughout.

Cash and his crew returned to the studio in December to rerecord the track without the horns. This time around, Charlie McCoy's harmonica features front and center, while Boots Randolph provides saxophone punctuation in the second half of the track. The decision was made to include the winter recording on the 1965 release of *Orange Blossom Special*; the earlier track wouldn't resurface in the States until the 2002 reissue of the album.

"It Ain't Me, Babe"

Recorded August 27, 1964

Cash got a lot of mileage out of this playful collaboration with June Carter. First released as a single in November, it went #1 on the Country Singles chart and #58 on the Pop chart. To announce the single, Columbia even placed a full-page ad in *Billboard.* The song was then released in 1965 on *Orange Blossom Special,* and again in 1967 on *Carryin' On with Johnny Cash and June Carter.*

"Don't Think Twice, It's All Right"

Recorded December 18, 1964

Cash's Newport performance of this song was captured on tape but wouldn't be released in the States until 1995 (by Vanguard). It was then issued again in 2011 as part of the Columbia/Legacy *Bootleg* series. This December recording was released as one of three Dylan covers on *Orange Blossom Special.* There is an unissued live version featuring Rosanne Cash on vocals that was recorded during a show at the Palladium in London, England. (Other tracks from the same show were released as *Strawberry Cake* in 1976.)

"One Too Many Mornings"

Recorded October 29, 1965

Tracked during sessions for 1966's *Happiness Is You,* this song lay unreleased until the 2011 release of *Bootleg Volume II: From Memphis to Hollywood.* Cash would pick up the song again in 1985, recording it as a duet with Waylon Jennings for their album *Heroes.*

"Wanted Man"

Recorded February 24, 1969, October 9, 1970, and September 4, 1986

Although the credit reads only Bob Dylan, Cash has said periodically that he co-wrote this song with him. It makes its recorded debut about halfway through the live recording *At San Quentin,* starting off by playing on the common theme of prisoners, until it becomes evident that the singer is actually talking about being wanted by a variety of women. The first studio recording came in 1970, for the soundtrack to the Robert Redford film *Little Fauss and Big Halsy.* In 1986, Cash returned to the well for his final Mercury release, *Mystery of Life.*

"Song to Woody"

Recorded late 1974/early 1975

Making his debut with Bill Monroe's Bluegrass Boys in the mid-1940s, Earl Scruggs helped to define the core bluegrass sound with his three-finger banjo style. Later, he and singer/guitarist Lester Flatt would form the duo Flatt & Scruggs and capitalize on the newfound popularity of bluegrass with the college crowd. The duo began to experiment in the studio by covering popular songs of the day, many of them by Bob Dylan, and many of them produced by Bob Johnston. Flatt didn't care for this new direction, but Scruggs saw the potential. They soon split up, and Earl Scruggs formed the Earl Scruggs Revue with his sons Gary, Randy, and Steve. "Song to Woody" appeared on the Earl Scruggs Revue's album *Anniversary Special*, issued to celebrate Scruggs' twenty-five years with Columbia, with Scruggs, Cash, and Ramblin' Jack Elliot taking a verse each. One of the two originals included on Bob Dylan's debut album, it is here performed as a tribute to both Woody Guthrie and Dylan himself.

"Forever Young"

Recorded 1994

Red Hot is a nonprofit organization dedicated to "fighting AIDS through pop culture." One of their weapons of choice is a series of compilations focused on one theme or genre. The fourth in the series was *Red Hot + Country*, which includes Cash's cover of this 1974 song of father-son advice. It is interesting to note that this was released months after *American Recordings*, but with production near identical to what Cash fans had been used to before he started working with Rick Rubin. He even uses many of the same session players of old, making it perhaps the last session to have that sound.

Dylan Covers Cash

The bulk of Dylan's Cash covers come from recordings made in one place—Big Pink, the house rented by the band soon to be known as the Band near Woodstock, New York—during April and May of 1967. Widely known as the Basement Tapes, these informal recordings capture Dylan and the Band running through seemingly every folk or roots song they know. That included four songs written by or associated with Cash: "Belshazzar," his first Sun Records gospel recording, from 1957; "Still in Town," written by songwriting giants Hank Cochran and Harlan Howard, which first appeared on Cash's *I Walk the Line* album; and "Big River" and "Folsom Prison Blues," Sun hits that Cash rerecorded for the same album.

The only Cash song Dylan ever recorded in a proper studio was "Ring of Fire," which he tracked for the soundtrack to *Feeling Minnesota* in January 1996. Dylan loses the Mariachi horns and brings in a gospel choir.

Nashville Skyline

Continuing his escape from the title "Voice of a Generation," Dylan continued to evolve creatively, doing so largely out of the public eye. In 1965, he traded his Gibson Nick Lucas Special for a Fender Telecaster and went electric. When he mounted a world tour in the early part of 1966 to publicly debut the sound, he was booed by fans and grilled by reporters. And he grew tired of it. In July 1966, he had a motorcycle accident (or did he?) and became somewhat of a recluse, shunning interviews, concerts, and television appearances. But he continued to record, putting out a steady stream of albums, each met with anticipation by fans and critics alike. By the time of 1966's *Blonde on Blonde* he had begun to temper the electric rock sound he had cultivated on *Bringing It All Back Home* and *Highway 61 Revisited.* His informal recordings with the Band saw him mellow further still, while his 1967 release, *John Wesley Harding*, shows further evolution.

Instead of returning to Columbia's New York studios, producer Bob Johnston suggested he and Dylan try the label's studios in Nashville, using session men like steel-guitar wizard Pete Drake and Charlie McCoy, who played bass on the session but was better known as a harmonica player. The resulting album has a much more laid-back sound than its predecessor, and fans could see Dylan slowly slipping toward the country end of the spectrum, although his vocals and playing (and, perhaps most importantly, his songwriting) remain intact.

Then, in February 1969, Dylan once again met Johnston in Nashville to begin work on the album that would become *Nashville Skyline*, perhaps his most country-sounding work. On the 17th, Johnston was pulling double duty, producing a session for Cash next door to Dylan's. That evening, Cash and Dylan went out to enjoy dinner, and when they returned to the studio to find that Johnston had set up stools and mics for them, they looked at each other and laughed. They were always game for a song swap, even if it was being recorded by their sneaky producer, and in front of the film crew that was following Cash for a documentary. Playing into the next morning, the two ran through twenty songs, including material by Cash, Dylan, Carl Perkins, and Elvis Presley, plus several country standards. It is interesting to note that Carl Perkins, who played on these sessions, has said that Dylan often visited Nashville after that, and that there were at least a couple of other sessions, although aside from bootlegs of this session, no tapes have circulated. Dylan confirmed this to be the case in a 1994 interview with Perkins biographer David McGee, adding that he has never heard the subsequent sessions.

The idea for the collaboration wasn't Johnston's alone. When Clive Davis—at the time the president of Columbia—was told that two of his top-selling artists would be working in the same studio at the same time, he conspired with Johnston to get them on tape together. If his hope was to create a collaborative album by two of his label's pillars, however, it was quickly dashed by the end result. While interesting in a historical sense, the material isn't something you'd want to spin on a regular basis—and certainly not ahead of anything either man produced individually. One song did make the cut, though: a duet of Dylan's "Girl from the North Country" was included on the final mix of his new album, for which Cash also contributed liner notes.

Dylan on *The Johnny Cash Show*

Nearly three months after their unfruitful Nashville recording session together, Dylan returned to Music City, USA, at the invitation of Cash to be a guest on his new ABC network variety show. Dylan had moved farther into his hermit lifestyle, growing a short beard and cropping his hair, and it was a testament to their friendship that Dylan agreed to make an appearance on the show. But it wasn't without a few stipulations, the main one being that the press be kept away from the rehearsals. One tenacious Nashville reporter, Red O'Donnell, did make it around security and confronted Dylan in a guerrilla-style interview that clearly freaked him out. A fan also made it through and had to be escorted out, further upsetting the now reclusive-singer, who at the time seemed almost overcome with shyness and self-doubt.

Even though he was trying to change his image, Dylan was still acutely aware of how he was viewed by his fans both inside and outside the music industry. During his first run-through of his set, with the band off-camera, he was placed in front of a backdrop of a shack. After he finished, he told Cash he would be made a laughing stock if people saw him singing in front of the prop. Cash simply asked him how he would rather be seen and then, per Dylan's request, had the scenery moved.

After rehearsals wrapped up, Dylan made his way to Cash's Hendersonville home, where a crowd was beginning to gather. And what a crowd! Sitting in the round and pulling out their guitars were Kris Kristofferson, Joni Mitchell and her boyfriend Graham Nash, and Shel Silverstein. Cash later recalled that Dylan sang "Lay Lady Lay" from his recently released *Nashville Skyline*, Kristofferson sang "Me and Bobby McGee," Mitchell did "Both Sides Now," Nash shared "Marrakesh Express," and Silverstein brought out his soon-to-be Cash hit "Boy Named Sue." (Cash's stepdaughter Carlene, then twelve years old, left Silverstein out of her recollection, but remembered James Taylor singing "Sweet Baby James.")

The next day, May 1, 1969, the audience filed into the Mother Church of Country Music to witness the first show. Cash opened—as he would every show in the run—and then introduced his first musical guest, Joni Mitchell. When Dylan's turn came, he performed two songs alone, the first being "I Threw It All Away" from *Nashville Skyline.* The second was a new song called "Living the Blues," which would appear on his 1970 release *Self Portrait.* It was the one and only live performance of the song. To wrap up the segment, Cash joined Dylan for "Girl from the North Country." They performed each of the songs several times to be sure of capturing a good take, and the crowd responded enthusiastically. When the show aired, on June 7th, everything went off without a hitch. In convincing Dylan to appear again on television, Cash had done the near impossible, while also putting their unique friendship directly in the public eye.

12

Pied Piper of the Desert, Roll On to the Sea

Columbia 1965

Cash's 1964 album *Bitter Tears* (discussed in chapter 13) was not only a commercial disappointment but also a polarizing album for country music radio, in terms of its subject matter and presentation. Its lack of success led Columbia and Don Law to steer Cash back to more familiar territory, toward something they could sink their programming teeth into. So, on December 17–20, 1964, Cash returned to the studio to put together a new album, to feature eleven songs plus his newest single, "It Ain't Me, Babe," the Bob Dylan–penned song he and June had recorded in August.

Orange Blossom Special (1965)

Orange Blossom Special was more of what listeners were used to—straightforward songs, free from controversial subject matter. *Orange Blossom Special* was Cash's first solid effort in some time. The album starts with a one-two punch of modern classics, "Orange Blossom Special" and "The Long Black Veil," both of which are often thought to be much older than they actually are.

Written in 1938 by fiddle-playing Florida native Ervin T. Rouse, "Orange Blossom Special" was an ode to the train that ran from Miami to New York, and would become a showpiece for fiddlers of all levels. (One-time Bill Monroe sideman Chubby Wise would also claim authorship, or at times co-authorship, of the song, although it is widely credited to Rouse.) Here, Cash eschews the fiddles for harmonica and saxophone, played by Charlie McCoy and Boots Randolph, respectively. To emulate the fiddle frenzy that usually occurs, McCoy switches between two harmonicas in different keys for the solo—a trick Cash would replicate in concert. Meanwhile, Cash, needing a conversation partner for the mid-song exchange, had stepped out into the hall and recruited studio custodian and security guard Ed Grizzard.

"The Long Black Veil" is often mistaken for a ballad in the old English tradition, but was actually written by two Nashville songwriters in 1959. Co-writer Danny Dill was intrigued by a story of a New Jersey priest who was killed under a streetlight while witnesses stood silent. To that he added the story of the woman in a long black veil who would leave a solitary red rose on the grave of the actor Rudolph Valentino. Unable to successfully merge the two ideas together, Dill took the elements to co-writer Marijohn Wilken, who helped him blend them into a cohesive story. The resulting song depicts a man who has clearly done something most people would deem unacceptable—sleeping with his best friend's wife—but then switches the point of view from the living to the dead, skillfully garnering sympathy for the man as he choses death rather than disgracing his lover and his best friend. Lefty Frizzell took the song to #6 on the Country charts in 1959, but the song would become most closely associated with Cash after its inclusion on *At Folsom Prison*.

The album also includes three songs by Cash's friend Bob Dylan. "It Ain't Me, Babe" is a playful warning to the woman in the singer's life, featuring June Carter on a harmony vocal, plus the horn sound that had helped make "Ring of Fire" a hit. The single was released in September of 1964 and reached #4 on the Country chart but stalled at #58 on the Pop chart. Dylan had recorded the song for his 1964 album *Another Side of Bob Dylan*, and the Turtles took it to #8 on the Hot 100 less than a year after Cash recorded it.

The B-side of the Cash single, "Time and Time Again," was the first Cash/Carter co-write to be released. (June had already recorded another co-write with a darkly comedic hook entitled "How Did You Get Away from Me," but it would remain unreleased for many years.) In "Time and Time Again," Cash sings of a lover who is "like the shifting sand" and who disappears from his life only to reappear later, making one wonder who Johnny and June had in mind as they wrote the song. At the time, they were both married to other people, and a constant source of argument was whether one of them was going to get a divorce to be with the other.

The second Dylan song on the album is "Don't Think Twice, It's All Right," from *The Freewheelin' Bob Dylan*. Peter, Paul & Mary had recorded the song in 1963 and had a #9 hit with it. The third is "Mama, You Been on My Mind," a song Dylan had recorded just prior to Cash's Newport Folk Festival appearance but decided to leave off *Another Side*. (His version wasn't released until 1991.)

"There's no doubt about Bob Dylan's influence on my music and myself," Cash told Anthony DeCurtis in 2002, in an interview to publicize the CD reissue of *Orange Blossom Special*. "We became friends, but I already was a fan of his. I still am. I go to the record shop with every release he has and buy his new CD—and his latest one, by the way, is the best yet. Bob is timeless. Invariably, before every day ends, there will be a Bob Dylan song that'll float through me."

The remainder of the material for the album came from a variety of sources. From Harlan Howard came "The Wall," the story of a prisoner's suicide disguised as a jailbreak attempt, and the song that Freddie Hart had

After the death of Johnny Horton, Cash and the Tennessee Three went into the studio to add music to two songs Horton had started. The single was released so that the royalties could help the family. *Private collection*

gotten his start with in 1959. Perhaps as a tribute to his lost friend Johnny Horton, Cash included Horton's former #1 "When It's Springtime in Alaska (It's Forty Below)." He also recorded versions of the Irish standard "Danny Boy" and the Carter Family's signature tune, "Wildwood Flower." The album closer is "Amen," a spiritual number written by black gospel songwriter Jester Hairston. It had recently featured in the 1963 Sidney Poitier film *Lilies of the Field*, which was where Curtis Mayfield first heard the tune. He and his group the Impressions released a version of the song in December 1964, taking it to #7 on the Pop chart.

Cash's last album, *Bitter Tears*, had brought out a couple of new songs from his pen, and he wrote two more for this project. The first was an ode to the Colorado River entitled "You Wild Colorado." Performing with only an acoustic guitar accompanying him, Cash shakes off the effect of the cigarettes and pills to turn in a characterful vocal. Although radio programmers were hoping for tracks that would be easy to swallow—and country DJs surely flinched at the inclusion of the three Dylan tunes—Cash then took up the case of the downtrodden and the disenfranchised once again with "All of God's Children Ain't Free."

The 2002 CD reissue of the album adds three more songs from the sessions: the Carter Family song "Engine 143," a second take of "Mama, You Been on My

Mind" (this time with horns replacing the harmonica and saxophone parts), and "(I'm Proud) the Baby Is Mine," in which the narrator of the song declares his love for his wife, and his pride for the unborn baby, even though it isn't his.

The second single from the album was "Orange Blossom Special," b/w "All God's Children Ain't Free." It didn't fare well on the pop chart, reaching only #80, but did reach #3 on the Country charts. The album just cracked the Top 50 of the Pop charts (peaking at #49) and reached #3 on the Hot Country Albums chart.

A Downhill Slide

Orange Blossom Special can certainly be considered a success, and that success helped Columbia overlook—or at least get away with being less enthusiastic about—Cash's more creative but not so commercially minded projects. One of those projects, discussed elsewhere in this book, was a double album of cowboy songs, *Sings the Ballads of the True West.* It proved to be a commercial disappointment, perhaps partly due to the double-album format and higher price tag.

Taking a stab at something a little more commercial, and with a broader appeal, Cash cut the song "Thunderball" during the same sessions. A potential title song for a forthcoming James Bond movie, the result would be more in keeping with a western, with a rhythm that foretold "(Ghost) Riders in the Sky." The film's producers passed, and the nod went to Tom Jones, who took his version of the song to #25 on the Pop charts.

A month later, Cash went back into the studio and, using virtually the same music and arrangement as he had on the unreleased Bond track, recorded the theme for the John Wayne movie *The Sons of Katie Elder.* This time, the song was a much better fit for the film, and the producers agreed. The single made it to #10 on the Country chart.

Cash and his band might have used the same instrumental track just so as not to let a good arrangement go to waste. Or it might have been because Cash was in no shape to be creative.

Back home in California, Cash was spending an increasing amount of time with a camper van he had nicknamed Jesse James and painted black. "I painted his windows black so I could sleep in him during the daylight," he writes, in his 1997 autobiography, "but also because I just liked to spray-paint things black." On June 27, 1965, he set off into the mountains to escape. The official story of what happened next is that Jesse backfired, as a result of a faulty exhaust, and set some grass on fire. "Oil from a cracked bearing dripped onto the wheel," he adds, "which by that time was red hot, and it set fire to the grass."

The resulting fire quickly swept through the Los Padres National Forest, burning 500 acres of trees. In public, Cash pushed the blame onto the truck. In family circles, he blamed his nephew, Damon Fielder, causing a rift between the once-close relatives that would last for decades. (In an interview with Robert Hilburn, Fielder claimed that Cash himself had started the fire because he was cold.) In 1967, the federal government filed a $125,000 suit against Cash, making him one of the few private citizens to be sued by the government. He would later negotiate that figure down and sue his insurance company for some of the related costs.

Members of Cash's band and family could see a disturbing pattern emerging in him—a reckless streak and a willingness to lie to those he loved in order to hide the extent of his drug usage. It would begin to come to a head on October 2, 1965, as Cash and his group were finishing up a stretch of tour dates in Dallas.

"John had been in really good shape for the whole outing," Marshall Grant writes in his autobiography, "and like everyone else, he'd had a lot of fun. When the tour ended, he said he'd take the tour receipts and deposit them in our bank account when he flew home to California the next day. Since he'd been in such good spirits and appeared to be straight, I gave him the money, all of it."

In fact, Cash was headed not for California but for Mexico, where he knew he could score some cheap pills without the hassle of a prescription. After making the deal, he flew back to the States. When he landed, he was pulled aside, and customs agents found 668 Dexedrine pills and 475 Equanils hidden in his guitar case.

Cash was arrested for smuggling and concealing illicit drugs. He spent a day and a night in jail before being released on $1,500 bond. By March 6th, the story was in newspapers across the country. Cash's only defense was that he "had had several beers, [and] I guess I was so tired that I lost my faculties."

It should be remembered that this was happening at a time when even casual drug use could severely damage a performer's reputation—and here was a country artist, splashed over the news pages, exposing his secret. Just after his arrest, Texas A&M University canceled a scheduled appearance by Cash. In a foreshadowing of the kind of youth appeal Cash would achieve later in the decade, a group of students led by James Baldauf and nine others circulated a petition in protest. Around 2,000 students signed the petition, but A&M president Earl Rudder refused to reverse his decision. The ten students then formed the Student's Committee for Johnny Cash and decided to honor Cash's contract by organizing an off-campus show. The committee then announced that it would "continue to function as a watchdog over controversial campus subjects."

While these students rallied in support of Cash, other forces were marshaling against him. Though their marriage was in serious trouble, Vivian flew to be with her husband upon his release from jail. Photographers crowded the entrance to the police station as they emerged, Johnny in dark glasses, Vivian by his side.

Marshall Grant hoped that the public humiliation of having been discovered as a pill-popper would straighten Cash out, but, as Cash writes in his 1975 autobiography, "I faced the shame from it sober for the next six weeks. But as humbling and defacing as it all was, the memory of embarrassment faded into the heightening schedule of demanding tours. And I returned once again to my shadows of death—the pills."

13

It's the Song, the Sign of the Weary

Concept Albums

The main reason Johnny Cash gave for moving to Columbia Records was a desire for more creative control and the ability to make albums the way he envisioned them. And the way he envisioned them was for them to be much like a 1947 album by Merle Travis. *Folk Songs of the Hills* consists of eight songs that Travis had either grown up listening to in Muhlenberg County, Kentucky, or written himself about his time there. Each one is introduced by a short spoken narrative, which taken together serve as the thread that weaves the album together. Cash would return to the album again and again, and would eventually record his own versions of five of the eight songs.

This chapter covers the more strictly themed albums Cash released between 1960 and 1977. (A few of his other broadly thematic releases, more song cycles than concept albums, are included in the chronological analysis of his recordings elsewhere in the book.)

Ride This Train (1960)

While 1959's *Songs of Our Soil* is widely considered to be Cash's first concept album, it was more a song cycle of loosely related songs. His first full-on concept album—the first based on the structure built by Travis on *Folk Songs*—is this one, from 1960, which was billed "a Stirring Travelogue of America in Song and Story."

Using the train as a device to move from scene to scene and song to song, Cash draws on some of his favorite writers: Merle Travis ("Loading Coal"), Leon Payne ("Lumberjack"), Tex Ritter ("Boss Jack"), and Red Foley ("Old Doc Brown," though Cash may have been more familiar with the version by his hero Hank Snow).

The three songs credited to Cash himself, meanwhile, find him in full A. P. Carter song-collector mode. Though the intro to "Slow Rider" retells a portion of the story of Old West outlaw John Wesley Harding, the song itself is based on an old western song called "I Ride an Old Paint." It tells of a man whose wife "died in a pool room fight" and whose daughters have left him (one went to Denver, "the other went bad"). Now he just rides, slowly, waiting to die.

"Dorraine from Ponchartrain" is in the ballad tradition, and recalls the old folk song "The Creole Girl of Ponchartrain." In Cash's telling, the narrator is engaged to marry Dorraine, and as the two sit together, holding hands and laughing, he jokingly asks if she is marrying him for his money. The question so offends her that she hops in a boat to row home, but the waters are stormy, and while the narrator at first believes she will turn back, she ends up losing her life to the storm.

Finally, "Going to Memphis" is attributed to Alan and John Lomax, with Cash getting an arranger credit. It came from another of his favorite albums, the Alan Lomax–produced *Blues in the Mississippi Night.*

The 2002 reissue of the album adds four bonus tracks, two of which, "Second Honeymoon" and "Smilin' Bill McCall," were released as singles in 1960. "The Ballad of the Harp Weaver," a recitation based on a poem by Edna St. Vincent Millay, was previously included on *The Christmas Spirit*; "The Fable of Willie Brown" had never before been released in the US.

Bitter Tears: Ballads of the American Indian (1964)

When Cash's work for the disenfranchised is assessed, three albums are generally noted: the two prison albums, *At Folsom* and *At San Quentin*, and this one. *Bitter Tears* grew out of a chance meeting with Peter LaFarge, writer of the album's centerpiece, "The Ballad of Ira Hayes." Hayes was a Pima Indian who joined the army to fight for his country, and was one of the men who raised the flag at Iwo Jima. After his service ended, however, he soon descended into alcoholism, and died after drowning in a ditch filled with less than two inches of water. LaFarge was part Native American and an active member of both the Red Power civil rights movement and the New York folk scene. He and Cash were first introduced by folksinger Ed McCurdy after Cash's disastrous Carnegie Hall debut in 1962.

Cash had first recorded a song about Native Americans in 1959 in the form of "Old Apache Squaw" from *Songs of Our Soil.* He even claimed in interviews that he was part Native American, sometimes suggesting that he had a bit of Native American blood and other times indicating that he was a quarter (or more) Cherokee. The claim, he explained to Larry Linderman in 1975, varied depending on the amount of drugs in his system: "The higher I got, the more Indian blood I thought I had in me."

For *Bitter Tears*, Cash recorded five LaFarge songs, wrote two himself, and added a song written by his old running buddy Johnny Horton. All of the songs were pointed commentaries on the treatment of Native Americans by the US government, stretching back to the days of George Washington. The combination of Cash's passion for his subject and the pills he was popping with alarming frequency gave his voice an almost menacing growl, as evidenced on "As Long as the Grass Shall Grow." A more hoarse voice serves the sarcastic "Custer," while the growl returns for "The Ballad of Ira Hayes."

"Ira Hayes" was the only single released from the album, and Cash watched as it was virtually ignored. Believing it to be a great song with a message that needed to be heard—and maybe looking for a bit of a fight, egged on by the drugs—Cash placed a full-page ad in *Billboard*, calling out the country DJs who wouldn't play the song. He accused them of not having any guts, adding that they should take a look at the sales figures for the song, which he claimed were more than double the "Big Country Hit" average. Responding to the claim that "teenage girls and Beatles record buyers" didn't want to hear a sad story, Cash let the DJs know that he had been welcomed at the Newport Folk Festival, where "Ira Hayes" "stole my part of the show." He ended the letter with "just one question: WHY???"

For many DJs, the issue was not so much the song's content but what they perceived to be Cash's abandonment of the country format for the shiny new folk sound. Whatever their initial reasoning, many of them then began to play the song, which was enough to make it a Top 5 hit. After two weeks on the chart, *Bitter Tears* itself hit #5, and for the next three months hovered between #2 and #6.

For an in-depth look at this album, and Cash's excursions into folk, *A Heartbeat and a Guitar: Johnny Cash and the Making of Bitter Tears* by Antonino D'Ambrosio is highly recommended.

Sings the Ballads of the True West (1965) and *Mean as Hell* (1966)

Amazingly, while Cash was at his highest, chemically, he was also in a creative high gear. Only one album and less than a year separate his Native American concept album and this, his Old West project.

The Old West had been a favorite subject of Cash's for many years, although according to the liner notes to *Sings the Ballads of the True West* it was producer Don Law who first encouraged him to record an album of western songs. It took a bit of time, but Cash eventually agreed, and with typical abandon dove deeply into the research to compile the right songs for the project. After combing through several songbooks, he decided to call in Tex Ritter, one of America's first singing cowboys, to advise him.

Though Cash went to some lengths in his search for authentic material, half of the album's songs would end up coming from the usual suspects—June Carter, Maybelle Carter, Harlan Howard, Merle Kilgore, Tex Ritter, Peter LaFarge, Ramblin' Jack Elliot, Shel Silverstein, and Carl Perkins. Six of them were arranged by Cash, including his adaptation of the Longfellow poem "The Song of Hiawatha" ("Hiawatha's Vision") plus a number of old western songs: "I Ride an Old Paint," "The Streets of Laredo," "Bury Me Not on the Lone Prairie," "Sweet Betsy from the Pike," and "Green Grow the Lilacs."

Cash also wrote three songs for the album. On "Hardin Wouldn't Run," he returns to the subject of John Wesley Hardin, whom he first mentioned on *Ride This Train*, basing the narrative here on Hardin's autobiography. "Mean as Hell" is more recitation than song, a long poem about a ranch hand and the reasons he needs to be mean, which transitions into a manic version of "Sam Hall." The closing track, another recitation entitled "Reflections," serves as a summary of the album.

The only track not written by Cash or someone from within his circle is "The Shifting, Whispering Sands," a two-part song by Mary Hadler and V. C. Gilbert. Country artist Rusty Draper took the song to #3 in 1955, and a year later Billy Vaughn & His Orchestra recorded it. It had also been recorded by Sheb Wooley (in 1960) and Jim Reeves (in 1961), and by western actor (and Johnny Cash Award of Merit winner) Walter Brennan. Cash himself had also recorded the song a few years earlier as a duet with *Bonanza* star Lorne Greene, but that version remained unreleased until 2011's *Bootleg Volume II: From Memphis to Hollywood.*

Many of the songs on *True West* are tied together with spoken introductions à la *Ride This Train*, and the overall result is an excellent album. The only downside came with Cash's insistence that it be a double. This was a time when singles still ruled, so the thought of a double album was one his record company initially resisted. With creative control having been part of the bait that snagged Cash, the label relented, but sales of the album were slow. The only single to be drawn from it, "Mr. Garfield," failed to reach the Top 10, while *True West* itself was the first Johnny Cash LP to miss the charts entirely. Realizing the quality of the material on offer, Columbia pared it down to a single album, *Mean as Hell,* which made it to #4 on the Hot Country Albums chart in 1966.

From Sea to Shining Sea (1967)

Never one to wear his political affiliations on his sleeve, Cash was always quick to affirm his allegiance to his country. With the powder keg of cultural change set to explode in 1968, Cash entered the studio to record an album of patriotic songs—or at least patriotic songs the Johnny Cash way. This was an album of America as Cash saw it, or wished to see it, reframed in the manner of the historical narrative of *Ride This Train.*

Cash wrote all of the songs for the album, and it flows in much the same way as his 1960 concept masterpiece. Beginning (and ending) with a recitation set to the strains of "America, the Beautiful," Cash, joined by the Carter Family and the Statler Brothers, invites listeners to remember the land that God had shed his grace upon. Elsewhere, the songs travel from Tennessee rivers to coal country, cotton fields and shrimp boats to prison. The journey reveals a few lost treasures left behind, from the sculptor's work of "The Masterpiece" to the "Flint Arrowhead" and even "Cisco Clifton's Fillin' Station," which has seemingly survived despite the progress of the interstates and highways that have started to cut it off from the main road network.

From Sea to Shining Sea reached #9 on the Country Album chart. "Another Song to Sing" was chosen as the single, but it failed to chart. It stands out on the album as not being about a particular place but instead about the traveler. Written and recorded while Cash was going through the prelude to a divorce, it is hard not to hear it as a series of questions to Vivian Liberto. "Is my name whispered in your bedside prayers?" he asks. "Do you feel a vacant spot beside you there?" Vivian had been holding out from divorce on religious grounds, but that resolve was quickly fading. Cash delivers his questions without remorse, as if he were simply an objective bystander, intoning, "Do you tell them I was wilder than the wind?"

America: A 200-Year Salute in Story and Song (1972)

The Johnny Cash Show ran for three seasons from 1969 to 1971. It took the success Cash had achieved with his two prison albums and their hit singles, and exploded it. Even after the show was canceled, his success continued unabated. So, in 1972, he decided to combine his patriotic view of America, as represented

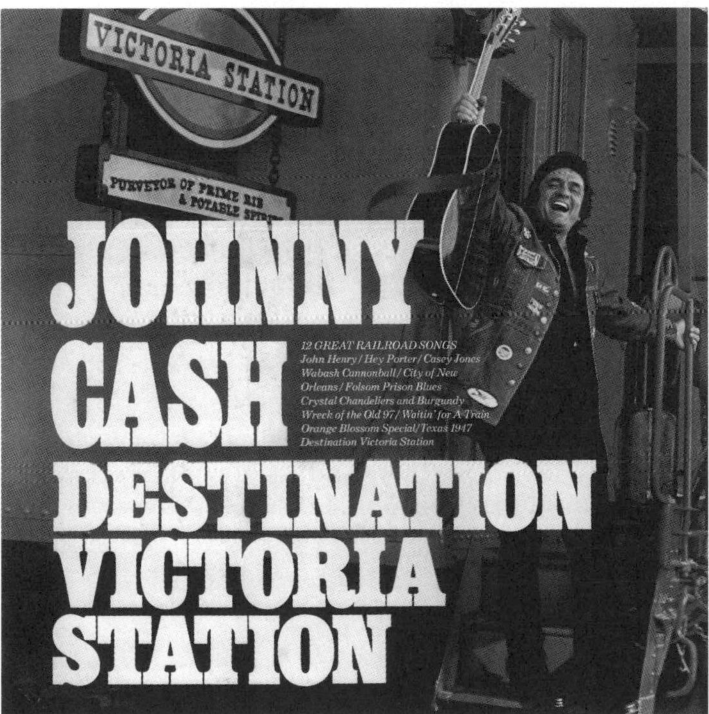

Commissioned in 1977, Cash re-recorded eleven of his favorite train songs and also included an original song focusing on Victoria Station.
Author's collection

on *From Sea to Shining Sea*, with the structure and storytelling of *Ride This Train*. The result was this album, which tells the 200-year history of the nation.

As with *Ride This Train*, Cash includes narration to help thread the songs together. There are a few new songs, like "Paul Revere," and also new recordings of songs from previous releases, such as "The Road to Kaintuck" and "Mr. Garfield" (from *Sings the Ballads of the True West*), and "Remember the Alamo" and "The Big Battle" (from *Ring of Fire: The Best of Johnny Cash*).

"The Battle of New Orleans," once a hit for his friend Johnny Horton, shows Cash in a playful mood, delivering the song with a smirk and slipping, at the end, into something akin to Doug Kershaw's "Louisiana Man." He trades playfulness for seriousness a few songs later to deliver a reading of the Gettysburg Address, before offering an unvarnished assessment of the ugly treatment of Native Americans in "Big Foot."

As the album nears its end, Cash sings a song from 1910, "Come Take a Trip in My Airship," to represent the beginning of the modern age, and then brings proceedings to a close with his own "These Are My People," which he had attempted to record on two other occasions in 1970. No singles were released from the album, but the LP itself reached #3 on the Country chart, where it remained for three weeks.

Destination Victoria Station (1977)

After connecting strongly with the youth culture in the late '60s and early '70s, Cash began to draw their criticism toward the mid-'70s. Aside from his public support of President Nixon and close association with the evangelical Baptist minster Billy Graham, what drew the most ire was his "selling out" to do commercials and endorsements for Pepsi and the American Oil Company (and to a lesser extent Hohner harmonicas and Lionel Trains).

These were simply radio, television, or print ads, however. Cash's biggest commercial endorsement came about after he was approached by executives for the San Francisco–based restaurant chain Victoria Station in 1975. The company, named after the London landmark, invited Cash—on the basis of the prior success of his train songs (not to mention his overall popularity)—to record a series of commercials in which he would sing a snippet of a song called "Destination: Victoria Station" and then tell listeners about how good the restaurant's food was. The spots were a huge success, netting the company record profits, and funding its previously stalled expansion plans.

According to Victoria Station executive Tom Blake, in his book *Prime Rib & Boxcars: Whatever Happened to Victoria Station*, Cash's then-manager Lou Robin approached him with the idea of recording an album of Cash's train songs. "VS would pay to have the album produced, $45,000 for 50,000 pressings," Blake writes. "We could use the records for promotions or whatever we chose, including selling the album in our restaurants. Our only payment to Johnny would be to give him 1,000 copies of the album."

The resulting album includes twelve songs, eleven of which had been previously recorded by Cash. The live hit single version of "Folsom Prison Blues" appears again here, while the original backing tracks of "Orange Blossom Special" (preserving Charlie McCoy's harmonica and Boots Randolph's sax) and "Wabash Cannonball" are adorned with newly recorded vocals. The remaining songs—"Casey Jones," "Hey Porter," "John Henry," "City of New Orleans," "Crystal Chandeliers and Burgundy," "Wreck of the Old 97," "Waiting for a Train," and "Texas-1947"—were all rerecorded. Cash also offered an original song, "Destination Victoria Station" (not the same as the one featured in the ads), which he had premiered on *Strawberry Cake* the previous year.

The Rambler (1977)

By the late '70s, it's debatable whether or not Cash knew what to do with himself. What's inarguable is that Columbia certainly didn't know what to do with him. The label had drawn only one single, the title track, from his recent album *The Last Gunfighter Ballad* (two other songs from the LP were issued as B-sides), and after it fell off the charts on April 23rd, no further Cash singles were released until "Lady," the first offering from *The Rambler*, came out three months later.

When Cash entered the studio on January 12, 1977, more than five years had passed since he last made a concept album (not including the soundtrack to *The Gospel Road*). In the interim, Merle Haggard had released a Top 10 concept album, *My Love Affair with Trains*, while Willie Nelson had a multi-platinum hit with his Columbia Records debut, *Red Headed Stranger*, the story of a man on the run after killing his unfaithful wife and her lover (and an album so sparse that the label originally mistook it for a demo).

The result of those sessions, *The Rambler*, is akin more to a radio play than a record, and features Cash's then son-in-law, Jack Routh. It tells the story of the Rambler, played by Cash, who responds to the pain of a broken love affair (with the Lady) by jumping in his car and just driving. He stops beside a river near Lafayette, Indiana, where he meets the Fisherman, played by Routh, who tells him about a woman he once loved in California. With nowhere else to go, the Rambler invites the Fisherman to join him, and head west together. "California, I guess, that's the way I'm heading," the Rambler says, sounding like the last stranger you'd want to jump in a car with. The pair end up in a bar in Denver, where they meet a couple of good-time gals played by Routh's wife (and Cash's stepdaughter) Carlene and Cash's daughter Rosanne. After several Coors, the Rambler excuses himself to go to his room, having convinced himself that the Lady was in the bar, too. Then, after the Rambler and the Fisherman make it to Phoenix (!), they pick up a hitchhiking girl—a "pinball freak" known as the Cowgirl—who turns out to have killed her "old man." After ditching the Cowgirl, the Fisherman decides that his girl, Calilou, is likely to have gone to

New Orleans by now. So, after a nearly 2,000–mile road trip in a car without air-conditioning, they decide, why not, let's head thataway.

The songs that sit between the narrative excerpts were all written by Cash, but while some of them—"Hit the Road and Go," "Lady," "After the Ball," and "Calilou"—serve to further the story, others—"If It Wasn't for the Wabash River," "No Earthly Good," "A Wednesday Car," and "My Cowboy's Last Ride"—sound like they were simply songs Cash had at his disposal at the time. Musically, the album stays close to the sound of the recent *The Last Gunfighter Ballad,* right down to Waylon Jennings–esque phase-shifted guitar. But if Cash's goal was for *The Rambler* to be a cohesive piece of art—just like *Ride This Train* or even *America*—the mix of songs that contribute to the narrative and songs that don't makes the whole thing a wash. And the dialogue, which should have been designed to push the story forward, is simply a collection of improvised scenes by Cash and Routh.

"John asked me to do that with him, and I was just going along with it," Routh says. "I felt like I was pretty horrible in it, but we had a good time. We actually had a mini-recorder, a nine-volt recorder, and the engineers, Charlie Bragg and Roger [Murrah], were in the backseat of the car, and John and I were driving down county roads recording dialogue. You can hear the car running. It was really a great experience, really unique."

Many saw the album as a vanity project—another self-indulgence of a superstar. Unwittingly, Cash fed that fire with his front-cover billing, which states, "Written and Directed by Johnny Cash." In the brief liner notes, he works hard to convince the listener that what is presented on the album is "a few slices of life as I remember them being served up," adding that he had been in each of these situations, and known these people in one form or another. That may be so, but it doesn't help much. Presented as a radio drama—something to be listened to once, maybe twice—it would be fine; as a stand-alone project, it was a tough sell.

"He had a hard time getting record companies to understand what he was doing his whole career because he was so different," Routh says. "Always different, always turning the corner, always picking a different road than anybody. It's what he was, you know?"

The album's first single, "Lady" b/w "Hit the Road and Go," spent the same amount of time (nine weeks) on the Country chart as "The Last Gunfighter Ballad" but peaked eight slots lower, at #46. The second single, "After the Ball," with "Calilou" as its flip side, spent twelve weeks on the chart, but peaked at #32. "Lady" was a soft ballad that leaned heavily on the orchestral backing—not your standard Cash fare. "After the Ball" brought back the guitar sound of Bob Wootton with an up-tempo swing, but there was nothing there, lyrically, to grab the listener.

With his momentum on the singles charts declining, Cash also found his album releases stalling, with *The Rambler* topping out at #31, two slots below *Gunfighter.* Cash felt the album had failed to live up to his potential, and he blamed his label for that. "It was one of my favorites," he told Bill Flanagan for

Musician, "but it didn't sell anything. . . . *The Rambler* was a concept I really felt good about at the time, but the record company was just totally negative about it. I don't think they pressed enough to even distribute it."

Critical opinion was mixed as well. For *Country Music*'s Billy Altman, *The Rambler* was "an interesting experiment for the Man in Black—and a successful one too," but for Michael Bane, writing in the same publication a couple of years later, it was an "ill-fated" release that caused Cash to rethink his musical direction.

14

You Know the Only Song I Ever Learned to Play

Columbia 1966

After a well-publicized run-in with the law that revealed to the world his battle with drugs, Johnny Cash now needed to rebuild his reputation with fans, radio programmers, and promoters. Back then, things like drug use were not as easily overlooked as they are now, but it is a testament to Cash's popularity and his connection with his audience that his fans did just that. Even so, now was a time to rescue a career that could have easily come to a screeching halt, had it happened to almost any other star.

Cash would later give varying accounts of when the final straw came, but one incident that certainly affected his decision to kick the drugs came when he drove his tractor off a small cliff on his Hendersonville property into a lake, nearly killing himself in the process. This was also the last straw for June, who felt she didn't have the strength or conviction to help him kick the habit. For help, she turned to Dr. Nat Winston, the Tennessee State Commissioner of Public Health, who devised a recovery plan to help Cash to kick the drugs. But it didn't last long at all. According to Marshall Grant, Cash remained clean for a total of thirty days after his first detox in Hendersonville. From there, the space between the days began to shrink.

Everybody Loves a Nut (1966)

In the midst of the chaos surrounding his arrest, Columbia released a new single to close out the year. Co-written by Cash, June Carter, and Merle Kilgore, "Happy to Be with You," with its swirling '60s pop organ carrying most of the musical weight, had a sound unlike any Cash single to date. Even so, fans responded positively, and the song started a slow climb up the charts, starting 1966 at its peak of #9.

Everybody Loves a Nut is the first album many fans of the dark and brooding version of the Man in Black eliminate from conversations about his career. It doesn't even warrant a mention in Michael Streissguth's *Johnny Cash: The Biography*, while Tony Tost, author of the *American Recordings* volume of the $33\frac{1}{3}$ series of books on individual albums, called it a record "no one currently sporting a Johnny Cash bumper sticker would like to admit actually exist[s]."

Cash himself would blame it on the drugs, and there is probably some truth in that—although not in the sense Cash likely meant it. After the bad publicity of his arrest, this "comedy" album was an attempt at lightening the mood. It wasn't a strict comedy album in the sense of something like those Ray Stevens had been recording and hitting the Pop charts with but instead a collection of "silly songs," as Ramblin' Jack Elliot put it.

One of Cash's influences, Bradley Kincaid, began selling songbooks in the late 1920s, with huge success. The gimmick caught on and country music stars sold books filled with photos and songs through the 1980s. *Author's collection*

Whoever followed that instinct to steer away from serious material toward novelty songs would soon be proved correct. While the album only made it to #88 on the Pop chart, it spent seven weeks in the Top 10 of the Hot Country Albums chart, four of them at #5.

Three singles were released from the album. The first, "One on the Right Is on the Left," was written by Cash's old running mate Cowboy Jack Clement. *Billboard* gave the single a "Spotlight" review, noting that "with 'Happy to Be with You' still climbing, Cash has a double-barreled chart contender. First side ['Cotton Pickin' Hands'] has hit potential for the country chart while the flip has equal hit appeal for both country and pop markets." A playful swipe at the popularity of folk (and faux-folk) groups, the song went to #2 in April of 1966 and spent a total of ten weeks in the Top 10. It even reached the mid-level of the Pop charts, at #46. The flip side was a non-album track, "Cotton Pickin' Hands," that offered a return to earlier themes and sounds.

The second single was the album's title track, also written by Clement. "Everybody Loves a Nut" is the quirky tale of people who have odd habits, like keeping a dead horse in a cave, but are still loved. One of the men, a "Columbia man" named Frank, tries to keep a tiger in a tank, while another is kicked out of the Queen's kingdom for not believing the world to be flat—a nod, perhaps, to producers Frank Jones and Don Law. In any case, the song didn't fare nearly as well on the charts, stalling at #96 Pop and reaching only #17 Country. The flip side was another track from the album, "Austin Prison," which tells the story of a prisoner who is helped to escape by his jailer. "Now all I want between me and there are a lot of friendly people," he says, "and miles and miles and miles and miles and miles and miles and miles." Cash wrote the song, and he must have felt a very personal connection with it, given that it was recorded soon after his release from jail in Texas.

The third single, "Boa Constrictor," was the second Shel Silverstein song Cash recorded (the first being "25 Minutes to Go"). It fared even worse than "Everybody Loves a Nut," reaching only #43 on the Country chart and #107 on the Pop chart (Cash's last Pop chart entry for over a year). The song would live on, though, in Silverstein's 1974 best-selling collection of poems, *Where the Sidewalk Ends.* The B-side was a non-album track called "Bottom of the Mountain," featuring the acoustic work of Norman Blake and Bob Johnson.

The rest of the album's songs came from various places, including Ramblin' Jack Elliot, who guests on "A Cup of Coffee." This is one track where Cash's drug use really seems to affect him. The lyrics are essentially a conversation between a truck driver and his friend, whose house he stops at to get some coffee before hitting the road again. Cash's performance is careening, and at times you wonder if he's going completely off the rails.

Like "Boa Constrictor," "The Bug That Tried to Crawl Around the World" was given a new life in literary form when Columbia released it in 1970 as part of a book/45 combo containing a second short story. (Cash is pictured talking to a cartoon bug on the cover.) The next track on the album, "The Singing Star's Queen" is a honky-tonk piano take on "Twinkle, Twinkle Little Star" with a lyric about a singing star named Waylon and his queen, who alerts the narrator to when Waylon has left for the road so they can spend time together. It was co-written by one Jackson King—a nom de plume for Waylon Jennings.

Cowboy Jack contributed two more songs to the project, "Dirty Old Egg-Suckin' Dog" and "Take Me Home," the latter not so much a comedy song as a heartfelt plea to go home, while Cash offered "Please Don't Play Red River Valley," probably the weakest track on the album. Rounding out the album is the dark humor of "Joe Bean," which would make a further appearance, a few years later, on *At Folsom Prison.* The song tells the story of a prisoner, Joe Bean, who is sentenced to hang on his twentieth birthday for "a shooting that he never did," although he had killed twenty other men during his short life. The song was written by the duo of Leon Pober and Bud Freeman, who had previously worked as a saxophonist with Tommy Dorsey and Glenn Miller. He and Pober wrote a number of humorous tunes together, including a set of comic songs about psychiatry for the 1957 album *Songs of Couch & Consultation* by Katie Lee. In 1960, they wrote and produced the short-lived Broadway musical *Beg, Borrow, and Steal* before going back to songwriting.

The album cover was created by artist Jack Davis, who was well known for his work on *Mad* magazine. Other notable country-music artists for whom Davis designed covers include Little Jimmy Dickens, Archie Campbell, Ben Colder (Sheb Wooley), and Homer & Jethro.

Happiness Is You (1966)

This is another of the albums that many want to forget exists (per Tost's comment above). Featuring the earlier single "Happy to Be with You," it kicks off with the title track, another sappy Cash/Carter co-write. Cash also returns here to "Guess Things Happen That Way," but in a version that is inferior to the original Sun cut.

Like much of Cash's non-concept '60s work, the album is marked by a heavy dependence on the songs of others—not just other writers' work but other artists' filler. "Ancient History" was a Don Law–produced album cut for Billy Walker in 1963, while "You Comb Her Hair"—in which the singer reassures his wife that the other woman in his life is in fact their young daughter—was a #5 hit for George Jones that same year. Cash's heart may have been in the right place, but his decision to record the song probably stemmed from his guilt about being an absentee father. (Jim Ed Brown also recorded the song in 1966 for his solo debut, *Alone with You.*)

One of the high spots on the album is Peter LaFarge's "She Came from the Mountain," in which the narrator takes a girl away from her home only to have her leave him and go back there. What should have been a bright spot was Cash's take on "For Lovin' Me" by Canadian singer/songwriter Gordon Lightfoot, who recorded the song for his debut disc *Lightfoot!* in 1965. Marty Robbins had taken the young songwriter's "Ribbon of Darkness" to #1 on the Country chart in 1965, but Cash was unable replicate that success. He hews close to Lightfoot's version, but his take sounds somehow more mean-spirited than Lightfoot's matter-of-fact reading. Cash's buddy Waylon Jennings took the same song in a slightly different direction, adding his patented swagger and walking it up to #9 on the Country chart just before the release of *Happiness Is You.*

Cash returns to the past for "No One Will Ever Know," a mid-1940s song written by Mel Foree and Fred Rose and recorded by everyone from Roy Acuff and Hank Williams to Don Gibson and Roy Orbison, although it wouldn't become a hit until Gene Watson took it to #13 in 1980. Helen Carter's "Is This My Destiny" was first popularized by the bluegrass group the Osborne Brothers & Red Allen in 1958, before making a resurgence in 1962 with versions recorded by Jan Howard and the duet pairing of Willie Nelson & Shirley Collie, and in 1965 with rockabilly queen Wanda Jackson's take on the song (as "My Destiny"). "A Wound

Time Can't Erase" was originally recorded in 1957 by Sky Johnson (possibly an alias of the song's writer, Bill D. Johnson), before Stonewall Jackson had a #3 hit with it in 1962. Closing the album is the standard "Wabash Cannonball."

Cash offers passable versions of all of these songs, but they lack the fire of his better recordings. Even some of the performances on *Everybody Loves a Nut* are stronger than what's on offer here, and so too were the recordings that would immediately follow *Happiness Is You*'s release.

On the way back to that fire, Cash recorded two songs for single release on November 1, 1966. The A-side was a Cash-penned tune called "You Beat All I Ever Saw," another run at using bold trumpets. The flip side was a co-write with Mother Maybelle Carter, "Put the Sugar to Bed." The most notable thing about both cuts is the extremely fuzzed-out guitar that bubbles in the background of the former and then takes center stage on the latter.

Columbia placed a half-page ad in *Billboard* to declare the single to be "Hard Cash. Country and Western and man of the world. A modern troubadour who doesn't mince words. When John cuts a single, it's an event. And everyone shares the experience." In the event, "You Beat All I Ever Saw" only made it to #20 before beginning to drop and make room for the next single, a duet with June Carter that would return Cash to the top of the charts.

15

You a Long-Legged Guitar Pickin' Man

Columbia 1967–69

Onstage, the pairing of Johnny Cash and June Carter was a big hit with crowds. Offstage, it wasn't all fun and games. They were both married, and that fact was common knowledge among fans. Johnny had been asking Vivian for a divorce for months, but she refused to grant it. Though his relationship with June is often portrayed as a romantic comedy in which they fell in love, left their spouses, and found true love in each other's arms, the truth is there was real pain involved for all concerned. The pairing of Johnny and June on records and onstage always came as a slap in the face to Vivian, and there was no escaping it.

Their chemistry was readily apparent, and their onstage banter playful and fun. June brought a sort of balance to Johnny's charismatic bad-boy persona, a light to his dark. The record company saw the pairing as a potential sales boost. The rough-cut king of country and the daughter of country's first family, the Carter Family, had all of the makings of a headline-generating machine. The next step was to get the two of them into the studio together. June had been included on other Cash cuts, but never as a duet partner. The key was to find a song that would capture their onstage chemistry, and translate it to vinyl.

Carryin' On with Johnny Cash and June Carter (1967)

The song in question came to Cash in 1963 through June's brother-in-law, Don Davis, who would bring him a few songs that became hits over the years. "One day I was driving down 16th Avenue South when I heard a song on the radio that excited me," Davis writes in his autobiography, *Nashville Steeler*. "It was a duet by a songwriter I knew, Billy Edd Wheeler, and a girl, Billie Joan Scrivner, called 'Jackson.' It occurred to me that it would be a great song for June and Johnny."

"June and I had probably been singing 'Jackson' for about three years before we ever recorded it, just for the fun of it," Cash told *Country Music* in 1980. "We hadn't thought about doing duets together or singing together until she was really firmly locked in as a part of my show. . . . I think about the first take was the one that was released, because we had sung it so much together."

Written by the Carter sisters, "Rosanna's Going Wild" was Cash's last single of 1967 and hit #2 by February of 1968. *Private collection*

Released early in 1967, the song quickly climbed the charts, and by May it had reached #2. The flip side of the single was another duet, "Pack Up Your Sorrows," written in 1965 by Richard and Mimi Farina and recorded the following year by Peter, Paul & Mary and Joan Baez. The single's success encouraged Columbia to release further duets, so on March 1st the duo went back to the studio to record a follow-up, "Long-Legged Guitar Pickin' Man."

The single featured the lead-guitar playing of Carl Perkins and had an infectious energy about it but fell short of "Jackson's" chart success, rising only to #6. The flip side, a Cash/Carter co-write entitled "You'll Be All Right," would also appear on the duo's upcoming album. Curiously, just prior to the album's release, Columbia issued another single featuring two songs—"Red Velvet" and "The Wind Changes"—that were not duets, with the latter stalling at #60 on the Country chart before quickly dropping off.

Released in the fall of 1967, *Carryin' On* brought together Johnny and June's two recent duet singles alongside 1964's "It Ain't Me, Babe." To those it adds two more Cash/Carter co-writes, "Shantytown" and "Oh, What a Good Thing We Had," plus Johnny's "No, No, No," and "Fast Boat to Sydney," written by June and her sisters, Anita and Helen. To round out the album, the pair recorded two Ray Charles songs, 1954's "I Got a Woman" and 1959's "What'd I Say."

Set against the backdrop of the behind-the-scenes drama of Johnny's volatile relationship with Vivian and his rather public affection for June, *Carryin' On* seems to signal the end of a chapter in Cash's personal life. Vivian had filed for divorce in early 1967, and as of January 1, 1968, the marriage was officially over.

Cash wrapped up 1967 by releasing a version of the Carter sisters' "Rosanna's Going Wild," a song about a young woman who is out to experience life to the fullest. The song climbed the charts as 1967 turned into 1968, peaking at #2 in February. The B-side was "Roll Call," which tells of an army platoon losing their final battle, culminating in the attendant roll call in the beyond.

At Madison Square Garden (2002)

The remainder of the decade is covered elsewhere in this book, but suffice it to say that for all of his (largely self-inflicted) troubles, Cash ended the '60s on a large upswing. In 1968, he had the biggest album success of his career with *At Folsom Prison*, and in a year-end letter to himself, he celebrated what was, "in many ways, the best year of my thirty-six years of life."

He would follow that success with the release in 1969 of *The Holy Land*, a very personally meaningful project, and *At San Quentin*, an album that had an impact in both the rock and country worlds and elevated his status to that of worldwide celebrity. He also debuted his weekly ABC television show, and continued to have huge successes on both the Country and Pop charts.

Before the year was out, Cash performed a sold-out show to a crowd of 19,342 at Madison Square Garden on December 5th. Though the recording of the show wasn't released until 2002—during a yearlong celebration of Cash—it is included here as a snapshot of Cash the performer at the pinnacle of his success.

In October 1969, Cash had walked away from the Country Music Association awards ceremony with five trophies, including Entertainer of the Year. His weekly television show was preparing to enter its second season, and his announcement from the stage that it would

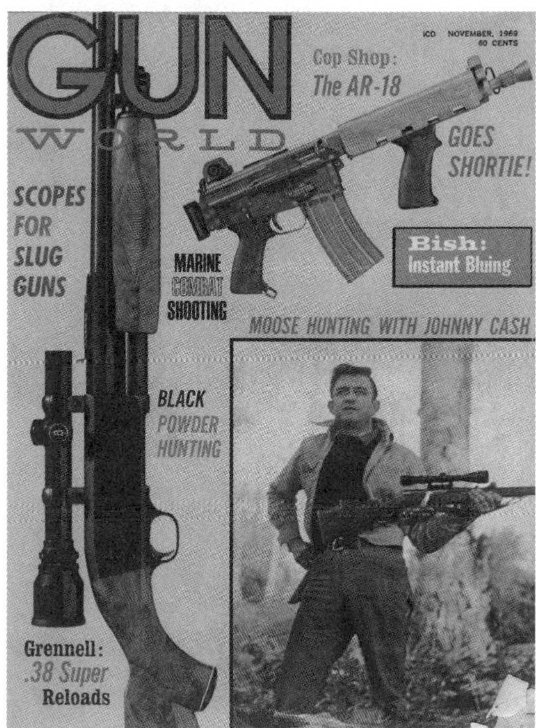

Cash's appearance on the cover of a magazine never hurt its sales. In this issue, a reporter follows Cash and Merle Travis to Canada for a moose hunt.

Photo copyright Gun World *magazine. Used by permission*

return in January is greeted with a roar that surpasses even the ovation he receives when he reveals John Carter's due date.

Something Cash rarely did in concert was speak about current events, but here, having previously taken some flak for his endorsement of Nixon's policies on getting out of Vietnam, he lets his feelings show a little more. Take his introduction to "Remember the Alamo": "History lesson: 1835, 5,000 men under Santa Anna crossed the Rio Grande. Davey Crockett left Tennessee with the volunteers. At a Spanish mission near San Antonio, he met a knife fighter, gambler named Bowie. 180 Americans against 5,000. *180 Americans against 5,000*—Mr. President, that's the kind of odds we got today."

Cash follows "Remember the Alamo" with Ed McCurdy's anti-war song "Last Night I Had the Strangest Dream." In introducing that song, he references how reporters would ask him his thoughts on the "Vietnam situation." He mentions that he and the Roadshow had been to Long Binh, Vietnam, in January to entertain the troops, and that a reporter friend had asked him if that made him a hawk. "No, no, it don't make me a hawk," he says, to a small amount of applause, before adding, "If you watch the helicopters bring in the wounded boys, and then you go in to the wards and sing for them, try to do your best to cheer them up so that they can get back home, it might make you a dove with claws." The phrase is met with more applause and, though Cash later recanted it, it offered a rare public glimpse of his political feelings.

The 2002 release of the concert contains the whole show, including songs by the Carter Family (minus June, who gave birth to John Carter three months later), the Statler Brothers, and Carl Perkins. Cash's performance is captivating, the audience hanging on his every syllable. The song choices cover the expected themes and material: growing up in Dyess ("Five Feet High and Rising," "Pickin' Time"), prison and crime ("Long Black Veil," "The Wall," "Send a Picture of Mother," "Folsom Prison Blues"), Native Americans ("The Ballad of Ira Hayes," "As Long as the Grass Shall Grow"), and gospel ("Jesus Was a Carpenter," "He Turned the Water into Wine," "Were You There [When They Crucified My Lord]," "Daddy Sang Bass").

Listening to the show today, it is evident why Cash was one of the most popular entertainers in the world in the late 1960s. The decade ahead held many ups and downs, in both his career and his personal life, but for now, he was at the top of his game.

16

Gotta Sleep on the Floor Once More at City Jail

Prison Albums

That Johnny Cash served hard time, be it at Folsom Prison or elsewhere, is one of the most persistent myths about him. To some, it gave him an extra boost of authenticity or credibility. Others chalked it up as marketing hype. To this day, there are fans who insist that he spent time in the hoosegow. It wasn't something Cash or his people actively promoted, but it wasn't something they discouraged, either. It added to the mystique. It justified his dark clothes and brooding persona. It helped some listeners understand how he could write a song like "Folsom Prison Blues."

The truth is, Cash only saw the inside of a cell on a few occasions, most of them just overnighters resulting from public intoxication or getting a little too rowdy while popped up on pills. His brief brushes with the law gave him a sense of empathy with the inmates, although he appeared in prisons first as a performer, rather than as a jailbird.

Cash's First Trip Inside

His first trip inside came in 1956 or 1957—it varies by the telling—at the Texas State Prison in Huntsville, Texas. The prison held an annual rodeo for the inmates and invited a musical guest as intermission entertainment. Cash and the Tennessee Two were set up in the middle, and just as they began to play, a surprise thunderstorm came up and drenched them. The trio continued to play as best they could, and the prisoners responded enthusiastically. It was a response that Cash held on to.

Cash remembered that first appearance in a 2000 promotional interview with the actor Tim Robbins:

> The next thing I knew, they were calling from California and wanted me on the New Year's show at San Quentin in 1957–58, so I did those and word spread that I was one of them. Then I started digging in to the

> repertoire from my childhood, you know, the songs that were already there, the prison songs, "I'm Just Here to Get My Baby Out of Jail," for one, and "Columbus Stockade Blues," Jimmie Rodgers' jail songs and Hank Williams' jail songs. And the classic tragedy songs of country music, I got into all of those and mixed them up and put them on a record. I knew if I could ever get a live recording at a prison, it was going to be something really worth listening to.

That live recording was still way off in the future, but Cash continued to play shows in prisons on a regular basis. After his appearance on the New Year's show at San Quentin in 1957–58, he was asked back the following year. The shows were a celebration for the inmates—something they could look forward to when they had nothing else. They included musical acts like Cash and the Collins Kids, Larry and Lorrie, who were paired up with magicians, jugglers, and strippers. You might think that strippers in prison would be the runaway success of the show, but Merle Haggard writes in his first autobiography that "Johnny was by far the most popular, which should give you some idea how impressive he was. . . . Anybody who can actually make a group of men forget they're in San Quentin is some kind of magician."

Merle Haggard

Haggard was speaking from experience. His father had died when he was nine, and after that, Haggard didn't care too much about what was going on around him, much less the future. That recklessness led him to a string of petty thefts and fights, with the end result being multiple stays in juvenile holding cells. In late 1958, with a wife and a new baby to care for and no prospects for steady, well-paying employment, Haggard and a buddy hatched a plan to line their pockets with a little cash for the upcoming holidays. Sitting around the living room, drinking and scheming, the two decided it was now or never and headed out to a small diner Haggard knew. The plan was to pull up behind the diner, pick the backdoor lock, slide in, get the money, and get out.

The flaw in the plan was the drinking. While Haggard and his friend were sure that it was between two and three o'clock in the morning, it was actually closer to nine or ten in the evening, and the diner was still open. The stunt landed Haggard in jail for the night, but he slipped out the next day and stole a car to get home. The police came for him soon after. That trifecta was enough to send Haggard to the big leagues, and in March 1958, he was sent to San Quentin.

Haggard had always had an interest in music, and he continued to dabble with it while in prison, filing away stories and situations that he would later turn into hits such as "Sing Me Back Home," about the 1940s serial-rapist Caryl Chessman being led to his execution. At the time, however, a successful music career was a distant dream for a wayward young man who didn't feel anyone cared at all.

Finally, the day of the New Year's concert came, and Haggard was front row center. "When we spoke a few years later I told him how much I loved seeing that show," Haggard later told Marshall Ward, "and Johnny said, 'You know Merle, I don't remember you playing that day?' He was thinking I was maybe a performer, and I told him, 'No man, I was in the audience.'"

The show was a turning point for Haggard. Watching Cash's confident and commanding performance, he was inspired to strive for his dreams of being a music star. First he joined the prison band to hone his chops and then, on his release from prison on November 3, 1960, he began to pick up any gig he could on the club circuit, even playing bass with Bakersfield legend Buck Owens for a few months. By 1962, Haggard had recorded his first solo single, and was on his way to a career in music. In early 1965, his third single, "(My Friends Are Gonna Be) Strangers," reached the national Top 10.

Jail Time on the Charts

Just a few months later, Porter Wagoner released his twenty-second charting single, "Green, Green Grass of Home." The song, written by an ex–shoe salesman named Curly Putman, comes from the perspective of a man looking at his hometown as he gets off a train to meet his parents. Over their shoulders, he sees the girl he left behind running to greet him and he thinks to himself, "It's good to touch the green, green grass of home." The house he grew up in remains the same, except for a few cracks in the paint, and the old oak tree that served as a childhood playground still remains in the front yard. Stealing another look at his girl, Mary, he is reminded again of how good it is to be home. Here, after this second verse, Wagoner breaks from the mold laid by the original cut of the song by Johnny Darrell and lays in one of his specialties: the recitation. With strings swelling in the background, and a lush chorus of female voices surrounding his spoken words, he tells us it was all a dream. He has awoken to greet the four gray walls that surround him, and, there, coming down the hall, are a guard and "a sad old padre" who will escort him down the long corridor where, finally, he will be laid beneath the green, green grass of home.

Wagoner took this prisoner's tale to #4 on the Country charts, where it was heard by Cash's old Sun labelmate, Jerry Lee Lewis. Lewis quickly recorded a version of his own for his 1965 album *Country Songs for City Folks.* The album did little business in the US, but one fan in England—where the Killer had a much stronger following at the time—heard the song while he was gathering material for his next album. Tom Jones had scored a series of Top 10 hits in 1963 and 1964 with songs like "It's Not Unusual," "What's up Pussycat?" and "Thunderball" (the theme for the James Bond movie of the same name, for which Cash had also attempted to write a song). In 1966, Jones was looking to become a more mature, well-rounded performer, and began to look to country for songs that might help accomplish that task. He felt "Green, Green Grass of Home" could help him do that, so in 1967 he released it as a single and as the

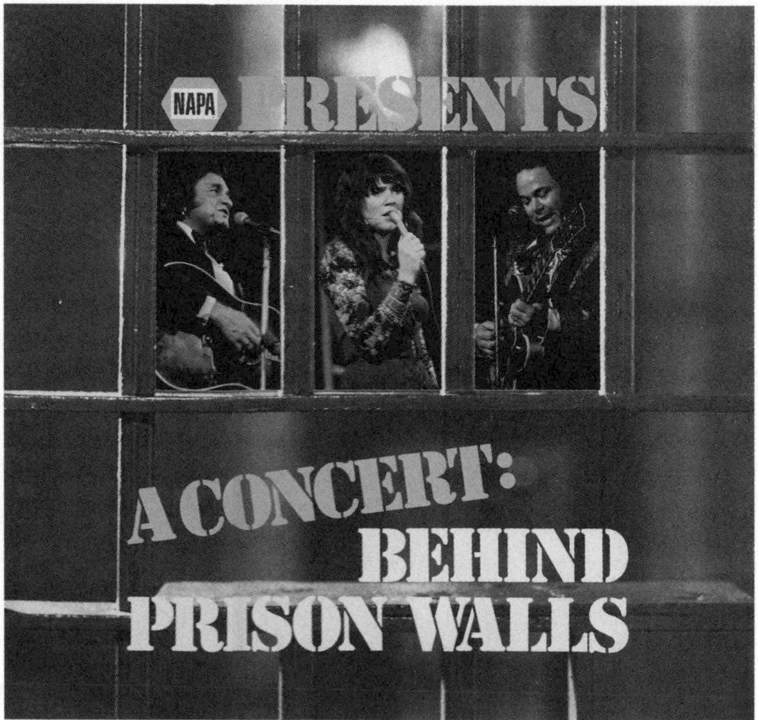

NAPA produced this compilation that was available in their auto parts stores. NAPA sponsored the syndicated run of *A Concert Behind Prison Walls*, an edited version of the television special *A Flower Out of Place*. *Author's collection*

title track on his new album. It was a #1 hit in the UK, and reached #11 on the *Billboard* Pop charts.

Perhaps to capitalize on Jones' recent success, Wagoner included the song on his 1967 album *Soul of a Convict & Other Great Prison Songs*, one of a series of concept albums he had started releasing in 1962. Like Cash, Wagoner dug back into the prison songs of his youth, including on the album songs of old like Karl & Harty's "I'm Just Here to Get My Baby Out of Jail" and Vernon Dalhart's 1926 hit "The Convict and the Rose." He also drew from more recent catalogues with Hank Williams' "I Heard That Lonesome Whistle," "The Snakes Crawl at Night" (a Mel Tillis cut from Charley Pride's 1966 debut album *Country*, which also included a version of "Green, Green Grass of Home"), and Cash's "Folsom Prison Blues."

Wagoner's album of prison songs slowly climbed the charts, peaking at #7 a few months after its release. Meanwhile, Merle Haggard, who had been successfully keeping his prison past a secret, had moved to Capitol Records and released his third single, "The Fugitive" (also known as "I'm a Lonesome Fugitive"), the song of a man constantly on the run from the law, afraid to slow down and always looking over his shoulder. The Fugitive can never stop for love, no matter how lonely he gets; the highway is his home, and he has to keep running.

It was a story Haggard had lived in spurts, although it actually came from the pen of Liz Anderson. That fact probably shielded him from questions about whether the song was indeed autobiographical. Three months after its release, the song became Haggard's first #1, and the LP from which it was drawn, which bears the same title, reached #3 on the Country chart.

Although somebody else had written "The Fugitive," the album track "Life in Prison" did draw on Haggard's own experiences. He would take things a step farther with his second #1 single, "Branded Man," from the album of the same name, which lays it all out in the open. "When they let me out of prison, I held my head up high, determined I would rise above the shame," he confidently proclaims. But he is a branded man, and "they" won't let him.

It was a real-life fear: would the public turn on him if they knew the truth? Fearful of people's reactions, he also included Tommy Collins' "I Made the Prison Band," a song celebrating the small victory of being able to pursue a dream within the walls of a prison, and how he had been planning to break out of the joint, regardless of the outcome, until he made the band. Regardless of who wrote it, the song is a real celebration of a turning point in Haggard's life. Its parent album stayed on the charts for thirty weeks. During this prolific period of Haggard's career, he released his fourth album, *Sing Me Back Home*, built around the single of the same name, which reached #1 in December of 1967 and stayed on the top into 1968.

There probably couldn't be a more disparate pair of singers to lay a sort of foundation for Cash's coming masterpiece—Porter Wagoner, with his flashy rhinestone suits and almost spoken delivery style, and Merle Haggard, the poet of the common man with real-life experience of that which he sings. Prison songs have always been a part of country music, but in 1967 and 1968 we had the unlikely duo of Wagoner and Haggard bringing them front and center to the country music listener's consciousness.

Johnny Cash at Folsom Prison

If singing songs about prisoners was nothing new, singing songs *to* prisoners was. Cash had been thinking about doing that very thing since 1957, and had even been talking to reporters about it since 1963, but there were obstacles to be overcome—mainly himself. Columbia had attempted to record a live album when Cash appeared at Carnegie Hall in 1964, but his voice was so dried up from the pills and cigarettes that he could barely croak, let alone carry a tune. As a result, producer Don Law never even turned on the recording unit.

This incident would surely have popped into the minds of Columbia executives whenever Cash suggested the prison idea. Add to that the fact that no one had ever attempted to record within a prison, and you have the kind of thing most labels avoid like the plague—a risky proposition. Those in charge often prefer to continue on the path of the tried and the true, and Don Law, while giving Cash as much creative leeway as possible, held to those standards.

On February 24, 1967, Law celebrated his sixty-fifth birthday, and received a gift from Columbia. "They've got a strict rule at Columbia, regardless of who you are: when you're sixty-five, you're through," he told Douglas B. Green in 1975, in an interview for the Country Music Hall of Fame. "But they made me a very good deal. They let me keep Carl Smith, Ray Price, Johnny Cash, and Flatt & Scruggs."

Law's position as head of A&R—and his Nashville territory—were now up for grabs, and Law hoped to use his influence to ensure that he be succeeded by his co-producer, Frank Jones. However, Columbia sales manager Bill Gallagher already had a successor picked out: another independent producer named Bob Johnston. When the two men met, Law voiced his opinion that this was a terrible idea, but it fell on deaf ears. "Then Johnston and Gallagher went to work," Law told Green. "My deal was that I could record these four artists, as long as they wanted me, as long as they asked for me. Then they started putting real pressure on all these four guys to leave me. They succeeded with Cash."

The pressure didn't come only from within the company, but also from Cash's manager, Saul Holiff. Although Cash was still well known to the public, and still charting with songs like "Jackson" and "Rosanne's Going Wild," from a record company perspective, he wasn't doing as well as newer acts like Merle Haggard, or acts of his tenure such as Buck Owens, Marty Robbins, or even Eddy Arnold. Even his biggest singles were peaking at #2—and that ain't #1. The last of Cash's songs to reach #1 was 1964's "Understand Your Man," which followed the #2 hit "The Matador" and the chart-topping "Ring of Fire." On the strength of those hits, Cash had renegotiated his contract with Columbia, signing a $500,000 deal that would expire in July 1969. By now, the pressure was beginning to build for Cash to come up with something to rejuvenate his career. Holiff believed that the first change they should make was to switch from the tried-and-true Law to the maverick Bob Johnston, who had built his reputation working with folk-oriented acts like Bob Dylan and Simon & Garfunkel. Cash was a very loyal man, but Holiff was able to convince him that this was what needed to be done.

At Cash's first meeting with his new producer, Johnston asked what he had always wanted to do. "Record a live show in a prison," Cash replied.

"I picked up the phone and I called Folsom and Quentin, and I got through to Folsom first," Johnston later told author Michael Streissguth, for his excellent book *Johnny Cash at Folsom Prison: The Making of a Masterpiece.* "And after six years of talking," Cash adds, in the liner notes to *At Folsom Prison*, "I finally found the man who would listen at Columbia Records. Bob Johnston believed me when I told him that a prison would be *the* place to record an album live."

While it probably wasn't that easy to schedule a recording session in the maximum-security prison, the groundwork had already been laid for Cash's visit. In 1955, Earl C. Green Jr. was convicted of murder and sent to San Quentin to await his execution. While he was there, he befriended the Reverend Floyd Gresset, who frequently went into prisons to minister to the inmates. Eighteen months later, Green's sentence was reduced to life, and he was transferred to Folsom, where Gresset continued to visit him. Green, a model prisoner, then became the host of a radio show on the closed-circuit station heard within the walls, on which he was known as "The Voice of Folsom Prison."

In an interview with journalist Gene Beley (one of only two journalists to accompany Cash into the prison for the concert), Gresset recalled that, during a visit in 1962, Green "asked me what the possibility was of Johnny visiting the inmates." It so happened that at this time, Cash had been sporadically attending services at Gresset's church, so Gresset told Green he would see what he could do. After two years of working to schedule something with Cash and the supervisor of recreation at Folsom, Coach Lloyd V. Kelley, Cash and his troupe—including original Carter Family member Sara—put on a show in the prison yard in November 1966. The concert was a success, and whenever Gresset visited after that, inmates and officials alike would ask when Cash might return. So when Johnston got the wheels rolling for a return engagement, the prison was ready for it, and the show was scheduled for January 13, 1968.

Cash, Carter, and Beley flew into Sacramento a couple of days before the show and settled into a hotel near Folsom to await the arrival of Johnston, Carl Perkins, the Statler Brothers, and the Tennessee Three. At the hotel, Cash began to learn a new song that he would perform at the concert, written by one of the inmates, Glen Sherley. Sherley had been in and out of prison for ten years, mainly for armed robbery, and had taken to songwriting as a way to cope with life inside the system. When Sherley heard of Gresset's connection with Cash, he recorded one of his songs to tape and gave it to Gresset to hopefully pass on to the singer.

Gresset took the tape, but months passed without any mention of it, so Sherley asked for the tape back. "I felt that it probably wasn't very good anyway," he told *Country Song Roundup* in 1972. "And if Cash never heard it, at least he couldn't turn it down. That way I could always think it was good." But the song, "Greystone Chapel," *was* good, and Cash didn't turn it down. According to Beley, he, Cash, and Carter met with Reverend Gresset at the hotel, where Gresset asked Cash to listen to the tape. Beley retrieved a reel-to-reel player, and the foursome sat quietly, listening to the inmate's song.

"As the lyrics filled the room, accompanied by a bass beat from the prisoner's guitar, Cash's usual straight-faced, deep-creased cheeks began changing to a smile, with his eyes glowing, radiating enthusiasm," Beley wrote. "When the tape was finished, Cash said, 'This has got to be recorded as a single, and I want to record it tomorrow on the album during the show.' Cash began scribbling the words down in a notebook and tried singing the phrase while beating out the rhythm with one hand on his knee, the other hand tapping a pen on the desk."

The rest of the troupe joined them the next day to rehearse the set and go through last-minute instructions. The rehearsal concluded after a brief visit from California governor Ronald Reagan, and Cash retired for the night. He got up early the next morning to go over the new song again before he, June, Johnston, and his father, Ray Cash, started the twenty-five mile trek to Folsom, with the rest of the group following behind in their traveling camper. The only journalists present were Beley, photographer Jim Marshall (who had come along to shoot pictures for the album release), and *Los Angeles Times* reporter Robert Hilburn.

Once inside the prison, the musicians were quickly searched before being escorted into a room that would serve as their dressing room. It was there that Marshall Grant opened the case holding his bass and realized that inside lay a small cap-and-ball pistol that he and Cash would use in a comedy routine during the show. "I started shakin' in my boots," Grant recalled. He closed the case and explained the situation to a guard, who took the gun for safekeeping until the group was outside the prison walls.

To ensure that they had enough usable material for an album, the group played two shows, one at 9:40 a.m. and a second at 12:40 p.m., both featuring more or less the same set list. The original album contains sixteen tracks—all but two, "Give My Love to Rose" and "I Got Stripes," are from the first show—but the 2008 Legacy Edition lays out both shows for the first time and fills in some interesting gaps. The first is the introduction by Los Angeles DJ Hugh Cherry. The original release simply starts with that famous "Hello, I'm Johnny Cash," followed by the thunderous applause of the inmates. On the expanded edition, we can hear Cherry tell the inmates that they are to be an important part of something that had never been done in prison. "If you hear something you like, react in kind," Cherry tells the audience, before introducing Carl Perkins, who fires them up with "Blue Suede Shoes," modifying the first line from "go, cat, go" to "go, men, go."

After Perkins finishes his performance, Cherry returns to remind the audience how important their response is to the album. "Let's see how loud 1,000 men from Folsom can be," he requests, before being answered by a roar from the crowd. Next, the Statler Brothers take the stage to sing a rousing version of "This Old House," which is met with whoops and cheers from the crowd. Then it is time for the main event, as Cherry introduces the Tennessee Three, throwing in a good-natured jab at Luther Perkins. Cherry tells the men not to make a sound until Johnny speaks, reminding them that everything will be recorded. The *Folsom Prison* album proper then begins with that memorable opening line, which Johnston claims to have suggested to Cash.

The Legacy Edition offers a complete look at the set list for the show, revealing that Cash had laid out his best prison-related material alongside songs about the prison of poverty and loneliness. A raw and stark "Folsom Prison Blues" kicks off the show, followed by Harlan Howard's "Busted," a song Cash took to #13 on the Country Singles chart in April 1963, and which Ray Charles took to #1 on the Pop chart just a few months later. "Dark as a Dungeon" and "I Still Miss Someone" keep the tone dark and the audience still, before Cash launches into a manic version of "Cocaine Blues," bringing the inmates alive with a murderous tale of drugs and the protagonist's downfall. Shel Silverstein's "25 Minutes to Go" and "I'm Just Here to Get My Baby Out of Jail" lighten the mood a little before Cash kicks up the excitement with "Orange Blossom Special," using the two-harmonica trick that session man Charlie McCoy had taught him. "I have to change harmonicas faster than I can kiss a duck," he tells the cheering audience.

The roller coaster takes a downturn here into songs of adultery and death ("Long Black Veil"), nostalgia ("Send a Picture of Mother"), and guard-assisted suicide ("The Wall"), all done by Cash alone, sitting on a stool strumming his slightly out-of-tune acoustic guitar. Between songs, he does a short bit asking for a drink of water—the same line he used at the Newport Folk Festival in 1964. With thoughts of botched escape, or suicide, heavy on the minds of the audience, Cash lightens the mood with three songs he introduces as "a couple of love songs." Two of the three, "Dirty Old Egg-Suckin' Dog" and "Joe Bean," were included on his 1966 album *Everybody Loves a Nut*, while the third, "Flushed from the Bathroom of Your Heart," was recorded for that album but never used.

The mood of the show completely lifts with the introduction of June Carter, who immediately has the attention of the audience, especially when she tells them she is glad to be back in Folsom. "I sure like to watch you talk," Cash tells her. "I'm talking with my mouth—it's way up here," she replies, before the duo launch into their #2 hit "Jackson." They then dive into Ray Charles' "I Got a Woman," which they had recently recorded for *Carryin' On*, and even though June forgets the lyrics of her first verse, the crowd doesn't seem to mind. June stays out to accompany Johnny on "The Legend of John Henry's Hammer" and then performs a comedy poem of her own before leaving the stage.

To bring the show to a close, Cash joins Wagoner and Haggard as an interpreter of Curly Putman's "Green, Green Grass of Home." Then comes the album's closing number, the song written by one of Folsom's own, "Greystone Chapel." To add a shot of realism to the album, the original release includes a callout to Rudolph Sandoval to come to reception. In 1974, just a few months after Sandoval was released from prison, he sued Cash, Johnston, Columbia, and their owner CBS for $5.25 million for invasion of privacy on the basis of the album including his name and prison number.

The second set shows Cash to be a little worse for wear, his voice hoarse, and lacks some of the energy of the first show. To give him a bit more rest, opening act Carl Perkins gets three songs ("The Old Spinning Wheel," "Matchbox," and "Blue Suede Shoes") as do the Statler Brothers ("You Can't Have Your Kate and Edith, Too," "Flowers on the Wall," and "How Great Thou Art"). Hugh Cherry returns to repeat his earlier announcement, and the show kicks off again. Cash trades out a few songs for this show, bringing in "Give My Love to Rose," "Long-Legged Guitar Pickin' Man," and "I Got Stripes." The crowd is also different, giving less of a reaction during the songs than the first audience did, but still responding at the songs' end. By the end of the show, when the time comes for "Greystone Chapel," Cash's voice is almost shot. He makes two attempts at the song, neither as good as the one from the first show. As the group leaves the stage, Hugh Cherry takes the opportunity to introduce Ray Cash and Reverend Floyd Gressett.

The recording of the album had gone off without a hitch, capturing Cash in top performing condition (for the first show, at least). Now all Columbia had to do was sell the album. The groundwork laid by Wagoner and Haggard (and years of prison songs by country performers) meant the album would easily make the Country charts, but Columbia had its sights set higher. The Country charts were fine, but the real money was on the Pop charts. The hard sell—on both charts—was that the album contained only two of Cash's previous hits, with the rest made up of new songs, album tracks, and B-sides.

Around the time of *Folsom Prison*'s release, there was a revolution going on in the radio world, originating from San Francisco—underground radio. Soon, underground stations were popping up all over the country, offering a "free-form" format that encompassed everything from jazz to country to rock. Columbia decided to court this new radio audience by placing ads in publications like *Rolling Stone* and the *Village Voice*, and just before the album was released, *Rolling Stone* founder Jann Wenner wrote an article endorsing the country singer to his rock audience.

"Johnny Cash, more than any other contemporary performer, is meaningful in a rock and roll context," Wenner wrote, before referencing Cash's friendship with Dylan as a way to bring his audience closer to the subject. He goes on to compliment country music in general, while at the same time extracting Cash from it. "It might seem like a truism, but at this point in time when the frivolous and the bullshit in rock and roll comes faster than royalty checks and thicker than 'pop music' critics, it ought to be re-asserted that the main thing is the music and understanding begins there. It always has been and should always continue to be the case that the best groups and performers are those who are solidly grounded in the music, who can play and perform well, and not those who just have timely, hip messages."

On May 25th—the cover date of the *Rolling Stone* in question—"Folsom Prison Blues" entered the Hot 100, *Billboard*'s Pop Singles chart, at #96, and the next week it popped onto the Hot Country Singles chart at #47. In mid-June, *At Folsom Prison* entered the Hot Country LPs chart at #24, and the Top LPs chart at #160. While the album leapfrogged up the Pop charts, it sprinted up the Country chart, reaching #1 after just five weeks, knocking Bobby Goldsboro's pop-country, big-hit-producing *Honey* off the top spot and resting there for three weeks.

Columbia capitalized on Cash's resurgence in popularity in 1968 by releasing a greatest hits set, drawing together a span of his Columbia singles, while Cash and company worked on his next release, *The Holy Land.* It was a year of extreme highs and lows for Cash. That spring, he finally persuaded June to marry him, but a few months later he lost one of his best friends and architects of his sound, Luther Perkins.

At San Quentin

As evidenced by much of his catalogue, Cash was the type of performer who liked to conquer a concept or idea and then move on, so when the British production company Granada Television reached out to request he replicate *At Folsom Prison* on film, the answer was a polite but immediate no. Undeterred, the producers kept returning to the idea, and decided to approach Cash's manager, Saul Holiff, one last time, only to be told once again that Cash had no interest in recreating his famous concert. But then, just as they were leaving, one of the producers, Geoffrey Cannon, later told Cash biographer Steve Turner Holiff said, "But Johnny is going to San Quentin. He'd be happy to make a film with you there."

The date was set for February 24, 1969, with the Columbia recording engineers and Granada Television crew members gathering at the prison a few days earlier to set up. It was then that the British crew got their first look at life inside an American prison. "It was full of chaos, the whole thing," director Michael Darlow told Turner. After being asked "What's in it for me?" by the warden, the crew came to an agreement whereby they would provide the prison with a new sound system and the warden with a new radio. Then they were approached by a group of inmates. "Twelve hard guys came and told us that we needed protection, and the senior guard advised us to accept the offer," Darlow continued. "So these guys looked after us, and they became the twelve guys in the front row at the concert!"

As with *At Folsom Prison*, there have been three separate releases of *Johnny Cash at San Quentin*. The original release, which appeared in June 1969, contained ten songs, five of which were making their recorded debut. In 2000, an expanded edition was released containing eighteen tracks, but was misleadingly dubbed *The Complete Concert*. In 2006, the Legacy Edition was released, offering thirty-one tracks, including those of opening acts and Johnny Cash Show members Carl Perkins, the Statler Brothers, and the Carter Family. The Legacy Edition also adds a DVD of the Granada Television–produced show—the first time it had been made available in the format.

As with *At Folsom Prison*, the Legacy Edition provides a better picture of the show than the television documentary or the original album allowed. There were several differences between the two shows, not least in terms of the overall presentation. Whereas at Folsom Cash had performed on a small stage decorated only with a banner reading "Welcome Johnny Cash," for the San Quentin show he appeared in front of a large, glittering "Johnny Cash Show" backdrop.

The performers also felt a difference between the shows—one that helped them make it better. Cash would later admit that he had had a few slip-ups after kicking his pill habit in 1967, and that one of them was at Folsom Prison, where he fell off the wagon in an attempt to calm his nerves. Now, however, he had cleaned up again, and was regaining his health. "If everyone had [previously] been giving 100 percent effort on our tours," Marshall Grant writes in his autobiography, "I think John's improved physical and mental state, coupled with the success we were having with the *Folsom Prison* album, inspired everybody—including John—to start giving 115 percent."

Just as at Folsom, Carl Perkins and the Statler Brothers open the show with "Blue Suede Shoes" and "Flowers on the Wall," respectively. The Carter Family—Mother Maybelle, Helen, Anita, and June—then sing two songs, Tom Paxton's "The Last Thing on My Mind" and Maybelle's signature tune "Wildwood Flower," with June talking to the audience in between and repeating the poem she had read at Folsom.

Five of the first seven songs of Cash's set are drawn from his Sun and early Columbia days: "Big River," "I Still Miss Someone," "Wreck of the Old 97," "I Walk the Line" (during which he chides a cameraman for picking something up, saying, "You're in the wrong place to be bending over!"), and "Folsom Prison Blues." "Give My Love to Rose," another early song, makes an appearance in a medley with "The Long Black Veil," from 1965's *Orange Blossom Special*. He then performs the title track from that album before reintroducing June to the crowd. The two sing a spirited version of "Jackson," followed by their take on the John Sebastian–penned "Darlin' Companion," the chemistry between them giving off more sparks than their Folsom performance. The Carter Family returns to perform their version of John D. Loudermilk's "Break My Mind," which had become something of a late-1960s standard, having been recorded by Linda Ronstadt, Glen Campbell, Jerry Lee Lewis, and Lee Hazlewood and Ann-Margret. Although this performance lacks the smooth flow of the Carters' other versions of the song, it serves as an attempt to bring the act in line with what June introduces as "a funky, western, folk sound of today."

Cash then pulls up a stool and, in an echo of the Folsom show, introduces the next song, "I Don't Know Where I'm Bound." "There's a young man here at San Quentin that wrote a song that I just saw wrote down on paper for the first time yesterday," he tells the crowd and the listeners. "He sent me the sheet music on it, and I don't know anyone that reads music, except maybe Helen. I liked the lyrics so much, I started singing my own tune to it—the first thing that came to my mind. Let's try a little bit of it right here." The song doesn't receive the fanfare of "Greystone Chapel," and nor would T. Cuttie, the writer of it, about whom seemingly no information has survived. Afterward, while his guitar is being tuned, Cash mentions another song with an odd title, "A Boy Named Sue," before asking the crowd if they want to hear it. The crowd responds with laughter and applause, and Cash replies, "I do, too. I'm anxious to hear it. I don't know how in the hell it's going to sound."

"Where's Luther?" someone yells. Cash breaks the news of Perkins' death and asks for some applause. Then, before he gets to "A Boy Named Sue," he recounts the story of one of the few times he spent time in jail, for disturbing the peace in Starkville, Mississippi—although he claims here that it was for picking flowers at two in the morning—and debuts "Starkville City Jail."

To follow this comical take on an overnight stay behind bars, Cash brings out a song he wrote the night before, "San Quentin." In one account of the song's origins, Cash reportedly wrote it after touring the jail and being asked what he thought of the place by one of the inmates. "It's a hellhole," he replied. June told him he should write a song about those feelings. In another telling, Granada director Darlow claimed to have suggested that Cash write a song for the occasion, only to be told what he could do with the idea. "I was crestfallen," Darlow told Steve Turner. "[But] June came over to me and whispered in my ear, 'That means he'll do it.'" Cash did do it, and the result was a song in which he puts himself in the mind of the inmates to reveal how he thought he would feel if he were one of them. With the opening line, "San Quentin, you've been living hell to me," he instantly has the attention of his captive audience—and of the guards, their rifles at the ready. As the song progresses, the inmates grow more enthusiastic, exploding at the words, "I hate every inch of you."

"The guards were scared to death," Cash told writer Bill Flanagan. "All the convicts were standing up on the dining tables . . . all I would have had to do was say, 'Break!' and they were gone, man." Cash thought better of it, although he admitted to being tempted by the power. Instead, before honoring the inmates' request to hear the song again, he tries to diffuse the situation by asking—"if any of the guards are still speaking to me"—for a glass of water, allowing a little time for the crowd to calm before launching into the song again, and having it met with the same wild response. After that, Cash waves off requests for a third performance of the song by introducing a new one he had recently co-written with Bob Dylan, "Wanted Man."

Carl Perkins is called back out to play his newest single, "Restless," shaking the jailhouse with the same rockabilly fervor that had propelled his initial burst of success in the '50s. Cash then asks Perkins to stay out to play guitar on the next song, "A Boy Named Sue"—a song they had not yet worked through even once. Cash kicks it off, and Perkins leads the band through a simple rhythm. "That song tore the crowd—and us—apart, because it was the first time any of us had ever heard it," Marshall Grant recalled. The prison audience's response is electric, accurately predicting the response the record-buying public would have to the song.

Cash then debuts a new song that he had tried in the studio just the week before: "Blistered," written by Billy Edd Wheeler, one half of the writing team on "Jackson." He would return to the studio to cut the song in the fall and include it on his next album, while also releasing it as a single. Here at San Quentin, in an archetypal Saturday night/Sunday morning turn, he follows it with a tale of following a beautiful woman from bar to bar and the classic spiritual "(There'll Be) Peace in the Valley (for Me)."

The show closes in a manner typical of a Johnny Cash Show date of the time, with Carl Perkins returning for the instrumental "The Outside Looking In," the Statler Brothers singing Glen Campbell's "Less of Me," and Cash performing "Ring of Fire," with the Statlers simulating the horn parts.

Perhaps the starkest difference between *At Folsom Prison* and *At San Quentin* is the inclusion of several gospel numbers. In the time between the two shows, Cash experienced a recommitment to his faith, and in addition to performing "Peace in the Valley," he and his group close the show with two songs from *The Holy Land*, "He Turned the Water into Wine" and the #1 hit "Daddy Sang Bass," as well as reach back to his first collection of gospel songs, *Hymns by Johnny Cash*, for "The Old Account Was Settled Long Ago." The gang closes the show in the customary manner: a medley of Cash's hits, with a member of the cast taking a verse of each. June takes "Folsom Prison Blues," the Carter Family do "I Walk the Line," the Tennessee Three play an instrumental break featuring a drum solo by W. S. Holland, the Statler Brothers go for "Ring of Fire," Carl Perkins sings the second verse of "Folsom Prison Blues," and Cash rounds things up with "The Rebel—Johnny Yuma."

At San Quentin was released on June 4, 1969, and entered the charts a month later, debuting at #38 on the Country LP chart and #52 in the Top LP charts. At the time, both *At Folsom Prison* and *The Holy Land* were still on the Country Top 20, with both albums also still lingering on the Top LPs chart. Propelled by the success of the lead single, "A Boy Named Sue," and the debut of *The Johnny Cash Show* on ABC during the week of the album's release, *At San Quentin* quickly shot up the charts. On August 2nd, the album hit #1 on the Country LP chart, knocking off Merle Haggard's tribute to Jimmie Rodgers, *Same Train, Different Time.* A couple of weeks later, on August 23rd, it topped the Top LPs chart, taking the #1 spot from *Blood, Sweat and Tears.* It stayed at #1 on the Top LPs chart for four weeks, and on the Country LPs chart for twenty weeks.

By the end of 1969, Cash had transcended genre labeling and become a worldwide pop-culture star, thanks to the success of his television show and a recent recording presence made up of a mix of prison albums, Columbia greatest-hits LPs, and Sun International repackages.

på Österåker

In 1972, Cash accepted an invitation from Olof Arvidsson, a high-profile Swedish lawyer, to come to Sweden and perform a concert in a prison there. He had played in Sweden before, in Gothenburg, on September 11, 1971, to a crowd of over 13,000, and shortly afterward in Stockholm.

At the time, Swedish prisons were among the most progressive in the world, operating along the lines Cash had been pushing for in his testimony to the senate (see chapter 17). Keen to see firsthand how the prison system was working, he agreed to do the show, while deciding he would also like for it to be recorded and filmed. The request to film the show was denied by prison officials, but Columbia's Swedish division arranged for the recording to take place on October 3, 1972.

Supplementing the Tennessee Three that day were Carl Perkins on guitar and Larry Butler on piano. Butler had joined the Roadshow in 1971, and his easy, Floyd Cramer–esque piano style gave the boom-chicka-boom a different dimension, as heard on the first song of the show, an instrumental version of "I Walk the Line." It is a distinction that sets this show apart from Folsom and San Quentin in moving along and updating Cash's sound. The set list for the concert differed from the previous shows as well, with Cash playing more new songs, or songs he had never recorded before and wouldn't again, with the original 1973 Swedish release of the album containing none of the previous hits that were performed at the show.

Cash opens the show with two of those hits—"A Boy Named Sue" and "Sunday Morning Coming Down"—before priming the crowd with a version of "San Quentin," reworked here as "Österåker." Maybe something is lost in the translation, or maybe it's just too early in the show, but the crowd reaction here pales in comparison to the response at San Quentin.

Drawing once again on the work of one of his favorite songwriters, Kris Kristofferson, Cash sings "Me and Bobby McGee," a song of freedom that would remind the prisoners of what it was like on the outside, and one that had previously been performed by everyone from Roger Miller and Janis Joplin to Hank Snow and the Grateful Dead. Then comes "Orleans Parish Prison," from songwriter Dick Feller's 1973 album *Dick Feller Wrote. . . .* It's followed by another new song, "Jacob Green," about a first-time offender in Virginia, whom Cash had mentioned in his senate testimony had been arrested for possession of marijuana. While the boy was awaiting trial, the prison guards had decided to shame him by stripping him naked and shoving him into a holding cell. Ashamed and fearful, the boy killed himself. This was illustrative of the stories Cash had heard over the years, and just the kind of thing he hoped to have others avoid in the future.

"Life of a Prisoner" offers an account of prison life from the pen of an inmate named Jimmy Lee Wilkerson, and here features Larry Butler's tinkling piano in the background. Cash follows it with another song from his youth, Guy Massey's "The Prisoner's Song" (made famous by Vernon Dalhart), before moving swiftly into his own "Folsom Prison Blues" at the request of a shouting inmate. While this version lacks the rawness of Folsom and the energy of San Quentin, it is still a fine performance of the song. Rounding out this stretch of prison songs is "City Jail," a song Cash would later record in the studio for his 1976 LP *The Last Gunfighter Ballad.*

Cash then returns to the Kris Kristofferson songbook to give a fine performance of "Help Me Make It Through the Night" before reaching back again to his childhood and Gene Autry's "That Silver-Haired Daddy of Mine," another song he would return to in 1976, and which he here dedicates to his seventy-year-old father Ray. The next song, "The Invertebrates," is a rarity for Cash: a poem, "written by a man in prison in America," and accompanied by Butler's piano. Staying on that theme, Cash introduces "Lookin' Back in Anger," which was co-written by the two men who had joined him to give their testimony to the senate subcommittee on prison reform earlier in the year, Glen Sherley and

Harlan Sanders. In his introduction, Cash says that Sherley can't be there with him tonight because the parole board won't let him leave the country. He tells the inmates that Sherley has now been out for a year and a half—"the longest time in his entire life that he has been out of prison."

Next, Cash mines *Hymns by Johnny Cash* for Arthur "Guitar Boogie" Smith's "I Saw a Man" before bringing out Carl Perkins—"the most underrated performer I know"—to do "High Heel Sneakers" and "Blue Suede Shoes." Cash then opens up the floor to requests, which come in the form of "Dirty Old Egg-Suckin' Dog" and the live favorite "Wreck of the Old 97," before dedicating "I Promise You," from 1972's *A Thing Called Love*, to June, who was absent for the show. With June still on his mind, he debuts "Nobody Cared," a Tom T. Hall–like tale of a man gone to jail that she wrote "just this week" and that he'd "never sung . . . before. I've never even had a chance to rehearse this song before." He then wraps up the show with another attempt at "San Quentin" (restricting the "Österåker" alteration to just one line this time), to which the crowd responds much more favorably than before.

The album was initially released in Sweden only, although Columbia did issue one single drawn from the recordings in the States. "Orleans Parish Prison" (b/w "Jacob Green") was released in February 1974 and crept up the chart, stalling out at #52 after seven weeks and lingering for one more week before dropping off. Germany's Bear Family label released the album in 1982, retitling it *Inside a Swedish Prison*, but it would not be released in the US until 2008, in an expanded edition containing all of the songs discussed here.

17

There's a Lot of Strange Men in Cell Block Ten

Inmates

Johnny Cash's ideas on prison reform can be summed up by saying that he hoped for meaningful rehabilitation to be provided to show prisoners that someone cared about them. Convict-turned–mystery-writer Albert Nussbaum wrote an article for a newspaper in Charleston, West Virginia, about a concert Cash put on at Leavenworth Prison in the early 1970s, and included the following exchange:

> "We came because we care," [Johnny] said. "We care. We really do. If there's ever anything I can do for you all, let me know somehow, and I'll do it."
>
> The guy in front of me turned to his buddy and whispered.
>
> "Do you think he means it?"
>
> The second man looked at Cash, studying him for a moment from hooded eyes. He nodded slowly. "Yeah. I think he does," he answered.

Cash wasn't just paying lip service to the celebrity cause of the hour. He truly believed that a man could change, and he put his beliefs into action on more than one occasion, bringing into his life ex-convicts that he hoped to help in some way.

Cummins Unit, Little Rock, Arkansas

Between the recording and release of *At San Quentin*, Cash played another prison show, this time in his home state of Arkansas, at the invitation of the governor, Winthrop Rockefeller. Rockefeller—an heir of *the* Rockefeller family—had become the very first Republican governor of Arkansas in 1966, and was seeking reelection in 1968 on a platform that included cleaning up the state's prison system, which had grown into a model of corruption. Helping to tout that fact on the campaign trail was Johnny Cash.

The media spotlight had been shone in recent years on two Arkansas prison farms, Cummins Unit and Tucker Unit. Following numerous complaints of brutal abuse and prostitution at the latter, Arkansas State Police launched an investigation, and in 1966 released their findings in a sixty-seven-page report containing an exhaustive list of grievances, the most infamous being the "Tucker Telephone." Prisoners described being "rung up" on an old-style crank telephone attached to two dry-cell batteries that would be hooked up by electrodes to an inmate—the ground wire to his big toe, the hot wire to his genitals. The phone would then be cranked, and the shock delivered. When it was deemed "necessary" by the guards, some prisoners received "long distance calls." These electric shocks were found to cause permanent damage, but despite the publication of the report, it came out in 1968 that the Tucker Telephone was still in use.

Meanwhile, that same year, Cummins Unit inmate Reuben Johnson, convicted in 1937 of killing his brother, began to talk to prison officials about memories he had of helping to dig unmarked graves for inmates he claimed were "shot with a pistol, a shotgun, or just beaten to death." He then led officials to the spot he remembered, which revealed the unmarked graves of three men. For years, there had been rumors of inmates being killed by guards or "trustees" (prisoners who had earned the trust of officials, and were granted special privileges) and then reported as escapees and never recaptured. Now they were proven to be true.

These two very public cases elevated Rockefeller's campaign platform, leading him to call for the state legislator to instigate a full reform of the prison system. Thinking that a bit more publicity never hurt a good cause, Rockefeller then reached out to Arkansas' favorite son, who happened to be perched on a fairly high platform at the time, shouting similar things.

The show was scheduled for April 10, 1969, and would be recorded for broadcast on KATV, the ABC affiliate in Little Rock. Very little of the show has been released since, save for a few clips of what would have been the end of the show, which have survived through tape traders and now reside on YouTube. The songs performed in those clips echo the end of the San Quentin show almost exactly, with the one exception being that, in the closing medley, after singing a verse from "The Rebel—Johnny Yuma," Cash goes back to "Folsom Prison Blues," changing the title phrase to "Cummins Prison Blues."

With *At Folsom Prison* and *At San Quentin*, Cash sang to the prisoners, bringing them relief from their daily existence. "For a little while he'd accomplished the impossible," Merle Haggard writes in *Sing Me Back Home*. "He had replaced our misery with music. He'd made us *forget* where we were."

To do so was definitely a goal for Cash. "A concert does relieve a lot of tension," he told Peter McCabe and Jack Killion in 1973, "because it makes them forget, it makes them happy, it makes them applaud, it makes them laugh, they tap their feet to the music. That's our purpose, to give them a little relief."

At Cummins Unit, while Cash was still there for the inmates, he was also there to talk to the people in charge. "There's a lot of things that need changin',

Mr. Legislator Man," he said, as cameras rolled. The cotton and other crops grown on the prison farm were sold for profit, which Cash said raised millions of dollars each year, but none of it was being used to improve the facilities or to help separate the boys from the men. Putting his money where his mouth was, Cash donated $5,000 toward the building of a chapel at the prison, challenging Governor Rockefeller to match the sum, chiding, "He can afford it."

The awareness raised by Cash and Rockefeller had an impact, and within a few months, nineteen prison officials and employees—from Tucker Unit's superintendent down—were indicted by a federal grand jury on charges of administering unconstitutional punishment. In the next year, the US Supreme Court ruled the Arkansas prison system unconstitutional, due to its various civil rights violations, and ordered it to be overhauled. "I heard later they got some things done," Cash told writer Paul Hemphill. "That's what I mean. I mean, I'm a musician. But if I can help out a little, well, it's a bonus."

The Call for Prison Reform

"Some people, even a lot of congressmen, tell me I should stick to my own business, which is music," Cash told a reporter in 1969. "But when you travel around and see things, you can't help but voice an opinion."

Cash's opinion on social justice stemmed from a deep place, someplace rooted in the renewal of his religious faith. In the New Testament book of Matthew, Jesus tells the parable of a king separating those who follow him from those who choose not to. To those who follow him, he says, "I was hungry, and you fed me. I was thirsty, and you gave me something to drink." And, finally, "I was in prison, and you came to see me." The puzzled followers ask the king, "I don't remember seeing you there?" The king answers, "Whatever you've done to the least of these, you've done to me." The king goes on to condemn those who did not do these things, noting their eternal punishment.

Cash's Baptist upbringing and his own deep study of the Bible would have highlighted the interpretation that, as a follower of God, he was to do what was in his power to help those who cannot help themselves. "If we make better men out of the men in prison," he told *Country Music* in 1973, "then we've got less crime on the streets, and my family and yours is safer when they come out. If the prison system is reformed, if the men are reformed, if they are rehabilitated, then there's less crime and there's less victims."

Cash's thoughts on separating the men from the boys lay at the heart of his ideas on prison reform. It wasn't that he was out to abolish prisons, or envisioning a Utopian society. He admitted that, while he wasn't a fan of the death penalty, he knew no other answer for criminals that had reached that point. "There have been some sentenced to death, that are dead and gone, that I know the world's a much better off place without them, that kind of evil," he told Tim Robbins. "I think about the victims, especially the little children. I have a hard time when a little child is a victim. And there are some of those people that I am glad are no longer around. But I still don't know if death is the answer though, I'm not sure."

Of seemingly more importance, Cash felt, was making sure that first-time offenders would be *only-time* offenders. "It's as if we're all saying, 'Okay, let's send this man who's offended society to the school for crime that we call our state joint,'" Cash said. "The result is that when the guy comes out, he'll be able to pull off a bigger-and-better robbery, or kill somebody, and that's what's been happening."

The first order of business he wanted to see addressed was why many inmates were there to begin with. "A lot of prisoners have been convicted of marijuana charges, and I personally don't think they should be in prison in the first place," he said. Many of these offenders, particularly in the late '60s, were young men who had committed no other crimes. In Cash's opinion, as long as it remained illegal to possess marijuana, those first-time low-level offenders should be placed in a separate facility, rather than being thrown in with the hardened murderers, rapists, and pedophiles.

It was this belief that led Cash to accept the invitation from Tennessee senator Bill Brock to testify before a senate subcommittee regarding the passing of a bill that would set up an early diversion program for first-time offenders. On July 26, 1972, Cash and Carter, accompanied by Glen Sherley and Harlan Sanders (ex-convicts who had served time in Folsom, San Quentin, and Vacaville Prison) were led by the senator to the witness table in front of the committee, where Cash stated, "Money cannot do the job. People have got to care in order for prison reform to come about."

To illustrate the need to separate classes of offenders, Cash referred to stories he had heard while performing in prisons over the past fifteen years. "At a Southern prison where I performed," he recalled, "the day before I arrived there, I was told by prison officials a fifteen-year-old boy was in prison for car theft and was raped continually all night long by his fellow inmates, and he died the next morning; fifteen years old and his bunk—these bunks are all jammed up together in this prison, and the young man, the first time living with three-time losers and sadistic killers, died."

Cash's idea for reform was split into two areas: logistical and spiritual. His wish was for these people to be housed in different facilities, and for young inmates to be trained to live a different life. Alongside that, he believed that faith could do for these men what it had done for him. "Another big thing that would help with these bills that the senator is working on here is a great spiritual revival," he continued. "I think the emphasis in a lot of these prisons needs to be on more religion, and the kind of religion that the man wants to hear about, ministers, rabbis, preachers that really care for these men, that are really concerned with them and not just somebody who comes here because he is paid $200 a week to do it."

Both Sherley and Sanders then took turns outlining what they had seen during their time inside. Sherley had been in and out of several prisons, mainly for armed robbery, during the previous fifteen years, while Sanders had served a shorter term for the same offense. Both men fully supported the proposed bill, stating that if people could be diverted from prison and into another form of rehabilitation before they became cogs in the prison's inner machinery, it would drastically reduce the rate of recidivism.

Glen Sherley

Soon after Sherley was born, in Oklahoma in 1936, his parents packed up—like droves of others—and headed to California, where they began picking fruit and vegetables in any grove or field they could find along the West Coast. It was a living, but not much of one, and growing up in that environment led young Glen to dream of a way out. That way out was similar to the one chosen by a young Merle Haggard—armed robbery of small shops and liquor stores. It earned Sherley an escape, but not quite to the paradise he dreamed about. Instead, he was behind bars, and every time he got out he found a way back in, eventually touring all that the California Department of Corrections had

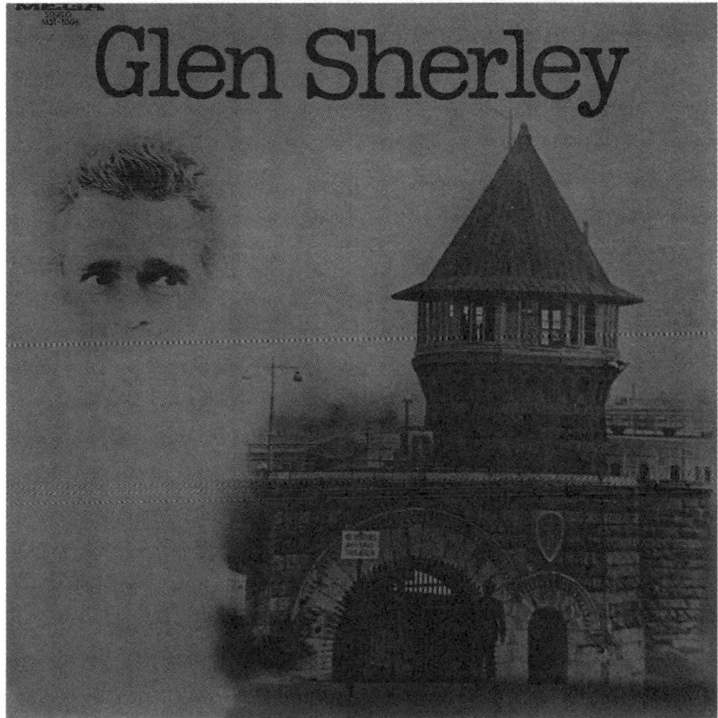

Perhaps the first album recorded in a prison by a current inmate, Glen Sherley's self-titled album showcased his songwriting and his hard-edged personality. *Author's collection*

to offer. Folsom Prison was to be his last stop, where he was scheduled to serve out the rest of his days.

To pass the time, he began writing songs, many of them dealing with life in prison or on the run. As with many other inmates and their art, writing songs offered him an escape from the day-to-day drudgery. "I don't really think that he ever saw it as anything, as a way to make a living," his stepson, Keith Sherley, told author Michael Streissguth. But Glen plugged away at it, perhaps thinking that, while it might not provide a living, it could offer a way out. It was then, with the help of recreation director Coach Lloyd Kelley, that he got a tape of his song "Greystone Chapel" to Reverend Floyd Gresset, who in turn got it to Johnny Cash. When the Cash troupe pulled in to Folsom, they planned to debut it during the concert recording as a surprise to Sherley—or at least a bit of a surprise. The prison grapevine had been buzzing, and Sherley had to have had at least an inkling that something was going to happen. He had been cleared to attend both shows that day, and had a seat in the front row. If that wasn't enough, Cash had tipped his hand a couple of times throughout the show by saying they would be doing a song written by someone in the audience a little later.

When the time came, at the close of the first show, Cash stepped to the microphone:

> The next song was written by a man right here in Folsom Prison, and last night was the first time I've ever sung this song. And we may be a little rough on it today. We may have to do it twice. We'll definitely do it again on our next show in order to try to get a new recording of it because it is new and it may be released as a single record out of the album, I'm not sure. Anyway, this song was written by our friend Glen Sherley. I hope we do your song justice, Glen. We'll do our best.

As Michael Streissguth writes in *Johnny Cash at Folsom Prison: The Making of a Masterpiece*, "It was a symbol of Cash's bond with convicts and the possibility of redemption." The response to the song dwarfed the response even to Cash's biggest hits. "I watched [Sherley] the whole time we were playing 'Greystone Chapel,'" Marshall Grant recalls in his book. "And he was so thrilled that it seemed as if he almost turned into a different person." As the applause rose after the song, Cash reached down and shook the hand of the man who wrote it.

Two hours passed between the first and second shows, during which time the Cash entourage was sequestered in a room off to the side of the cafeteria. An exception was made, and Sherley was allowed to come back and meet Cash. "This is the happiest man I've ever seen in my life when they allowed him to come backstage," Grant continues. "It had to be the biggest day in his life, because he liked to have died when John did 'Greystone Chapel.'"

Cash stayed in contact with Sherley after the show, putting him in touch with Larry Lee, who was in charge of the House of Cash publishing house, to encourage his songwriting. He also set him up with independent producer Jim Malloy, who worked with artists like Sammi Smith and Eddy Arnold. Over the next two years, partly through the efforts of these friends, Sherley was transferred from the maximum-security Folsom to the minimum-security Vacaville Prison.

Nineteen seventy-one was a big year for Sherley. He had continued to write songs, and now, with the help of Lee and Malloy, he had placed one with country legend Eddy Arnold. Although his career was beginning to slow down, Arnold had been a superstar since the mid-'40s, and to have him record your song was an honor. It got even better for Sherley when Arnold decided to name his new album after the song, "Portrait of My Woman." Although the single didn't chart, the album reached a respectable #17 on the Country LPs listing, gaining Sherley some exposure outside of Cash's immediate circle. That small success prompted Jim Malloy to work out a deal for Sherley with Mega Records, and with that, Sherley was set to record his first album.

Johnny Cash had made history by being the first major artist to record an album in a prison. Other country and blues artists followed: Mack Vickery with *Live at the Alabama Women's Prison* (1970), B. B. King with *Live at Cook County Jail* (1971), John Lee Hooker with *Live at Soledad Prison* (1972), Freddy Fender with *Recorded Inside Louisiana State Prison* (1975), Big Mama Thornton with *Jail* (1975), Leona Williams with *San Quentin's First Lady* (1976), and Sonny James with *In Prison, in Person* (1977), to name but a few. But in 1971, Glen Sherley made history as the first person to record an album inside a prison as a *prisoner*.

Sherley's album was recorded live at Vacaville prison on January 31, 1971—his first time in front of an audience doing all his own songs. Jim Malloy had arranged for a crack group of Nashville's best studio musicians to accompany him, so the day before the recording, Chip Young (lead guitar), Jerry Carrigan (drums), Lloyd Green (steel guitar), Bobby Thompson (rhythm guitar and Dobro), and Henry Strzelecki (bass) arrived for rehearsal. The band had learned the songs in Nashville prior to arriving, so all Sherley needed to do was plug into the groove.

Sherley was nervous that, because it wasn't a mandatory activity, no one would show up for the show, but he was excited by the opportunity. But by the time the show started, 800 men had crowded into the makeshift concert area—and that was just for the first of the two shows. The liner notes state that it took one and a half hours to record the thirteen songs picked for the recording, probably due to Sherley's nervousness. "At the end of the show," the notes add, "the prisoners would not leave, so the show was repeated in its entirety for the first group. The second group was then let in, another full house, the reaction equal to the first, Glen Sherley was a hit in his home."

Of those thirteen songs, eleven made the album, each of them written or co-written by Sherley, the majority about life in prison. He also did songs about his mother ("Mama Had Country Soul") and love (the aforementioned "Portrait of My Woman"). One of the songs he debuted was "Looking Back in Anger," co-written by Harlan Sanders, and soon to be recorded by Cash at Österåker. The finale was a fine number called "Measure of a Man," which Sherley introduces by saying, "This next song here was written in an effort to try and express my respect and appreciation, so I'd like to do it now, especially for you, John. And from the bottom of my heart, man, I thank you. You're something else. You really are."

Sherley's voice is expressive, and the passion for what he is singing about is quickly and easily evident. A few overdubs were added later, including a little piano in places, and a Cash cameo on "If This Prison Yard Could Talk."

In February 1971, the popular TV show *This Is Your Life* paid a visit to Cash as he wrapped up a taping of *The Johnny Cash Show* at the Ryman Auditorium in Nashville. During the show, various people from Cash's life, each representing different points in his life story, came out to honor him. At one point, after mentioning the *At Folsom Prison* album, host Ralph Edwards introduces a taped message from Sherley, who says:

> I'm sorry I can't be there today to be a part of *Your Life*, but I can't even begin to tell you how thankful I am that you've been a part of mine, man. I know that you've been a great inspiration to a lot of people, but none more than me. Because I can honestly and truthfully say that you were the major turning point in my life. And maybe someday soon I can justify that faith and encouragement that you've given me by making a success and a productive life out of mine and maybe pass on a little bit of the kindness you've shown me.

Cash is visibly moved throughout, at one point appearing to fight back tears. And you can tell that Sherley means every word he is saying.

One week after the show was broadcast, Sherley would get the chance to try to make that life. Cash, Malloy, Lee, Reverend Gresset, and Reverend Billy Graham had been working to get Sherley paroled, even taking their case to Governor Ronald Reagan. On Saturday, March 7, 1971, Sherley was released from Vacaville, and the next day he was on a plane to Nashville.

"You guys down here in this end of the country are too much," he said, as he was met at the plane by Cash, Carter, and Malloy, who loaded him into a black Cadillac. "We're gonna take him home with us right now," June told a reporter. "He's going to be a writer for the House of Cash and sing with us on the concert tour."

What came next was a crash course in the music business. On the March 24th episode of *The Johnny Cash Show*, our host devotes nearly eight minutes to promoting Sherley's upcoming album. He begins the segment by performing "Greystone Chapel," before introducing a clip of Sherley from the live recording. The segment wraps up a montage of "Portrait of My Woman," begun by Sherley on tape and finished by Cash live at the Ryman.

The next week, Mega placed a full-page ad for the album in *Billboard* that also announced that Sherley would be added to the Cash roadshow. His debut show came on April 10th in Chattanooga, Tennessee, and from there he made every stop on the tour, as well as appearing on *CBS Evening News*, *The Mike Douglas Show*, and other TV shows over the next few months. It was a whirlwind for Sherley, who went from spending most of his life behind bars to playing in front of crowds of thousands, and then being able to walk free offstage each night.

In mid-May, *Glen Sherley* entered the Hot Country LPs chart at #44, peaking a few weeks later at #32. Having observed how *At Folsom Prison* was marketed, Mega launched a special campaign to underground FM stations. The first single from the album, Sherley's live version of "Greystone Chapel," was released in July, and stayed on the lower level of the Hot Country Singles chart, peaking at #63. In September, a new studio single was released, but "Pud'n' Tane" failed to gain any traction at radio. Mega gave it one more try in February 1972 with "Robin (One of a Kind)," but it too failed to do much.

To its credit, Mega continued to stand behind Sherley, who had been booking solo shows with his band in addition to his stops with Cash. One of the more innovative things the label did was form Alias, Inc., headed by Nickie Dobbins, the former personal assistant to Mega boss Brad McCuen. Taking its cue from Cash, Alias was a music publishing company that would work exclusively with incarcerated songwriters, working to place their songs with artists and getting royalties paid to them or their families. The initiative was launched in June, with a concert at Nashville's Tennessee State Prison, headlined by ex-cons Glen Sherley and David Allen Coe. Others on the bill were Sammi Smith, who had earlier in the year broken out with her version of Kristofferson's "Help Me Make It Through the Night," plus the Kendalls (still years away from their big hit, "Heaven's Just a Sin Away") and steel-guitar whiz Pete Drake.

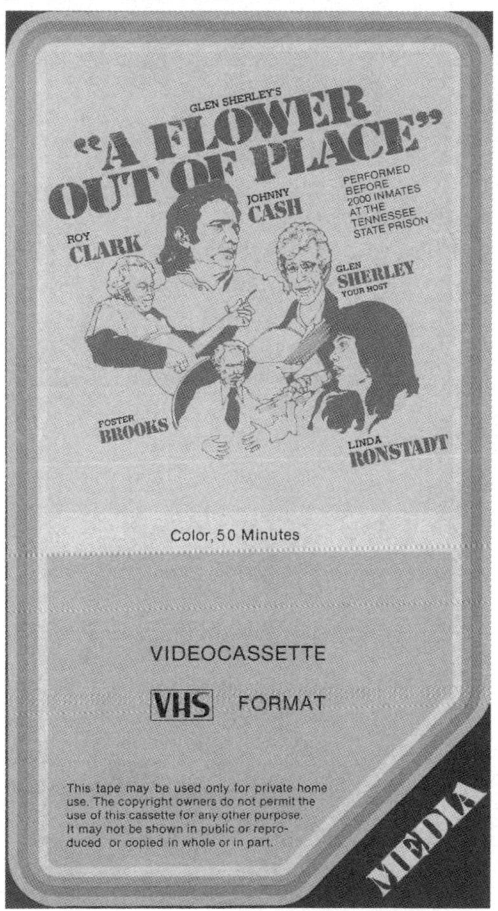

The original edit of *A Flower Out of Place* was distributed on VHS in the early 1980s. The edited version that remained in syndication for several years was released in 2003 as *A Prison Behind Prison Walls.* *Author's collection*

Sherley capped off his big year in December by marrying Dobbins in a ceremony held at Cash's Hendersonville home, with Cash as his best man. Dobbins became Sherley's personal manager, and over the next couple of years, with the help of Lee and Malloy, Sherley continued to place songs with other artists, including Cash and Faron Young. His own recording career began to fizzle out, but Cash continued to do what he could to promote him, including recording with him in prison one last time.

A Flower out of Place was recorded in Tennessee State Prison in Nashville in 1974 and, unlike Cash's earlier prison albums, was set up as a variety show, with Sherley serving as MC on a bill that featured comedian Foster Brooks, Linda Ronstadt, Roy Clark, and Cash. He was obviously nervous, and even a bit uncomfortable, but was the perfect host for the show. Having previously played to the same audience—and sat in a very similar one—he had a level of comfort that comes across on screen.

The show also gave airtime to inmate and singer/songwriter Jerry Jernigan, and the Outlaws, an African American band fronted by four singers who here work their way through a choreographed arrangement of Bill Withers' "Use Me." The show was syndicated throughout the US as well as being broadcast in various other countries over the next two years before eventually being released on VHS. It was subsequently reissued on CD and DVD in 2003, but without Sherley and the other two inmate acts, leading to speculation that Sherley had been edited out because of his tragic passing in 1978. In fact, though, it had first been reedited a year earlier, with the inmates and Sherley removed and the show itself given a new title for resyndication, *A Concert: Behind Prison Walls.* That edition was sponsored by the auto parts store NAPA, which also offered a record compiling hits by Cash, Ronstadt, and Clark, though they were not live cuts from the concert.

Being thrown into a whirlwind of fame can take its toll, with the pressure of making albums and performing concert dates, not to mention trying to live up to the ideals set by an idol who has now become a friend. For Sherley, the pressure was starting to build. In his autobiography, Marshall Grant recalls that at one point he had to speak to Sherley about the fact that he was staying up too late at night and sleeping too late into the morning, causing problems with the troupe's tight travel schedule. Shirley's reply "scared the hell out of" Grant:

> "Marshall, let me tell you something," he said. "You know I love you like a brother; I really love you. I love everybody on this show, but do you know what I'd really like to do to you?" I said, "I got no idea." Glen said, "I'd like to take a knife and start right now and just cut you all to hell. It's not because I don't love you, because I do. But that's just the type of person I am. I'd rather kill you than talk to you."

Grant had no choice but to tell Cash. Several years had passed since Cash himself had told the audience at the Swedish prison Österåker how Sherley had been out of jail for eighteen months, and how that was the longest time he had spent out of prison in his entire adult life. Since then, Sherley had turned to drugs and alcohol to help with life on the road, and now, following this threat to one of his closest friends—and the thought that another threat, or worse, could come to any member of the roadshow at any time—Cash had to make the tough call to remove Sherley from the show. As much as this was disheartening to Cash, it had to be a devastating blow to Sherley, who had spoken over and over again of how much Cash meant to him. As he had told the senate subcommittee in 1972, it was "Johnny . . . [pulling] me out of the muck [that] made me want to try, it gave me the strength and the courage to try and only that."

After being removed from the tour, Sherley slowly slipped out of sight, eventually moving his family to Utah, but he soon left them there to travel around California. By now, he had progressed to a full-blown heroin addiction. He continued to wander, not knowing where he was going, but knowing there was one place he was *not* going—back to jail. Through a haze of the drugs, Sherley could only see one way out, and on the morning of May 11, 1978, he put a gun to his head and ended his troubled life.

The news hit Cash hard. His brother Tommy later recalled that Johnny didn't speak a word for two days. It was a tough blow to the beliefs he had been preaching about rehabilitation for those several years when he was so close to Sherley, and perhaps something he never quite came to terms with. Speaking to Tim Robbins for a promotional interview in 2000, he described how Sherley "lived a very good productive life for many, many years until he had a tragic ending from, well, actually cancer."

Harlan Sanders

Two men walked with Cash into the senate subcommittee hearing on July 26, 1972. Glen Sherley was one; Harlan Sanders was the other. Paroled only six days earlier, this one-time armed robber was appearing in Washington with one of his heroes. He and Sherley were friends and even co-writers on some of the songs Sherley had been performing, including "Looking Back in Anger." But while they came from similar circumstances, in the end they could not have been more different.

Sanders was born in Weedpatch, California, where his parents, like Sherley's, were itinerant laborers in the fields. Music was always on his mind, and he dreamed of writing and singing songs like his idols in nearby Bakersfield. One day, he was bumping around the city when he ran into Red Simpson, the singer/songwriter who had written a #1 hit for Buck Owens, and who later became best known for his truck-driving songs. Sanders was having a hard time getting anyone to listen to his songs, so Simpson told him he needed to make a demo to pass around to try to get people to record them. "How much does that cost?" Sanders asked him. Simpson told him he could do a song for a few hundred dollars. Sanders thanked Simpson and went on his way, knowing he didn't have a few hundred dollars. But he did know where he could get it.

By now, Sanders had already visited several of California's correctional facilities for knocking over liquor stores and anywhere else he thought might have a few bucks. But one fateful attempt that left a man dead ended that career and earned Sanders a ninety-nine-year sentence. "After that, I didn't think I'd ever get out of jail," he told a reporter in the mid-'70s. But instead of resigning himself to bitterness, he turned even more to his songwriting. "All the prison guys called me a nut because I was happy all the time," he continued. "But why not? I was writing my songs, and as long as I didn't have to be by myself and think, it was a good deal."

It was there, in Vacaville, that Sanders met Glen Sherley. The two became fast friends, and they would write songs together until Sherley was granted parole in March 1971. "I was so happy writing songs all day, I didn't really care if I ever got out, but when I went before the parole board they said there was a chance," Sanders told UPI's Paula Schwed. That chance came about because of his positive attitude, plus several good words from Johnny Cash, who said he had a job waiting for him at House of Cash. "Here I am a convict, expecting nothing but the worst," Sanders recalled. "And what this man has done for me nobody ever did. I just cried and cried."

Working at House of Cash, Sanders was able to ease into life on the outside (as opposed to Sherley, who jumped straight into the glare of the spotlight). But he promised Cash that he would repay him by making it big one day. He also wanted to give back—to encourage those that were in the position that he had been in—so in January 1973, he and fellow ex-cons Sherley and Earl Green performed a show at the Tennessee State Prison, with Johnny Cash, Johnny Rodriguez, Don Wayne, Jeanne Pruitt, and Jackie Burns rounding out the bill.

"People ask me what I'm doing for the guys back in prison," he told a reporter after the show, "and this is what I'm doing—writing songs, working hard and trying to get ahead. Doesn't do much good for them if I go sing to them. But if I make it—that's good for those guys." Sanders got married that same year, and began to find more work in the music publishing industry. He went on to work for Willow Fair and Willow Green Music, as well as taking over the country wing of House of Cash when Larry Lee moved departments to look after the gospel material that was now increasingly the focus of Cash's attention.

Sanders signed with the small Shannon label in 1974 and released his first single, "She Says I Look Like Daddy," that summer. The song didn't chart, but it received a good review from *Billboard*, which said, "A star is born! . . . He's one of the most exciting new artists in some time. The singing is great and the song is outstanding. . . . Now a part of the Nashville community, 'Sandy' has made scores of friends and is highly thought of as an artist and an individual."

Two years after his release from what was originally a ninety-nine-year sentence, Sanders was finding his place in the world. When his second single on Shannon, released in early 1975, failed to get any action, he left for Epic. His first major-label release, *Off and Running*, came out in 1976 and increased his profile beyond the songwriting community. Two singles were drawn from the album, but they too failed to excite anyone in radio, even with the endorsement of Cash, who wrote the liner notes.

Sanders continued to place songs with other artists throughout the late '70s and early '80s. In 1976, he had told a reporter, "I'm just starting to write good songs, and I've got lots of good songs left in me. I just love writing songs." One of the songs he had left in him was "If Drinkin' Don't Kill Me (Your Memory Will)," which he co-wrote with Rick Beresford and Karl Sanders. George Jones put the song on his 1980 album *I Am What I Am*, which also contained the career-revitalizing "He Stopped Loving Her Today." The album went Top 10, and the song was released as a single, peaking at #8 and becoming one of Jones' most popular songs of the 1980s.

Building on that success, Sanders recorded a follow-up album for the small independent label Brylen in 1982, but for the most part he kept to songwriting, and working with young singer-songwriters, like Mila Mason, who charted with a few minor hits of her own in the late 1990s.

Cash extended a helping hand when he could, and when he believed it might make a difference, as it did in the three following examples:

David "Cuz" Powers

Sherley and Sanders weren't the only songwriting inmates in Vacaville. In early 1973, Sanders brought Cash two songs written by a friend of his, David "Cuz" Powers. Soon, Cash sent a letter to Powers' publisher, which read, "Dear Cuz, I'd say you are the best songwriter I've heard in a year, and I hear a lot of songs. I have just recorded two of your songs for my next album which will be released at the end of July." The songs, "Tony" and "Godshine," were included on *Johnny Cash and His Woman* in 1973.

Jerry Jernigan

Jernigan was one of the talents showcased on *A Flower out of Place*, where the Tennessee State Prison inmate sang a song he wrote called "Make My Mama Proud." He met Cash during rehearsals for the show, and got the chance to talk with him a bit.

"I told him that I was trying to write songs, and that I had written a song for him and June, and would he listen to it," Jernigan told *Country Music* in 1980. "He said sure, and even let me play the song on his personal guitar." Cash liked the song enough to take a tape of it home with him. A few days later, he called Jernigan and offered him a songwriting contract with House of Cash.

In a move similar to the Alias, Inc. program, Cash was able to bring Jernigan to the studio to record demos, and had him appear on *The Grand Ole Gospel* show in 1975. Jernigan continued to write while serving his ninety-nine-year sentence. Cash's impact came less on his work and more on his life—or, as Jernigan put it, "not only monetary, but real things, things that count and will last a long time."

Larry Hilton

Not everyone Cash helped was a songwriter. He had a very simple reason for helping the twenty-four-year-old Hilton: "I saw myself in that young man," he told Bob Battle in 1975. Hilton had been convicted, in 1972, of selling $900 worth of drugs to an undercover officer, for which the first-time offender was sentenced to eleven years.

Hilton's own drug addiction is what had landed him behind bars, and Cash knew something like this could easily have happened to him. In fact, if it hadn't been for the fame and the money, it probably would have been him when he was arrested in El Paso, Texas, in 1965 for carrying a guitar case full of pills—much more than $900 worth.

"I was probably a worse victim than Larry," Cash told Hilton's parole board panel, in what was the first such hearing he had ever attended. ("He has written some letters for people," June told *Country Song Roundup*, "but he has never gone before a parole board."). Hilton's remorse, plus Cash's testimony, led to him being paroled in 1976.

But It Isn't My Masterpiece

The 1960s #1s

Johnny Cash got a slow start to the 1960s, with the pills threatening to drag him down. On top of that, he was also touring almost nonstop, dipping his toes into the acting stream, and moving his family across the country. All of this had an effect on his music, and Columbia began to worry that it had made a poor decision in scooping him up from Sun. That turned around just a few years into the decade with an enduring #1 hit in 1963, followed by another in 1964. After that, it would be another four years before Cash hit the top spot, but when he did, he stayed there, with a line of successive hits.

"Ring of Fire" b/w "I'd Still Be There" (1963)

Knocked out "Act Naturally," Buck Owens; knocked out by "Abilene," George Hamilton IV

The early '60s were a trying time for both Cash and Columbia. On the personal front, Cash was sinking deeper into addiction, and it affected every aspect of his life, including his judgment—particularly when it came to June Carter. He was spending less and less time with his family in California, and more and more time on the road, with June there along for the ride. During that time, Columbia released ten singles, but only three—"Frankie's Man, Johnny," "I Got Stripes," and "In the Jailhouse"—reached the Top 10 on the Country chart, and none of them even touched the Pop chart.

The tenth of those singles, "Busted," was one that Cash and his producer Don Law felt could be a hit. Written by the great Harlan Howard, it was a semi-comedic look at a man who was down on his luck and looking to provide for his family, even if it meant turning to a life of crime. Folk singer Burl Ives had recorded the song in May 1962, and Cash went into the studio to record his version on August 21st of the same year for the album *Blood, Sweat and Tears.* Columbia released it in April 1963, but it only reached #13—a disappointment to all involved. Later that fall, Ray Charles released his version, which went to #4 on the Pop chart. It showed, perhaps, that Cash and Law still had an instinct for what could be a hit, and they hoped to prove that with their next release. As far as Columbia was concerned, they needed to. The label's contract with Cash

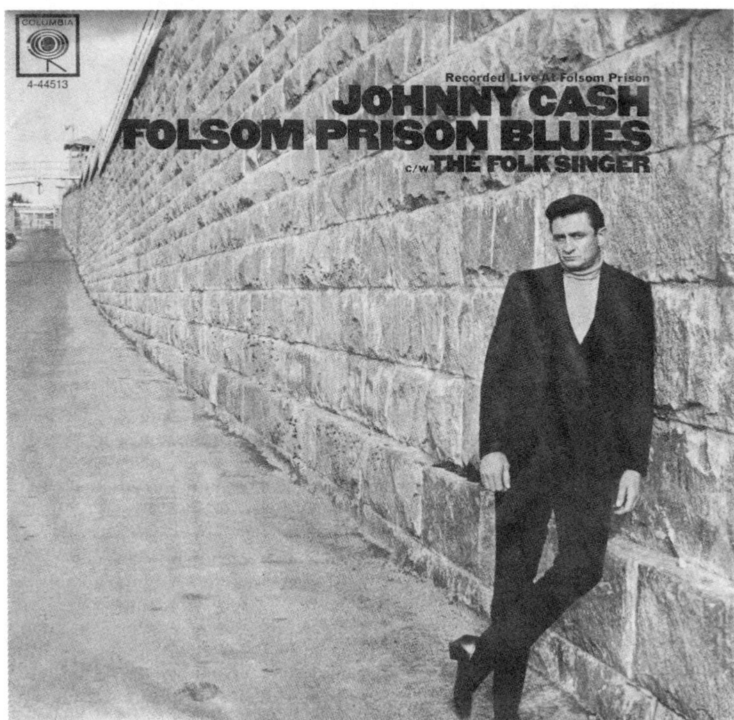

The second release of "Folsom Prison Blues" proved to be even more successful than the original Sun release. *Private collection*

included yearly options, and those in charge were ready to exercise the clause to release him.

Earlier that year, June Carter and her co-writer Merle Kilgore had written a song inspired by her feelings for Cash. Based on a line from a book of Elizabethan poetry, the song, "(Love's) Ring of Fire," was a folky number about temptation and desire. In her memoir, Vivian Cash claims that Cash told her that he had written the song with Kilgore and only given his part of the writing credit to Carter because "She needs the money and I feel sorry for her." By now, Vivian was starting to piece together what was happening with Johnny and June, but she was helpless. "The truth is," she writes, "Johnny wrote that song, while pilled up and drunk, about a certain private female body part." In his excellent Cash biography *Johnny Cash: The Life*, Robert Hilburn maintains that Kilgore wrote the song with June, although Vivian's co-writer Ann Sharpsteen lays out a pretty convincing case for Cash to be the co-writer in an epilogue included in the paperback edition of *I Walked the Line.* Sharpsteen asks questions about other songs written by June and their lack of similarity to the hit, notes contradicting dates on the copyright filings that list Cash as a co-writer of the song, and draws on eyewitness accounts by friends of Cash that back up Vivian's story.

Regardless of who actually wrote the song, the first person to record it was June's sister Anita. Her version is an earthy, folky take, with rolling acoustic guitar and her beautiful soaring alto voice. In 1980, Cash told Ed Salamon for *Country Music*:

> I said, "Anita, I'll give you about five or six months, and if you don't hit with it, I'm gonna record it the way I feel it." She said, "OK." Well one night, not that I [claim] any psychic powers or anything, I dreamed I heard "Ring of Fire" with trumpets, which is an outlandish kind of innovation for country music. I called Don Law, who was producing my records, and I said, "I want to record a song with trumpets with a Tex-Mex sound of trumpets." And he said, "Are you sure?"

It might have been outlandish, but it wasn't unprecedented. Bob Moore, bass player for the famed A-Team of Nashville studio musicians, had reached #7 on the Pop charts in 1961 with a Tex-Mex-inspired instrumental called "Mexico," and for the "Ring of Fire" session, Law brought in the two trumpet players who had played on that recording, Bill McElhiney and Karl Garvin.

The result struck a chord with the record-buying public, and over a two-month period the song climbed to #1 on the Country chart, remaining there for seven weeks. Better yet, in Columbia's view, was that the song spent ten weeks on the Pop chart, peaking at #17. It was enough to restore some of the label's faith in Cash, prompting them to re-sign him to a profitable new recording contract.

"Understand Your Man" b/w "Dark as a Dragon" (1964)

Knocked out "Saginaw, Michigan," Lefty Frizzell; knocked out by "My Heart Skips a Beat," Buck Owens

Columbia wasted no time after the success of "Ring of Fire." As soon as it dropped out of the Top 10, the label released a new single. "The Matador" was a co write between Cash and June that brought McElhiney and Garvin back with their trumpets for a tale of a matador walking into an arena where he acts strong for the crowd but is distracted by the fact that his ex and her new love are in the stands watching. It reached #2, but was kept off the #1 slot by Buck Owens' "Love's Gonna Live Here" and its sixteen-week run at the top.

As "The Matador" dropped out of the chart, a new single was waiting in the wings. *The Freewheelin' Bob Dylan* had recently been released, and Cash was spending a lot of time listening to Dylan's songs, soaking in the lyrics and sounds. He was so inspired by the music, in fact, that he essentially lifted the melody of "Don't Think Twice, It's All Right" for his new song, "Understand Your Man." Lyrically, though, the inspiration came from somewhere closer to home—from home, in fact. Things hadn't been good between Johnny and Vivian for some time. He would sporadically ask for a divorce, but she would always say no, both because she still loved him and because her Catholic upbringing forbade it. Cash's resulting hit had to be devastating to her. "Understand Your Man" was aimed squarely at her, just as "I Walk the Line" had been, back when times were better for them.

For the "Understand Your Man" session, held in Nashville on November 12, 1963, Cash retained McElhiney and Garvin but added a new sound, the Dobro of Norman Blake. Blake had played on a few shows with June Carter in the past and was friends with session guitarist Bob Johnson. He had been invited along to the session after visiting Johnson in Nashville. When Blake arrived, June remembered him and recommended him to Cash, who invited him to add his Dobro to the song.

"Saginaw, Michigan," by Bill Anderson and Don Wayne, was a clever song about a gold miner who tricks his greedy father-in-law-to-be into leaving for riches that aren't really there so he can marry the man's daughter. Lefty Frizzell had been sitting at #1 with the tune in early April, until "Understand Your Man" bumped it out of the way. That ride lasted six weeks before Buck Owens, who was enjoying a string of #1s, took over the spot with the bouncy "My Heart Skips a Beat."

"Folsom Prison Blues" (Live Version) b/w "The Folk Singer" (1968)

Knocked out "D-I-V-O-R-C-E," Tammy Wynette; knocked out by "Heaven Says Hello," Sonny James

By 1968, four years had passed since Cash's last #1 single, and as the 1960s wound down, his personal life was a series of extreme lows (generally caused by his drug use) and highs (June finally agreeing to marry him, and his decision to kick the pills—or at least try to). In the interim, he had continued to release a few singles a year, some of which were well received and landed in the Top 10, like "The Ballad of Ira Hayes" (#3 in 1964) and his duets with June Carter on Dylan's "It Ain't Me, Babe" (#4 in 1964) and "Jackson" (#2 in 1967). His next trip to the top would be with a song he had released as one side of his second single in 1956, "Folsom Prison Blues."

Cash got the idea for the song while stationed in Germany with the Air Force, when one day the men were shown a film called *Inside the Walls of Folsom Prison*. The images sparked his imagination, and he began to toy with the idea for the song. As many fledgling songwriters do, Cash borrowed the melody, structure, and many of the words from a song he had heard in the barracks called "Crescent City Blues." The song came from a 1953 album called *Seven Dreams* by bandleader Gordon Jenkins, who was also a successful arranger and composer. *Seven Dreams* was a concept album about a man who has, yes, seven dreams, the first being that he is a botany professor and is joined by his class as they escape the classroom. The second dream, subtitled "The Conductor," depicts the man as a train conductor. In the first part of the song, a politician is giving a speech from the observation deck of the train; the train then pulls into a station, and the conductor gets off to have a cigarette, when he hears "a voice from the shack across the way." The voice is that of Beverly Mahr, who sings "Crescent City Blues," the melody for which was borrowed from an earlier instrumental song of the same name by Little Brother Montgomery. The singer "hears the train a-comin', rollin' round the bend" and laments how "she ain't been kissed since I don't know when." The two songs aren't just similar—they are essentially the same tune with different lyrics. (Cash would draw on the album once again for "The Caretaker," from *Songs of Our Soil*, which "borrows" the theme, chorus, and melody from "The Third Dream: The Caretaker.")

"At the time, I really had no idea I would be a professional recording artist; I wasn't trying to rip anybody off," Cash told a Canadian magazine in the mid-'90s. "So when I later went to Sun to record the song, I told Sam Phillips that I rewrote an old song to make my song, and that was that. Sometime later, I met up with Gordon Jenkins and we talked about what had happened, and everything was right."

In fact, it was less of a meeting and more of a lawsuit, and everything was made right by an undisclosed cash settlement and a co-writer credit. Curiously, Jenkins didn't come calling during the first run of "Folsom Prison Blues," even though the original version inspired the recording of several other renditions (none of which were very high-profile, save perhaps for the 1966 versions by Porter Wagoner and Charley Pride). Problems only arose after the second release of the single, when it proved to be a huge success.

"I think the excitement on that record is what I had been trying to say for years to the record people," Cash told Ed Salamon about the live prison recording from which the single was taken. "If you can capture that excitement on record—that energy—then you got a hit record. And it was once in my life I was right."

Boy, was he right. The album and single became Cash's breakthrough to a larger audience, and his performance on both is mesmerizing. Of the single, Bill Friskics-Warren, co-author of *Heartaches by the Number: Country Music's 500 Greatest Singles*, would later write, "That corrosive snarl of his sounds like it could be just enough to send that locomotive barreling straight to hell." In *The Best of Country Music: A Critical and Historical Guide to the 750 Greatest Albums*, John Morthland writes, "From the opening cut, a version of his old favorite 'Folsom Prison Blues,' with the band bearing down harder than usual, this album is all rapport. Quite simply, Cash identifies with these inmates and they with him."

The single's release also marked the point when the rock press and listening public began to identify with Cash, and soon he was climbing both the Country and Pop charts. "Folsom Prison Blues" would stall out at #32 on the Hot 100, but it knocked Tammy Wynette's "D-I-V-O-R-C-E" from the top spot on the Country chart, holding on to it for four weeks before being ousted by "Heaven Says Hello," a happy, shiny sing-along by Sonny James that is almost the antithesis of "Folsom." The new success of the track inspired a new spate of recordings, and in 1968 and '69 alone there were eighteen versions of the song recorded by a range of artists like Merle Haggard, Waylon Jennings, Chet Atkins, Flatt & Scruggs, and bluesman Slim Harpo.

"Daddy Sang Bass" b/w "He Turned the Water into Wine" (1969)

Knocked out "Wichita Lineman," Glen Campbell; knocked out by "Until My Dreams Come True," Jack Greene

The success of "Folsom Prison Blues" and *At Folsom Prison* raised Cash's profile tremendously, and everyone was eager to keep that success coming. After making such a gritty, hard-hitting album, most artists would strive to put out something very close to whatever it was that had grabbed everyone's attention—and their management and label would be all for it. But Cash wasn't like most artists. He had already begun work on a project he had wanted to do for a long time: another gospel album, and one that would use actual sounds from a recent trip he and June had taken to Israel. The resulting double album, *The Holy Land*, came out in early 1969, but its lead single was released at the end of 1968.

"Daddy Sang Bass" was one of the three songs on the project not written by Cash. It came instead from his former Sun labelmate and current roadshow member Carl Perkins. Inspired by Cash's attempt to kick his drug problem, Perkins had decided to kick his alcohol habit and rededicate his life to God. With that idea on his mind, he began to write the song backstage while warming up by going through the Carter Family's "Will the Circle Be Unbroken." Cash overheard him and encouraged him to continue the song. Harold Reid of the Statler Brothers also heard it, and asked if his group could record the song. Perkins told him that he believed Cash was going to record it, but if that didn't happen, the Statlers were welcome to it. In the event, Cash got there first.

"Carl Perkins was really looking inside my head when he wrote 'Daddy Sang Bass,'" Cash writes, in the liner notes to his second volume of *Greatest Hits*. "He knew the song would be as much a part of me as it would if I had written it."

The song showcases all of the current members of the Johnny Cash Roadshow, with the Carter Family, the Statler Brothers, Jan Howard, and Perkins all included on the catchy recording. The sing-along quality—and maybe a dash of nostalgia—carried the song to #1 in January of 1969, where it met up with the melodic "Wichita Lineman" by Glen Campbell. It remained there for six weeks, before making room for Jack Greene and "Until My Dreams Come True."

"A Boy Named Sue" (Live Version) b/w "San Quentin" (Live Version) (1969)

Knocked out "Workin' Man Blues," Merle Haggard; knocked out by "Tall Dark Stranger," Buck Owens

Columbia got its wish granted for a follow-up to *At Folsom Prison* with the release of *At San Quentin*. The album exceeded the success of *Folsom*, spurred on in part by Cash's new television show. *The Johnny Cash Show* aired on Wednesdays on ABC and became a hit nationwide after the first episode aired on June 7, 1969, just one week before another country-music variety show, *Hee Haw*, premiered on CBS. Shortly after the show's debut, Columbia released the live version—the only version, in fact, and a spur-of-the-moment decision at that—of "A Boy Named Sue."

The origins of the song lie in two seeds of inspiration and the fertile imagination of Shel Silverstein. One of them was a real-life boy named Sue: Sue Kerr Hicks. He was born in 1895, the youngest of nine children, and named Sue by his father in honor of his mother, who died during childbirth. At age thirty, Hicks was an assistant prosecutor in the 1925 "Scopes Monkey" trial, which challenged a Tennessee law stating that only creationism be taught in the classroom. After one term in the State House of Representatives, Hicks went on to serve as a criminal judge for twenty-two years. One afternoon in the late '60s, Hicks was attending a bar association meeting in Gatlinburg, Tennessee, at which he was scheduled to speak. Shel Silverstein was also in Gatlinburg that same week, and he overheard Hicks' name over the loudspeaker. "It is an irony of fate that I have tried over 800 murder cases and thousands of others," Hicks once said, "but the most publicity has been from the name Sue."

Judge Hicks wasn't the first man Silverstein had encountered with a feminine-sounding name. One of his best friends was Jean Shepherd, the author perhaps best known for the perennial holiday favorite *A Christmas Story*. Lisa Rogak, in her 2007 book *A Boy Named Shel: The Life and Times of Shel Silverstein*, notes that Shel "wrote the song after hearing Jean Shepherd complain about his name, because he was often teased as a child for having a girl's name. Shep turned his experiences into rich farce on his radio show, among them a teacher in elementary school who always spelled his name Gene, and once when he was automatically put into a gym class for girls because of his name. 'I fist-fought my way through every grade in school,' said Shepherd. 'How do you think I got so aggressive? So wiry?'"

Although Cash often recalled that he first heard Shel play the song during a guitar pull at his house in Hendersonville, he more likely heard it on another occasion, according to steel-guitar player, songwriter, and music publisher Don Davis, in his memoir *Nashville Steeler: My Life in Country Music*. Davis had also been married, twice, to Anita Carter, so he and Cash knew each other well. In fact, he was the man who brought "Jackson" to Johnny and June. One day, Shel Silverstein stopped by the office of Davis' Wilderness Publishing Co., took out a guitar, and began to play a new song. "I knew immediately the only person who could cut it was Johnny Cash," Davis writes. He called Cash right away and told him about the song. "Bring it out now," Cash replied.

At the time, Silverstein was gaining some commercial recognition, as the Irish Rovers had had a Top 10 Pop hit in 1968 with "The Unicorn," his quirky song about Noah's Ark. Cash had also recorded songs by Silverstein before, most notably "25 Minutes to Go," which he originally cut for *Ballads of the True West*, and which received a great reception at Folsom Prison.

"The song wasn't even demoed," Davis continues, "so when I took Shel out to John's house, he sang it to him live. When we left, all John had was the lyrics." This was the day before Cash and crew were scheduled to leave to record the album at San Quentin. As they were packing, June reminded him of the folded piece of paper containing the lyrics.

"I got a brand new song that I grabbed just as I was leaving home to go to California," Cash later explained to *Country Music*'s Ed Salamon. "I didn't even know the lyrics. When I got to San Quentin Prison, I had to put the words on a music stand in front of me."

"I thought then and still think that it is the most cleverly written song I have ever heard," Cash writes, in the liner notes to *The Johnny Cash Collection—His Greatest Hits, Volume II*. "And the rendition that you hear here is that same one and only recording where I was reading the words off as I sang it. Maybe the recording doesn't have a lot of polish, but it sure has a lot of honesty."

It was not only the first time Cash had performed the song but also the first time the band had heard it. Cash instructed them to do a shuffle in A; Carl Perkins led the charge, with Marshall Grant on bass and W. S. Holland on drums, while new recruit Bob Wootton jumped on board on guitar. The music never goes along perfectly with Cash's recitation and occasional singing, but that is part of why it works so well. The unpolished performance, spurred on by the energy of the prisoners' laughter and whooping, takes the song somewhere it would have never reached in a studio setting.

On August 2, 1969, the eighth episode of *The Johnny Cash Show* was broadcast. Among the featured guests was Merle Haggard, who performed "Lonesome Fugitive" and "California Blues," with the crowd cheering him so loudly that parts of "Lonesome Fugitive" are barely audible. Haggard's current single, which he didn't perform, was "Workin' Man Blues." David Cantwell, in his book *Merle Haggard: The Running Kind*, states that Haggard wrote the song as "an identity-solidifying, common-man anthem of his own" in response to "Folsom Prison Blues." Just a couple of weeks after his *Johnny Cash Show* appearance, Haggard's song went to #1, but one week later, "A Boy Name Sue" took over and held onto the top spot for five weeks.

During that time, *Hee Haw* was developing a strong following of its own, and co-host Buck Owens was riding that success. Owens and his band, the Buckaroos, typified the Bakersfield sound with its bright, in-your-face guitars and jangly quality, and their songs were a natural fit for the upbeat production of the show. In early 1969, he went into the studio to record a new song he had written, "Tall Dark Stranger."

"The song wasn't like anything I'd ever written before, but I thought it was one of my better ones," Owens writes in his autobiography, *Buck 'Em!* "I admit I was going against my usual way of thinking, but I felt like it was the kind of song that needed strings and background vocals. Ninety-nine percent of the time I didn't think that sort of thing was right for the kind of records I was making, but this was that other one percent." Owens' instinct paid off, and "Tall Dark Stranger" became his third #1 single of 1969.

"A Boy Named Sue" went on to sell over one million copies and spent three weeks at the #2 spot on the Hot 100, held off #1 only by the Rolling Stones' "Honky Tonk Women." It was the most commercially successful single of Cash's career, and it won Single of the Year at the 1969 Country Music Association Awards, where Cash also won Entertainer of the Year, Male Vocalist of the Year, Vocal Group of the Year (with June Carter), and Album of the Year for *At San Quentin.* Before long, "A Boy Named Sue" had become a cultural touchstone, even showing up as a catchphrase in classified ads, one of which sported the title as the top line of its bold headline, followed by the words, "didn't build this house, but Manley did," and a description of the company's new homes. At the twelfth annual Grammy awards in 1970, Bob Newhart called the song "a phenomenon" and went on to do a bit about Silverstein's pitch to Cash, incorrectly calling it the first song that Silverstein had ever written. Later in the ceremony, Silverstein won his first Grammy for Country Song of the Year, while Cash won Best Country Vocal Performance, Male for the song.

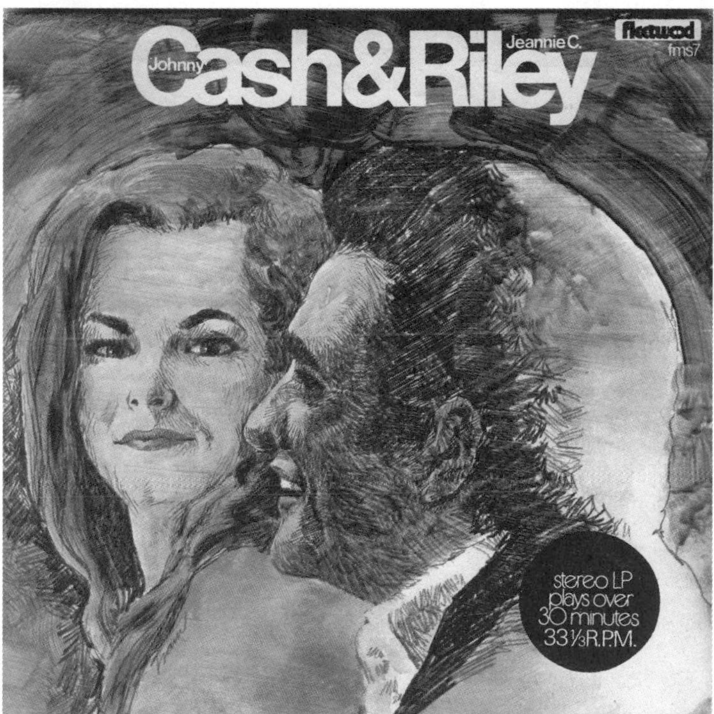

Johnny Cash and Jeannie C. Riley were two of the biggest music stars in the early '70s. Fleetwood Records released this 33⅓ RPM EP, featuring four songs from each artist, to capitalize on Cash and Riley's popularity.
Private collection

In *The Man Called Cash*, Steve Turner notes that, while "[Cash] naturally enjoyed its staggering success, he didn't relish the idea that his most commercially successful song was a novelty number written by someone else." Even so, the song remained a part of his set list for many years. As he told reporter Mary Dickie in 1987, "When I get requests for songs from young people, it's always for the early-'60s songs, or the Sun years. No later than 1970, 'A Boy Named Sue.'"

That was still the case in 1993, when, in an interview with *Country Music*'s Michael Bane, Cash let his feelings show a little more. "What's the one song you wish you never had to sing again, and why?" Bane asked.

"If you really want to know, 'A Boy Named Sue,'" Cash replied. "It's a hard song to do right. It's an acting job. I have to play the father and the son, and you really have to be up for it. There was a live audience there when it was recorded. It was new. The laughs were spontaneous. Now everyone knows what's coming, so it's hard to get a real reaction. I still try to do it in every show."

19

Keep the Chilly Wind Off My Guitar

Columbia 1970

Musically speaking, the 1970s were an odd period for Johnny Cash. The decade started strongly, with the momentum of his late-1960s hits pushing him along. But somewhere in the middle, his interests and energies were directed elsewhere, and his music suffered. Then, toward the end of the decade, he began to rally. But as uneven as Cash's '70s output could be, the biggest problem—at least in the minds of many critics and fans—was simply that it wasn't his 1950s work. During this decade, Cash worked to grow as an artist, expanding his musical palette, incorporating new songwriters, and attempting to stay current among swiftly changing radio formats.

He was beginning to straighten out his personal life, too. On March 3, 1970, John Carter Cash was born, prompting Cash to lay off the pills for around eight years. He also returned to the big screen, co-starring with Kirk Douglas in a western entitled *A Gunfight.* The younger fans he had attracted grew a little critical of him when he appeared at the White House on April 17th, at the request of President Richard Nixon, but Cash made clear that he was appearing out of respect more for the office than the person, and he wasn't shy with his feelings as he performed. In November, Washington society columnist Betty Beale reported that First Lady Pat Nixon was surprised to learn that Cash had recorded his performance for possible release. According to Beale, after learning that the record would be called *Johnny Cash at the White House*—and would follow *At Folsom* and *At San Quentin*—Mrs. Nixon "took a dim view of that sequence and put a stop to it."

There were further voices of criticism when Cash appeared at his first Billy Graham Crusade on May 24th in Knoxville, Tennessee. He would continue to appear at Crusades with some regularity through the early 1990s (as detailed in chapter 49).

Hello, I'm Johnny Cash (1970)

With millions tuning in to ABC to see his show every week, Cash's profile was higher than ever. The title of his first album of the decade served as a reintroduction of sorts. David Vaught, writing in the *Village Voice*, said, "Despite [his] recent middle-class sellouts on Pepsi commercials and statements of Nixon support on network TV, Cash remains a country artist, deriving and absorbing his own music and writing from that of his own country background in Arkansas and from the many country writers and singers he has come to know in his years in the business. . . . 'Hello, I'm Johnny Cash,' his latest release, illustrates this in a return to the classic country of his earlier albums."

Here, instead of simply depending on songs other country artists had already recorded, as he had in the past, Cash draws on a variety of new songwriters (plus a couple of his old favorites). He also contributes four new songs of his own.

The album kicks off with his "Southwind," which tells the story of a man losing his girl to a train. This was the first session to feature new guitarist Bob Wootton, and fans would be hard pressed to notice much of a difference between Wootton's style and that of Luther Perkins. Overall, the major difference in sound between this and earlier albums is the increased presence of acoustic guitar and Dobro. The two acoustic guitars playing in harmony that open Cash's version of Merle Travis and Leon Rusk's "The Devil to Pay" bring a new dimension to his sound, as do the harmony vocals on the chorus.

The second of Cash's contributions, "'Cause I Love You," was the B-side of the album's second single, "If I Were a Carpenter." Acoustic guitar again leads the way as Johnny and June affirm that they will be there for each other throughout life's journey. The B-side of the first single ("Blistered") was a song Cash co-wrote with Roy Orbison called "See Ruby Fall." Inspired by signs they saw painted on barn roofs in Chattanooga urging travelers to visit the local attraction Ruby Falls, Cash and Orbison used the phrase to weave together the story of a love gone wrong. The singer knows his other half is on her way out of the door, so he lets her go, only to tell someone else where he can find her. It's classic country love-gone-wrong, covered up a bit by the almost ragtime piano that lessens the emotional impact of the song.

The next song is largely built on emotion. In 1970, the war in Vietnam was fully raging, and there was scarcely a family in the US that wasn't affected by it in some way. Well-known celebrities were no exception. Jimmy Howard, the son of singer and Cash family friend Jan Howard and songwriter Harlan Howard, had been drafted and was stationed in Vietnam. In 1968, Jan wrote a letter to him that she then turned into a recitation entitled "My Son." Two weeks after the release of the song, Jimmy was killed in action.

In 1969, Cash went to Vietnam to entertain the troops, and took the chance to talk to many of the men serving there. "Route #1, Box 144" was a reaction to his experiences of the war. "His dying barely made the morning paper," the song begins, before filling in the backstory of the kind of man who would give all he could to a fight he didn't start.

What follows is a melodic and catchy song about moving on written by a young songwriter who was also close to Cash, as he explained from the stage during a 1969 concert at Madison Square Garden (a recording of which was released in 2002). "One of the songs on the new album *Hello, I'm Johnny Cash* was written by a young man, fifteen years old, Kenny Jones, who was the son of Helen Carter," he announces. "We do this song tonight as a tribute to Kenny Jones who was killed in an automobile accident at the age of sixteen. And to give you an idea of the talents of this young man while he was with us, here was a song that he wrote when he was fourteen."

Another newer songwriter that Cash drew on was Tim Hardin, whose "If I Were a Carpenter" was the album's second single, and a song Bobby Darin took to #8 on the Pop chart in 1966. Cash's version—a duet with June—went to #2 on the Country chart and #36 on the Pop chart. The song also won the Grammy for Best Country & Western Vocal Performance, Duo Or Group, beating out records by the Statler Brothers, Waylon Jennings & Jessi Colter, Porter Wagoner & Dolly Parton, and Jack Blanchard & Misty Morgan.

Next, Cash takes on another Kristofferson tune, the story song "To Beat the Devil," which tells the tale of a guitar-picker who seeks shelter from the cold in a tavern. There, he encounters an old man who quickly points out that the singer isn't making any money with his guitar. The old man buys him a beer

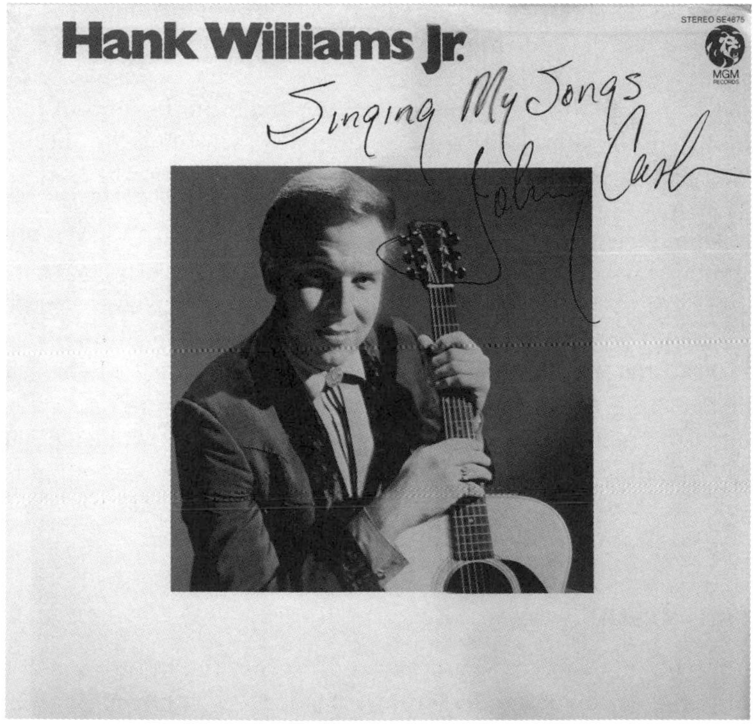

When he was younger, and performing his daddy's songs, Hank Williams Jr. toured with the Cash show occasionally. After he began to break away from his father's image, Jr. recorded a tribute to Cash featuring eleven of Cash's most popular songs from his Sun and early Columbia days. *Author's collection*

and borrows the guitar, singing him a chorus and then leaving. Before singing the same chorus, the singer tells us that while he isn't saying he beat the devil, he did drink his beer for nothing. On his 1970 debut album, Kris Kristofferson introduces the song by recalling:

> A couple of years back I come across a great and wasted friend of mine in the hallway of a recording studio. And while he was reciting some poetry to me that he had written, I saw that he was about a step away from dying and I couldn't help but wonder why. The lines of this song occurred to me. I'm happy to say he's no longer wasted and he's got him a good woman. I'd like to dedicate this to John and June who helped show me how to beat the devil.

The album's first single, the raucous "Blistered," came from Billy Edd Wheeler. It was something a little different than Cash's usual material—a little more carnal, with a beat that leaned more toward Ray Charles than Jimmie Rodgers. Another new songwriter that Cash called on was a discovery by Cowboy Jack Clement named Vince Matthews. Cash recorded "Wrinkled, Crinkled, Wadded Dollar Bill" for the album, and had Matthews guest on *The Johnny Cash Show* to sing "Melva's Wine," which Cash would also later record. He also recorded one of Clement's songs for the album, "I've Got a Thing About Trains."

Finally, in what would become something of a trend for him in the early '70s, Cash ends the album with a gospel song. For this album, he chose "Jesus Was a Carpenter," written by Christopher Wren, who was at the time writing Cash's life story.

The album was a great start to the new year, landing at #6 on the Pop charts among competition such as Miles Davis' *Bitches Brew*, the Beatles' *Let It Be*, Paul McCartney's *McCartney*, Jimi Hendrix's *Band of Gypsys*, the Jackson 5's *ABC*, and Van Morrison's *Moondance*. That made Cash one of four country-oriented acts to be on the Hot 100 at the time, the others being Glen Campbell, Merle Haggard, and Charley Pride. On the Country LPs chart, *Hello, I'm Johnny Cash* spent four weeks at #1 and a total of thirty-eight weeks on the listings (seventeen of those in the Top 5), fending off a slew of Sun releases containing various configurations of his hits and Columbia's own two-volume retrospective, *The World of Johnny Cash*. "Greedy bastards," Cash told Wren.

"What Is Truth"

As the '60s became the '70s, Cash was wildly successful, but for much of the rest of the country it was a different story. The US was still deeply entrenched in Vietnam, student protests were increasing and spreading across the country, and the divide between the working class and the idealistic youth seemed insurmountable. Cash saw evidence of this wherever he did shows—and sometimes within his own show.

"I was sitting around at a TV rehearsal watching the First Edition and really digging it," Cash told Christopher Wren. "Merle Travis said, 'They sure play funny music, don't they?' I decided to write a song with that."

With that idea still bumping around in his mind, Cash was visited in his Hendersonville home by the Reverend Billy Graham. Graham was searching for a way to reach his somewhat wayward teenage son, Franklin, whom he knew was a Cash fan, and hoped that connecting with Cash might help make the breakthrough. Graham felt that the music in the church was out of touch with what the youth were listening to, and he wanted to encourage Cash to write something that could fill that void.

"So he talked to me about myself and other song writers like Kris, who think along that line," Cash explained, in an interview with Peter McCabe and Jack Killion for *Country Music*, "and he kinda challenged me to challenge others, to try to use what talent we have to write something inspiring, that would inspire people to sit up and take notice of religion and Jesus. Well, the first thing that happened, the night after he left, I wrote 'What Is Truth.' Just him coming to the house inspired me to write that, if you want to call it inspiration."

"I'd read a book on Pontius Pilate and wanted to write a song on what is truth," Cash told Wren. "I got up at 6:30 and the wheels were still turning, so I made some coffee and sat and wrote the song. It just came real fast, as long as it takes me to write it down. . . . I felt it, and I thought about that line, 'what is truth?' and I thought about the youth of today, and a lot of them—not all of them—are searching for truth."

Merle Haggard had risen to superstardom in the late '60s, and closed out the decade with his controversial anthem "Okie from Muskogee," a song that poked fun at the hippie culture and, to many, spoke for the "silent majority." The song went to #1 on the Country charts as 1969 drew to a close and stayed there for four weeks. As it fell from the charts in 1970, Haggard released a follow-up, "The Fightin' Side of Me." While the two were aimed at the same audience—and the same targets—there was a stark difference between them.

"The most obvious difference was in tone," music critic David Cantwell notes in his 2013 book *Merle Haggard: The Running Kind*. "Where 'Okie' had condescended to any and all listeners, and done so with enough aw-shucks humor and good old-fashioned irony to leave it at least a slightly open question as to just who was being condescended to, 'The Fightin' Side of Me' addressed one audience by unambiguously laying into another. 'Okie' had been playful and at least partially in jest where 'Fightin' Side' sounded mad as hell."

Haggard performed both songs on the March 18th episode of *The Johnny Cash Show*, which was broadcast around the same time as "Fightin' Side" reached #1 for a three-week stay. Later in the same show, against a black background, standing in a single spotlight, Cash introduced a new song of his own:

> A few months ago, June and I were driving down Sunset Strip in Hollywood one Saturday night, and I commented to her about all the young people milling around in bunches—in groups of ten, twenty, then

> twos and threes and fours—walking up and down the sidewalk. Some people call these young people "hippies." Well, now, if that many young people had been out on the streets together back in my part of the country, say thirty years ago, damned if there wouldn't have been a fight every twenty feet. But those young people out there seem to be the nonviolent variety. They may look strange to us—the way they dress, they look strange to a lot of people—but a lot of them are wearing clothes that would have looked just right a few short years ago. And, you know, maybe they're trying to hold on to that part of our American heritage that they believe was good and beautiful. Now, granted, there will always be a few bad apples making the headlines, and violence in any form is destructive and should not be allowed. However, I do believe that most of our young people are good, and that all they desire is to be listened to. They're only exercising their freedom of speech, and God help you if that's ever taken away from 'em, America.

On October 21, 1970, during the fifth episode of the third season of the show, Cash performed the song again, but this time with a visual illustration of the message. Sitting in the dark, with only his guitar as accompaniment, Cash sings the first verse of the song and then stops as the Canadian group Guess

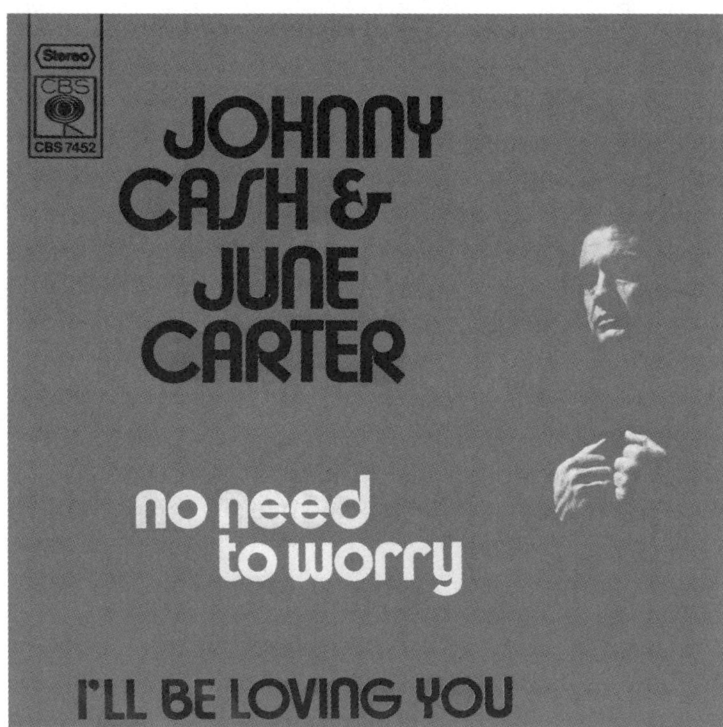

Johnny and June were a popular duet pairing in the era of great country duets like Porter Wagoner and Dolly Parton, Conway Twitty and Loretta Lynn, and George Jones and Tammy Wynette. *Private collection*

Who—with the Canadian flag draped over Burton Cummings' piano, and a psychedelic logo hanging behind them—launch into the first verse of "Hand Me Down World." Cash and the Guess Who then repeat for the second verse, with Cash laying out the questions and the youthful group answering back that they don't want the world as it is being left to them.

Cash had taken up the cause of Native Americans, the workingman, and prisoners. Now he was picking up the cause of another disenfranchised group: the youth of America. It was the first time in years that he had spoken out about a particular issue, though he still hesitated to label the song a "message song." That said, the song meant so much to Cash that he had originally written twelve verses for it, placing himself in the shoes of the youth he was deeply thinking about. He performed it three times on his TV show in 1970, and also performed it for President Nixon during his April 17th engagement at the White House. Less than a month later, Ohio national guardsmen opened fire on student protesters at Kent State University, killing four and sparking further campus protests around the country.

"What Is Truth" rose no higher than #19 on the Pop chart, but reached #3 on the Country chart.

A couple of years after Cash had a huge hit with Shel Silverstein's "A Boy Named Sue," Silverstein recorded this tribute featuring Cash himself. *Author's collection*

The Johnny Cash Show (1970)

With the popularity of *The Johnny Cash Show* on television, it made sense to release an album of performances taken from the show. Issued just as the second season began, the result was a perfect representation of the show: there's a song from a hot young songwriter, a new Cash song, two country classics, and two medleys taken from the "Come Along and Ride This Train" segment (one of Cash's favorite parts of the show, in which he combined a contemporary song and an old favorite, hooked together by a story or theme).

The first single was "Sunday Morning Coming Down," written by Kris Kristofferson, and a huge #1 hit for Cash (as discussed in chapter 29). It was backed with the Cash original "I'm Gonna Try to Be That Way," a declaration of his ambition to live a life that benefits those around him.

From the country classics Cash liked to feature on the show, he chose "These Hands," an Eddie Noack song Hank Snow had ridden to #5 in 1956, and the gospel album closer "Here Was a Man," written by Tex Ritter and Johnny Bond and recorded by Ritter in 1957. (By the time of the show's final season, it would include a segment dedicated to country classics performed by the original artist.)

The album, like the show, was a hit, reaching #1 on the Country LPs chart and #44 on the Pop chart.

Little Fauss and Big Halsey / I Walk the Line (1970)

Fans who couldn't get enough of the various albums Cash was releasing, or the television show, were in for a treat in late 1970/early '71, when he was featured on a pair of movie soundtracks.

The first was the soundtrack to the Robert Redford motorcycle movie *Little Fauss and Big Halsey*. The movie didn't make any real impact, but the soundtrack is full of great music, including the first studio recording of Bob Dylan's "Wanted Man." While the two songs Cash contributed—"Rollin' Free" and "The Little Man"—were good, the shining star of the album is Carl Perkins. Cash may have sung the theme, but Perkins wrote it, and his instrumental version, featuring his signature rockabilly licks, shows the song to be solid even without Cash's voice. There's also another solid instrumental, "7:06 Union," that's more in the Tennessee Three vein, and Cash voices another Perkins tune, "Movin'," begging the question of why he didn't pull more songs from Carl. Perhaps Perkins' greatest contribution to the album is "True Love Is Greater Than Friendship." Recorded without the Tennessee Three and featuring a swelling steel-guitar part, it shows the direction Perkins would head in when he left the Cash roadshow a few years later. Arlene Harden recorded the song for the single release, covering up most of the steel guitar with strings and vocal choruses, and the guitar with piano. Harden's version made it to #22 on the Country chart, though Perkins' version should have been the single.

I Walk the Line tells the story of a small-town sheriff and married man, played by Gregory Peck, who falls in love with a country girl, played by Tuesday Weld, only to find out later she is using him to protect her moonshine-making father and brother. All of the songs on the album, except the gospel closer, were written by Cash, including the single, "Flesh and Blood," which went to #1 Country and #54 Pop. The reworking of "I Walk the Line" included here lacks the power of the original, but is a step above the version included on the 1964 *I Walk the Line* LP. The version of "'Cause I Love You"—featuring only Cash and guitar—is an excellent take on the song.

Interestingly, both albums were recorded in October 1970 (*I Walk the Line* on the 8th and *Little Fauss and Big Halsey* on the 9th) and hark back to the Cash sound of the early-to-mid '60s rather than the sounds he would move toward in the '70s. These two albums also mark the end of Cash's work with producer Bob Johnston, a relationship that lasted seven albums, including three of the biggest of Cash's career. Johnston had been appointed Columbia's Nashville A&R director in 1967, but his brash style rubbed many in the country community the wrong way. Much of the resentment stemmed from the way Clive Davis had given the A&R role to Billy Sherrill and appointed Johnston "Executive Producer at Large," allowing him to keep working with Cash, as well as Marty Robbins, Bob Dylan, and Flatt & Scruggs. Ironically, it was a similar arrangement as was given to Don Law when he was ushered out the door to make room for Johnston.

20

A Cowboy Met a Fiery Carny Queen

Columbia 1971

The third season of *The Johnny Cash Show* premiered in September 1970 and ended the following March. In January 1971, midway through the run, it was announced that the format of the show was to change. In recent months, it had slipped to #63 in the weekly ratings, while *Hee Haw* sat at #23 and Glen Campbell's variety show was #31. According to Associated Press writer Jerry Buck, a major element of the change was that the show "strayed from its country music origins." This followed tweaks during the previous season that included centering each episode on a theme, among them a circus-themed episode that quite literally put Cash in the middle of a three-ring circus.

That same month, Cash made his way to Arizona to tape a new television special, *Johnny Cash: A Ballad of the West.* The special aired in February, and amounted to a tribute to the singing cowboys of old, hosted by Cash and his *A Gunfight* co-star Kirk Douglas and featuring Roy Rogers, Dale Evans, and the Over the Hill Gang, a group consisting of one-time cowboy sidekicks Walter Brennan, Edgar Buchanan, Andy Devine, and Chill Wills.

The Johnny Cash Show was canceled soon after the completion of its third season. Cash received the news as he toured Australia, and he was relieved in many ways. "Doing a weekly show for television is brutal," he told an AP reporter. "TV is a man-eater, it wears you out mentally and physically." Instead, he turned his energies to recordings, touring, and re-energizing his spiritual side (as detailed in chapter 49).

Man in Black (1971)

During the early '70s, a number of new, young songwriters were drawn to Cash, and he began signing them to his publishing company, House of Cash. This had two benefits. The first was that he would be first in line to see new, fresh songs. The second was that being around these young creatives inspired him to create as well. Both factors are in evidence on *Man in Black*: six of the ten songs came from Cash, and four came from newer writers.

The title track became the first and most successful single from the album, peaking at #3 Country and #58 on the Hot 100. The song put a personal spin on the message of "What Is Truth," retrofitting an ideology behind his choice in clothing. The B-side was a non-album track called "Little Bit of Yesterday," about the bitterness of breaking up a love affair.

While "Man in Black" wore its political overtones on its dark sleeve, the next single from the album was perhaps Cash's most political to date. "Singin' in Viet Nam Talkin' Blues" is about a trip Cash and his crew took to Vietnam to entertain the troops, detailing the "livin' hell" he witnessed, and ending with a hope that, if ever he is to return, it will be after the war is over, by which time all of "our boys" will be home and safe.

When asked by a journalist if he thought he was becoming a political radical, Cash answered, "No, I sure don't. I look at it the other way: I'm just tryin' to be a good Christian." Continuing in that line of thinking, Cash opens this album with an unlikely duet with Reverend Billy Graham. The song, "The Preacher Said, 'Jesus Said'," is like a religious sequel to "What Is Truth," with each of Cash's verses followed by Graham reading a series of lines of scripture about truth, love, heaven, and trouble.

"Orphan of the Road" was by one of Cash's newer writers, Dick Feller. Feller had been kicking around Nashville since 1966, playing guitar in various touring bands, though songwriting was his first love. Tex Williams had a minor hit with one of his songs, "The Night Miss Nancy Ann's Hotel for Single Girls Burned Down," which tells a funny story of a town's judgmental elite being exposed as hypocrites by a fire at the local whorehouse. The song's success led to a contract with House of Cash.

Cash himself contributed "You've Got a New Light Shining in Your Eyes," on which he sings about the glow surrounding his lover. The next track, "If Not for Love," feels like another autobiographical glimpse, but in fact came from the pens of Larry Lee and Glen D. Tubb. The song lists a series of circumstances—all ending badly—that Cash escapes thanks to the love of his woman. "Singin' in Viet Nam Talkin' Blues" comes next, and then, after Cash offers his take on a legend of Australian folklore on "Ned Kelly," that woman, June Carter Cash, makes an appearance on "Look for Me," written by Glen Sherley and Harlan Sanders, two ex-cons who knew where they would be without the helping hand extended them.

Inspired by stories Cash heard while performing his prison concerts, "Dear Mrs." is a recitation for solo acoustic guitar. The song is addressed to a woman who never came to visit her husband while he served his time, though he continues to proudly carry her picture. Finally, overwhelmed by the loneliness, he dies alone and is buried outside the prison walls. The narrator's intention is both to let the woman know her husband has died, and to let the listeners know of the dangers and loneliness of life behind bars.

As on his previous album, Cash closes proceedings with a gospel number, calling again on Glen D. Tubb for "I Talk to Jesus Every Day." Joined by June,

Cash sings of needing only to talk to Jesus, rather than wanting to be out trying to rub elbows with self-important people.

Man in Black was Cash's first self-produced album, and he opted to strip things back down to just the Tennessee Three, removing even the background voices of the Carter Family and the Statler Brothers. The sound is very much like his two preceding soundtrack-album releases, and the stark sound of the original band, much like it was on Cash's early (and often most-loved) sessions. It was, Cash wrote in the liner notes, "A product of change." Record buyers agreed with that change, and the album quickly rose to #1 on the Country chart, though it hovered around the middle of the Pop chart, peaking at #56.

"No Need to Worry" b/w "I'll Be Loving You"

Columbia released these two songs to radio in August to capitalize on the pairing of Johnny and June. The A-side is an up-tempo Southern gospel number written by J. S. Cooper and G. P. White, featuring June on harmony vocals and the Carter Sisters backing them up. It was another step towards the second audience Cash was cultivating in the area of Christian events. In the secular arena, the song made it to #15 on the Country chart. The flip side, by Cash, is another declaration of love and devotion, written during the cleanest stretch of his life, and just before he and his wife welcomed their son John Carter Cash to the family.

21

Stay Away from Crazy Horse

Columbia 1972

In 1971, Johnny Cash had recommitted his life to God, and by 1972 he was devoting more time to Billy Graham's Crusades and pursuits like finishing the epic labor of love *The Gospel Road*, his story of the life of Christ. The movie made its debut in October 1972, with a double-album soundtrack following in 1973.

This year also saw a change of management, with Saul Holiff resigning and Lou Robin, who had been Cash's booking agent, taking over the position (one he continued to hold until Cash's passing).

A Thing Called Love (1972)

Despite making a strong debut as producer on *Man in Black*, Cash turned over the reins to Larry Butler for his next album. Butler—who was producing acts on Capitol, Columbia, and the short-lived Opryland label, working with artists like Ferlin Husky and Jean Shepard, among others—had been encouraged to get together with Cash by Columbia's new Nashville A&R man, Billy Sherrill. It proved to be a good relationship, with Butler not only signing on as Cash's producer but also taking the role of studio and touring pianist. Butler's first sessions with Cash, in December 1970, were for what would become *America: A 200-Year Salute in Story and Song* (discussed in chapter 13). He then returned to the producer's chair on May 18, 1971, to begin work on *A Thing Called Love.*

Cash contributed four of the album's ten songs, drawing on a mix of hit songwriters and up-and-comers for the remainder. "Kate," the opening track and the third single released from the album, was written by superstar Marty Robbins. *Billboard* noted that Cash had "gone back to prison songs" with this tale of a man imprisoned for shooting his girl but continuing to blame her for it because she had been cheating on him. The song's up-tempo beat took it to #2 on the Country chart and #75 on the Pop chart, while also winning Robbins a BMI Award.

"Melva's Wine" came from the pen of a new songwriter, Vince Matthews, while the album's title track was by veteran music guy Jerry Reed Hubbard,

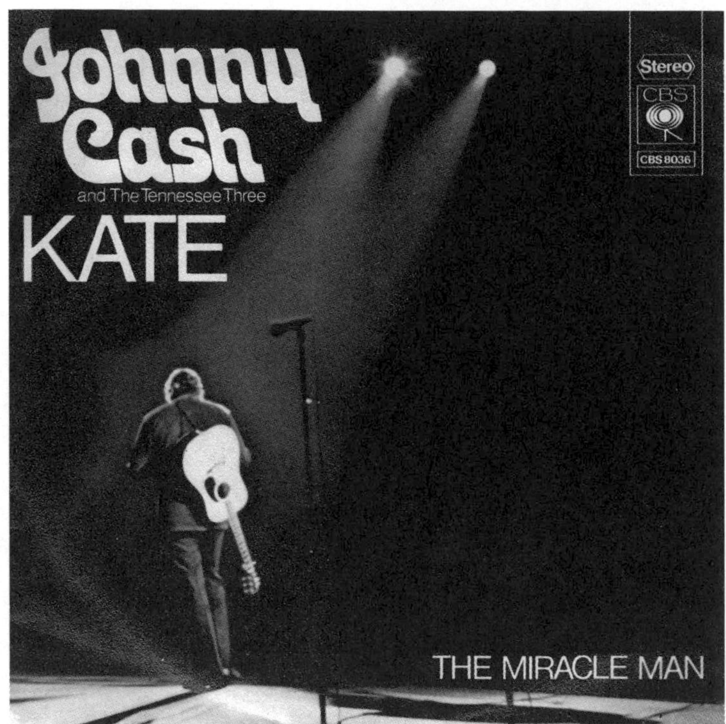

Written by Marty Robbins, Cash took "Kate" to #2 on the country charts.
Private collection

better known as Jerry Reed. Reed had been recording for several years with modest success before hitting a hot streak in 1971, when he took "Amos Moses" and "When You're Hot, You're Hot" to the Pop Top 10. "A Thing Called Love" was released as the second single from the album, with *Billboard* predicting similar success for Cash: "Jerry Reed's infectious rhythm number serves as potent pop-country material for Cash. Will hit heavy in both areas." But while the song did reach #2 on the Country chart, it spent only one week, at #103, on the Pop chart.

"I Promise You," one of the Cash-penned tunes and the B-side of the album's first single, is a promise of devotion to June. The message is sweet, but the whole thing comes off a little schmaltzy, and it's not on par with the other songs on the album. The A-side of the single, "Papa Was a Good Man," is by songwriter Hal Bynum, who had written some songs for Ernest Tubb (under the name Hap Howell) and would go on to co-write the huge Kenny Rogers hit "Lucille" in the late 1970s. "Papa" is told from the perspective of a son whose father is struggling with alcoholism. It was the lowest charting of the three releases from the album, peaking at #16 Country and #104 Pop. It featured additional vocals from the choir of the Evangel Temple, the Nashville church Cash was now attending, pushing the song close to the point of overproduction.

In stark contrast, Cash's "Tear Stained Letter" starts with only guitar, bass, and voice. It is a strong song that shows that Cash is still a songwriter at heart. He uses strings to sweeten the sound and add an extra dimension, but the overall effect is much more subtle than the overblown "Papa." It's followed by a song from June's pen, "Mississippi Sand," about the hard times of growing up.

"Daddy," written by Don and Harold Reid of the Statler Brothers, is a sentimental remembrance of a father who has passed on "just two days before." "Arkansas Lovin' Man" is by Red Lane, who had written several hits for others, including Merle Haggard. It finds Cash in a playful mood, delivering the slow rocking number with a wink.

Once again, the final song on the album is a gospel one, co-written this time by Johnny and House of Cash writer Larry Lee. "The Miracle Man" tries to put into perspective our troubles by comparing them to those Jesus endured. Cash sings with conviction, accompanied only by Butler's piano and the Carter Sisters' soft vocal chorus.

Billboard noted that the album had "all the ingredients of a top seller," predicting "this entry will be an instant addition to both the country and pop charts" and noting specifically the appeal of "The Miracle Man" and "Papa Was a Good Man." The magazine was half right, with the album hitting #2 on the Country chart and staying there for five weeks (plus an additional five at #3), but it never made the Pop Albums chart, merely bubbling under at #112.

22

I'm Doin' All Right for Country Trash

Columbia 1973

Johnny Cash's biggest accomplishment of 1973 was the wide release of *The Gospel Road*, a project he had poured a lot of time, energy, and money into (and which is discussed further in chapter 49). That aside, he continued to tour on a regular basis, though this time out, as of February, he disbanded the Roadshow. "John wants to go back to performing as he was with June and the Tennessee Three," his sister, Reba Hancock, told *Country Music*. "He's been with the Statlers, the Carter Family and Carl [Perkins], and sometimes an additional act, for eight years. When you carry a show of that magnitude, you have to play larger houses. John wants to go back to the little towns like Joplin, Missouri, and Mark Tree, Arkansas, and be with the people."

On the recorded-music front, Cash released three albums in 1973, including the soundtrack to *The Gospel Road*.

Any Old Wind That Blows (1973)

Before 1972 was out, Columbia began releasing singles from Cash's next album, which was set for release early in 1973. The first single drawn from the album, "If I Had a Hammer," features harmony vocals by June. It was co-written by Cash favorite Pete Seeger and originally recorded by Seeger's 1950s group the Weavers. Johnny and June's version rocks harder than the original (and most of the other many versions that followed), propelled by Carl Perkins and Bob Wootton's hot guitars and punctuated by Perkins' stuttering solo. Peter, Paul & Mary took the song to #10 on the Pop chart in 1962, while Trini Lopez had a #3 hit with it in 1963, but Cash's version couldn't replicate that success, never even touching the Pop chart. It fared little better on the Country chart, topping out at #29, making it Cash's lowest-charting single in some time. The B-side was the non-album track "I Gotta Boy and His Name Is John," a playful song about Cash's newborn performed with June, who was able to bring out some of her comedic chops on record. It would later turn up on *The Johnny Cash Children's Album*.

Cash's tribute to the working man, "Oney" found Cash playing the part of a disgruntled factory worker with glee and precision. *Private collection*

"Oney" was a song dedicated to the workingman—"any man that puts in eight or ten hard hours a day," Cash sings. The narrator is set to retire, and recalls the torment handed down to him daily by his supervisor, Oney, who feels that his pushing is what has caused the man to rise to the occasion. On his last day of work, he looks forward to giving Oney what he's got coming to him, calling out as the song fades, "Oney? Oooney?" This tale of knocking out the boss struck a nerve with listeners, who pushed it up to #2 Country for two weeks, though it dropped off the charts within two weeks of that peak and barely scrapped the Pop charts at #103. The anthemic "Country Trash"—a loping list of the high points of country living—served as the flip.

As winter set in, Cash released his next single, "Any Old Wind That Blows," written by Dick Feller, who Cash predicted was "going to be a big artist," adding, "I think as long as people like him keep coming along, country music's got a great future." The song seemed custom-fit for Cash, with a catchy melody that takes advantage of every nuance of his voice. As with many of the songs on the resulting album, it features a full orchestral backing that complements both the song and Cash's vocal. It hit #3 on the Country chart. The B-side, written by Cash, was "Kentucky Straight," in which he compares his partner to the best Kentucky Straight Bourbon.

A fourth single was released to close out the year, with both sides written by Kris Kristofferson and featuring June. "The Loving Gift," which only made it to #27, has Johnny and June publicly thanking each other for the gifts they have given each other throughout their life together. "Help Me Make It Through the Night" served as the flip side, though it lacks the intensity or loneliness of the 1971 #1 version by Sammi Smith or the 1980 version by Willie Nelson.

By the time the album was released, six of the album's eleven tracks had been issued as either A- or B-sides—an unprecedented number for Cash. He already had a Christmas album in the can, as well as *America*, and had spent the bulk of his 1972 studio time working on his ambitious *Gospel Road* album and film. Nonetheless, the rest of *Any Old Wind That Blows* stands up well among the songs selected as singles.

"Good Earth" was written by another new Cash discovery, Larry Gatlin, a young songwriter and singer who also contributed songs to *The Gospel Road* and went on to a long career as a singer, scoring several hits both solo and as Larry Gatlin & the Gatlin Brothers. Cash also recorded songs written by old friends, such as Roy Orbison's 1967 "Best Friend." "Roy Orbison wrote a song called 'My Best Friend,'" he told Anthony DeCurtis in 2002, "and there's a line in there that says, 'A diamond is a diamond / And a stone is a stone / But man is part good / And part bad.' I've always believed that the good will ultimately prevail, but there's a bad side of us that we have to keep warring against. I know I do."

During this period, Cash began making frequent trips to Jamaica, eventually buying a family home there. On one of those trips, he wrote "The Ballad of Annie Palmer," based on local stories of a woman who was said to have killed three husbands and several male slaves before being murdered by a slave. Two further Cash originals round out the album: "Too Little, Too Late," the story of a man whose girl expresses regret after having left him, and "Welcome Back Jesus," a personal song of rededication.

Producer Larry Butler struck a nice musical balance on the album, as noted in a *Country Music* review by Robert Mitchell, for whom *Any Wind* was "really two albums on one disc. The first view we have of Johnny is the essence of 'The Man in Black' in the presence of a full orchestra. Neither party intimidates the other. There is an almost divine sense of cooperation between banjo and soft violin, between the full arrangement and Johnny's singular talent to always seem as if he were doing a one-man show."

Though the album only flirted with the Pop chart, stalling at #188, it reached #5 on the Country chart, serving as an excellent start to 1973.

Johnny Cash and His Woman (1973)

Nineteen seventy-three was largely dominated by *The Gospel Road*, with the Cashes spending much of their time promoting the album/film project. A new single unrelated to it was released in the middle of the year, though no one seemed to notice. "Praise the Lord and Pass the Soup," written by Albert

Hammond and Michael Hazelwood, is one of those odd little entries in the Cash catalogue. Against a backdrop of funky piano and wah-wah-like guitar, Cash extols the virtues of the local soup kitchen, accompanied by the gospel shouts and harmonies of the Oak Ridge Boys and the Carter Sisters. The B-side—a 180-degree turn from the A-side—was "The Ballad of Barbara," Cash's rewrite of the old English ballad "Barbara Allen." Few noticed the single as it crept from #85 to #57 across seven weeks and then dropped immediately off the chart.

The single was followed by a new album of duets entitled *Johnny Cash and His Woman.* It opens with "The Color of Love," one of two songs by Billy Edd Wheeler, writer of "Blistered" and "Jackson," and finds Cash in fine form, while June careens quite freely through the melody. Cash then flies solo on the self-penned "Saturday Night in Hickman County," a gentle song describing a typical night out in Tennessee.

One side of the only single released from the album was "Allegheny," written by one of Cash's young songwriting friends, Chris Gantry, who recalls:

> A lot of my songs start with a guitar sound and I had tuned my guitar down into C tuning, which is a very low tuning for a guitar. But it makes a beautiful sound. I started experimenting with that tuning and trying to write some songs on it. That song just fell out of me, out of the blue, because of the way the guitar sounded. It evoked a feeling and an attitude, and me being a writer, I just kind of received what was coming in to my head and wrote it down. That song fell out in about half an hour.
>
> Myself, [Kris] Kristofferson, and Shel Silverstein were all out at John's house, and we were all playing him new songs. We had dinner—June made a big dinner, John Carter was a little boy—and after dinner we all went in the other room and played songs. I played "Allegheny," and it just knocked him out. It's funny, somebody took a picture of the four of us, and it's in John Carter's coffee-table book about his Dad [*House of Cash: The Legacies of My Father, Johnny Cash*].

Cash sounds like he is having a good time on the song, while June whoops and hollers in the background before coming in perfectly as the wild woman her husband is singing about. But despite the impassioned performance, "Allegheny" reached a high of only #69 on the Country chart.

Cash then turns in a fine performance of "Life's Little Ups and Downs," written by Margaret Ann Rich and previously recorded by her then-husband Charlie Rich in 1969. As if to prove the staying power of the sentiment behind the song, Ricky Van Shelton took it to #4 in 1991.

Cash's "Matthew 24 (Is Knocking at the Door)" is his summation of the "end times" prophesized in the Gospel according to Matthew, making it, with "The Man Comes Around," from *American IV,* one of Cash's most apocalyptic songs. It's followed by Steve Goodman's "City of New Orleans," a train song on which Cash sounds very much at home. Goodman's Kris Kristofferson–produced version had been released in 1971, followed by Arlo Guthrie's #18 Pop version in 1972. Cash's version was inexplicably never released as a single, although it is one of the strongest performances on the album. (Ten years later, Cash's buddy Willie Nelson took the song to #1 on the Country chart.)

Accompanied only by his guitar, Cash turns in another riveting performance on "Tony," written, along with album closer "Godshine," by David "Cuz" Powers, a prisoner at San Quentin. Between those two tunes rests a second Billy Edd Wheeler composition, "The Pine Tree," which compares love to the flexibility and strength of a giant pine tree, and "We're for Love," co-written by Cash's sister Reba Hancock. The latter song was chosen as the single from the album, though it didn't touch either chart.

Johnny Cash and His Woman marked the return of producer Don Law, who had helmed many of Cash's earlier successes, and was released to positive press coverage. In a "Spotlight" review, *Billboard* said, "Every now and then one of those albums comes along in which every single cut is outstanding. This is one of those rarities. Johnny and June have that empathy, to put it mildly, and here they have the material and the great production work." *Country Music* echoed the sentiment, with Robert Adels asking, "Tell the truth. When was the last time an album hit you over the head with the effect of a carefully wielded two-by-four? Well, that's what it's like listening to this LP for the first time . . . this record jumps out at you. Then it tones down to unravel a series of documentary-type sagas which cannot help but keep your undivided attention."

Wrapping Up a Good Year

Though the album was a critical success, it peaked at #36 on the Hot Country LPs chart and produced only one non-charting single. Around the same time, Cash released two non-album singles, the first of which featured Mother Maybelle Carter on both sides. "Pick the Wildwood Flower," written by Joe Allen, tells the story of a young man leaving home with his guitar and pausing to play the Carter Family's signature tune "Wildwood Flower" whenever he gets the chance. Just as it seems to be coming to an end, Maybelle speaks up, instructing him to "Play it like this, son," and laying down her trademark guitar style. The other side of the single pairs Johnny and Maybelle on the Carter Family song "Diamonds in the Rough." Neither side stirred much interest, with "Wildwood" reaching only #34 on the Country chart.

In time for Christmas, Cash teamed up with his brother Tommy for "That Christmassy Feeling," backed by a solo recitation of "Christmas as I Knew It," by Jan Howard and June Carter. Both songs offered reminiscence of childhood Christmas activities and family, but listeners seemed to take little notice.

In October 1972, Cash had recorded another prison album in Österåker, Sweden (detailed in chapter 16). Columbia opted to release the album only in Sweden, but did pull a single from it in 1973: "Orleans Parrish Prison" b/w "Jacob Green." It was another minor success, lingering on the Country charts for nearly two months and peaking at #52.

23

I Like My Honey from the Hives of Home

Columbia 1974

Johnny Cash toured consistently throughout the early 1970s, but his television appearances had been sporadic since his weekly ABC television show ended in 1971, with only one special to his name. Then, in 1974, he jumped back in with both feet.

First up was a late-night showcase for NBC called *Johnny Cash's Country Music*, which aired on Sunday, February 24th. The ninety-minute show featured performances by Johnny, June, the Carter Family (Mother Maybelle, Anita, Helen, and Lorrie Davis, daughter of Anita and steel guitarist Don Davis), the Statler Brothers, Tommy Cash, Tanya Tucker, Bill Monroe & His Blue Grass Boys, Larry Gatlin, Carl Perkins, and Brush Arbor.

On April 26th, Cash hosted another NBC special, *Country Comes Home*. In March, the *Grand Ole Opry* had moved from its longtime home at the Ryman Auditorium to the newly built Grand Ole Opry House, and this was celebration of the move, featuring performances by Chet Atkins, Tennessee Ernie Ford, Tom T. Hall, Dolly Parton, Charlie Rich, and Opry staples Roy Acuff, Ernest Tubb, Minnie Pearl, and Porter Wagoner.

Cash also made an appearance on *Columbo*, starring as a country singer caught in a murder mystery, and on *Sesame Street*, for which his guest spot was spread over two episodes. But the project with which he became most deeply involved was *Johnny Cash: Ridin' the Rails—The Great American Train Story*. Shooting for the film took place in twelve locations across the US throughout the summer and fall, with the results airing on November 22nd on ABC.

The purpose of the documentary-style show was more than just to showcase pivotal moments in US history that involved trains—though it certainly did that, too. "We hope to show how the railroads helped to build America," producer Nick Webster told Fae Cline Carroll. "We need to re-evaluate America. We want to show the promise that the future holds."

For the producers, Webster and Dyann Rivkin, Cash was the perfect host. "Johnny is a figure that fits into any period of history and in this he is, in our eyes, in a part of history as we might have seen in it around 1830," Rivkin told

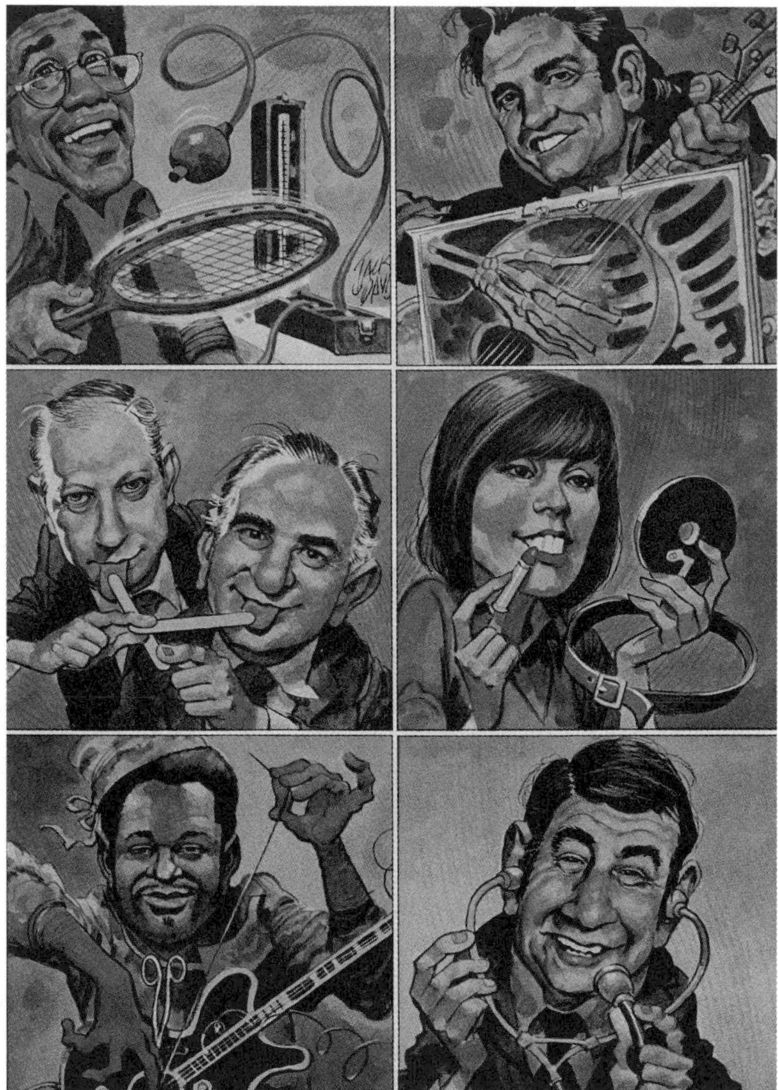

Beginning in November of 1974, PBS aired *Feeling Good*, a show featuring various guests and focusing on health and well-being. Cash appeared on the first episode and discussed mental health. He sang "Helping Hands."

Author's collection

Carroll, referring to one location shoot that told the story of James J. Andrews' theft of a Confederate train, the General.

Cash himself told reporter Sidney C. Schaer that he tried not to travel by airplane or the interstate highway system as he moved around the US, preferring to go via routes that would connect him with more people. "I think what I'm trying to do by getting off the interstates and airplanes is to get back to some roots," he said. "We need to slow down and live a little more in the country. I guess that's why I have such a feeling for trains. It represents a slower pace, it represents a kind of freedom."

Ragged Old Flag (1974)

In the mid-'70s, Cash stood at a cultural precipice. Except for a few sporadic appearances on shows like *The Tonight Show* and comedian Flip Wilson's variety show *Flip*, he had pulled back a little from the televised public eye, and had left longtime fans wondering about his direction as he continued to pull in young songwriters and give their revolutionary songs a platform. But the generation that had embraced him after his smash prison albums—and whom he had once championed—remained skeptical of Cash because of his public support of President Nixon, the object of much of their venom.

Maybe he wasn't so much standing on *a* precipice as straddling on the one representing the growing generation gap, looking down from there to everyone else. He was the wild-eyed Memphis guy who shook up the country charts with his sparse arrangements and songs that didn't chirp along with illusions of perfect love. He was the man who stood alongside presidents with no fear to tell them what he thought should be happening in our prisons—even our country. Here, on the cover of his new album, he stood before all of the people—young and old, country music fans and rock 'n' roll fans—pointing at a ripped and torn American flag. No words were required; the look on his face said it all: "I don't give a damn who you are or where you come from—by God, we're all Americans."

The title track, and the album's only single, was not presented in the spirit of Haggard's "Fightin' Side," with its directive to "love it or leave it." "I wrote 'Ragged Old Flag' to remind myself of how many and how often this country's been involved in wars," Cash said in 1987. "It seems to me like the politicians and the military just can't wait for another one. And that really bothers me."

The recitation was recorded live at a Columbia luncheon; after it received the ovation that remains on the record, Cash took it into the studio, where the orchestration and Earl Scruggs' banjo were added. The message was clear: the flag, the concept of being an American at that time, was in all of us. But this wasn't a song you'd put on again and again and listening to over and over, and that was reflected on the charts, where it reached only #31 Country.

The flip side of the single didn't even chart (as many of Cash's previous B-sides had). If some listeners—especially those in younger age groups—might have found "Ragged Old Flag" jingoistic, "Don't Go Near the Water" takes to task those in the older group who don't believe the concerns being raised by environmental movements. "See the fish all dead upon the shore?" Cash asks, before lamenting that he won't even be able to enjoy taking his young son fishing the way he used to, because they wouldn't be able to eat their catch for fear of what toxins the fish might contain.

In the liner notes, Cash writes, "I got so excited writing the songs in this album that you'd think I just started in the music business. It's something I always wanted to do, write an album of all my own songs and for some reason, I just never got around to it. One reason, I suppose, is that I have so many friends that are good songwriters and their songs just kept coming along."

Cash also co-produced the album, alongside engineer Charlie Bragg, and as on *Man in Black* he takes the sound back to the bare essentials, with the Tennessee Three, Carl Perkins and session ace Ray Edington adding some guitar, a little piano supplied by Larry McCoy, and the occasional vocal support of the Oak Ridge Boys, brought in to fill the void left by the departure of the Statler Brothers, whose own careers had started to explode.

Dave Dudley and Red Sovine had made huge career gains in the early '70s with truck-driving songs, and a little more than a year after *Ragged Old Flag*, "Convoy" and the CB radio craze would sweep the nation, catching even Kris Kristofferson, who starred in the movie adaptation of the song in 1978. With "All I Do Is Drive," Cash plants his tongue in his cheek to sing about those songs glamorizing the trucker's life, to which the truck solemnly replies, "All I do is drive."

That wry humor carries over into "Southern Comfort," the story of a man who is trying to survive life in Nashville, but with little to look forward to save for his job making snuff at a tobacco plant. He finally meets a woman, but she soon tires of "tobacco, at least the regular kind," and leaves him to "grow her own" in Sumner County.

"King of the Hill" takes Cash back to his cotton-picking and coal-mining songs, while "Pie in the Sky" finds him longing to leave the toil of earth for the escape of Heaven. "Lonesome to the Bone" is sang from the point of view of a homeless man warmed only by the memory of someone who once loved him.

The humor returns in "While I Got It on My Mind," an ode to sex in marriage, and perhaps Cash's most innuendo-laden song. "I like my honey from the hives of home," he sings, "and berries from my own vine."

"Good Morning Friend" is a testimony of Cash's life since he rededicated it to God, and the second of three gospel songs on the album. The last of these is the album closer, "What on Earth Will You Do (for Heaven's Sake)," an exhortation on how sitting around simply waiting to die won't help the cause.

June joins proceedings for the bouncy "I'm a Worried Man," with Cash later recalling the writing of the song during his 1998 appearance with Willie Nelson on VH1's *Storytellers*:

> I was walking along the streets of Falmouth [Jamaica] one day and this bum came up. He said—he recognized me—he said, "Mr. Cash, I'm a worried man, I'm a very worried man." I thought, here's a new approach—I've never had this one before. I said, "OK, what are you

worried about?" He said, "I've got a wife and nine kids, and no job. That's makes me a worried man." So after I left him, on the way back to our home, I wrote ["I'm a Worried Man"].

The next song, "Don't Let Me Out," tells of a prisoner who has been granted parole but, having spent eleven years behind bars, doesn't really want to be released into the wide world. It's a song that displays the nuanced qualities of Cash's writing, as listening to the verse can bring an amused smile—until the words sink in fully, and the truth is heard.

The title track aside, *Ragged Old Flag* represented a return to form for Cash, here reaching back to his Sun days and forward to his future as a musical icon. It is the work of a man standing firm in the knowledge that he was releasing the music he wanted to release, how he wanted to release it. The country-music world of the time was in the midst of big changes. When the album reached its

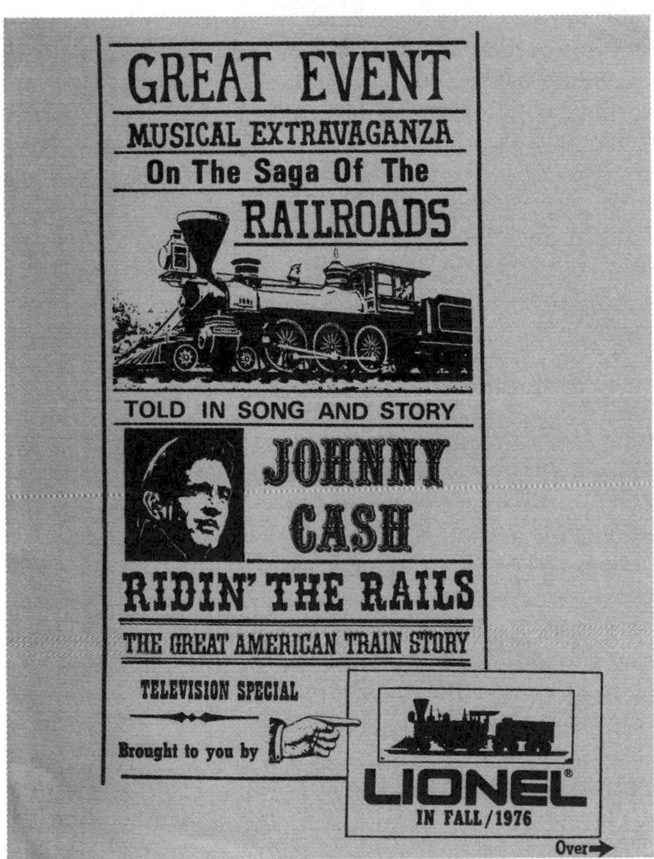

Originally shot and aired in 1974, Lionel Trains sponsored a rebroadcast of Cash's documentary *Ridin' the Rails* in 1976.

Author's collection

peak of #16 on the Country chart, the slots above it were filled with pop-country amalgams by acts like Olivia Newton-John (who held the #1 and #11 spots), Cash's fellow Memphis refugee Charlie Rich (who mixed in elements of soul with his pop-country, and held #2, #3, #4, and #6), Freddie Hart, Ronnie Milsap, and Mac Davis. Loretta Lynn and Conway Twitty served as the only representatives of an older style of country (though often with their own blend of pop).

In among them all stood Cash's old pal Waylon Jennings, with *This Time*, an album he co-produced with Willie Nelson. In 1972, Waylon had turned up the heat in his fight for independence in the Nashville system, while Willie headed for the higher ground of Texas. A year later, Nelson released his laid-back *Shotgun Willie*, while Jennings made two albums, *Lonesome, On'ry & Mean* and *Honky Tonk Heroes*, the second of them being the record many point to as the start of the "outlaw country" movement.

As they are wont to do, record labels followed suit with pseudo-outlaws in an attempt to match that initial success. Cash couldn't help but notice the success his friend Waylon was having—a success he had achieved essentially by following the blueprint drawn by Cash. It also couldn't have escaped his view that, even without charting, Willie had managed to connect with the younger generations—and, with the help of Cash friends like Waylon and Larry Gatlin, among several others, was able to draw 100,000 fans to a field in College Station, Texas.

Even with all of the changes going on around him, though, Cash stayed true to his vision of honest music that drew from the folk and country traditions, which he would continue to follow, with very little variation in theme or instrumentation, for the rest of his career.

The Junkie and the Juicehead Minus Me (1974)

Cash remained completely clean until late 1976, his priorities in life being his wife, his God, and his children. He lived with tremendous guilt for leaving his four daughters with Vivian at the time, and in the manner, that he did. John Carter's birth was the spark that got him to clean out his system and devote his time to his family.

Kicking things off with a Kris Kristofferson song, "The Junkie and the Juicehead (Minus Me)," Cash set out to build a record that showcased his family, namely June, daughter Rosanne, and stepdaughters Rosey and Carlene. The title track is, as the *Country Music* review put it, a "slice of low-life, abounding in moral and brittle-clever lines that made Kristofferson's reputation." That may be true, but the single version didn't even get to the charts.

Also included on the album is a wholly unnecessary take on "Don't Take Your Guns to Town" that does nothing to improve on the original. The public likely agreed, as it too failed to chart when released as a single. Luckily, it is followed by another Kristofferson song, "Broken Freedom Song," here performed by Rosanne, making her recording debut. The marked difference with this track is that it doesn't utilize the Tennessee Three (augmented elsewhere on the album by Gordon Terry on fiddle and Larry McCoy on piano), but rather an entirely different group of musicians, including Elvis' drummer D. J. Fontana, session guitarists Randy Scruggs and Jerry Shook, piano by Jerry Whitehurst, and the sinewy steel guitar of Stu Basore. Rosanne does a good job with the song, but her voice is a shadow of what it would become by the time of her 1981 breakthrough album *Seven Year Ache*.

After that, Cash contributes a song and solo performance on the broken-hearted "I Do Believe." June swings in next with the old-timey "Ole Slewfoot," based on Marjorie Kinnan Rawlings' 1938 novel *The Yearling*, which becomes a Cash family sing-along when, after Johnny sings the hook of the first chorus ("Some folks say he looks a lot like me"), the girls join in the second time around to yell, "Looks a lot like Daddy!" The whole group continues in the same vein on the Carter Family staple "Keep on the Sunny Side," before Rosey Nix makes her recording debut with a spin on the Cat Stevens 1970 hit "Father and Son," here retitled "Father and Daughter (Father and Son)," in which a father seeks to understand his child's desire to rush out into the world, to which his daughter explains that it is simply something that has to be done.

The album also includes three songs by Jack Routh, who had moved to Nashville in 1973 to pursue songwriting, and soon made his way to Cash's Hendersonville office. Cash's sister Joanne told him Johnny wasn't in but that Jack might be able to catch him at a local revival service that evening. Cash didn't turn up, but Routh was undeterred. He returned to Hendersonville the next day, but this time went straight to Cash's home rather than the office. Seeing Cash working in the yard, Routh stopped and approached the fence. When Cash noticed him, Routh said he wanted to play some songs for him. Cash told him he would be glad to listen, and to just leave a tape at the office. Routh said he would rather sing them to him in person. Impressed by the man's moxie, Cash told him he would need thirty minutes to clean up, and then they could go over to the office. Once they got there, Cash listened to a few songs and immediately signed Routh to an exclusive contract.

"To be signed by Johnny Cash is a real treat," Routh says. "But to have him record something was beyond words. If it was the last I ever did, it was all I needed. He was into my writing, and into helping me develop and was real generous with his time."

Routh has three songs on *The Junkie*: "Crystal Chandeliers and Burgundy," "Friendly Gates," and the closer, "Lay Back with My Woman." The second of these is sung by his wife, Cash's stepdaughter Carlene (credited in the liner notes as Carlene Smith). It's a decent enough performance, but much like Rosanne's turn earlier on, Carlene's voice is not as strong as it would be by the time of her 1978 self-titled debut.

Elsewhere, borrowing liberally from the melody from Billy Joe Shaver's "Willie the Wandering Gypsy and Me," Cash wrote a tribute to the leading evangelists of the time, "Billy & Rex & Oral & Bob." Then, in a tribute to the real object of his worship, Cash, joined by his wife, gives a spirited reading of Loney Hutchins' "Jesus."

Though the singles from the album didn't chart, the album itself did, briefly, for the month of November, peaking at #48 on the Country LPs listing.

24

All of My Songs Remain Unsung

Columbia 1975

As the '70s reached their midpoint, Cash's career hit a plateau. While he was still a revered figure in the entertainment world, his albums had begun to slide in popularity, and would barely see any chart action. That August, he told Patrick Carr:

> It's not that I'm frantically groping around for a hit. I'm not. Everything that I have released, I was proud of it at the time I released it. It was exactly what I thought I should release—but the public has a way of proving you wrong, you know. If they don't want it, they ain't going to buy it, and you don't try to cram it down their throats. You haven't seen a lot of big ads run by Columbia Records or anyone else on my latest product, and maybe they shouldn't have run big ads. Maybe they knew it wasn't what I should put out, and maybe I didn't know. But when I made a mistake I always knew it. I didn't make the same mistake twice. I made a lot of *different* mistakes, which is a good thing to do, because I know not to make *them* anymore, see.

Unfortunately for Cash—and, perhaps, his fans—a few more mistakes, or at least missteps, awaited in the second half of the decade. To start the year, Cash released two pet projects: another album of hymns, *Sings Precious Memories*, that had been recorded over two June days in 1974, and a children's album.

In August, the large religious publishing house Zondervan released Cash's first autobiography, *The Man in Black.* Writing with the Christian market strongly in mind, Cash put a religious slant on nearly every event in his life up to that point, though he doesn't hide his addiction or its consequences. Some of the stories in the book show him at his worst (while building up to his eventual redemption). He dedicated the book to his father-in-law, Ezra "Pop" Carter, who died on January 22, 1975.

The Johnny Cash Children's Album (1975)

Being a parent changes a person, and it was no different for Cash. Even though he was already the father of four daughters and the stepfather to two others, it was the birth of his son in 1970—at a time when his girls were all approaching their teenage years—that solidified it all for him.

"John Carter kind of brought him together as a family man, and he was really enjoying doing that," says Jack Routh. "He was starting to approach his career and making decision around his son. He was offered huge sums of money to go play the Fourth of July, but he'd turn it down so he could spend it with his kids, which was great, he loved it."

Cash started recording songs for a children's album in August 1971, continuing sporadically until October 1973. The album showcases a side of Cash that many never knew: his playful, silly side. Story songs, like "Nasty Dan," "Tiger Whitehead," and "(The) Timber Man," sit alongside silly songs like "One and One Makes Two" and "Dinosaur Song." Cash also included a couple of sentimental songs, "Little Magic Glasses" and "Miss Tara," which he wrote for his daughter when she was twelve. He also recorded a version of "Old Shep," first performed by Red Foley (who wrote it) and later recorded, in 1956, by Elvis Presley, which was a sad choice of song for a children's album since it is about the death of a beloved family dog.

The Johnny Cash Children's Album never reached the charts, but the reviews were positive. In his review for *Country Music*, Jerry Liechtling called it "very competent and entertaining and a good gift for the kids or anyone else. Johnny Cash is like a force of nature, too good and too strong to ever turn out really bad records."

The album was rereleased as part of a spate of Cash reissues in 2006, adding four extra tracks that had been recorded for the original LP but not included on it: "There's a Bear in the Woods," "Ah Bos Cee Dah," "Why Is a Fire Engine Red," and "My Grandfather's Clock," which Cash had originally recorded for *Songs of Our Soil* in 1959. At the time of this writing, seven songs tracked during the same sessions remain in the vault: "Mystery of No. 5," "The Very Biggest Circus of Them All," "Watermelon Song," "Billy Goat Song," "Oh Boys, Oh Girls, Do You Love Jesus," "Jesus Loves Me," and "Ben Dewberry's Final Run." The last of these seven has been released, though not officially in the States, by the excellent Bear Family reissue label on the 1999 album *It's All in the Family*. Cash also returned to the song in 1982, while working with Cowboy Jack Clement on *The Adventures of Johnny Cash*, but that version wasn't released until 2013's *Cash Unheard*.

John R. Cash (1975)

A lack of chart success is something that will always raise the concern of a record label, and by now Cash, too, had noticed it. "I've been using my own group to record with me—you know, the ones I use for concerts—but I'm going to use a lot of other people, and try different things, because it's apparent that what I've been doing is not what people really want to hear," he told Patrick Carr. "So I'm going to try to do something that they want to hear."

To do that, Cash went into the studio with his old partner in crime, Cowboy Jack. In June 1974, the pair cut four songs with a stripped-down band that included Joe Allen on bass, Charlie Cochran on keyboard, Jim Isbell on drums, and Reggie Young on guitar: "I Like Having You Around," "Rosalee's Good Eats Cafe," "Just the Other Side of Nowhere," and a new take on "You Remembered Me," originally from 1962's *The Sound of Johnny Cash.*

At the time, Cash told Patrick Carr:

> Jack Clement and I work very well together sometimes. Sometimes we don't agree on *anything,* and I never know from one minute to the next whether we're going to be able to have a session together and work together for an hour. I don't know which direction his head's going, and he don't know where I'm going, and we're both a little egotistical and temperamental. We're going to have another session, and it may last for three days and nights—or it might last for three minutes. I don't know. But we're going to give it a try. We're going to give it everything we got. We both respect each other quite a bit. I certainly respect him. If I didn't, I wouldn't work with him.

The next session came in October 1974 and lasted for two days, with nine more songs recorded. Two of them—"So Doggone Lonesome" and "No Earthly Good"—were new recordings of previous Cash songs. Others included "Mose Rankin," "Love You," "Hang Out," and "My Ship Will Sail," written by Allen Reynolds and later made popular by Emmylou Harris. Cash contributed two new songs, "It Comes and Goes" and "Committed to Parkview," the latter turning up again in 1976. Waylon Jennings contributed "That Old Time Feeling."

"We're not going to release anything out of those sessions until we have something we know is *it,*" Cash said. As of this writing, however, all of these tracks remain unissued. Whether that was the decision of Cash and Clement or their label is unclear.

At the same time, Cash was also working on another album at Columbia's behest. The first single from those sessions was released in late 1974. "The Lady Came from Baltimore," written by Tim Hardin, had been recorded in 1967 by both Bobby Darin and Joan Baez, and told the story of a con man set to marry a woman with the intent of stealing from her, only to be thwarted by falling in love with her.

"It's a great song," Cash said. "The Columbia Records people in New York requested that I do that song, and they're putting together twelve songs for me to record." This label-initiated direction differed greatly from any approach Cash had taken in the past, or that would follow in the future.

"The sound is going to be produced somewhere else," Cash told Carr. "I'll put down my voice, and what they're going to do with it I don't know yet. But

Though Cash wasn't an official member of the Grand Ole Opry since the mid-1960s, he still made occasional appearances and was always game to help them promote the show. Soon after this show, he was asked again to be a member, but declined the invitation due to their restrictive appearance requirements. *Author's collection*

they have a man producing the music that has produced some fine stuff. I think he knows what he's doing: If he doesn't, I won't fool with him anymore. His name is Gary Klein."

Gary Klein got his start in the music business as a songwriter in 1963, before eventually moving into producing. He was appointed a Columbia staff producer in 1973. Prior to that, he had produced the Osmond Brothers, Tim Hardin, and Charlie Daniels, as well as Mac Davis' hit record *Stop and Smell the Roses.* His productions in country music tended to lean in a pop direction, best evidenced by two 1977 pop-country smashes: Glen Campbell's *Southern Nights* and Dolly Parton's *Here You Come Again.*

On paper, *John R. Cash* looks like an update of the formula Cash and Don Law used for *Now There Was a Song*—pick a batch of good songs, most of them released by others in the recent past, and a couple newer ones, and have Cash give his interpretation of them. The first track, and the second single to be drawn from the album, is "My Old Kentucky Home (Turpentine and Dandelion Wine)," a Randy Newman song that had been recorded by Newman and also by bluegrass legends the Osborne Brothers in 1970, and by Three Dog Night in 1974. Cash's version reached only #42 Country—a disappointing showing, especially given that "The Lady Came from Baltimore" had reached #14. (Neither song reached the Pop chart.)

Jack Routh was able to land one song, "Hard Times Comin'," about the importance of the support of a good partner when life's troubles begin to pile up. Cash's "Lonesome to the Bone" comes next, though this rerecording, with added gloss and polish, dulls the message of the song by comparison to the original cut from *Ragged Old Flag.* To close out the original album's first side, Cash turns in a fine performance of the Band's "The Night They Drove Old Dixie Down." The song had reached the charts twice before: on the Pop chart for Joan Baez in 1971 (#3), and on the Country chart that same year for Alice Creech (#33).

"Clean Your Own Tables," on which the singer tells a bar full of people they'll have to take care of themselves as he takes the barmaid home to make her a housewife, was written by Chip Taylor, best known for writing the Troggs' "Wild Thing" and Juice Newton's "Angel of the Morning." Taylor himself had recorded it in 1974, while Stoney Edwards cut a version a year later.

Another new songwriter to the world of Cash was the Texan Billy Joe Shaver. Shaver had made a name for himself when Waylon Jennings recorded almost an entire album of his songs (nine of the ten tracks on *Honky Tonk Heroes*). "Jesus Was Our Savior (Cotton Was Our King)" is a great fit for Cash, the content and tone making it seem like he could have written it himself.

Of the remaining songs, "Reason to Believe," written by Tim Hardin, had been a #1 hit for Rod Stewart in 1971, while "Cocaine Carolina" came from the pen of David Allan Coe. For the first time in several albums, Cash doesn't end things with a gospel song, instead singing the workingman's lament "Smokey Factory Blues" by Albert Hammond and Michael Hazelwood.

John R. Cash received generally positive notices. For music critic Nick Tosches, it was "a reassuring album, for it shows that Cash is just as interesting, and just as good, today as he was twenty years ago." And in a review of Cash's *next* album, critic Rich Kienzle wrote, "If there's one thing Johnny Cash does better than just about anyone else, it's interpreting other writers' material," noting the "excellence of his last effort, *John R. Cash.*"

It seems Cash didn't agree. He had reluctantly gone along with the process of how the album was made—laying his vocals over music that was produced and played elsewhere—because, as he said of his label's heads, "it was their idea of an album to restore my sales potential." But if that was the goal, it wasn't achieved: the album didn't even touch the charts.

Cash was left with a dilemma. All of the songs on the album were strong, and he was in great voice, turning in heartfelt performances. The music was contemporary for the time and fit in with other albums on the charts. At this point, he had been in the music business, and in the public eye, for twenty years. Many of his fans—particularly the casual ones—wanted to hear more of what they heard on the sparse prison albums and the early Sun (or even Columbia) recordings.

Cash was caught in a snare of his own design, one that has caught many artists over time—he desires to grow, but his audience wants him to stay the same. It's a snare that still exists: it's what gave birth to the "classic rock" format, and it continues to frustrate artists to this day. Of the sessions with Clement that Cash had spoken of before the release of *John R. Cash,* he said, "I'm not sure how bad the people want to hear the boom-chicka-boom. If they want to hear it, that's what we'll give them." *John R. Cash* went a long way to proving to Cash that the people did, indeed, want to hear the boom-chicka-boom.

Look at Them Beans (1975)

Before his point was proven with *John R. Cash,* Cash had already headed back to the studio, this time with producer and ex-brother-in-law Don Davis (once married to Anita Carter), the man who had brought him such great songs as "Jackson" and "A Boy Named Sue." Here, Davis' contributions started with the first single.

"He had been having some extremely lean times," Davis writes in his autobiography. "I guess he thought he'd better call me to find another hit. I got to rambling around up at Tree [the publishing company] and found a Joe Tex song called 'Papa's Dream.' It knocked me out; I loved it and talked to John. He listened to the song and said, 'Hey, I like that, but can we change the name?' I asked him what he wanted to change it to, and he said, 'Look at Them Beans.'"

After asking Tex if the name change was okay, Cash and band went in to cut it, but soon ran into trouble. Cash called Davis, who brought in some additional musicians, and on June 6, 1975, they recorded the song, plus another that would end up on the album, Dave Kilby's "What Have You Got Planned Tonight, Diana" (which Merle Haggard would record the next year), and "Beautiful Memphis," which remains unreleased.

On June 10th, Cash and the band returned to the studio to do a few overdubs on the previous session, and to cut three more songs, two of which made the album: Jack Routh's "All Around Cowboy" (a song Waylon Jennings cut around the same time, and would include on his Clement-produced album *Dreaming My Dreams*) and the Johnny/June composition "Gone," which features some great steel guitar work by Curly Chalker. The session also produced another song that hasn't been released, "On the Way Home."

The single release of "Look at Them Beans" b/w "All Around Cowboy" began to climb the charts, and after it peaked at #17, Columbia wanted an album to follow it. Cash went back in the studio with Davis to add to the four songs they already had. Among the material they recorded was a new train song by up-and-coming young songwriter Guy Clark called "Texas-1947." They also pulled a song called "No Charge"—which had been a hit for Melba Montgomery in 1974 and a bigger hit for Shirley Caesar in 1975—from Don's business partner (and Cash's old friend) Harlan Howard. The song talks about a young boy wanting to be paid for every little thing he does around the house, only to have his mother turn it around and list all of the things they have done for the boy at "no charge."

JOHNNY CASH
ON WHEELS.
Here's a collector's album of 12 great Johnny Cash railroad songs with exciting originals and unique versions of old favorites. Just $3.95 for "Destination Victoria Station," available only at Victoria Station restaurants or by the convenient coupon below.
Side one includes Casey Jones, Hey Porter, John Henry, Wabash Cannonball, City of New Orleans, Folsom Prison Blues. Flip it over for Crystal Chandeliers and Burgundy, Wreck of the Old 97, Waitin' for a Train, Orange Blossom Special, Texas 1947 and the special new song Destination Victoria Station. Be sure you cash in on this unique Johnny Cash offer.
Send check or money order for $4.30 (includes 35¢ handling) to:
VICTORIA STATION INCORPORATED
150 Chestnut Street
San Francisco, Ca. 94111
Name
Street
City
State
Zip
(Allow 3 weeks for delivery)
cm

In 1975, Cash was commissioned by the restaurant Destination Victoria Station to record an album of train songs. The album was only available in the restaurant or by mail order.
Author's collection

More recently, the song's message has been turned into a sappy cliché after being passed through thousands of emails and social media posts, but at the time it was a new sentiment. *Billboard* columnist Gerry Wood called it "the best and most meaningful song Howard has ever written"—and Howard had written a bunch by that time. "'No Charge' was my most gratifying work," Howard told *Country Song Roundup*. "A lot of music friends that I greatly respect called and complimented me. I was really touched. It took me six months to write the song. One month just to end it."

Elsewhere on the album, Cash contributed a tongue-in-cheek look at honky-tonk songs with "I Hardly Ever Sing Beer Drinking Songs," while Don Williams' 1974 composition "Down the Road I Go" sits perfectly alongside Cash's other road songs. "I Never Met a Man like You Before" is one of Rosanne Cash's earliest songwriting efforts, so it makes sense that Cash would want to record it, but it comes off a little clunky. The lyrics concern the strength a woman gets from a good man, and Cash sings it just as it is written (perhaps changing the man to God) but the results come off odd.

The closing song is the most disappointing on the album. Those who currently complain about the proliferation of "list songs" in country music today need only look at "Down at Dripping Springs" to find an early example. This is Cash's look at the 1973 Texas concert headlined by Willie Nelson and Waylon Jennings (and featuring many others) that drew 100,000 fans. The problem is that Cash wasn't there, which is obvious from the way the song simply lists the performers, while musically, with its bopping horns, it couldn't have been farther from what was going on at Dripping Springs.

The eventual second single from the album was "Texas-1947," though Davis had been pushing for "What Have You Got Planned Tonight, Diana." His instincts may have been correct. "Texas-1947" made it to only #35, while Merle Haggard's cut of "Diana" (coupled with the Bob Wills tune "Cherokee Maiden") made it to #1. *Look at Them Beans* made it to #38 Country, but failed to register on the Pop chart.

25

Get Your Dark Clouds off of Me

Columbia 1976

Johnny Cash found himself in a familiar place in 1976. Just as in the mid-1960s, his songs had dropped off the charts, and it was harder to get them there. It wasn't that he was out of sight, out of mind: Cash had been making appearances on *Dinah Shore*, *Mike Douglas*, and *Hee Haw*, and his guest spots always drew ratings. In the fall, he returned to weekly television for a limited time with *Johnny Cash & Friends*, a show that ran for four weeks in August and September. His profile was still high enough that KRAFT foods, sponsor of the Country Music Awards televised award show, insisted he be brought in as host. The CMA had balked at the request in 1975, but this time it was more of a demand than a request. The ninety-minute event aired on October 11th and captured 41 percent of the overall ratings, making it the highest-rated CMA awards show to date.

In his autobiography, Buck Owens theorized that once an artist had a regular network television presence (as he had, with *Hee Haw*), their album sales would drop off sharply. When *The Johnny Cash Show* was on the air, from 1969–71, Cash seemed to be the exception. During that time, he consistently placed albums at #1. After the show ended, his television presence consisted only of sporadic variety-show appearances and a pair of television specials in 1971 and 1974. Without a regular show from 1971 to 1975, his album sales actually declined. And the rise of "One Piece at a Time" up the singles chart actually corresponded with the run-up to *Johnny Cash & Friends*.

Cash's name didn't just help television ratings. It also sold albums, though not all of them for Columbia. Sun International was still pumping out regular releases of repackaged '50s hits, and in 1972 Cash took the company to court, claiming he was owed royalties. The court awarded him over $204,000 and set up Sun International with a payment plan.

In 1976, Cash filed another suit, claiming that SI had stopped making its payments in 1974 and that the company was using the money that should be going to him, and which amounted to $15,000 a quarter, to operate its business, which including making "new" Cash albums. Cash's attorney, Ben Cantrell, told the press, "The plaintiff's patience has come to an end."

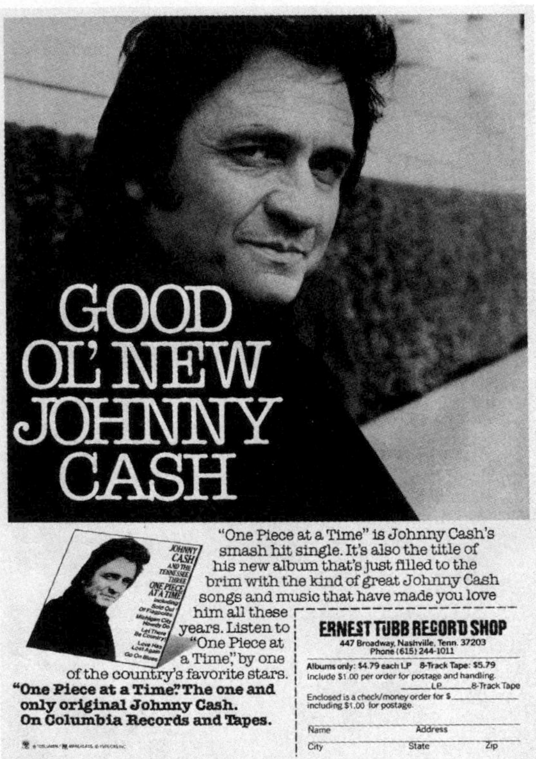

To help promote country music, and his own records, Ernest Tubb opened his Record Shop in 1947 with a Nashville location and a large mail-order business. This ad, placed by the store, touted Cash's return to form.
Author's collection

Alongside his many television appearances—which included a guest spot for Johnny and June on *The Little House on the Prairie*, playing a con man and his wife—Cash and Columbia released two albums, one of them a live set.

Strawberry Cake (1976)

In 1976, Bob Dylan released *Hard Rain*, a live album that received very mixed reviews, while around the same time, Lynyrd Skynyrd released *One More from the Road*, which kicked off a new (though short-lived) era of the band. Waylon Jennings released *Waylon Live!*, and RCA reissued a 1966 Willie Nelson live set to piggyback onto it. Paul McCartney & Wings released *Wings over America*, and Peter Frampton released his live double *Frampton Comes Alive*.

In the midst of all these, Johnny Cash released a new live album of his own, *Strawberry Cake*. It's interesting to compare the live albums by Cash and Jennings, or by Cash and Dylan. Jennings' was recorded in 1974, and contained songs that were, for the most part, no more than a couple of years old, plus a few that hadn't even been released yet. Waylon's manner is relaxed as he chides the audience, sounding more like a guy at an open-mic night than a superstar. By contrast, Dylan split his album between older songs and newer songs, though the older songs had been rearranged to fit the Rolling Thunder Revue, his traveling troupe. Both approaches contrast strongly with Cash's effort. What causes the biggest problem with *Strawberry Cake* is that it comes across more as a stage show—with Cash as curator of his own material—than a regular live performance.

The show was organized to touch on various stages of his career, starting at the beginning. While Cash sounds relaxed, seasoned entertainer that he was, he also sounds scripted, and at times as if he is going through the motions, as he talks between songs. The album stands as a snapshot of Cash at a particular time and a particular crossroads. With the outlaw country movement barreling forward, he remained where he was, unmoved, either by choice or confusion, and backed by the Tennessee Three of Wootton, Grant, and Holland (augmented at that time, and on this recording, by Jerry Hensley on guitar and Larry McCoy on piano).

The album was recorded at the Palladium in London, England, over two nights. Twelve songs from the two shows are included on the album, but thirty-two were played during the first show, including performances by Jerry Hensley (June's cousin, who had joined the band as a second guitarist after Carl Perkins left the group), and Rosanne Cash, singing "Don't Think Twice, It's Alright." Certainly, there is enough material to warrant an expanded reissue, or an entry in the *Bootleg* series.

The biggest maker of model trains at the time, Lionel Trains enlisted Cash as a spokesman and produced a line of trains with his image and song titles on them in 1976. *Author's collection*

Of the twelve songs that made the cut for the album, the Sun days are represented by an updated "Big River," "Doin' My Time," and "Rock Island Line," dedicated to skiffle king Lonnie Donegan, who was in the audience. From his early Columbia years, Cash presents "I Still Miss Someone," "Another Man Done Gone," "I Got Stripes," and "The Fourth Man." June and her sisters perform "Church in the Wildwood," though the first run-through is interrupted after a bomb threat is called in to the venue.

Cash does take the opportunity to bring out three new songs: "Destination Victoria Station," a love song centered on a train station, taken from an album commissioned by the restaurant Victoria Station; "Navajo," a tribute to the spirit of the Native American tribe; and the title track, "Strawberry Cake." Cash calls the latter, the story of a homeless man who eyes a large strawberry cake in a hotel lobby and runs in to snatch a piece before heading out the door, enjoying every bite, a "contemporary American folk song," while also noting, "I don't expect it to be as big as 'Folsom Prison Blues.'" It wasn't, topping out at #54 Country, while the album had a brief two-week chart run, peaking at #33 on the Country LPs chart.

One Piece at a Time (1976)

Cash returned to the studio in October of 1975, but with no direction or plan except a desire to record some gospel songs, plus a few other odds and ends. When "One Piece at a Time" became a hit (a story covered in chapter 29), many of those songs were swiftly cobbled together for an album. Musically, all of the songs rely on a more stripped-down sound, with the occasional augmentation of some fiddle, or Charlie McCoy's harmonica.

Opening track "Let There Be Country," co-written by Cash and Shel Silverstein, is a celebration of other country artists, carried along by the "list song" formula. "One Piece at a Time" follows as an example of the back-to-basics boom-chicka-boom, while "In a Young Girl's Mind," by Hoyt Axton and Mark Dawson, looks back at youthful love affairs.

Feeling a resurgence of creativity, Cash wrote six of the album's seven remaining songs. "Mountain Lady" is a thinly veiled tribute to June, while "Michigan City Howdy Do" relates the tale of a convict, Johnson Van Dyke Grigsby, who was given a seven-hour furlough and related how happy he was to be free in Michigan City, Indiana. Grigsby, at age ninety-two, had, according to an Associated Press story, spent "more time behind bars than any person on record."

Released in the bicentennial year, "Sold Out of Flagpoles" was a nostalgic directive to look at the bright side, no matter what was going on with the country. It was a poor choice of a follow-up single after the huge success of "One Piece at a Time." "One Piece" featured the steel-coil-tight trademark Cash guitar sound; "Flagpoles" is riddled with a Jew's harp solo. It reached only #29 Country, and didn't make it to the Pop chart.

"Committed to Parkview" (which would have been a much better follow-up single) talks about the country music artists and Nashville residents who spent time in the local nervous hospital. Before recording it himself, Cash had offered the song to Waylon Jennings, who apparently passed, though they would record it together with the Highwaymen in 1984. A few years later, Cash sent the tape to Porter Wagoner, but, so the story goes, it was misplaced until 2006, when Wagoner recorded his swan song, *Wagonmaster* (produced by Cash's ex-son-in-law Marty Stuart).

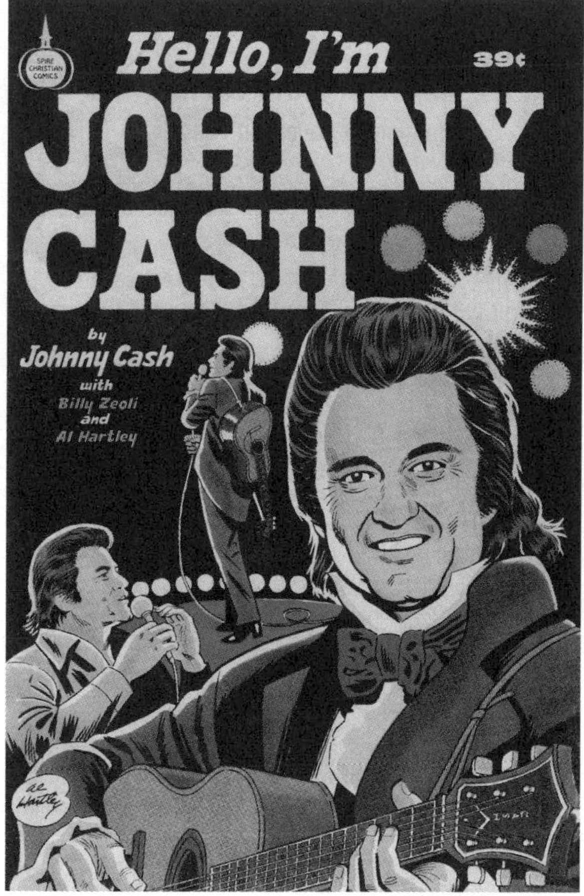

Published by Spire Comics, who released Christian themed comics, *Hello, I'm Johnny Cash* told Cash's biography in comic form with a religious slant. *Author's collection*

"Daughter of a Railroad Man" could be a continuation of the story of the girl Cash chased in "Big River," though her preferred mode of travel here is the railroad rather than the rolling river. "Love Has Lost Again" is another early songwriting effort by Rosanne Cash that shows her to still be working in the vein of her father's songwriting as she begins to grow into the performer who would make her recording debut in 1979. The album closes with "Go On Blues," a strong Cash song that shows how his songwriting could still be as strong in the mid-'70s as it was two decades earlier. He would later return to the song for the *American* sessions.

The response to the album—the first to be billed to Johnny Cash & the Tennessee Three—was overwhelmingly positive, with critics and fans alike proclaiming it a return to form. Cash, in his liner notes, felt the same way, even including a poem entitled "Here I Am Back Again." In his review of the album, Nick Tosches wrote, "And he is back. The first time I heard 'One Piece at a Time,' I knew that. Here was the old Cash, the Cash who forged that strident

Sun sound, the Cash who sang of gentle things in a tough voice. 'One Piece at a Time' is reason to celebrate Cash anew. He hasn't lost anything, just been waylaid, and he's back harder than ever."

The public agreed, and though it stalled out at #185 on the Pop 200, *One Piece at a Time* went to #2 on the Country chart. Cash had returned to the top—now all he needed to do was keep the momentum going.

26

I Woke Up This Morning with a Song in My Heart

Columbia 1977

In 1977, after several years of regularly attending the Evangel Temple, Cash felt he had no choice but to stop going to services there. He hadn't been shy, or quiet, about his beliefs, or about what that church had meant in his journey, and as a result, fans and hopeful artists had begun to make their way to services in the hope of meeting Johnny Cash. Not wanting to impede others' worship, Cash started holding his own services at the House of Cash, but they too were plagued with the same problem, so he stopped those, too.

When Cash stopped going to church, it took away the support system that he had built around himself, and soon after that, drugs began to creep back into his life. Their effects would soon enough be felt by all around him. Marshall Grant first noticed it on January 29, 1977, when he showed up at a venue a few hours before a show to find that Cash was already there. "John never showed up for a sound check when he was straight," he writes in his autobiography. "So naturally I feared the worst."

"Why John? Just please tell me why?" he remembers asking. "You've had all these good years. You've got the world by the tail. You're *THE* Man in country music. You have a great family, a great wife. You've got everything a man could possibly dream of. Why have you turned your back on them?"

Cash told him he was going "through the change of life" and that it was a one-time relapse, that he would be fine. But a few hours later, he took the stage in even worse shape. "I just wanted to stop the whole show, go backstage, and sit down and cry," Grant writes. Cash still put on a decent show, but it had begun again—the battle with addiction that would affect his career and the lives of those around him.

The Last Gunfighter Ballad (1977)

"One Piece at a Time" had taken Cash back to the top of the Country Singles chart in 1976, and now he had to maintain that success. He was under a lot of pressure—from his label and from within. The follow-up, "Sold Out of Flagpoles," hadn't had the same appeal. To end the year, he released two new singles. The first, "It's All Over," stayed close to the sound he had reestablished on *One Piece at a Time*, but with his singles momentum having been slowed by "Sold Out of Flagpoles," and it topped out at #41. The follow-up, "Old Time Feeling," was a love-ballad duet with June that fared a little better, making it to #26 as the New Year rolled around. The B-sides to both singles were to be included on the first of three new albums for 1977, *The Last Gunfighter Ballad* (the other two, *The Rambler* and *Destination: Victoria Station*, are discussed in chapter 13).

Throughout the '70s, Cash was a spokesman of Hohner Harmonicas and appeared in several ads and displays promoting the instruments. *Author's collection*

With *One Piece at a Time*, fans and critics rose up to praise Cash for going back to the boom-chicka-boom sound that every one loved. "I think I did something they wanted to hear, and what they wanted to hear was what I've done best all along—and that's the three-chord ballad with the Tennessee Three," Cash told Patrick Carr in 1976. "I'm glad that's what they want, because I know how to do that."

Knowing how to do something and actually doing it are two different things. Filling an album with songs whose sound recalled the past—no matter how many times it was praised in exuberant, breathless reviews—was still, to Cash, a backward step. He still wanted to try something else, to make his music sound contemporary. But the Johnny Cash sound wasn't contemporary. In 1977, the Country LPs chart was topped by the country-pop of Kenny Rogers' *Daytime Friends* (produced by Larry Butler), Dolly Parton's *Here You Come Again*, and Glen Campbell's *Southern Nights* (both produced by Gary Klein). That wasn't a direction Cash could go—in as *John R. Cash* had shown, though it didn't take him too far down that road.

Another well-traveled road led toward the outlaw movement—a movement pioneered, at least on the business side, by Cash, with the idea of recording what you want, when you want, with whom you want. Two of the biggest-selling albums of the year were Waylon Jennings' *Ol' Waylon* (produced by Chips Moman and buoyed by the huge hit "Luckenbach, Texas [Back to the Basics of Love]") and Johnny Paycheck's *Take This Job and Shove It* (produced by Billy Sherrill and featuring the hit title track).

Among those five releases—which were helmed either by producers Cash had worked with before (Butler, Klein) or that he would come to in the future (Moman, Sherrill)—there were four platinum-selling albums and one gold. But there, amid them, stood Cash. Rugged individualist? Trend bucker? Man without a direction? Going through the motions? It gets muddy right through here. Perhaps he might have done well to look to the other half of the outlaw power duo, Willie Nelson. Bucking the pervading outlaw formula, Willie self-produced a musically stripped-down tribute to Lefty Frizzell titled simply *To Lefty from Willie*. It didn't go platinum or gold, and it only produced one Top 10 single, but it was what he wanted to do.

Instead, Cash leaned a little more toward the outlaw road (at least initially). Patrick Carr, in his 1976 interview with Cash, notes, "Scratch today's Waylon Sound and you'll find the Cash/Clement style of the late fifties." Cash puts a fine point on it here. There is a little more twang to the phase-shifted guitar that opens "I Will Dance with You," while the loping rhythm and overall sound could have been an outtake from *Ol' Waylon*.

Cash performs a kind of aural course-correction with the album's first single and title track. His dark, deep voice brings to life Guy Clark's vivid description of a dying outlaw who, as it turns out, doesn't meet his end in a gunfight, but instead by reliving the past in the wrong place at the wrong time.

"Far Side Banks of Jordan," a spiritual love song, is one of the album's shining moments. The goal of the devout Christian is to make it to heaven to see the face of God. But here the narrator, having arrived there, announces to the world that he will still be waiting, patiently, for the other to join him. After the raucous fun of "Jackson," a somewhat goofy take on "I Got a Woman," and the silliness of "I Got a Boy Named John," nothing speaks to the end goal of a couple working through times that have devastated other couples as does this song. It found deeper meaning as the years passed, and they continued to sing it in concert, night after night. During a 1996 performance, June called it "my favorite of all the songs I get to sing with John."

"It was what my parents' love was about," John Carter Cash told *CMJ* in 2007. "They sang it from the moment they learned the song throughout the rest of their life. It was their onstage, on-camera proclamation of their love for each other—their undying love. When I listen to those recordings, it brings me back in contact with them more as parents than any of the other recordings and duets that they did together."

"Ridin' on the Cotton Belt" has Cash going home—literally, as he explains in the spoken intro to the song. He and the Cash family had been honored at a homecoming celebration in Rison, Arkansas, that the whole family attended. Cash says the homecoming was really a celebration of his parents, and prompted him to write a song based on the times his father would hop the rails to find work to feed the family before they moved to Dyess.

"Give It Away," a Tom T. Hall song about smiling ("smiles don't cost money") is a bit overrun with honky-tonk piano, which distracts from the otherwise back-to-basics sound. "You're So Close to Me," by Mac Davis, brings the record closer to the sound Cash said he was working toward, or back to it. He delivers the song with an edge in his voice that nobody—not even Davis—could have matched.

The second half of the album is built around a trio of original songs. On "City Jail," Cash returns to prison songs, stringing together a few spoken comedic asides that he had used in concert over the years during "Orange Blossom Special." He wrote "Cindy, I Love You" as a present to his daughter on her eighteenth birthday. The lyrics serve as an apology, an admission of the guilty feelings Cash harbored for having been the father he had been throughout her life. Then, returning to his song-collecting ways, he offers a rewrite of the old ballad "Barbara Allen," here called "Ballad of Barbara."

Joined by brother Tommy, Johnny ends the album with "That Silver-Haired Daddy of Mine," written and recorded in 1931 by Gene Autry—his first hit, issued before he became famous as a singing cowboy. It's thick with nostalgia, and a touch of irony, given the complicated relationship Johnny had with his dad, Ray, whose treatment of him bordered at times on mental cruelty.

Only "The Last Gunfighter Ballad" was released as an A-side, and it couldn't recapture the success of "One Piece at a Time," getting only to #38 Country. The album itself made it only to #29 on the Country LPs chart.

Nelson Allen, in a review for this album, notes that it is "inevitable (although probably a little unfair) that a man of Cash's stature will always be compared against his best work." Cash himself told Patrick Carr that his engineer and co-producer Charlie Bragg "harped on" him to "go back to the old sound," but said he wouldn't allow it. "Oh, I can always do that. I want to do something else."

In retrospect, it is easy to dismiss much of Cash's 1970s work as that of a once-great artist adrift in a sea of changing tastes and trends, but it would be shortchanging him to do so. It must be remembered that, by 1977, Cash was approaching twenty-five years in the business. Others who had been in the business for much less time—artists who are still considered great, like Merle Haggard, Conway Twitty, and Buck Owens—weren't playing the exact style and sound of music they were playing in the beginning. What we see in the 1970s is a Johnny Cash who is at the pinnacle of his success and using that luxury to explore his art, and maybe even indulge himself a little.

27

Baby, I Will Rock and Roll with You

Columbia 1978

Between touring and recording dates in 1977, Cash found the time to go to Texas to star in the made-for-TV movie *Thaddeus Rose and Eddie.* The movie, which aired on February 24, 1978, stars Cash and Bo Hopkins as "two no-accounts who are forever chasing women and pipe dreams." Journalist Jerry Buck called it a diamond in the rough, praising both the story and the acting. The movie was filmed in Floresville and Harlingen, Texas, using local sites and people. One pivotal scene was filmed in a local bar filled with half-drunk locals, and the director nearly left the set out of fear once he saw the crowd. But Hopkins told Buck they had a secret weapon: "Johnny kept everybody in a good mood. He picked up his guitar and sang to entertain the people there. It was going to be a long night."

The script, by first-time screenwriter William D. Wittliff, had been turned down numerous times before producers Rod Sheldon and Dan Paulson got hold of it. "It wasn't written in the correct script form," Sheldon told Buck. "The story was a little clumsy, but it was warm and charming. I said, 'Holy mackerel, we have a rare talent here,' and hopped on the next plane to Austin."

Wittliff would go on to write the screenplays for three Willie Nelson movies (*Honeysuckle Rose*, *Barbarosa*, and *Red Headed Stranger*), the television mini-series adaption of *Lonesome Dove*, and feature films including *Legends of the Fall* and *The Perfect Storm.*

I Would Like to See You Again (1978)

Back in 1970, when Cash wrote "What Is Truth," he based the line about kids playing "funny music these days" on a comment Merle Travis had made while they were watching the group First Edition rehearse. (The lead singer of the group was Kenny Rogers, while the drummer was Mickey Jones, who had played with Dylan on his infamous 1966 world tour and would later become a well-known character actor.) Although it was "funny music," there was a country tinge to some of their tunes. In the fall of 1975, the group broke up, leaving Rogers, for the first time, without a group to play with.

Larry Butler had last worked with Cash in 1973, on the Swedish prison album *På Österåker*. After that, they had a disagreement about the thing most artists and producers fall out over: money. Soon, Butler had left his job as a staff producer at Columbia and become the head of the Nashville division of United Artists Records. Butler signed new acts to the label, including Loretta Lynn's little sister, Crystal Gayle, who released her debut album in 1975. He also went to bat for the guy leading that band playing the funny music.

"The executives at United Artists Records thought I was too old, creeping up on forty, and too pop to have much success in country at this stage of my life," Rogers writes in his autobiography, *Luck or Something Like It*. "Fortunately, Larry had his own power with the label, and between Larry and Ken [Kragen, Rogers' manager], the executives finally caved and let Larry try to make me into a country star."

Their first album together "was pretty much uneventful," according to Rogers. "We had some success but nothing you would remember." *Love Lifted Me* rose no higher than #28 on the Hot Country LPs chart, but it included several decent songs, one of which was "I Would Like to See You Again."

In the late summer of 1977, Butler called Cash, and the two began to formulate a plan to work together again, setting aside September 13th and 14th to meet in the studio. Joined by the Jordanaires and the Tennessee Three plus Earl Poole Ball on piano and Jerry Hensley on guitar, Cash and Butler recorded six songs on the 13th and three more, including a re-cut of one of the songs, on the 14th. The group reconvened on October 4th to cut four more songs. The title track, and first single, was the song Rogers had recorded a couple of years earlier. Cash sounds almost wistful as he sings about an old girlfriend and times left behind. The Jordanaires swell behind him, singing occasional words as punctuation.

The album's second track, "Lately," is a Cash composition about the feeling of being in a relationship that is slowly ending. "Who's Gene Autry?" is another Cash tune, and finds him nostalgic once again, as he schools John Carter (making his recording debut) on the great Singing Cowboy. "Hurt So Bad" continues the alternating themes of nostalgia and dying love, this time with a light pseudo-Calypso beat, missing only the "cha-cha-cha" at the end. Cash also contributed a third song, "Abner Brown," about a vagrant whose spirit lifts a whole town. Again, the song has him looking back, as he asks the Lord to "take me back to the cotton land" and "let me be the boy that I had once been."

Among the other songwriters Cash draws on are members of his band. "I Don't Think I Could Take You Back Again," co-written by Earl Poole Ball and Cajun artist Jo-El Sonnier, was recorded at the end of the session, and Cash's voice reflects that, although it is hard to notice for the piano and backing vocals that tend to dominate. "I'm Alright Now" came from Jerry Hensley, and finds Cash in better voice and the sound closer to that of his last couple of albums. "After Taxes" is a silly song written by Billy Edd Wheeler and Jerry Leiber about what's left of a paycheck, with Ray Walker, the bass singer of the Jordanaires,

This German release featured Cash singing "Five Feet High and Rising" and "I Got Stripes" sung by Cash in German. *Private collection*

sounding more and more goofy as he checks off the various different types of taxes. Larry Butler and Roger Bowling wrote "That's the Way It Is," a soft song that wouldn't have been out of place on one of Butler's Kenny Rogers albums, but here Cash does a fine job with the tender melody.

Probably the most talked-about songs on the album were the two duets Cash recorded in 1976 with Waylon Jennings. "We cut two tracks for a single together, 'I Wish I Was Crazy Again' and 'There Ain't No Good Chain Gang,'" Cash told Patrick Carr. "I guess we're just going to call the record companies' bluff. They say we can't record an album together, but I think we're going to do it anyway, and then say, 'Here it is. Work something out.'"

By 1978, Columbia had worked something out. The label would have been foolish not to—Waylon was on fire. "Luckenbach, Texas (Back to the Basics of Love)" had been at #1 for six weeks, and the follow-up, "The Wurlitzer Prize (I Don't Want to Get Over You)," for two. Waylon kicked off 1978 with another #1, "Mammas Don't Let Your Babies Grow Up to Be Cowboys," a duet with Willie Nelson. At the same time, Cash's sales were slipping, so the chance to pair him with such a hot artist—especially one he had emulated on a few songs in the recent past—was something the label couldn't pass up.

The first single released from the album, "I Would Like to See You Again," made its way to #12—twice as high as either of Cash's previous singles. An even bigger boost came with the release of the first Waylon duet, "There Ain't No Good Chain Gang." Written by Hal Bynum and David Kirby, the song is a raucous story of what two men learned from their time in jail for trying to pass bad checks. Both singers sound like they were having a blast recording the song—just two old buddies doing what they did best without the pressures of a record label breathing down their neck. The single spent two weeks at #2, making it Cash's highest-charting single in two years.

As a collection of songs, *I Would Like to See You Again* plays to Cash's strengths, with only a couple of missteps. The duets with Waylon are superb, showing Cash to be loose and comfortable. "This record is a good example of how Cash is growing and striking out in new musical directions," Beck Foster, a reviewer from Kingman, Arizona, remarked. "Unlike many of today's artists, he does not rely on his past efforts and continually 'sing the same old stuff' that is tried and true," he added, showing that not all Cash fans were pining for the Sun days.

Nelson Allen's review for *Country Music* was a bit more revealing. Discussing the Cash/Jennings duet on "I Wish I Was Crazy Again," he writes, "Well I wish he was crazy again too, because Johnny Cash singing about the old Johnny Cash is not Johnny Cash. But he's the best Johnny Cash we've got, and this is hardly a bad record. The man couldn't make a bad record if he tried." That same phrase had been repeated in nearly every review, in some way or another, for several years. It wasn't that the new albums were *bad* albums, but each reviewer prefaced it with some form of wishful thinking that Cash would return to what he had done before. "Anytime I criticize Johnny Cash I feel like a fool," Allen concludes, "'cause he's done more than me or any ten of my friends will probably ever do. Still, *I Would Like to See You Again* ain't gonna get played as much around my house as, for instance, *Ride This Train*."

And there stands the crux of the problem: an apathetic and sometimes chemically influenced Cash may have been looking to the fans to give him some idea on his direction, but those fans couldn't—or, more to the point, wouldn't—do it. He was Johnny Cash! Whatever he did was fine with them. His latest might not be a great album, "but he's the best Johnny Cash we've got."

Perhaps on the strength of Waylon Jennings' participation, *I Would Like to See You Again* spent fourteen weeks on the Hot Country LPs chart—only one week less than *One Piece at a Time*—but only made it as high as #23.

Gone Girl (1978)

From time to time, Cash's momentum would be killed by a problem that befell many artists—the wrong choice of follow-up single. A good example would be what happened after "There Ain't No Good Chain Gang" hit #2 in 1978. Instead of releasing Cash's second duet with Waylon Jennings as a separate single, Columbia tacked "I Wish I Was Crazy Again" on the flip of "Chain Gang," waiting more than a year to release it as a single (by which time it was too late).

Cash and Butler returned to the studio on May 4, 1978, to record two songs for a new album, plus two songs that remain unissued (a retake on "A Thing Called Love" and a song called "Teeth, Hair and Eyeballs"). On July 6th, the crew came back to the studio for a further two days of sessions for the album. During that first day of sessions, Cash recorded a total of six songs, two of which stood out: one was "Gone Girl," by Cowboy Jack Clement, and the second was a song that had been making its way around town called "The Gambler."

"I wrote it in August of '76," writer Don Schlitz told *American Songwriter*, "walking home from a meeting with my mentor, Bob McDill. I walked from his office over on Music Row to my apartment, and in that twenty minutes I wrote most of it in my head. I didn't write a last verse, had no idea what was gonna happen, thought it was an interesting story but it was a throwaway. I spent about six weeks trying to figure out what was gonna happen after the chorus."

"Nobody would touch it," Schlitz added of the song, so he decided to record it himself. His original version sounded more like a folk song, with a lilting delivery and an altered chord structure and melody. The song eventually came to the attention of Bobby Bare, who decided to include it on his self-produced 1978 LP *Bare*. Changing the melody and a few of the chords, Bare uses a stripped-down backing, accented by acoustic slide guitar. His voice is gruff and a little scratchy, like he's sitting on a bar stool near closing time, telling the guy next to him this story that happened to him on the way into the city.

Cash cut his version of the song on a Thursday; Kenny Rogers claims to have cut his version (also with Butler) the previous weekend. Cash's band was pleased to hear the song, and Marshall Grant felt that their version "came off well, which made me happy, because it was the first thing that we had cut in a long time that had any commercial value whatsoever. And we really needed a hit record."

Cash's drug use changed the atmosphere of the session, however. "[John] kept going into the bathroom, and every time he'd come out he would be a little higher," Grant recalled. As Butler did his best to get a good performance out of his artist, Cash—who had been paying much more attention to "Gone Girl" than "The Gambler"—bristled and lit into him. The session was effectively over at that point, though the band kept on recording, capturing a few more songs, most of which would need multiple overdub sessions to fix the problems.

Whether it was "payback time," as Grant would later claim, or simply that Cash's apathy toward the song had doomed its potential as a single, Butler made the call to release Rogers' version as a single, but there were more tracks to get ready for the album. Seeking refuge, or maybe a creative refilling, Cash went into Clement's studio, with Butler, to work on "Gone Girl" on August 1st, and recorded the rest of the album there, too, with Clement on hand.

"Gone Girl" was certainly worth the extra time, with a smooth melody that gives Cash the room to glide into the low notes, and a rhythm that is infectious.

Cash was a favorite host of the annual Country Music Association Awards. Former music director Bill Walker said that when producers wanted a ratings boost to their show, they called Cash. *Author's collection*

"The Diplomat," by Roger Bowling, is a broken-love song set inside a train song, where a man has chosen his train life over his wife but now faces a lonely existence after being forced to retire. "Cajun Born" was co-written by Jo-El Sonnier, a Cajun-country artist who would later have a moderate solo career in the late 1980s. "You and Me" returns Cash to his favorite duet partner: his wife. While both turn in nice performances, it is essentially interchangeable with any duet the couple had recorded in the past several years (with the exception of "Far Side Bank of Jordan"), with its well-worn theme of "Hey, we're in love, and it's great!"

The surprise of the album came in the form of "No Expectations," a song written by Mick Jagger and Keith Richards that originally appeared on the Rolling Stones' 1968 LP *Beggars Banquet.* Here, Cash speeds up the tempo and uses more electric instrumentation than the Stones did on their version. The lyrics are a great fit for Cash, who delivers them with the conviction of a man who had lived them a hundred times over.

Cash wrote two songs for the album, one of them being "I Will Rock and Roll with You," a rocked-up retelling of his Memphis origins, featuring one of the best lead-guitar breaks to appear on a Johnny Cash tune since Carl Perkins left the group in 1973. "It Comes and Goes," the second Cash-penned tune on the album, mines much the same territory as "No Expectations" and suffers, again, from over-dominant piano in the arrangement (what else do you expect when the producer is a piano player?).

The album's closing track is an excellent song by Cash's soon-to-be son-in-law, Rodney Crowell: "A Song for the Life," a gentle piano ballad with a lush string arrangement that plays against Cash's rough voice. Cash tells us he has found a peace that helps him to keep his "feet on the ground," and we believe him—or we want to, because we want the same thing, for us and for him. Daughter Rosanne, just a year or so away from releasing her own Crowell-produced debut album, joins her father on the choruses, and you can hear that she is hoping, too, for her father and herself.

Now, let's get back to the singles. When the first single from *Gone Girl* was released, Waylon Jennings was just coming down from the #1 spot, where he'd recently been camped out with "I've Always Been Crazy." Instead of putting out a second Cash/Jennings duet, Columbia—no doubt prodded by Cash—released "Gone Girl," a great song that peaked at #44, held on to #71 the following week, and then dropped out of sight.

In October, with "Gone Girl" going nowhere, Waylon's "Don't You Think This Outlaw Bit's Done Got Out of Hand" made the Top 5. Even more upsettingly for Cash, Kenny Rogers' version of "The Gambler" was also released that month and began its climb to #1 on the Country chart, where it stayed for three weeks. The song crossed over to the Pop chart in December, reaching #16 and becoming a million-seller.

Though Marshall Grant's assessment that the song had hit potential had been proven correct, it's hard to tell whether Cash's version would have been able to pull it off. Cash's performance lacked the energy that Rogers brought to his, for one thing. At the start of the song, Cash changes the line "On a warm summer's evening" to "Twenty years ago," taking much of the immediacy out of the song. As on "Down at Dripping Springs," Cash has become a spectator rather than a participant, and it takes the drama out of the song. In any case, Cash and Columbia had had three months to put out his version of the song before Rogers did, but they didn't take the chance. Nevertheless, Cash felt betrayed by Butler, while his manager, Lou Robin, felt it was, at the very least, a breach of etiquette.

It would be the last time Butler and Cash worked together, though Butler held no ill will. He looked back fondly on his work with Cash in a 2012 interview with Kevin Sport for the television show *The Right Place*, conducted several months before he passed away:

> I got a call one day from Billy Sherrill, who was head of Columbia/Epic. He called me over for a meeting. He said, "I like what you're doing. I like the way you produce music. Would you like to come to Columbia? The first artist I'd like you to work with is Johnny Cash." That didn't take much thinking. I said, "Where do I sign?" Four of the greatest years of

> my life working for one of the greatest men that has ever walked the face of the Earth. Johnny Cash did so much for me, not as a producer, but as a man, as a person. His code of ethics that he lived by was incredible.

Cash's follow-up to "Gone Girl," "It'll Be Her," reached only #89, and was gone from the charts after two weeks. The year closed with the release of the album's final single, "I will Rock and Roll with You" b/w "A Song for the Life." While it remained on the chart for quite a bit longer, it only reached #21.

Reviews of the album were overwhelmingly positive, especially when it came to "No Expectations." Several reviewers also pointed out "The Gambler" as a high spot on the album. "When the song was first reviewed in the *New York Times*, it was Johnny's version and not mine," Rogers writes in his memoir. "But, for whatever reason, mine is the one that lasted."

Also popping up in many reviews—as it did nearly every time Cash made an album during the 1970s—was some variation of him being "back on track." The problem is, when every album is "back on track" or "back to basics," it's hard for anyone—especially for the artist—to tell where he was *off* track. *Gone Girl* is an interesting example of this. In his review of the album, Michael Bane refers to *The Rambler* as ill-fated, but commercially, it was a more successful album than *Gone Girl*, which didn't even touch the album charts. While it is true that *commercial* success does not always equate to *artistic* success, in the minds of the executives at Columbia, which was in the music *business*, a little more commercial success was needed.

28

No Fools, No Fun, Bull Rider

Columbia 1979

Regardless of Columbia's desire for another hit record, Cash went back into the studio in January of 1979, spending nearly every day that month working on a new gospel album (the double LP *A Believer Sings the Truth*, covered in chapter 49).

Gospel albums weren't high on Columbia's list of hit-making ideas, but there was a sense of therapy in it for Cash. On August 16, 1977, Cash's old Sun Records labelmate Elvis Presley passed away. Cash saw a reflection of his own life in Presley's death, even if he would often downplay its impact. Then, on October 23, 1978, he was dealt a tough blow when Mother Maybelle Carter died, aged sixty-nine. She had been a guiding light for him, even before he became an official member of the family. She was an inspiration to him, a cherished friend—somebody who had been there for him in the worst of times as "a fishing buddy, a darlin' mother-in-law, and a country music legend."

Less than two months later, on January 8, 1979, Sara Carter—the last of the original members of the Carter Family—also passed away. As he continued work on *A Believer Sings the Truth*, Cash's own mortality was very much at the forefront of his mind.

Silver (1979)

In February, Columbia got its wish as far as new albums were concerned when Cash brought in Brian Ahern to produce *Silver*, titled to celebrate the twenty-fifth anniversary of the start of his recording career.

Cash's path to working with Ahern was a long one, so hold on. In 1975, Emmylou Harris launched a solo career, two years after the death of her mentor, Gram Parsons, and hired Rodney Crowell to play rhythm guitar and sing harmony in her backing group, the Hot Band. Brian Ahern produced Emmylou's debut album in 1975, and soon after that they were married. Running in those same circles was Rosanne Cash, who soon began a romantic relationship with Crowell. And it was through that association that Cash became familiar with Ahern's work.

"(Ghost) Riders in the Sky" was Cash's biggest hit from his *Silver Anniversary Album.* *Private collection*

Brian Ahern had started producing records in his native Canada in 1968, beginning an association with a young new talent named Anne Murray that would continue through her first ten albums. In 1974, he worked with Emmylou Harris on her debut album, *Pieces of the Sky.* The album went gold and spawned a Top 5 single with the Louvin Brothers' "If I Could Only Win Your Love." Harris' second album, 1976's *Elite Hotel,* also went gold and produced two #1s and another Top 5 single. (In the meantime, Ahern also produced *Gypsy Boy* for Billy Joe Shaver, one of Cash's favorite songwriters.)

Cash and Columbia were looking to Ahern to bring him back to the top of the charts. Unfortunately, Ahern was walking into a situation where the cards were somewhat stacked against him. Cash was still working hard on his gospel album, and between recording dates, he was still touring, which left him depending heavily on the pills for the extra energy to get it all done.

Going back to the train songs that had been so successful for Cash in the past, *Silver* kicks off with "The L&N Don't Stop Here Anymore," written by Appalachian folk artist Jean Ritchie. The song gives Cash a showcase for those low notes, but the unfortunate horns distract from the otherwise stripped-down arrangement. It is also the arrangement that drags down Cash's third pass at "Lonesome to the Bone," leaving it miles behind the original 1974 cut. Something that affects the whole album is the guitar sound, which relies on a

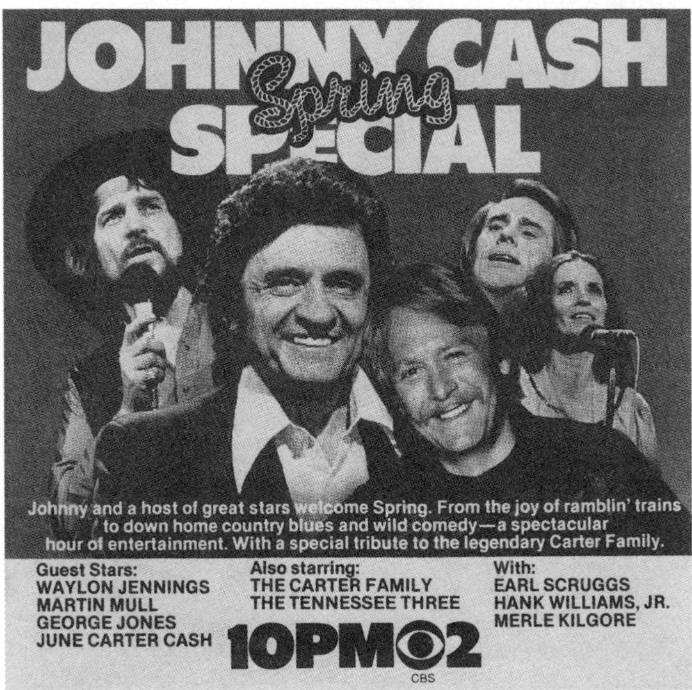

JOHNNY CASH
Spring
SPECIAL
Johnny and a host of great stars welcome Spring. From the joy of ramblin' trains to down home country blues and wild comedy—a spectacular hour of entertainment. With a special tribute to the legendary Carter Family.
Guest Stars:
WAYLON JENNINGS
MARTIN MULL
GEORGE JONES
JUNE CARTER CASH
Also starring:
THE CARTER FAMILY
THE TENNESSEE THREE
With:
EARL SCRUGGS
HANK WILLIAMS, JR.
MERLE KILGORE
10PM 2
CBS

Starting in 1978, Cash did two seasonal specials each year for CBS. One was a Christmas special; the other was a spring special. *Author's collection*

few too many effects and now sounds dated. Most of the arrangements would have been better served with the straight-to-the-amp sound of a few albums back.

Not all of the arrangements present a problem. "Bull Rider," written by Rodney Crowell, plays to Cash's strengths with excellent fiddle and banjo (both provided by Ricky Skaggs) and a deep guitar/bass riff that punctuates the song throughout. Likewise, "I'll Say It's True," for which Cash is joined by George Jones on harmony vocal, finds him having a little fun with many of the myths that surround the Man in Black. "I've never been in prison," he sings with a wink. "I don't know much about trains."

The effects-laden guitar sound actually works on the album's biggest hit, "(Ghost) Riders in the Sky." Written in 1948 by Stan Jones, the song was a big hit in the 1960s for Frankie Laine. Cash's voice settles nicely into the song, and while the arrangement recalls another time it still places itself squarely in the present. A song that fails in that regard is the retake of "Cocaine Blues." Cash's voice suffers from the amount of work it was undertaking during this time, and in contrast to the gruff rasp of the 1968 *At Folsom* version, this sounds like a karaoke version.

"Muddy Waters," written by Phil Rosenthal, finds Cash remembering a devastating flood, while "West Canterbury Subdivision Blues" brings misery to the suburbs. Billy Joe Shaver brings "Lately, I've Been Leanin' Toward the Blues" to the party, and Cash leans into it with a tired voice that sounds oddly perfect for the song. The album ends with "I'm Gonna Sit on the Porch and Pick on My Old Guitar," which was recorded at the first session for the album. The difference in Cash's voice between this and the preceding cut, which was recorded at the last session, shows the amount of strain it endured from being used so much (not to mention to the drying effects of the pills).

The 2002 reissue of the album includes two bonus tracks, both duets with George Jones. The first is a take on "I Still Miss Someone" that offers an interesting pairing of two legends and friends. The second is a killer cut of "I Got Stripes" that is so good it begs the question of why it was left off the original release.

"(Ghost) Riders in the Sky" was the album's first single, and gave all concerned a little hope as it peaked at #2, but those hopes proved short-lived after the release of "I'll Say It's True." Even the presence of George Jones—who would

Columbia made a big push to celebrate Cash's twenty-five years of music, but the company's relationship with Cash was a rocky one as both parties entered the new decade. *Author's collection*

experience a resurgence of his own in 1980—couldn't save the single, which peaked at #42.

With "I'll Say It's True" dying on the chart, country DJs began to spin Cash's second duet with Waylon Jennings, which had already been released as a B-side a year earlier, but now, as the year ended it was on its way to a peak position of #22. Columbia then released "Bull Rider," but it stalled at #66, killing any forward momentum Cash might have had on the chart.

"The pendulum's swung full circle in both Johnny Cash's personal life and his music," critic Rich Kienzle wrote in *Country Music*. "With the latter, he's gone from the spare, rough-hewn slapback of the Sun and early Columbia days to the dull, smothering orchestrations of the mid-seventies, and wound up back with the sound that got him started."

In the end, Brian Ahern had done the job he had been brought in to do. As he had on Emmylou's work, he found the right balance, most of the time, between traditional and contemporary elements. Buyers agreed, and though the album rose no higher on the charts than #28, it still did better than Cash's last album.

Silver was a fitting opening to the celebration of Cash's twenty-fifth year in the business. The next twenty-three would be filled with a lot of ups and downs—and more than a few surprises.

29

Lately I've Been Leanin' Toward the Blues

The 1970s #1s

Johnny Cash scored five #1s in the 1950s and another five in the '60s. With his attention often elsewhere in the '70s, he still managed three more chart-toppers.

"Sunday Morning Coming Down" (Live Version) b/w "I'm Gonna Try to Be That Way" (1970)

Knocked out "There Must Be More to Love Than This," Jerry Lee Lewis; knocked out by "Run, Woman, Run," Tammy Wynette

As with many of Cash's hits, there are a few stories around the song "Sunday Morning Coming Down," perpetuated by both Cash and writer Kris Kristofferson. Many (as with Shel Silverstein and "A Boy Named Sue") make it out to be Kristofferson's first song. Another tale was one of Cash's favorites, in which Kristofferson lands a helicopter on his front lawn and steps out with a beer in one hand and a tape containing the song in the other. The story, it turns out, is only partly true (as related in more detail in chapter 35).

"I remember mine and June's reaction to the song," Cash writes, in the liner notes to *The Johnny Cash Collection*. "It's one of those songs that you just know is a classic, and you know it so well that you are almost afraid to record it because you are afraid you will mess it up, so I didn't—not for two years after I heard it."

In the meantime, Ray Stevens had been building a career through the early '60s with songs like "Jeremiah Peabody's Polyunsaturated Quick-Dissolving, Fast-Acting Pleasant-Tasting Green and Purple Pills," "Ahab, the Arab," "Harry the Hairy Ape," and others on Mercury Records. In the late '60s, he signed to Monument Records, and, while still turning out novelty numbers like the Top 10 hit "Gitarzan," decided to move toward more serious material. *Have a Little Talk with Myself* was released in December 1969, and contained versions of Bob Dylan's "I'll Be Your Baby Tonight," Joe South's "Games People Play," and three songs from the Beatles ("Fool on the Hill," "Help," and "Hey Jude") along with other more serious-minded material. Among them was "Sunday Morning Coming Down." Stevens' version of the song is full of emotion and little touches that bring the song to life. One of those comes when he reaches the line "Stopped beside a Sunday school," and the background vocalists softly sing a snippet of the hymn "Bringing in the Sheaves"—a touch that Cash would later include in his live performances of the song.

"At the time Ray cut it, nobody had ever put that much money and effort into one of my songs," Kristofferson told *The Boot* in 2009, after being honored with the BMI Icon award. "He's a wonderful singer. The first time I heard it, I had to leave the publishing house. I went out and sat on the steps and wept. Of course, the record company didn't want him to put it out and go in that direction, because he was having success with those novelty songs at the time he cut it. Then John did it, and he had the hit with it."

The third story that is often told is that when Cash was preparing to perform the song on *The Johnny Cash Show* and record it for release as a single, the network suits objected to the line "Wishing, Lord, that I was stoned." They suggested it be changed to "Wishing, Lord, that I was home." Maybe they were nervous about that line coming from the mouth of someone who, just a few years earlier, had had his photo circulated around the country, with his hands in cuffs, beneath a headline announcing his drug arrest. Now he was a family man, and the star of a ratings-grabbing variety show.

Cash listened patiently and nodded. Kristofferson was disappointed, but he understood that his friend had to do what needed to be done. But while it might seem like a simple change, in many ways it would take away from the loneliness conveyed in the song. It's easy to be lonely away from home—another thing entirely to be lonely *at* home.

Kristofferson took his seat in the Ryman Auditorium's balcony and awaited Cash's performance of the song. When Cash reached the disputed line, he left it intact. Kristofferson maintains that Cash looked up at him in the balcony as he did so, and that it instantly made Cash his hero.

If the conversation with the network ever did happen, then the story above is an amalgam of truths, or half-truths. "Sunday Morning Coming Down" made its *Johnny Cash Show* debut on February 18, 1970, but it wasn't Cash who sang it. Instead it was Vikki Carr, a Liberty recording artist who had cut a version of the song for her new album, *Nashville by Carr*. Her version, too, keeps intact the line about being "stoned."

The next time the song appeared was February 25, 1970, as a part of the "Ride This Train" portion of the show, the segment where Cash would generally do a medley of thematically linked songs. Once again, Cash sang the word "stoned," and he did so again when he performed the song on the episode airing April 8th.

If the suits were nervous about the word, they must have gotten over it quickly. On April 29th, Kristofferson made a guest appearance on the show, and he and Cash sang "The Pilgrim, Chapter 33," the chorus of which also references being stoned. Cash performed "Sunday Morning" again as part of a "Ride This Train" segment on the second season opener, on September 23rd, and the following week Dennis Hopper joined him for a run-through of "The Pilgrim, Chapter 33." In the show's final season, after the song had become a hit, Kristofferson made an appearance to perform the song on November 18, 1970, and Cash sang it twice more, on February 17th, and on the final episode airing March 31, 1971.

No matter what the network thought, the song struck a strong chord with the fans. After "A Boy Named Sue," Cash had released three Top 5 singles: "Blistered" (#4), "If I Were a Carpenter" (a #2 duet with June), and "What Is Truth" (#3). The mix of loneliness and longing in "Sunday Morning" pushed the song to #1, where it met Jerry Lee Lewis' "There Must Be More to Love Than This." "Sunday Morning" stayed on top for two weeks before giving way to "Run, Woman, Run" by Tammy Wynette. But while two of Cash's other recent singles, "If I Were a Carpenter" and "What Is Truth," made it to the Hot 100, "Sunday Morning" never did.

"Flesh and Blood" b/w "This Side of the Law" (1971)

Knocked out "Rose Garden," Lynn Anderson; knocked out by "Joshua," Dolly Parton

Riding high in 1970, Cash was asked to do two movie soundtracks, *I Walk the Line*, which co-starred Gregory Peck and Tuesday Weld, and *Little Fauss and Big Halsy*, starring Robert Redford and Michael J. Pollard. The only single released from either was the tender love song "Flesh and Blood." *Billboard* gave the song a Spotlight review, saying, "Cash follows 'Sunday Morning Coming Down' with a strong piece of ballad material . . . an original and featured in the film *I Walk the Line.* Headed for a high spot on the Hot 100 and the top of the Country chart."

Cash first recorded the song, as "You're the One I Need," on August 20, 1969, and it made its public debut, briefly, in the movie *Johnny Cash: The Man, His World, His Music.* Cash performed the song again on *The Johnny Cash Show* on February 11, 1970.

He had written the song one afternoon on the farm with June, and the tenderness of the tune was unlike anything he had written for some time. He gives an account of the writing of the song on the *Storytellers* album with Willie Nelson. "June and I went for a drive down through the country and went to a place called Smithville, Tennessee . . . to Cedar Hill Lake," he recalls. "Spent the whole afternoon there. It was one of those magic days, you know, where the sun was just right and the temperature was just right, the breeze was just right, and she was just right." The crowd laughs, and Cash does too. "Uh, I wrote a song—I let her drive on the way back."

Billboard turned out to only be half right in its prediction for the single. The song went to #1 on the Country charts, knocking off Lynn Anderson and her career-making million-selling hit "Rose Garden," which also went to #3 on the

Hot 100. Cash spent a week there before giving it up to "Joshua" by Dolly Parton. "Flesh and Blood" spent only seven weeks on the Hot 100, peaking at #54.

"One Piece at a Time" b/w "Go On Blues" (1976)

Knocked out "After All the Good Is Gone," Conway Twitty; knocked out by "I'll Get Over You," Crystal Gayle

Nearly five years had passed since Cash's last #1 single. He had changed producers, and released some decent music, but nothing that struck a nerve with the public. "John called and said, 'Don, do you think you can come up with something else again?'" Don Davis, who had previously brought Cash "A Boy Named Sue," writes in his autobiography. "So I went through the songs and found 'One Piece at a Time.'"

After Davis found the song he discovered that the writer, Wayne Kemp, had recently been signed by Mercury Records and was planning to record and release the song for himself. Kemp had recorded a few low-level hits for MCA in the early 1970s, and was looking to come back strong on a new label. Davis tracked him down and told him that Cash wanted to record the song, telling

With the release of *Silver*, the House of Cash offered several pieces of memorabilia through mail order. *Author's collection*

Kemp that, if he let him, "you'd make a hell of a lot more money." Kemp couldn't say no to that, so he told Davis to go ahead.

"I got the idea from an old story an Air Force sergeant who told me about a guy that had stolen a helicopter piece by piece from an Air Force repair base," Kemp told a reporter in 1976. "The guy got caught sneaking the rotor blade out . . . it was the last piece he had to have."

Back in the studio, Cash was running through songs, but nothing was exciting him, so he decided to call it a day—until Marshall Grant stopped him and said they should work on "that song about the car." Grant describes the scene in his memoir, *I Was There When It Happened*: "'You think so?' he asked. 'I really do,' I told him. 'It's real catchy, and it's original.' He said, 'Ah, you just relate to it because you used to be a mechanic.' I told him that was probably part of the reason I liked it, but I said I really thought it had potential to be a hit for us."

According to Grant, Cash then laid down a scratch vocal and departed for the day, leaving the band to record the rest of the track before coming back later to add his final vocal. Don Davis disputes this account, saying that he was there to produce the session and that Cash remained the entire time, recording his part along with everyone else (John L. Smith's exhaustive discography seems to back up this version of events). Davis says that a concert promoter named Gene Ferguson was also on hand, and that he told Cash, "John, you just got through cutting a smash!" Grant had told him much the same thing, so the only one not seeing the song's potential was Cash.

Kemp had switched the song's setting from an air base to an auto plant in an effort to produce a hit. "I was trying to aim for a particular audience and I settled on the car industry," he reasoned. "I'm a believer that you really have to aim a song toward a ready made audience with a common interest before you have a hit. Let's say you've got sixteen million truck drivers in the country. If you make a million of them happy, you've got it made."

"One Piece at a Time" became Cash's thirteenth #1 single on May 29, 1976, and spent two weeks on top. Although the song features multiple guitars and piano, the overall feel evokes Cash's stripped-down earlier hits, and listeners, it seems, were in a nostalgic mood: the song it knocked from #1, Conway Twitty's "After All the Good Is Gone," sounded like a tribute to 1950s sock hops, while the song that supplanted it, "I'll Get Over You" by Crystal Gayle (her first #1), features crying fiddles reminiscent of many of her sister Loretta Lynn's early hits. Cash's song also spent ten weeks on the Hot 100, climbing to #29 before quickly dropping down.

In an amusing postscript to the hit, a car was commissioned from a local Nashville mechanic to accompany the song. "Johnny's producer phoned me in April of 1976 and said he thought 'One Piece at a Time' was going to be a hit and could we come up with a car to use in publicity shots," Bruce Fitzpatrick, the owner of Abernathy Auto Parts and Hilltop Auto Salvage, told Keith Martin for the book *Strange but True Tales of Car Collecting*. Fitzpatrick's crew went to work with what they had ("He knew I had a lot of Cadillacs"), and using parts from

1949 to the 1970s, they had it done in eight to ten days. The finished product was a multicolored and truly mismatched piece of work. The doors, which came from the different models, didn't even fit properly. The car was used for some publicity stills, and was then moved to the House of Cash museum, until it closed its doors in 1985. At that point, Fitzpatrick picked up the car and sent it to the great car show in the sky. "Today it's probably a Nissan or something," Fitzpatrick said.

While the Fitzpatrick Cadillac was still residing in the House of Cash, the owner of a coal company in Oklahoma started to build his own. Bill Patch always loved to tinker with cars, so he looked at the project as a challenge. He sent crews out to scour local salvage yards and eventually came up with all of the pieces, taken from cars built between 1949 and 1973, to assemble it. Patch finished the project and friends told him he should give it to Cash. After some thinking, he decided he would do just that, so he drove to Cash's Hendersonville home and waited by the gates until someone came out to check on him. Cash was curious, so he went out to have a look. What he saw wasn't the patchwork ensemble that he had on display at House of Cash, but a beautifully built black Cadillac. At first glance, you wouldn't notice the two headlights on one side opposite the one on the other, or that there were two doors on the driver side and one on the passenger side.

Patch told Cash he wanted to give him the car—no strings attached. It was a little hard for Cash to believe, but after a few weeks, and several phone conversations with Patch, he accepted the gift. In their conversations, Cash learned that Welch, which at the time had a population of around 750, was building a new civic auditorium. Patch was a member of the Lions Club, and they were working to raise $43,700 as part of a matching fund on the way to paying off the $218,000 project. Cash offered to do a benefit for them, so on October 7, 1977, Johnny, June, and the car, made their way to Welch for two sold-out performances.

Bill Patch passed away in the early '80s, and the car was sold in 1985 after the House of Cash closed. It can now be seen at Historic Auto Attractions in Roscoe, Illinois. It made its television debut on the 1979 NBC special *Country Stars of the '70s* (available on DVD from Shout Factory), in a music video of Johnny and June pantomiming as if in a silent movie, as they cruise around Hendersonville.

30

Her Body Was Made like a Song to Be Played

Columbia 1980

Musically, Johnny Cash's 1970s were a decade of experimentation, even as each turn was met with the joyous cry that he was back where he started. It was a frustrating reception for an artist who was striving to branch out. In the 1980s, he would continue in the same direction, always keen to change it up, even if just slightly.

Cash started the year with the release of his double-album gospel project, *A Believer Sings the Truth*. Columbia, still working *Silver*, hadn't wanted the album, so Cash took it elsewhere (as discussed in more detail in chapter 49).

Changes were made in Cash's band, too. Original Tennessee Two bassist Marshall Grant was fired as the year began, and in his place Cash brought in multi-instrumentalist Marty Stuart, who would become his son-in-law and a close friend for the rest of his life. The band, which had previously consisted of the Tennessee Three plus an extra guitarist and piano player, was expanded to eight members and rechristened the Great Eighties Eight.

"Song of the Patriot" (1980)

"Song of the Patriot" was released as a single, apropos of nothing, and reached #54 on the Country chart. It was written by Marty Robbins, who receives a vocal credit on the single, though it doesn't actually sound like his voice singing harmony.

"Mother Maybelle" and "What's Good for You (Should Be Good for Me)" (1980)

Marty Stuart had come to Nashville at age thirteen to play mandolin for bluegrass legend Lester Flatt and his band the Nashville Grass. By the time he put out his first solo album in 1977, he had been traveling and playing for over five

★★★★★ "THIS ALBUM IS A CLASSIC, IT WILL SET THE STAGE FOR COUNTRY MUSIC FOR THE DECADE."
THE LEGEND OF
Jesse James
AN ALBUM FEATURING PERFORMANCES BY
LEVON HELM
AS JESSE JAMES
JOHNNY CASH
AS FRANK JAMES
EMMYLOU HARRIS
AS ZERELDA JAMES
CHARLIE DANIELS
AS COLE YOUNGER
WITH ALBERT LEE AS JIM YOUNGER
"THE LEGEND OF JESSE JAMES," THE ALBUM.
ON A&M RECORDS & TAPES.
WRITTEN AND COMPOSED BY
PAUL KENNERLEY
© 1980 A&M Records, Inc. All Rights Reserved
PRODUCED AND ENGINEERED BY
GLYN JOHNS

Produced by Paul Kennerly, *The Legend of Jesse James* told the outlaw's story in song, with the help of Cash, Emmylou Harris, Charlie Daniels, and Levon Helm. *Author's collection*

years. Flatt disbanded his group the following year, due to his declining health, and died in 1979. After that, his group reassembled and continued on under the supervision of Curly Seckler. Their second album, *Take a Little Time*, included a tribute to Mother Maybelle, and they asked Cash to guest on the song (as well as a second number).

"I was producing an album on Lester's band," Stuart told *Country Music*. "And I remembered hearing John sing one of Lester's songs. So I called him and asked if he would come and sing on the record. He did, and it was great!"

"I believe God sometimes lays people on your heart early on just so you can prepare to know them later," Stuart later said, in a monologue included with his book of photos, *Country Music Masters*. "I met him in 1979 and when we shook hands, I literally heard thunder." It was the beginning of a long friendship.

To celebrate Cash's career, CBS brought together a large roster of country artists for a two-hour special on May 8, 1980.

Author's collection

Rockabilly Blues (1980)

Cash's first album of the new decade was once again heralded as a return to form, though this time it might actually have been true. Interestingly, instead of relying on one producer, or even self-producing the album, Cash worked with three different people on the record. The bulk of the album was produced by Cash's piano player, Earl Poole Ball (finally, a piano-playing producer who didn't put piano all over it!), who was able to represent the sound of the new expanded road band while still recalling the best of what had come before.

Cash brought four songs in for the recording. The first, "Cold Lonesome Morning," showcases Ball's arranging prowess, using a guitar sound that's contemporary, with few effects, and a musical break reminiscent of "Big River" that rocks up the song a bit. "W-O-M-A-N" would have been a perfect fit for country radio of the time, while "Rockabilly Blues (Texas 1955)" is a throwback to a rockabilly sound that Cash never really had in 1955. "She's a Goer" turns

One side of this 12-inch single contained "Without Love," which Cash recorded with Nick Lowe and Dave Edmunds. The other side was blank except for a laser-etched Johnny Cash signature.

Author's collection

the slash phrase "a goer" into a warning that the woman of the title is prone to leave her lovers.

One of the album's high points came via England. After her divorce from Jack Routh, Carlene Carter moved to the UK, where she met and soon married Nick Lowe, then a member of the pub-rock group Rockpile. The British pub-rock scene had given birth to several roots-oriented artists like Graham Parker, Elvis Costello, and Dave Edmunds. While touring the UK in late 1979, Cash recorded Lowe's "Without Love," which had appeared on Lowe's second album, *Labour of Lust*, released that year. Backed by Rockpile, plus Bob Wootton, Cash sounds confident, bouncing through the melody.

The remainder of the songs on the album draw from the best writers bouncing around Nashville. Billy Joe Shaver gets two cuts, the story song "The Cowboy Who Started the Fight" and the weeper "It Ain't Nothing New, Babe," the latter produced by Jack Clement. "The Twentieth Century Is Almost Over," written by Steve Goodman and John Prine and originally released on Goodman's 1977 LP *Say It in Private*, shows the wit of its writers.

"The Last Time" was the first Kris Kristofferson Cash had recorded in six years. The way his voice slips into it, like a body into a comfortable chair, suggests he shouldn't have waited so long. (In fact, a few years prior, the two had discussed recording an album together, where Cash would sing Kristofferson songs, and Kristofferson Cash's, but the album never came to be.) The final track on the album, "One Way Rider," came from Cash's son-in-law Rodney Crowell, and is a duet with June.

"Cold Lonesome Morning" was released as the album's first single, but even though it was stronger than much of Cash's recent output, it followed his last couple of singles in stalling outside the Top 50, at #53. As the year ended, "The Last Time," another strong song, performed even worse, halting at #85, while "Without Love," issued as Cash's first single of 1981, rose only to #78. And just like *Gone Girl*, the album didn't even make the chart at all.

Sometimes I Go Crazy, Sometimes I Go Sane

Columbia 1981

Johnny Cash had a rough start to the 1980s on the charts, but that didn't slow his momentum. Throughout 1981, he continued to tour the world, making stops in Germany and Australia. He also continued to make appearances on television shows, including *The Mike Douglas Show* and *The Muppet Show*, and on two CBS specials called *Country Comes Home*.

In March, Cash debuted another made-for-TV movie, *The Pride of Jesse Hallam*. He stars as Hallam, a Kentucky coal miner who sells his farm after the death of his wife and moves to Cincinnati, where his daughter needs an expensive operation. The problem is that Hallam is illiterate, and in the big city, that can't be hidden so easily as in the small coal-mining town he comes from.

It was a role that Cash identified with, and he was eager to help bring the problem to light. "When I was a kid back home in Arkansas," he told reporter Dick Kleiner, "I worked in the cotton fields and there were a lot of men I worked next to who couldn't read or write. And I saw how they got cheated because they were illiterate."

"Among singers who have been associated with Nashville, Cash is not the best actor," a syndicated review concluded. "But there is a rocklike integrity about Cash, a rugged and honest strength, that makes him totally believable as Jesse Hallam." Cash was honored by various organizations throughout the year for his work in helping bring more publicity to the problem.

Cash also hosted a special of his own in April. *Johnny Cash and the Country Girls* featured turns by June Carter Cash, Rosanne Cash, Emmylou Harris, Minnie Pearl, and *Hee Haw* "Honey" Misty Rowe. In one segment, twenty-eight female country singers—including Skeeter Davis, Jeannie C. Riley, Connie Smith, Kitty Wells, and Penny DeHaven—appear together on the *Opry* stage. One missing Grand Lady of the Opry was the feisty Jean Shepard, who decided she didn't need the exposure badly enough to stand in a crowd of other performers for such a brief time.

"They set it up with my booking agent," she told writer Jack Hurst. "When I got the contract, I read it: 'Such-and-such a day, Jean Shepard, *Johnny Cash Show*, blah, blah blah.' And then in parentheses it said, 'Cameo appearance.' I just chuckled to myself, tore the contract in half and threw it in the garbage."

By now, Cash was struggling in his personal life. One day, during some rare downtime at his farm in Hendersonville, he was walking through the small animal reserve on the grounds when an ostrich attacked him. The animal (whose mate had recently been removed) lashed out at Cash with its large talon, tearing into his stomach. The belt Cash was wearing prevented the ostrich from completely disemboweling him, and he was able to fight back with his walking stick before making it to safety. The surgery necessitated that Cash take prescription pain medication, which further fueled his slump back into addiction.

On top of that, as the family sat around the table for Christmas dinner at Cinnamon Hill, their Jamaican estate, three masked men brandishing weapons burst through the door, demanding money. Mistaking a friend of the family for John Carter, the leader of the men put a gun to his head, saying he would be shot unless their demands were met. Thankfully, everyone survived the ordeal, and the three men were brought to justice by the local law enforcement.

The Baron (1981)

As 1980 drew to an end, Cash was a part of a concept project called *The Legend of Jesse James*, which featured Levon Helm, Emmylou Harris, Rodney Crowell, and Charlie Daniels. Conceived by producer Paul Kennerly, it was a western epic focusing on the true cowboy outlaw story. At the same time, though, another "cowboy" threat was sneaking up on Cash.

With disco fading in popularity, the people who populated the dance clubs were looking for something else to do. John Travolta, star of *Saturday Night Fever*, lit the match with the movie *Urban Cowboy*, the backdrop of which was Gilley's, a large, modern, western-themed bar in Houston, Texas, owned by country artist Mickey Gilley. Seemingly overnight, all across the country, bars were installing mechanical bulls, while men and women alike bought cowboy hats and boots. The soundtrack raced to the top of the charts, with the main song, "Lookin' for Love" by Johnny Lee, going to #1 Country and #5 Pop.

Cash had seen two big trends come through country music. The first, the "Nashville sound," was a period when many in country music sweetened their records with strings and vocal choruses, forsaking the fiddles and steel guitar. Cash never fully succumbed to the temptation, although he did add (or at least allowed to be added) those same elements. Then, in the mid-to-late '70s, came the outlaw movement, and, again, many of the key musical elements—particularly those associated with Waylon Jennings—made their way into Cash's music.

The "urban-cowboy" era, however, was something different. With the Nashville sound and outlaw periods, the response came within the format of country music, but the urban-cowboy movement was taking place outside of

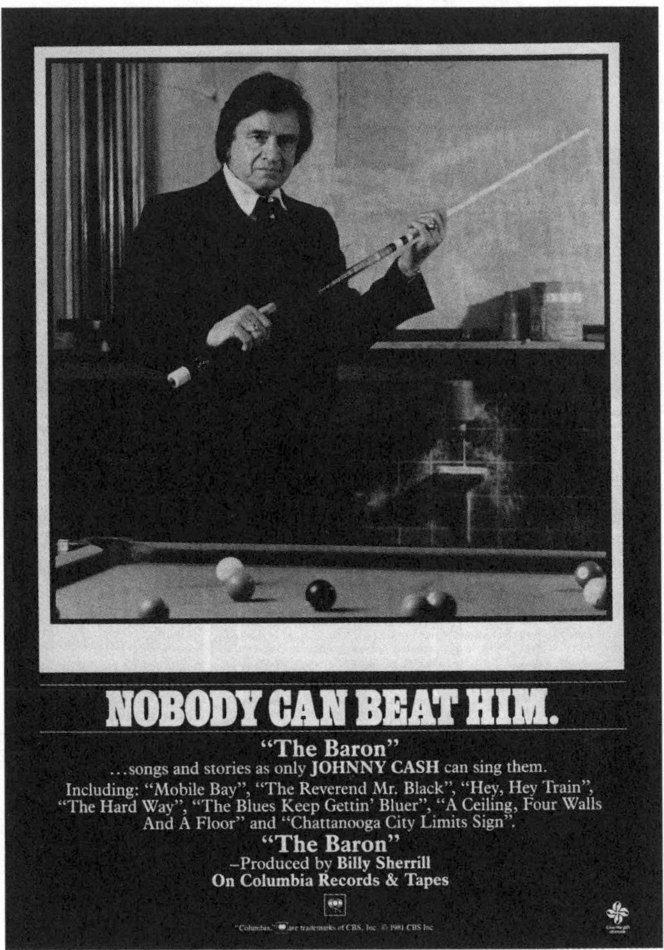

NOBODY CAN BEAT HIM.
"The Baron"
...songs and stories as only JOHNNY CASH can sing them.
Including: "Mobile Bay", "The Reverend Mr. Black", "Hey, Hey Train", "The Hard Way", "The Blues Keep Gettin' Bluer", "A Ceiling, Four Walls And A Floor" and "Chattanooga City Limits Sign".
"The Baron"
–Produced by Billy Sherrill
On Columbia Records & Tapes

Though the music isn't up to Cash's usual high standard, *The Baron* is one of Cash's highest charting albums of the 1980s, maybe on the strength of famed-producer and Columbia A&R man Billy Sherrill.

Author's collection

country, and making an impact in pop. Within a year, country music was selling almost 50 percent *more* albums than before—largely thanks to artists who were continuing the pop-country crossover work started in the Nashville sound era. And, as labels are wont to do, they followed the money—and wanted their artists to follow the money, too. Columbia decided Cash needed to produce a hit album, and, in order to do that, paired him with the head of A&R in Nashville, Billy Sherrill. With two albums out of his last three not even charting, and his life nearly overtaken again by the pills, Cash didn't have much fight left in him to protest.

Sherrill was known for producing luxurious arrangements, and as he and Cash entered the studio on September 5, 1980, George Jones was coming down from #1 and moving back to #2 with two Sherrill-produced singles, "He Stopped Loving Her Today" and "I'm Not Ready Yet," respectively. The former had been Jones' first #1 in nearly four years, and Columbia had hopes that Sherrill could repeat the feat with another of the aging acts on its roster.

Unfortunately, *The Baron* was a repeat of the *John R. Cash* scenario, where Cash had little input and wrote none of the songs for the album. The title track is a story song about a pool hustler who discovers that the kid he's trying to hustle is his own son—one he didn't know he had. Cash delivers it convincingly, with an authoritative voice—something that didn't come across in the album's second song, "Mobile Bay," the story of a bunch of hobos sitting around a trashcan fire, thinking about old times and places. "The Hard Way" is ill-suited to Cash, with an arrangement that would have been a better fit for, well, just about anyone else.

Tom T. Hall's "A Ceiling, Four Walls, and a Floor" comes the closest to being the sort of record Cash had been moving toward throughout the late '70s, while "Hey, Hey Train" is really what the whole album should have been. A rocking train song featuring a blistering guitar break from its writer, Marty Stuart, it gave Cash a little more energy, though he still sounds reserved as he shouts that the train is taking his girl from town.

"The Reverend Mr. Black" is another story song that weaves the Carter Family's "Lonesome Valley" throughout. "The Blues Keep Gettin' Bluer" is almost as ill-fitting as "The Hard Way," though this one at least gives Cash a pleasant melody to work with. One song that he could really sink his teeth into was "Chattanooga City Limit Sign." Borrowing liberally from both "One Piece at a Time" and Charlie Daniels' "Uneasy Rider," it tells the story of an unfortunate hitchhiking experience, and was obviously designed to duplicate the success of the former.

"Thanks to You" is a generic song of thanks to someone—the listener is never quite sure if it is the audience, or a woman—for the hit songs about heartache. But even that sounds good next to the final song, "The Greatest Love Affair," which is mainly a recitation, in which Cash talks about a love affair, sharing good times and bad, over a lavish background. In the end, it turns out that the song is not about a woman but his country. Yep.

If the point of the album was to generate more chart success, "The Baron" nearly achieved it by hitting the Top 10 (at #10) after a slow, two-month climb. The follow-up single, "Mobile Bay," took Cash right back down, stalling at #60. The last hit attempt of the year was the double-sided single "Chattanooga City Limits Sign" b/w "Reverend Mr. Black," but both petered out at #71.

Even with reviews like Bill Flanagan's ("This is a real disappointment") and Dave Mulholland ("Solid, but lacking spark"), the album entered the Hot Country LPs chart at #29—Cash's highest debut since 1976's *One Piece at a Time.*

But after two weeks of ticking up, it dropped down and off the chart over the next month and a half.

Perhaps because of Sherrill's involvement (rather than the overall strength of the album), Columbia promoted *The Baron* with a tie-in to the urban-cowboy movement, holding contests at the four biggest country radio stations in Dallas. Two of the stations held pool tournaments, while the other two accepted mail-in entries. The winners from each station met for another tournament at Billy Bob's Texas, competing to win a new pool table.

The label also sprung for a music video for "The Baron," starring Cash as the pool shark who, in living color, goes to hustle the kid, played by Marty Stuart. For whatever reason, the song and video were strong enough to convince someone in Hollywood to produce a made-for-television movie starring Johnny and June the following year, although Stuart gave up his role as Billy Joe.

In a 1988 interview with Bill Flanagan, Cash took partial blame for the album's failure by saying his mind was elsewhere—on television shows, movies, "and crap like that." But he placed most of the blame with Sherrill, saying, "Sometimes you go in a direction that your producer convinces you you need at the time, you know? And I listened to too many of those people. I know what I want when I get in the studio, and I let too many people tell me otherwise."

It certainly wasn't the last time he would do so.

32

John Taught Me a Whole Lot About Country Music

Columbia 1982

After the disappointment of *The Baron*, Cash made a slight comeback in 1982, powered in part by his teaming up with old friends. But before any new records were released, he recorded another CBS television special, *Johnny Cash: Cowboy Heroes*. Unlike his salute to the more fictionalized West from 1971, this special focused on the real-life cowboys from history, and those who still worked the ranches of Texas. The special included appearances by June Carter Cash and friends the Oak Ridge Boys and John Anderson.

Cash's second special of the year was for HBO and brought together songwriters John Prine, Steve Goodman, and Rodney Crowell for a patriotic show called *Johnny Cash America*. The seventy-five-minute show was recorded at the Kennedy Center in Washington, DC, and relived through song some of the highlights of the country's history.

"One More Ride," "Hey Porter," and "Get in Line Brother" (1982)

Just before Marty Stuart joined the Cash band full-time, he recorded an album for Sugar Hill called *Busy Bee Cafe*. Cash guested on three songs: the Sons of the Pioneers' "One More Ride," Cash's own "Hey Porter," and the Lester Flatt song "Get in Line Brother," where Cash is part of a vocal trio. On all three songs, Cash sounds as if he is having a blast—especially compared with tracks from *The Baron*. Stuart's excitement for the material (and in particular the material by his heroes, like Cash and Flatt) is infectious, and you can tell Cash had been infected.

"The General Lee" (1982)

Waylon Jennings served as narrator for *The Dukes of Hazzard*, and the show's producers decided to capitalize on that by releasing a soundtrack album of music used on and inspired by the show, featuring Waylon, Willie Nelson, Johnny Cash, and Doug Kershaw, along with series stars John Schneider, James Best, Catherine Bach, Tom Wopat, and Sorrell Brooks. Cash's contribution was "The General Lee," though it is not about the former Confederate general but about the car the Duke boys drove. Thanks to the popularity of the television show, the single reached #26, a higher chart placing than the last couple of Cash singles.

The Survivors (1982)

Just days after recording those three tracks for Marty Stuart's *BusyBee Cafe* in April, Cash and his crew left for a European tour. Also on tour at the time, and performing near one of the stops, were Carl Perkins and Jerry Lee Lewis. At the Sporthalle in Stuttgart, West Germany, fans were treated to a regular Johnny Cash show, featuring twenty-nine songs. Then, in a sort of surprise reprise of the Million Dollar Quartet, Perkins and Lewis joined Cash onstage.

On the album recorded that night, the first two songs come from Cash's solo portion of the show, and the most interesting thing to note is the band's new live dynamic, with Stuart giving "Get Rhythm" and "I Forgot to Remember to Forget" an extra dimension by playing the mandolin, an instrument not normally heard on Cash albums.

Carl Perkins then joins Cash for "Goin' Down the Road Feelin' Bad" and "That Silver-Haired Daddy of Mine," before going solo on "Matchbox." Then the Killer makes his grand entrance, and the trio launches into the gospel sing-along standard "I'll Fly Away," with Lewis—feeling the spirit, or maybe just the spotlight—shouting and hollering his way through the song. His solo turn comes with "Whole Lotta Shakin' Goin' On" and "Rockin' My Life Away," before Perkins returns with "Blue Suede Shoes." The trio rounds out the album together with three spiritual songs: "(There'll Be) Peace in the Valley (for Me)," "Will the Circle Be Unbroken," and "I Saw the Light."

At the time of the recording, Cash's career was on autopilot, while Carl Perkins hadn't released an album since 1974's *My Kind of Country*. Jerry Lee Lewis, on the other hand, had had a Top 10 hit the previous fall with his rendition of "Over the Rainbow," and a Top 5 hit earlier in 1981 with "Thirty Nine and Holding." When *The Survivors* came out, it was an exercise in nostalgia. All of the songs performed were decades old, but it made it to #21 on the Country chart, where it stayed for three weeks.

In the liner notes for the album, Cash says that the three had been crossing paths in Europe, and that their collaboration in Stuttgart was spontaneous, but in truth, the trio had met up first a few days earlier, in Rotterdam, the Netherlands. That night, rather than playing separate songs, they ran through a few medleys of the same material instead. A bootleg (entitled *Rockabilly Reunion*) exists of that whole show, featuring both Cash's solo part and the trio ripping the roof off of the Ahoy Hall, with the crowd chanting, "We want more!" Both this show and/or the full concert from which *The Survivors* was extracted would make excellent additions to the official *Bootleg* series released by Legacy Recordings.

The Adventures of Johnny Cash (1982)

"I was five years old the first time I heard Johnny Cash's voice," Marty Stuart recalls, on the CD that accompanies his book *Country Music: The Masters.*

> It crept into my heart, and it has lived there ever since. What drew me into his world was the fact that he wasn't your ordinary hillbilly singer. He was dark. He sounded to me as though he was singing from a room that had seen better days, maybe with only one light bulb hanging down from the ceiling. I felt like too much light shining on him made him uncomfortable. I saw him as a shadow on the wall—a mystery, regal as they come, yet common as a biscuit. I had the feeling that if I were to ever run with him, I'd see my share of trouble, but I didn't care. Seemed like it'd be worth it.

In 1982, after spending six years with his hero Lester Flatt, Marty Stuart was traveling the world with another childhood hero. "I started in his band in the early 1980s," he said, of playing with Cash, "and I played there for six years. I was around him all the time. During this time I had a microscopic view of his world. Following him around was an amazing adventure, no doubt about it. And he was, without a doubt, the most charismatic man that God ever made."

What Stuart saw on that tour—in front of crowds who were on their feet shouting, like the one in Rotterdam—was the Cash he had envisioned as he listened repeatedly to *At Folsom Prison.* Stuart challenged Cash to find that energy again. But at the same time, changes were afoot at Cash's record label, and indeed within the whole music industry. The old-school record men—or at least the few who remained—were being replaced by bean counters, people who didn't hear the music but simply saw the numbers. Along with the emphasis on numbers came marketing reports and studies on what listeners wanted to hear, and which artists they wanted to hear singing it. The days of a good song by an unknown artist breaking out over the airwaves were almost gone. The landscape of radio was shifting, largely under the weight of the urban cowboys. Cash responded in much the same way that he had in the past: by starting a gospel project with Stuart, and another new album with Jack Clement.

Clement and Cash had been recording together sporadically over the past several months, when Cash wasn't on the road, so by February 1982, they already had three songs in the can. The rest of the album took shape over two sessions in early February, on the 4th and the 8th.

In the studio, Cash's band was augmented by John Hartford on fiddle and banjo and Chuck Cochran on keyboards. "We're in the fun business," Clement was fond of saying. "If we're not having fun, we're not doing our job." On *The Adventures of Johnny Cash*, they were doing their job.

To open the album, the band kicks into Billy Joe Shaver's "Georgia on a Fast Train," and Cash lets loose an unbridled, and uncharacteristic, yodel. The song's freight-train rhythm and loose arrangement set the tone for the rest of the album. "John's," written by Marshall Grant's replacement, Joe Allen, looks back fondly at times spent hanging out at a local gas station, learning life lessons from the owner. While not a bad song, it seems out of place in the context of the album, a piece of filler among a clutch of strong songs.

"Fair Weather Friends," a co-write by Allen and Cash (and Cash's only songwriting contribution to the album) quickly puts things back on track. Cash was singing from a deep well of experience of a business filled with fair-weather friends—friends who don't seem to be around when the hits aren't coming. And the hits hadn't come for Cash for some time.

Next, Cash tees up John Prine's "Paradise," the story of the demise of a town (or even a region) due to the strip-mining of coal. It comes in stark contrast to the Bob McDill and Allen Reynolds' song "We Must Believe in Magic," which offers further evidence of Clements' quirky influence on Cash. The song was

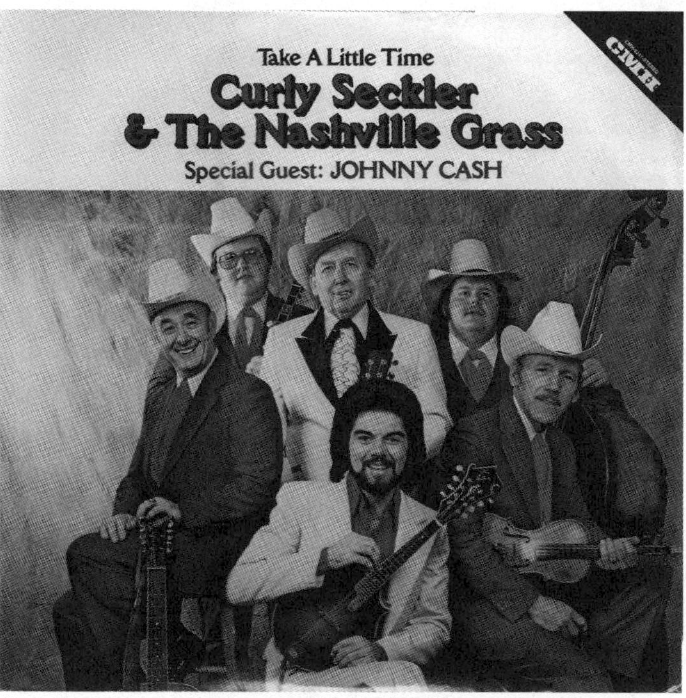

Cash guested on two songs on the 1980 album released by Lester Flatts's old band, fronted by Curly Seckler and featuring Marty Stuart. It was the beginning of many years of collaborations between Cash and Stuart, who joined his band full-time a short time after.

Author's collection

originally recorded by Crystal Gayle in 1977, its space-age mysticism layered with Moog synths. A year later, Clement stripped the song down, replacing the synths with a throbbing bass and adding whispering background voices for a version of his own. For Cash's version, the whispers remain, except only on the word "magic," with strings replacing the synths. The song served as Cash's third single from the album, but just as with the two previous versions, it failed to hit with audiences, staying on the charts for two weeks and peaking at #84. (At least Crystal Gayle got to perform her version on *The Muppet Show*.)

Cash returns to the work of John Prine, this time with co-writers Roger Cook and Sandy Mason, on "Only Love," before moving on to the work of Merle Haggard with "Good Old American Guest." Haggard had released the song on his 1981 Epic Records debut, *Big City*, before Cash, ever fully comfortable with train songs, put out a version that rivaled Merle's own.

"I'll Cross Over Jordan Someday," written by Peck Chandler, is a counterpart to "Far Side Banks of Jordan"—"If God loves me like I love you, I'll be in Heaven for sure." Don Devaney's "Ain't Gonna Hobo No More" focuses on another favorite Cash topic, the train-hopping hobo, and features a Buck Trent/Clarence White–inspired guitar break by Marty Stuart.

"Sing a Song" is one of the most interesting songs on the album, showing Cash's commitment to a good song in more ways than one. Back in the mid-1950s, his buddy Carl Perkins had a friend named Edd Cisco, who would play guitar with him on occasion. Cisco eventually went into radio, but he kept in close contact with Perkins, with the pair even going in together to buy property for both families to live on. In 1981, Edd brought his son Tommy, an aspiring songwriter, with him on a trip to Nashville, where he was able to play a few songs for Cash. "Sing a Song" jumped out: Cash wanted to record it, and it's no wonder. After more than twenty-five years of performing music all across the world, constantly fighting the addiction that began as a way to be able to do that very thing, the feelings in the song had to speak to him. The song's narrator knows people have come to see him, even as he "looks so tired and old" and struggles to stand still. "Try not to think," he sings in the chorus. "Act like it don't hurt."

Columbia released three singles from the album, but with little success. "Georgia on a Fast Train" reached only #55, while "Fair Weather Friends" did not chart at all, and "We Must Believe in Magic" stalled at #84. The album itself failed to chart.

I Tell You Folks I'm Ragged but I'm Right

Columbia 1983

Before trying to get his career back on track with a new album in 1983, Cash released yet another made-for-TV movie. *Murder in Coweta County* tells the true story of a small-town sheriff, played by Cash, working to bring down a rural kingpin, played by Andy Griffith.

It was during the filming of the movie, in Georgia, that Cash's drug use came to a head. One day, John Carter found his father unconscious and unresponsive in his hotel bed. He and June managed to get Johnny's large frame into a bathtub, where they ran a shower of cold water over him. When Cash woke up, his son, then only twelve years old, unleashed on him, telling him what he was doing to his family. But nothing changed. (In fact, after the incident with the ostrich, it got worse.)

Incidents like the one in Georgia became more frequent. June, pushed to the limit, went to spend time in England with Carlene. She even contemplated filing for divorce and moving herself and John Carter out of the worsening situation. Then, on November 22, 1983, Cash was admitted to the hospital in Nashville with a bleeding ulcer. Things looked grim, and June came home to him, even though he was still hanging on to his pills. While he was in the hospital, the family decided it was time for an intervention. And after realizing how much pain he was bringing on his family, Cash agreed to check into the Betty Ford Center (then fairly new) to begin a period of rehabilitation.

Johnny 99 (1983)

After Cash's last album with his chosen producer had failed, Columbia wanted to pair him with a hit-maker, suggesting he work, once again, with Brian Ahern. Cash was not thrilled with the idea, but he went along with it—publicly, at least. During a 1983 appearance on the *Country Close-up with Glen Campbell* radio show, he explained:

> Brian Ahern produced the *Silver* album, and we felt like we didn't really get completed with the project that we wanted to do. We wanted to do

> more songs than ten—we had a list of about forty that we wanted to do. I had a couple of other producers in between, but finally I was able to get to California and work with Brian. And as it turned out we called the album *Johnny 99*, which is the title of a Bruce Springsteen song, which is on the album. We did songs that we'd talked about doing back when I did the *Silver* album. Songs like "I'm Ragged but I'm Right," "Brand New Dance," "New Cut Road," and some of those. But then when I heard "Highway Patrolman" and "Johnny 99" I said, "Well, I'm ready to cut that new album with Brian." I thought he'd be the producer for that project.

The Springsteen songs were two of five Cash brought to the sessions. His label thought it was a bad idea. "I don't want to hear you do Springsteen," Columbia president Rick Blackburn told him, "I want to hear you do Johnny Cash." It was an interesting sea change from the early '60s, when Columbia had taken out an ad in the music trade press to promote the fact that Johnny Cash was recording his labelmate Bob Dylan's songs. Now, Cash couldn't get support to record the songs of another labelmate who was being hailed as the future of rock 'n' roll. But Cash felt strongly about doing the songs.

"[June] had heard 'Highway Patrolman' somewhere," he recalled, "and she suggested I get it. I bought it, and I played the whole tape and I kind of zeroed in on 'Highway Patrolman' and 'Johnny 99' as being songs that would be right for me. I felt like they were. 'Johnny 99' is the kind of thing I was writing twenty-five or more years ago—well, maybe not as good, Springsteen is a great writer. I feel good about recording it and I feel good about performing it."

The album was recorded in North Hollywood in April of 1983, with Ahern assembling a crack team of musicians, including legendary Wrecking Crew drummer Hal Blaine, guitarist James Burton, and keyboardist Glen D. Hardin. From Cash's camp came only Bob Wootton, Marty Stuart, and Jo-El Sonnier. Cash's cut of "Highway Patrolman," which opens the album, uses that team to full effect, building a moody sound that expands on Springsteen's stark guitar-and-harmonica original.

Bigger changes follow on "Johnny 99." In keeping with *Nebraska*'s bleak tone, Springsteen opens his version of the song with an off-mic bellow that brings to mind the mournful singing of a chain gang, before launching into a feisty, almost rockabilly story of a laid-off autoworker who decides to take it out on those around him, going off on a killing spree before being sentenced to death. Cash's full-band version removes some of the rawness of the original, but in doing so makes it almost too sing-songy.

Among the other tracks Cash brought in were "That's the Truth" and "Brand New Dance," which he sings here with June. Both were written by Paul Kennerly, of whom Cash explained:

> Paul Kennerly is an Englishman and he wrote the Jesse James album of which I was a part of along with Emmylou Harris, Levon Helm and Charlie Daniels. Paul Kennerly is one of those unique writers who can write on assignment. You can tell him what you want written and he can

> write it. Like he wrote the Jesse James album, and he also wrote *White Mansions* that Waylon was on. But he's written all these songs, and these two of his that I recorded—"Brand New Dance" with June Carter, and "That's the Truth"—we didn't ask him for 'em, but we had about six or eight Paul Kennerly songs to pick from. He's got some really good songs that I have on hold—course a lot of other people do, too, because he's such a great writer.

Cash's final pick was George Jones' 1956 hit "I'm Ragged but I'm Right." Ahern brought in "God Bless Robert E. Lee"—a story from the end of the Civil War told from the perspective of a soldier thankful that Lee has called off a battle they were sure to lose—plus a grab bag of songs that show the interesting interconnectedness of the music scene.

Emmylou Harris had recorded "New Cut Road" in 1978 for her Ahern-produced LP *Quarter Moon in a Ten Cent Town*, although it wasn't released until it was included on the 2004 reissue of the album. Rodney Crowell, Harris' rhythm guitarist, produced the 1981 album *The South Coast of Texas* by the song's writer, Guy Clark, as well as a version by Bobby Bare that went to #18 in 1982.

Steven Rhymer, who wrote "Ballad of the Ark," had played guitar on Anne Murray's 1974 album *Love Song* and written songs recorded by Jonathan Edwards, who was from Harris' old stomping grounds in the DC/Virginia area, and whose albums Ahern produced. Likewise, "Girl from the Canyon" was written by Jonathan Edwards and included on his Ahern-produced 1977 album *Sailboat.* (Keith Whitley, a friend of former Hot Band member Ricky Skaggs, recorded the song for his 1982 album *Somewhere Between.*)

"Joshua Gone Barbados" was a Jamaica-tinged tune by Eric Von Schmidt, who had been a part of the 1960s East Coast folk scene with Bob Dylan. It was something different for Cash, but while he didn't want to alienate his fans, he felt strongly about doing the album his way.

> It's more trying to keep track of who my fans are and where they are, you know, and what they want to hear. I have limitations. I know they like Alabama and they like Shelly West and this one and that one, but I don't do music that way. I do Johnny Cash style music. Sometimes I reach out and get a new song like "Joshua Gone Barbados" that just happens to feel right to me. Or "Highway Patrolman" or "Johnny 99" . . . they're right down my street, as they say. I don't record a song unless I feel like I can deliver it. I don't record a song unless I feel like I can work it up in concert.

Though the album met with positive reviews (many of them leaning heavily on the Springsteen songs), the fans' reaction didn't match Cash's enthusiasm. The first single, "I'm Ragged but I'm Right" stalled at #75 Country, while the second and third singles, "Johnny 99" and "That's the Truth," failed to chart at all. The album didn't chart either.

Cash, as he was becoming wont to do, placed the blame on Ahern. "That album was produced in California by Brian Ahern," he told Bill Flanagan. "I didn't have all that much control over the material on that album. He played producer with me, you know?"

Koncert V Praze—In Prague Live (1983)

Consisting entirely of live versions of previously released Cash material, plus Earl Poole Ball's take on Floyd Cramer's "Last Date," there is nothing particularly to distinguish this recording. It was actually recorded on April 11, 1978, and initially released only in Europe, not appearing in the States until 1983. Mostly, it stands as a document of how Cash's live shows had sounded just a couple of years before the release of Marshall Grant and the formation of the Great Eighties Eight.

Warm Up My Limousine, Take Me to the Top of Some Ol' Mountain

Columbia 1984

The Baron had been Johnny Cash's highest-charting album of the past five years, which is perhaps what led someone—maybe inspired by the video for the title track—to decide to expand it to a made-for-TV movie. The plot follows that of the song, so there aren't any surprise twists—just another CBS vehicle for Cash to indulge another facet of his creativity.

This year, for the first time since 1962, Cash did not release a single album of new material. His only album release for the year was a compilation of songs assembled from his 1980 gospel album *A Believer Sings the Truth.* Cash had entered the studio with Billy Sherrill, hoping to capture a little of whatever it was that nudged *The Baron* up the charts, but after recording more than an album's worth of songs, the project was shelved, and both parties moved on without a word. (Those recordings, with new instrumentation, were released in 2014 as *Out Among the Stars.*) Only one song from the sessions was released as a single, and boy, was it a doozy.

"Chicken in Black" (1984)

There are a couple of periods of Cash's career that many fans choose to ignore completely. One of the biggest entries in that category is his 1984 single "Chicken in Black"—one of only two solo singles released by Columbia that year. Written by Gary Gentry, the song tells the story of an ailing Johnny Cash going to a doctor, who performs a brain transplant that gives Cash the brain of a bank robber. When he starts demanding money from the audience of the *Opry*, he calls the doctor to get his old brain back, only to find it has been put in a chicken, which is now touring the circuit as the Chicken in Black.

While the song is as goofy as it sounds—and the video twice that—it is interesting to take a closer look at it. When Cash recorded the song on April 11, 1984, his career was certainly on the downward trend. Not only that, but he had been battling his addiction, and the health problems that came with it, to the point that there were times his family feared for his life. As he got stronger, physically, he entered the studio with Billy Sherrill to begin work on another album.

It is fairly easy to see the line of thinking the record executives used here. They wanted a hit, and for all its failings, "The Baron" had been Cash's highest-charting song in nearly five years—since 1979's "(Ghost) Riders in the Sky," in fact—so it seemed natural for them to want to bring in Sherrill, since he had helmed that project, and was a known hit producer.

The song selection itself was a Hail Mary. Remember, Cash's two biggest hits, "A Boy Named Sue" and "One Piece at a Time," were novelty songs, although granted both are much cleverer than the goofy "Chicken." But Nashville is a big place with a small-town mind set, meaning word travels fast, and Columbia had heard that Ray Stevens had signed a new contract with Polygram and was readying a new album of his signature novelty tunes.

In June, the label rolled the dice and released "Chicken in Black" as a single. While many—including Cash himself—would want to deny the whole thing ever happened, the fact is the song spent eleven weeks on the chart—only one week less than 1982's "The General Lee," a novelty song about a car—and peaked at #45, making it also his highest-charting single since "The General Lee." In a concert recording taped just three weeks after Cash cut the studio version of the song (but just before its release), the audience responds positively to it, whooping and laughing, just as those convicts did during "A Boy Named Sue."

But after hearing the thoughts of friends and family, Cash turned his back on the song, and, in the record company's eyes, killed its chance at becoming a hit. Who's to say? It is certainly an aberration in Cash's catalogue—even compared with *Everybody Loves a Nut*—but if that audience reaction was any gauge, it was always a possibility that it might have become a hit. Meanwhile, Ray Stevens' Polygram debut, *He Thinks He's Ray Stevens*, went to #3 on the Top Country Albums chart and #118 on the Pop 200, spawning the Top 20 single "Mississippi Squirrel Revival," and its 1985 follow-up, *I Have Returned*, which went to #1.

The B-side to "Chicken in Black," "Battle of Nashville," tells a different story. Named for the famous Civil War battle, the song is about a man losing the battle for a woman's heart and in doing so thinking about leaving town to avoid the pain. But the conviction in Cash's voice during the chorus suggests he may have had even a third context in mind as he sings of how there's "a troubling deep in my soul" and his "forces are out of control."

The sentiment is similar to the one expressed in "Crazy Old Soldier," the Paul Kennerly/Troy Seals song Cash recorded with Ray Charles for *Friendship*, Charles' 1984 album of duets. In perhaps the most telling evidence of Cash's commercial cachet at the time, five singles from the album charted in the Top 20, with Charles' duets with Willie Nelson, George Jones, Mickey Gilley, B. J. Thomas, and Hank Williams Jr. reaching #1, #6, #12, #14, and #14, respectively. But though the Cash-Charles pairing produced an excellent take on the song, it failed to chart at all.

Like Desperados Waiting for a Train

The Highwaymen

Sometimes you just need a little support from your friends—even if you're Johnny Cash. In 1985, with his recording career stalling out after more than thirty years, those friends helped carry him back to the top of the charts with a dream collaboration by country music's biggest rebels.

Kris Kristofferson

After spending time in the army and as a Rhodes Scholar, Kristofferson decided to try to make it as a songwriter in 1965, moving to Nashville and picking up whatever jobs he could that would get him close to the music business. One of those jobs was as a janitor at Columbia Studios, where he would see the likes of Johnny Cash and Bob Dylan recording, though he was forbidden by his bosses to approach them. Soon enough, people began noticing his songs, including Dave Dudley, who recorded "Viet Nam Blues" in 1966. Others quickly followed, among them Ray Stevens, Roger Miller, Jerry Lee Lewis, and Faron Young.

Like every songwriter in the late 1960s, Kristofferson wanted to get a song on a Johnny Cash album. He had first met Cash backstage at the *Grand Ole Opry*, which he was attending as a guest of songwriter Marijohn Wilken, a relative of a friend.

Since he was forbidden from speaking to Cash at work, Kristofferson decided to slip tapes of his songs to guitarist Luther Perkins and June Carter Cash. This had little effect, however, as Cash was given so many tapes that he would just pitch them into the lake behind his house without listening to them. So Kristofferson decided to take another approach. To make ends meet, he had joined the National Guard, and as such had access to the helicopter he would pilot on his weekend duties. He decided maybe a grand statement would help, so he landed the chopper on Cash's front lawn.

Now, over the hundreds of retellings of this story, the details have shifted and changed, grown and expanded. The way Cash and his wife often told it, Kristofferson stepped out of the helicopter with a beer in one hand and a tape in the other, and on that tape was "Sunday Morning Coming Down." In June's telling, Cash, fuming, met Kristofferson midway across the yard, took the tape, and threw it in the lake.

Years later, after both Johnny and June had died, Kristofferson admitted that it didn't happen quite that way. "The story about me getting off the helicopter with a tape in one hand and a beer in the other isn't true," he told Rob Hughes for *Uncut.* "Y'know, John had a very creative imagination. I've never flown with a beer in my life. Believe me, you need two hands to fly those things."

In an interview with Chet Flippo, he added:

> I don't believe that ["Sunday Morning Coming Down"] was the one that I gave him that day. I don't think he ever cut that one, but I'm sure that John heard me singing it to him out at his house because . . . there were three or four of us that could call up John when we really felt needy, and we could show him what we were doing and he would raise our spirits. He never let us down, and every time that I can remember, I wouldn't overdo it to bother him or invade his privacy, but it was one of the great experiences for us at the time because we weren't getting any songs recorded, but just to have him listen and give us encouragement was the great thing.

Cash invited Kristofferson to the Newport Folk Festival in 1969 and gave part of his stage time to him. It was one of Kristofferson's first high-profile live performances. Based on his success as a songwriter, Monument Records signed Kris to an artist deal in 1970. The posthumous release of Janis Joplin's version of "Me and Bobby McGee" saw his profile rise further, and he began to branch out into movies. He continued as a performer throughout the 1970s, before turning his attention back to films following the release of 1981's *To the Bone.* One of those films, *Songwriter,* paired him with Willie Nelson, with whom he collaborated on the soundtrack. *Music from Songwriter* was released in October 1984, just prior to the formation of the Highwaymen.

Willie Nelson

After moving to Nashville in 1960, Willie Nelson found that his unique vocal style made him a hard sell to record labels looking for smooth, crooning voices to feed into the Nashville sound machine. While his singing was an acquired taste, his songwriting was immediately recognized as something that could, and should, be latched onto. Soon, his songs were topping the charts for artists including Faron Young ("Hello Walls"), Ray Price ("Night Life"), and Patsy Cline ("Crazy").

While his songs were becoming hits for others, Nelson continued to make records of his own, though they met with little success. His voice just didn't mesh with the prevailing formulas of the day. From 1970 onward, his albums started to exhibit a little more of his musical personality, and in 1973 he broke away from RCA and became the first country artist to sign to Atlantic Records. Known more for its rock and soul rosters, the label had decided to open a new country division, although it wouldn't last long. Nelson's relationship with the label was a brief one—lasting only two records—but formed an important part of his journey.

Soon afterward, Willie—or, perhaps more accurately, his manager Neil Reshen—struck a deal with Columbia records, this time one that included full creative control. Though Columbia had its reservations upon hearing the results, the new relationship resulted in Nelson's first #1 album, *Red Headed Stranger*. He followed it up with three more #1 albums and a #2. By now, he was at the center of the outlaw movement spearheaded by Willie and his pal Waylon.

But while Waylon continued on with the phased-out boom-chicka-boom, Willie blazed his own trail within the movement, reaching back to the Great American Songbook and his other formative influences. In 1980, he too began acting, appearing in several movies, including the seemingly autobiographical *Honeysuckle Rose*. At the time the Highwaymen gathered, he was still consistently charting in the Top 10.

Waylon Jennings

Of all the Highwaymen, Jennings was the one with whom Cash had the most history. They had shared a small apartment for a brief period of time just after Johnny moved to Nashville, and their friendship continued through the years. They finally recorded together two decades later, hitting the charts in 1978 with "Ain't No Good Chain Gang."

Waylon Jennings started out in radio and soon moved on to being a musician, but his career was almost cut short on "the day the music died," February 3, 1959. He and Buddy Holly had become friends as a result of Holly's regular shows at KLLL, the radio station where Jennings worked. When Holly and his band, the Crickets, split up, Holly recruited a new band that included Waylon on bass.

Years later, Jennings made his way to Nashville, and while he had some success, he grew disillusioned with the music business. Willie Nelson then turned him on to the scene in Austin, Texas, where long-haired hippies and rednecks could be found in the same clubs, enjoying the same music. Together, Willie and Waylon became branded the leaders of the outlaw movement, and *Wanted: The Outlaws*, which featured songs by both alongside material by Tompall Glaser and Jessi Colter, became the first platinum-selling country album.

By the time of the Highwaymen collaboration, Jennings had moved record labels, and though he was no longer the multimillion-selling artist he had been in the 1970s, he was still charting Top 10 singles.

Christmas on the Road

Cash had been producing an annual Christmas television special each year since 1976. In 1984, he was in the middle of a two-year tour, with the last date set for November—just in time to film that year's Christmas show. Cash's tour

WILLIE NELSON
KRIS KRISTOFFERSON
JOHNNY CASH
WAYLON JENNINGS
Highwayman
38-04881
Produced by CHIPS MOMAN
From the Columbia Records album, HIGHWAYMAN, FC 40056
Illustration: BILL IMHOFF/ Photo: JIM McGUIRE/ © 1985 CBS Inc./ ℗ 1985 CBS Inc./ Manufactured by Columbia Records/CBS Inc./51 W. 52nd St., New York, N.Y. / "Columbia" and are trademarks of CBS Inc. WARNING: All Rights Reserved. Unauthorized duplication is a violation of applicable laws.
Columbia

Johnny Cash, Willie Nelson, Waylon Jennings, and Kris Kristofferson had been friends for many years, though they rarely recorded together until the Highwaymen. *Private collection*

was due to wrap up in Europe, so it was decided that he would film the show in Montreux, Switzerland. The best way to celebrate, he thought, was to bring in his friends—Kris Kristofferson, Willie Nelson, and Waylon Jennings—as guests.

The history of this foursome goes back more than twenty years, and during that period they had played and recorded together in various combinations. Now, for the first time, they were all going to share a stage.

Marty Stuart, a member of Cash's band at the time, described the scene in an article for *Country Music* in 1985. "As songs and stories were swapped," he wrote, "it was clear that these guys have appreciated each other's work down through the years, and now, for the first time ever in this combination, they were in the midst of a musical gathering. Collectively, their singing and their songs represent a major portion of serious country music as it is known today. It fell together so naturally that you got the feeling that this wouldn't be the last time you'd hear them sing together."

The show opens with each of the three friends saying "Hello, I'm Johnny Cash" in turn, just as Cash had opened his earlier *Johnny Cash and Friends* television shows. The band starts "On the Road Again" and the camera pans out to reveal everyone. What follows shows a group of friends enjoying themselves as they tour Switzerland, and as they stand together on the stage. Cash even shows the video for his recent single "Chicken in Black" before Willie sings "Pretty Paper." Cash then joins him for their first-ever duet, "I Still Miss Someone."

Waylon and his wife, Jessi Colter, keep up the Christmas spirit with "Silent Night" before introducing the video for Waylon's new single, "America." June then joins Johnny for a duet of "Baby Ride Easy," a song Carlene Carter had recorded with Dave Edmunds for her third album, *Musical Shapes*. Cash then dedicates the next video, for his song "I Believe," to those who had recently competed in the Special Olympics.

Comic relief follows, as the Highwaymen wives—June, Jessi, Lisa Kristofferson, and Connie Nelson—are joined by Anita Carter and Tammy (the wife of the musical director) to perform a song accompanied by a video of them sightseeing and shopping throughout the city, while being followed around by Waylon.

Kristofferson dedicates a new song called "Good Morning, John," about his friend's triumph over addiction, to Cash, whose last public battle with drugs had come just a couple of years earlier. (Cash would go on to record the song himself in 1988, though it was never released.) Next comes John Carter Cash's video debut, "Old Time Rock and Roll," featuring Robert Duvall and Roy Orbison. Jessi Colter then takes a solo turn at the piano for "I'd Rather Have Jesus," before the group joins in to finish the song. The whole group then performs a new song by Kristofferson, "Love Is the Way," before closing the show out with a reprise of "On the Road Again."

"The road always offers a new beginning," Stuart wrote in his *Country Music* article. "Montreux felt like the beginning of something. The world enjoyed the Christmas special and shared in some of the good will that went around there. But I hoped with all of the creative seeds dropped there, something more would spring forth."

Highwayman (1985)

Prior to filming the Christmas special, Cash had been working in the studio with producer Chips Moman, and in October he invited in Kristofferson, Jennings, and Nelson to record two songs, "Highwayman" (covered more extensively in chapter 38) and Bob Seger's "Against the Wind."

According to Marty Stuart, the first seeds of the collaboration took root while Cash was recording "Love Is the Way," which Kristofferson had given him in Switzerland. "John asked Waylon to sing on it," Stuart recalled. "Around the same time, Willie and Kris were in town working with Brenda Lee and Dolly Parton on a TV show, *The Winning Hand*, on which Cash was the host. Plus Willie and John had just recorded 'I Still Miss Someone' as a step toward the duet album idea they'd discussed in Switzerland. But, instead of standing in line for another duet album, John was looking for a different idea."

That idea became the Highwaymen, and what would be their first album was recorded over just a few days in January, when they added eight more songs to the two they already had in the can. Surprisingly, only two of the ten songs they recorded were by a member of the group—and both of them were Cash's. Kristofferson insisted that "Big River" be included, with the version they recorded restoring the fourth verse of the song that had been trimmed from the original due to time constraints. The other Cash original was his ode to the psychiatric hospital, "Committed to Parkview," which he had originally pitched to Waylon before cutting it himself in 1976. The remainder of the songs came from some of their favorite writers: Ed Bruce, Charlie Walker, Guy Clark, Steve Goodman, John Prine, Paul Kennerly, and Woody Guthrie, whose "Deportee (Plane Wreck at Los Gatos)" features a guest appearance by Johnny Rodriguez.

While none of the members of the group were at the peak of their popularity, the release of *Highwayman* was an event. It was treated as such in the review by *Country Music*, which ran two and a quarter pages and featured a discussion of the importance of the album by two of the magazine's editors, Michael Bane, who had published a biography of Nelson in 1984, and Patrick Carr, who had interviewed Cash extensively in the past, and would go on to help Cash write his 1997 autobiography. "This record ought to have been called *The Last Cowboy*

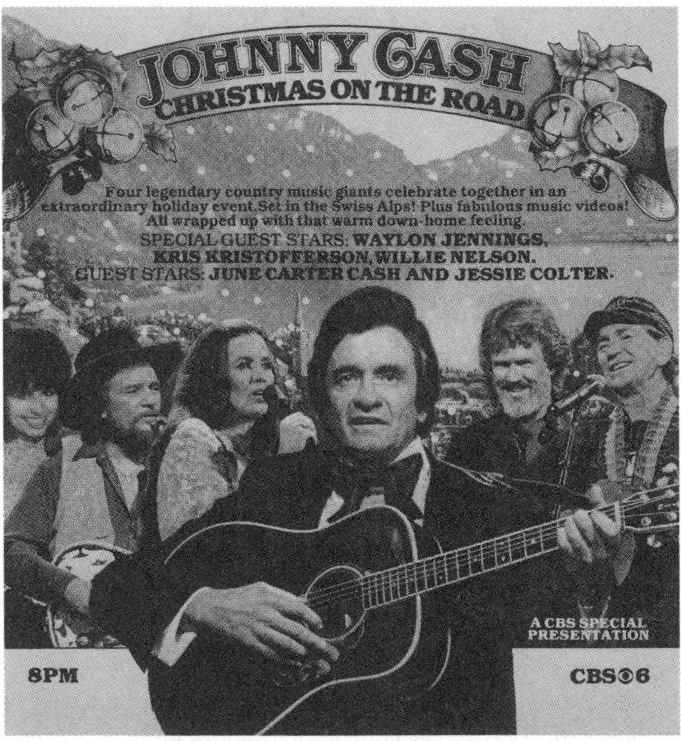

Johnny Cash: Christmas on the Road was one of Cash's annual Christmas specials, and this 1984 show was the genesis of the Highwaymen.
Author's collection

Album," Bane concluded. "It's wrapped it all up. It's the closing parenthesis on the Outlaw Movement."

Listeners who had slowed down on buying the foursome's solo recordings quickly picked up the new album. After "Highwayman" hit #1 in August, the album of the same name followed it to the top of the charts for one week in September, remaining in the Top 10 for four months.

The group made its first public appearance in July, at Nelson's annual Fourth of July Picnic. "The guaranteed highlight of the day came with the onstage appearance of Nelson, Cash, Jennings, and Kristofferson, who publicly re-created the characters from their well-received Columbia album *Highwayman* for the first time," *Billboard* noted. "Kristofferson was flown in especially to round out the superstar quartet."

On January 27, 1986, the group won two American Music Awards: Video Duo/Group (for which they went up against Alabama and the Oak Ridge Boys) and Video Single for "Highwayman" (for which they were pitted against Alabama's "40 Hour Week" and Hank Williams Jr.'s "All My Rowdy Friends").

Highwayman 2 (1990)

After the success of the first album, a second was inevitable. It continued what the first one had started, but it fell short in some areas. Whereas the first album was essentially a Johnny Cash project, from song selection to assembling the crew, the second was more of a collaborative effort.

"As an album, it could have used a little more time spent on it," Jennings writes in *Waylon: An Autobiography*. "We ran in and out too quick, and we didn't have that one great song. It's hard to find material that goes over with four people, each with strong let-it-all-hang-out opinions."

Sure enough, the songs on *Highwayman 2* showed signs of being chosen by committee. Cash got one new song (hey, he got two last time!), Jennings got one, and Kristofferson and Nelson got two each (not that there is much to complain about in that). During the time just prior to recording the album, Willie and Waylon's chart success had begun to drop off considerably, so they must have looked at this as a chance to rise back up with the power of numbers.

The album's only single, "Silver Stallion," dashed those hopes pretty quickly, peaking at #25 after two months on the chart, and making it clear that "Highwayman's" success wouldn't be replicated. It wasn't as if they weren't trying, as the group's recording of Rivers Rutherford's "American Remains" showed. Rutherford would go on to become a popular and commercially successful songwriter, but here his song sounds like a desperate attempt to recapture what the group had achieved with "Highwayman," even down to the reincarnation theme and similar melody and arrangement.

"Born and Raised in Black and White" suffers from crowding all four singers together and then adding additional voices, drowning out both the characteristic qualities of the group and the song itself. One of the important things about the first album is that all four sing together only when appropriate. Fortunately, this is not the case throughout the album, and by the next song, "Two Stories Wide," written and sung by Nelson, the other voices are placed deeper in the background, enhancing the song rather than smothering it.

"We're All in Your Corner," while a little syrupy, finds the group back on track as far as arrangements go, before running straight into "American Remains." Talk then turns to love on Kristofferson's "Anthem '84" and Jennings' "Angels Love Bad Men." Cash recalls the epic guitar pulls that took place at his home in "Songs That Make a Difference," while "Living Legend" brings the foursome back together, before Nelson closes the album with a solo turn on "Texas."

Although "Silver Stallion" performed poorly, the album fared much better. Though it never hit #1, it did remain in the Top 10 for nearly three months, peaking at #4, and brought *Highwayman* back to the charts for three weeks.

The Highwaymen in Concert

Although all four members of the group were busy with projects of their own, they decided to embark on a tour in 1990, beginning at the Houston Astrodome on March 3rd. Their set lists included only two songs from the first album ("Desperados Waiting for a Train" and, of course, "Highwayman") and none from the second. The rest of the show consisted of songs made famous by each of the four Highwaymen individually, with the others helping out here and there. Three of these shows were documented, and two are available for fans to buy.

Highwaymen Live!

The first Highwaymen live release was recorded in 1990 and issued on VHS in 1991, as well as being shown on the Disney Channel. Recorded at Nassau Coliseum in Uniondale, New York, the show captures the foursome in a playful mood as they wind through their hits, intercut with interview segments that give a good idea of what each member felt about playing with the others.

Highwaymen at the Mirage

Recorded during a five-day engagement in June 1991, the set list for this show is nearly identical to the band's performance at the Nassau Coliseum. The concert was broadcast by TNN on May 25, 1992, but has yet to be released commercially, though it is easily accessible online.

Perhaps the most notable thing about the show is Cash's appearance. In early 1990, he developed a cyst after undergoing a dental procedure, with the resulting surgery weakening his jaw. Not long after that, while eating a steak, his jaw broke, though he didn't realize it at the time. As a result, he appears to have aged five years or more between the two filmed concerts, and in the second his face is swollen and his voice gruff. Being the consummate showman, however, he doesn't allow the pain to impede his performance.

On the Road Again

Taped on April 15, 1992, in Aberdeen, Scotland, this performance wasn't given a commercial release until July 15, 2003. As with all of the Highwaymen's shows, they seemed to be having a ball onstage. Most importantly, Cash looks healthier than he did at the Mirage, though his hair is a little longer and lighter, in both color and weight.

The Highwaymen in Central Park

On May 23, 1993, the Highwaymen participated in "Country Takes Manhattan," an eight-day concert series in Central Park (for which *New York* magazine condescendingly printed a checklist of items attendees might want to bring, including a "feathered hairstyle, Jim Beam, chicken-fried-steak dinner, rear-window-mount gun rack, and Dodge 4 × 4.") The concert series also brought in Clint Black, Wynonna Judd, Travis Tritt, Trisha Yearwood, and a solo performance by Willie Nelson the night before the Highwaymen's show. TNN later broadcast the Highwaymen portion on November 10, 1993.

***The Road Goes On Forever* (1995)**

After two-plus years of shows, the Highwaymen took a break in 1993. During that time, Kris Kristofferson returned to his film work, Willie Nelson made three solo albums, Waylon Jennings recorded a one-off album with RCA, and Johnny Cash was busy reinventing himself with Rick Rubin. Then, in 1994, they circled the wagons for what would turn out to be the last time.

To produce the album, the group called in Don Was, who had overseen records by Willie, Waylon, and Kris during the previous few years. He proved to be just what the group needed. His production dialed back Moman's *Highwayman 2* sound to something closer to *Highwayman*, but with a more rough-hewn feel. And like any good movie trilogy that dips in the middle so that the heroes can be triumphant in the end, *The Road Goes On Forever* would provide the backdrop for a wonderful swan song.

All four Highwaymen and Was brought in songs for the album, and from that large pool twelve tracks were selected, though only eleven made the cut for the initial release. Introducing the album is a song by a modern-day country-music outlaw, Steve Earle, whose "The Devil's Right Hand" is an anti-gun song in the mode of Lynyrd Skynyrd's "Saturday Night Special" in that it never explicitly states its anti-gun message but instead tells a story of guns being used for wrong.

Next comes "Live Forever," one of the most beautiful songs from the catalogue of another outlaw, Billy Joe Shaver, which slows things down and provides a fitting anthem for the foursome, while "Everyone Gets Crazy," by Kevin Welch, shows a more empathetic side to the group.

"It Is What It Is," the album's only single, puts the group back into a rowdier space. It was one of Waylon's favorite songs from the album because, he said, it allowed the members to "pass the song around like a hot potato.... Part of the fun is guessing who sings where; others rely on the ensemble effect. We're making so much noise, it doesn't matter that one's starting on a verse while the other is ending up a chorus." It was co-written by John Fleming and Stephen Bruton, Kristofferson's guitarist, who in fact is the only songwriter to have two songs on the album. The second, "Waiting for a Long Time," is another raucous number, this time about waiting for the perfect girl.

The four principles also contributed a song each. Waylon's "I Do Believe" is personal statement of faith, while Willie's "The End of Understanding" was a song he had written in the late 1950s, with Was giving it a suitably retro feel. Cash brought "Death and Hell," about a cowboy and a prostitute with supernatural powers, which he co-wrote with his son, John Carter Cash. Kristofferson's offering was one of Cash's favorites, "Here Comes That Rainbow Again."

In an interesting bit of kismet, the group recorded "True Love Travels a Gravel Road," a song written by Dallas Frazier and A. L. Owens, and previously recorded by Elvis Presley for *From Elvis in Memphis*, produced by Chips Moman. Cash's ex-son-in-law Nick Lowe also released a version of the song the same year the Highwaymen recorded it. Unfortunately, their arrangement veers from the soul-inspired mood of past versions and closer to the radio country of the time.

The closing title track, an outlaw tale that made for a perfect pick for the group, came from Texas songwriter Robert Earl Keen. It was originally recorded by Keen himself in 1983, before being brought to a wider audience in 1993 by veteran Texas performer Joe Ely.

As good as the album was, it arrived in the midst of major changes in the country-radio landscape. With deregulation in progress, stations were now driven primarily by ad sales. As a result, playlists were shrinking even tighter, and the first to go were "old" artists—a category into which the Highwaymen fit. The newfound success Cash was enjoying with a younger audience following the release of his *American Recordings* (discussed elsewhere) didn't translate to his other projects, and *The Road Goes On Forever* reached only #42 on the Top Country Albums chart, while its lone single failed to chart at all.

In 2005, to commemorate the album's tenth anniversary, Capitol/Liberty reissued *The Road Goes On Forever* with six bonus tracks. The first is "If He Came Back Again," a song about Hank Williams that was recorded for the album but left off the final track listing. There are also four acoustic demos—of "Live Forever," "I Ain't Song," "Pick Up the Tempo," and "Closer to the Bone"—recorded when the musicians were playing each other songs for the album, and a forty-nine-second clip of Gene Autry's "Back in the Saddle Again."

Packaged with the reissue was a DVD containing a documentary, directed by Don Was, entitled *Live Forever—In the Studio with the Highwaymen.* Clocking in at just over a half hour, the documentary combines studio footage with interviews with each member of the band. In one segment, they sit down for a talk with their idol, Gene Autry, and it's fun to see how icons like Cash and Nelson interact with a hero of their own. Also included on the DVD is the music video for "It Is What It Is."

CMT Presents American Revolutions: The Highwaymen

Broadcast to coincide with the tenth anniversary of *The Road Goes On Forever*, this CMT documentary uses much of the same footage as Don Was' film, but offers a few different or extended cuts. It also includes new interviews with Kris Kristofferson, Jessi Colter, Waylon Jennings' son Shooter, and a few others.

The film was released on DVD the following year. Just as interesting as the main feature are the uncut interviews included on the disc, one of which is an extended version of the segment featuring the crew with Gene Autry. There's also a video for "If He Came Back Again."

By now, of course, two of the Highwaymen were no longer with us, with Waylon Jennings having passed in 2002, and Cash following the next year. Thinking back on his time with the group, Kristofferson told *Uncut*'s Rob Hughes, "When we all got together for *Highwayman*, it was incredible. I loved it, but I just wish now that I'd realized how short it was going to be. It's like life in that respect. It was such a blessing, because every guy up there was my hero. I got to stand next to Johnny Cash and sing harmony every night. Now Willie and I are the only ones left. I wish I'd appreciated it more."

You Know All the Songs as Well as I Do

Columbia 1985

As 1985 rolled around, Johnny Cash's relationship with Columbia was beginning to crumble. His work with Billy Sherrill had been shelved, but he returned to the studio with Chips Moman, who had been highly recommended by Waylon Jennings, among others. The resulting album, *Rainbow*, would be Cash's last solo effort for the label.

"The Three Bells" b/w "They Killed Him" (1985)

Several months passed before Columbia issued a follow-up to "Chicken in Black," and it made little impact. While not as wacky as "Chicken," it was still an odd choice of single for Cash. "The Three Bells" had been a #1 hit for the Browns in 1959, with Jim Ed Brown's smooth voice making it a signature tune for the group. Cash's version doesn't have the same happy sound to it, instead dragging the song down. If Cash had really wanted to put out a hit from 1959, he might have done better rerecording one of his own.

The flip side, written by Kris Kristofferson, while not a bad performance, was another odd song for Cash to record. "They Killed Him" ticks off a list of peaceful men who were killed for their beliefs: Gandhi, Martin Luther King Jr., and Jesus Christ. Neither song touched the charts, and the single went completely unnoticed by the general public.

Rainbow (1985)

Chips Moman got his start at Stax Records, just as the label was getting off the ground in the early 1960s. From that time, his producing career climbed steadily upward until 1969, when the afterburners kicked in with his production of *From Elvis in Memphis*, the album credited with putting Elvis Presley back on the right path.

In 1977, Moman produced Waylon Jennings' top-selling album *Ol' Waylon*, and that association would put him at the helm of several collaborative projects featuring Jennings and Willie Nelson, along with solo projects by both artists. It wasn't long before the continuing chart and sales success of the duo was noticed by Columbia, leading to the suggestion that Cash team with Moman for his new album. Knowing Waylon and Willie the way he did, Cash took their endorsement as a good sign and gave the project the green light.

In November 1984, Cash filmed his annual Christmas special in Switzerland with guests Waylon Jennings, Willie Nelson, and Kris Kristofferson. The grouping was an inspiration to the participants and their producer, who had flown out to watch it. Once they returned to the States, they entered the studio to begin recording an album together. *Highwayman* was released in May 1985, and according to *People* magazine, "If Mount Rushmore could sing, this is the way it would sound." By July, it was in the Top 10 of the Country chart, and heading for #1. A month later, the album's first single, "Highwayman," hit #1. (For more on the Highwaymen, see chapter 35.)

Hopes were high, then, for the Cash/Moman collaboration that became *Rainbow.* Cash contributed two songs to the project: the opening "I'm Leaving Now" and a song he had written twenty years earlier, "You Beat All I Ever Saw." There are also two by Kristofferson, "Here Comes That Rainbow Again," which he had recorded in 1981 for the album of the same name, and "Casey's Last Ride," which he had cut in 1970, and which both Waylon Jennings and John Denver had recorded in 1971.

Cash also included a song by Willie Nelson, "They're All the Same." In the liner notes, he says he dreamed Willie had a song for him back in 1965—a story he had related in longer form in his notes for an obscure 1982 compilation called *Kris, Willie, Dolly & Brenda . . . The Winning Hand.* There, he says he dreamed that one day in 1962, he was playing Nelson "The Ballad of Ira Hayes," to which Willie replied that he should do "an album of Indian songs." Then it was Nelson's turn, and he played Cash "They're All the Same." When he woke up, Cash tracked down Nelson, who at this time was still bouncing around Nashville but starting to hit his stride as a songwriter, and asked him if had a song by that name. Confused, Nelson said that he did, and sent a tape to Cash—who then lost the tape. Twenty years later, while the two were swapping songs in a late-night session, Cash remembered the song and asked for it again.

"Easy Street," written by Moman and Bobby Emmons, was originally recorded by Tammy Wynette for her Moman-produced album *You Brought Me Back* (and also by another act Moman produced, Jessi Colter, on *Rock and Roll Lullaby*). Here, Cash switches the order of the first and second verses, which slightly alters the song's message. Whereas Wynette's version sounds like it is about the end of a love affair, Cash's sounds more like the end of a career, or at least the end of a chapter of one.

"Love Me like You Used To" is another song co-written by Emmons, this time with Paul Davis. Coming from Cash, it sounds odd, but from the female perspective of Tanya Tucker a few years later, the song went to #2. With its references to mystery trains and sing-along chorus, Emmons and Moman's "Borderline" (with the parenthetical subtitle "A Musical Whodunit") is another odd choice of song for Cash to perform.

Elsewhere, he does a strong version of John Fogerty's 1970 composition "Have You Ever Seen the Rain?" (another song suggested by Moman), while "Unwed Fathers," written by the team of Bobby Braddock and John Prine, talks to men about the responsibility of fathering a child and the societal tendency toward shaming young unwed mothers while allowing unwed teen boys to run free.

Overall, *Rainbow* is a strong album, one that's able to stand alongside *Highwayman* and hold its own. But the group's album overshadowed Cash's new solo effort, and neither it nor its only single, "I'm Leaving Now," made it onto the charts.

It was bad timing. While riding high as a part of a group, Cash was tanking as a solo artist—just as it came time to talk to Columbia about renewing his contract. Cash, buoyed by *Highwayman*'s success, asked for more money upfront, but the label refused, pointing to the weak performance of his recent solo albums. The writing was on the wall.

Ain't Gonna Hobo No More

Columbia 1986

Throughout his career, Johnny Cash had always been viewed as a loner, but in the mid-1980s he was regularly seen alongside his old friends Willie Nelson, Kris Kristofferson, and Waylon Jennings, both in the Highwaymen and in other related projects.

Two of those projects were more made-for-TV westerns. The first to be broadcast was *The Last Days of Frank and Jesse James*, which recounts the last years in the lives of outlaw brothers Frank (Cash) and Jesse (Kristofferson). It was produced by Joseph Cates, who had directed many of Cash's TV specials over the years. The second was a new version of John Ford's 1939 western, *Stagecoach*, originally starring John Wayne. The new version starred all four members of the Highwaymen, plus TV actor John Schneider. Neither made great waves, but they were entertaining ways to keep the group in front of their audience.

Class of '55 (1986)

Nineteen eighty-six saw the release of three new Cash projects, but only one, the gospel album *I Believe in Him*, was a solo project. The other two were released almost simultaneously, and both were produced by Chips Moman. The first teamed Cash with his one-time Sun labelmates Carl Perkins, Jerry Lee Lewis, and Roy Orbison, and was Moman's tribute to the town where he (and they) got their start.

Class of '55 is essentially an act of nostalgia, but it comes nowhere close to being a rockabilly Highwaymen. Cash gets the lead vocal spot on only one song, a mawkish Elvis tribute entitled "We Remember the King." Orbison, inexplicably, was also kept in the background, with only one lead vocal, "Coming Home," though it's a fine one. Jerry Lee Lewis sang "Sixteen Candles" and a rockin' "Keep My Motor Running." Carl Perkins came away as the star of the album, nailing his two leads, "Birth of Rock and Roll" and "Class of '55." The group numbers, like "Waymore's Blues" and "Rock and Roll (Fais Do Do)" were simply songs that allowed them all to sing together. The closing "Big Train (from

Memphis)" is really the crowning jewel, with the four men joined by Marty Stuart, the Judds, Dave Edmunds, and the song's writer, John Fogerty.

The album was released by the newly formed and short-lived America label, which put a lot of effort behind it, including organizing a huge press conference at the Peabody Hotel in Memphis that was filmed by Dick Clark Productions. "I think it will shake a few memories loose for people my age," Perkins said, in a *Billboard* article on the album release. "But at the same time, there seems to be a movement around young people today to find out who was the inspiration for so-and-so who they dig so well."

The album did well, rising to #15 on the Top Country Albums chart and #87 on the Pop chart, but there was nothing there to follow it up. Orbison, Perkins, and Lewis would pick up recording again, separately, in the late 1980s, with Orbison becoming the most prominent of the three. As for Cash, well, he was in for a rough year.

Heroes (1986)

For years, Johnny Cash and Waylon Jennings had been talking about recording together, and they had done so sporadically, releasing one single together in 1978. Now, taking advantage of Waylon's move from RCA to MCA, they were able to release an album together. Produced by Chips Moman, the resulting *Heroes* was only partially worth the wait. While there are some standouts, like "Field of Diamonds," "Even Cowgirls Get the Blues," "The Ballad of Forty Dollars," and "One Too Many Mornings," most of the other songs are simply just there. Ken Tucker, a syndicated music critic, described the album as "a session of self-congratulation, paying feeble homage to the 'Folk out on the Road'—i.e., the folks who buy the tickets and albums that keep Cash and Jennings in black leather. Lushly orchestrated, mawkish and dull."

While Tucker's conclusion may be a bit strong—especially to the Cash or Jennings fan—the album did lack the spirit of the pairing's earlier work with creative sparkplug Cowboy Jack Clement. Of the two singles released from the album, "Even Cowgirls Get the Blues" and "Ballad of Forty Dollars," only "Cowgirl" had any chart action, making it to #35. The album, however, kept pace with *The Class of '55* and made its way to #13 on the Country chart.

The End of an Era

The mid-1980s were a time when landscape of country music began to shift. As the urban-cowboy movement died out, it left behind a legacy of pursuing a youth audience—something the country-music industry hadn't actively tried to do before. Occasionally, an artist would strike a chord with the youth-oriented rock audience, just as Cash had done in the late '60s, but to aggressively market a whole strand of the music to that audience was something new. But as the bean counters took over the record labels, the emphasis was more and more on how and what would bring in new audiences (and more money). It was a shift that was noticed across the industry.

Midway through 1985, Charley Pride left RCA after twenty years at the label. "It appeared to me that RCA Records wants to concentrate on younger and newer acts," he told *Billboard*, "and must therefore invest inordinate amounts of time and money in the publicizing and promotion of those acts, while giving less and less attention to the older acts on the label. As a result, I figured it was time to move on."

Coming from another artist, this might have looked simply like a case of sour grapes, but Pride was a different story. As an African American in country music, he made huge strides in breaking down racial barriers. Joel Whitburn, who is the expert at tracking chart movement and success, places Pride at #3 on his list, by chart success, of the Top 25 Artists of 1970–79 (Cash ranks #14). Between 1980 and '84, Pride had seven #1s, three #2s, and four Top 10 hits. But after that, during the period where Pride says he lacked label support, his singles dropped from #9 to #32.

A week after Pride's comments appeared, his label bosses fired back, sort of, in another *Billboard* article, but their best defense was to offer up examples of other older artists who were still working. RCA pointed out that it had recently signed Mel Tillis, an artist who had been in the business for five years longer than Pride. Roy Wunsch, then vice president of marketing at CBS, pointed out that the label had "ample activity" from "Willie Nelson, Merle Haggard, George Jones, Tammy Wynette, Chet Atkins, and Johnny Cash." He went on to note, "What you might call our 'classic' artists, such as Merle Haggard and George Jones, are probably selling greater today than they were ten years ago."

Just one week later, another *Billboard* headline proclaimed, "Younger Acts Dominate CMA Nominations." Beneath it, writer Edward Morris noted how Ricky Skaggs and George Strait (who would become known as neo-traditionalists) led the nominations at the Country Music Association Awards, and that Alabama, Reba McEntire, and the Judds were also nominated. "Overall, this seems to be the year of opportunity for younger acts," Morris wrote. "Even those nominated for the top award, entertainer of the year, are all acts that have come into prominence within the past five years."

But it wasn't just the shift to younger acts that was affecting older artists. In business, there are a few ways to make money. One way is to sell a lot of product (which, in this case, meant getting the hits). Another is to increase profit margins, which for record labels meant offering smaller advances (the fight that Cash was busy fighting with Columbia), or getting more control over the product.

"When my contract came up for renewal in July 1985, I didn't re-sign with RCA," Waylon Jennings writes in his autobiography. "It was no longer a delivery of masters in their eyes. The contract had words like 'mutual consent,' which translates into more partnership, less money. . . . I passed on it."

Now, a year after Jennings had made the move from RCA to MCA, he and Cash had two albums on the chart, *Highwayman* and *Heroes.* Cash also had the *Class of '55* project, but none of those records were solo albums—and that, so the thinking went, was where the money was. So the decision was made: Johnny Cash would no longer be a Columbia recording artist.

When the news broke, there was a groundswell of outrage, mostly directed at Columbia's Nashville boss, Rick Blackburn. Dwight Yoakam, one of the brightest new stars in the country galaxy, called Blackburn a "prick" and took the whole town to task in an article, published in the *NME*, that drew the ire of Blackburn and company. "Well, if you don't want the murder rap, then don't bludgeon somebody over the head with a baseball bat," Yoakam told *Spin.* "Blackburn wanted to dump on Johnny Cash, but then he doesn't want anybody to say anything about it."

Cash didn't say anything about the matter to the press. Through his manager, Lou Robin, he simply announced that he had a new gospel album out on Word Records, and that they were already in talks with other labels for a new home for Johnny Cash.

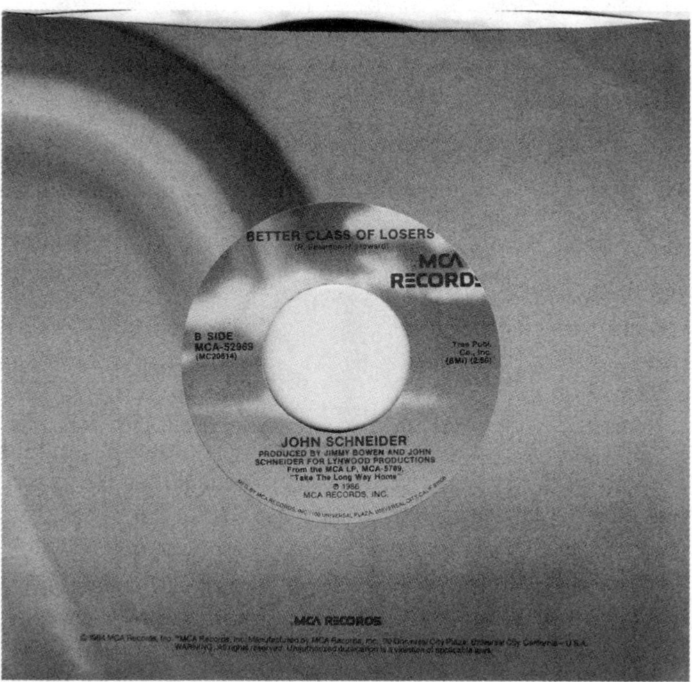

Known also as Bo Duke, John Schneider started a recording career in 1981. His biggest success came in 1986, with a pair of well-regarded albums. Though it failed to chart, "Better Class of Loser" got attention for the appearances of Cash and Waylon Jennings. *Private collection*

The Time Has Come to Sing a Traveling Song

The 1980s #1

Johnny Cash was fond of saying that he was invisible in the 1980s, and as far as chart presence is concerned, that's pretty spot-on. Throughout the decade, he only reached the top spot once, not as a solo performer but with the Highwaymen (whose origins are discussed in chapter 35).

"Highwayman" b/w "The Human Condition" (1985)

Knocked out "I'm for Love," Hank Williams Jr.; knocked out by "Real Love," Kenny Rogers & Dolly Parton

While recording his 1977 album *El Mirage* in London with Beatles producer George Martin, Jimmy Webb answered his apartment door to find his friend Harry Nilsson. The pair spent the night engaged in what Webb would later describe as "professional drinking," and then Jimmy crashed into bed.

"I went to sleep and had an incredibly vivid dream," he told *Performing Songwriter* in 2007. "I had an old brace of pistols in my belt, and I was riding, hell-bent for leather, down these country roads, with sweat pouring off of my body. I was terrified, because I was being pursued by police, who were on the verge of shooting me. It was very real. I sat up in bed, sweating through my pajamas. Without even thinking about it, I stumbled out of bed to the piano and started playing 'Highwayman.' Within a couple of hours, I had the first verse."

From there, Webb wasn't sure where to go, until he realized that the highwayman of the first verse didn't die—he was reincarnated. He returned first as a sailor, then as a dam-builder, and finally as a starship pilot. Webb recorded the song in the studio with Martin, but nothing came of it. Two years passed before his friend Glen Campbell, who had enjoyed great success with Webb songs like "By the Time I Get to Phoenix" and "Wichita Lineman," decided to cut the song for his new project. Campbell loved the song enough to make it the title of his 1979 release, but changes were on the horizon.

"When a new regime took over at Capitol, things went downhill pretty quickly," Campbell told an interviewer in 2008. "They didn't understand me at all. This was the late seventies, and I'd finished 'Highwayman' and they wouldn't release it as a single. They said, 'We don't want that, why don't you do something more like this?' and they played me 'My Sharona' by the Knack. That's when I knew I had to get off the label. I said, 'Screw you! Who the hell are you, telling me to do a song like that?'"

The single was never released, and the song remained a hidden gem until 1984, when Cash was putting together some ideas for a loose collaboration with his old friends Willie Nelson, Waylon Jennings, and Kris Kristofferson. Marty Stuart suggested "Highwayman" to Cash and producer Chips Moman. They took it to the group, and the four agreed that the song would be a good fit—good enough to name the group after, even.

"I don't know how they decided who would take which verse, but having Johnny last was like having God singing your song," Webb said. ("Glen Campbell had even stopped by to record a demo to help us to learn 'Highwayman,'" Stuart wrote in a 1985 *Country Music* article. Campbell subsequently took the place of an absent Kristofferson to sing the song with the group at the first Farm Aid concert in 1985).

The song entered the Hot Country Singles chart on May 18, 1985, and began a steady rise, reaching the Top 10 after eight weeks. The top of the Country charts in 1985 was a real mix of "older" acts, like Merle Haggard, Conway Twitty, Willie Nelson, and the Oak Ridge Boys, and artists who had broken through in the previous five years, like Alabama, Exile, Lee Greenwood, and Rosanne Cash. Sitting in the #1 spot when the group of outlaws arrived was a friend and fellow outsider, Hank Williams Jr., with "I'm for Love." It was a rarity at the time for any song to stay in the #1 position for more than a week (in fact, only two records spent more than one week at the top during the whole year), and "Highwayman" was no exception, riding on to make room for "Real Love" by Kenny Rogers and Dolly Parton.

Sometimes I Reckon I Got Here Too Soon

The Mercury Years, 1987–91

After twenty-eight years at the same label, Cash was now a free agent. But with his record sales in a downturn, few labels were willing to take on a potential non-seller—even if that non-seller was widely considered to be an icon.

One of the first places Cash turned was MCA. One year before Columbia set Cash free, Waylon Jennings had left his label of twenty years, RCA, and moved to MCA, which was headed at the time by Jimmy Bowen. Bowen had made his name helping to revive the careers of Frank Sinatra and Dean Martin in the 1960s, before eventually moving to Nashville. He was also working with another of Cash's friends, Hank Williams Jr., who was riding high on the charts. So, with Waylon's encouragement, Cash called Bowen.

"I was running MCA Records in Nashville when he called me about signing a deal," Bowen writes in his autobiography, *Rough Mix*. "I was open but I told him I'd need to get a feel for the songs he was into, to see if I could work him properly." In a repeat of his visit to Sam Phillips and Sun Records nearly thirty years earlier, Cash took his guitar to Bowen's office and played him several songs. But for whatever reason, Bowen decided to pass.

While other labels considered making an offer, it was Polygram that showed the most interest. Both the head of the label, Dick Asher, and the head of its Nashville subsidiary Mercury, Steve Popovich, had worked with Cash at Columbia. They both felt that he was one of the most recognizable stars in the world, and still viable in the marketplace. Popovich reached out, and in August 1986, Cash signed a contract with the label.

Johnny Cash Is Coming to Town (1987)

"There were times when I didn't care. It was, like, complete apathy from the record company, and I guess I got that way too," Cash told *Rolling Stone* in 1992 of his final few years at Columbia. Now, though, he was back.

"Highwayman" marked a vocal event that brought together the outlaw movement's biggest stars and took Cash back to the top of the charts, but it was the last time that happened. *Private collection*

To produce his new album, Cash called Cowboy Jack Clement, as he had often in the past when looking for an extra creative spark. The two set about assembling a collection of songs that would make a statement that Cash was ready to commit fully to his music career.

"The Big Light" opens the album and immediately shows Cash to be back in the swing, full of energy and experience, in a song about waking up regretting the night before. It was written by Elvis Costello, but though Cash knew him through Nick Lowe, he had actually been turned on to Costello's new album, *King of America*, which contained the song, by a DJ in Grand Rapids, Michigan. Two Cash originals follow: "The Ballad of Barbara," which he had also recorded for *The Last Gunfighter Ballad* in 1977, and "I'd Rather Have You," a new song that shows the quirky side that Clement often encouraged.

The rest of the material came, as usual, from an assortment of Cash's favorite songwriters. From Guy Clark comes "Let Him Roll," about a man who befriends a wino who dies of a broken heart years after being jilted by a "whore in Dallas," and "Heavy Metal (Don't Mean Rock and Roll to Me)," co-written with Jim McBride, which tells the story of a workingman who drives a bulldozer. Only Cash and Clark could make a song about driving a bulldozer sound both romantic and ominous. Clement's tendency to throw a lot at a production really comes out here in the horns that swell in controlled chaos mid-song.

In "The Night Hank Williams Came to Town," Cash, joined by Ol' Waylon, sings of the excitement that accompanied an appearance by Williams, and the memories they'll always have of him. "Sixteen Tons," written by Merle Travis, fits, as one would expect, like a coal miner's glove, while "Letters from Home," by Jack Wesley Routh and John Charles Crowley, finds Cash in a sentimental mood.

"W. Lee O'Daniel (and the Light Crust Dough Boys)" came from the pen of James Talley. Though he had been around Nashville since the late 1960s, Talley didn't record his first album—*Got No Bread, No Milk, No Money, but We Sure Got a Lot of Love,* which includes this song—until 1975. Influenced by Woody Guthrie, Pete Seeger, and Hank Williams, Talley wrote songs that offer an intriguing blend of nostalgia, sentimentality, social issues, and pain. (Playing the armchair A&R guy, it would have been interesting to see Cash record an entire album of Talley material à la Waylon Jennings' set of Billy Joe Shaver songs, *Honky Tonk Heroes.*)

Echoing the structure of his 1970s work, Cash ends the album with a gospel number, "My Ship Will Sail." Written by Allen Reynolds, this was a song Cash had originally recorded, with Clement, in 1974, while working on the ill-fated *John R. Cash.* He had also recorded it with the Earl Scruggs Revue for the Bob Johnston–produced *Earl Scruggs Anniversary Album, Vol. 2* in 1975, and again in 1976, with the Carter Family, for *Country's First Family.*

While Cash would later complain about a lack of promotion for the album, and even a lack of product released, Polygram/Mercury put a lot into the album, pushing it as his great comeback and releasing a total of four singles from it. But even with the label's excitement (and Cash's, too), some great new tunes, and the heavy promotion, the singles couldn't find traction in radio. Radio was changing, with newer acts finding greater favor.

The selection of singles was an obstacle that Cash had to overcome. Consider the first two singles from the album. The first, "The Night Hank Williams Came to Town," is about an artist who, though legendary, had been dead since 1953, and who to many newer listeners was simply the long-lost daddy of chart-topper Hank Williams Jr. The song's chart history bears that out: it reached its lowly chart peak of #42 after six weeks, and remained on the listings for only eleven weeks total.

For the next single, Cash and Mercury moved the song selection a little farther into the future, but only by two years, releasing a song that had been a million-selling #1 hit for Tennessee Ernie Ford in 1955. Both "Sixteen Tons" and its flip side, "Ballad of Barbara," failed to chart in 1987, as did the subsequent, more contemporary choice, "Let Him Roll."

It wasn't for lack of trying. Although Country Music Television had yet to become a major, image-making force (it was only three years old at the time), Mercury produced videos for both "Sixteen Tons" and "Let Him Roll." They must have been shot back to back, because Cash, sporting a nice mustache, is wearing the same outfit in both. "Sixteen Tons" has him singing the song against a black backdrop, with archive footage of miners fading in and out. "Let Him Roll" is a more elaborate production, portraying the story of the song, with Cash joined by songwriter Guy Clark, Jim Varney (best known for the popular film and TV character Ernest), and Waylon Jennings as the wino.

If audiences had trouble remembering the real Hank Williams, the final single from the album—as good a song as it was—probably led a lot of listeners to wonder, "Who?" W. Lee O'Daniel & the Light Crust Doughboys hadn't been popular since the mid-1930s, and the single named after them lingered at the bottom of the chart for five weeks, rising only to #72.

The album itself made little movement either, rising to only #36 on the Country chart, though it stayed on the chart for twenty-six weeks, longer than any Cash solo album since 1970's *The Johnny Cash Show* (which had benefited from weekly television exposure).

Classic Cash (1988)

The Country Music Hall of Fame was established in 1961, and, in the words of *The Encyclopedia of Country Music,* honored "performers, songwriters, broadcasters, and executives in recognition of their contributions to the development of country music." On October 13, 1980, that honor had been given to Cash, then aged forty-eight, making him the youngest ever living inductee. Eight years later, the Country Music Hall of Fame and Museum opened an exhibit in Cash's honor. As part of that exhibit, Cash went into the studio on October 12th and 14th, and then on December 2nd, 3rd, and 9th, to record twenty of his previous works, encompassing both hits and personal favorites.

Initially, the album was only going to be available at the Hall of Fame and Museum gift shop, but it was then decided to give it a wider release. As such, it can't be called a proper follow-up to *Johnny Cash Is Coming to Town,* but more of a side trip down memory lane. That said, all of the versions included on the album are good, with a few, like "Get Rhythm," switching up the arrangements a bit, but no listener would turn to these takes over the originals. Like his live recordings, the album provides a snapshot of how Cash and his road band—all of whom appear here—performed these songs live. Cash acted as the album's producer, selecting songs he felt were most representative of his career, which makes for an interesting look at his career through his own eyes.

Water from the Wells of Home (1988)

Cash went back into the studio with Clement at the end of 1987 armed with a batch of new songs for the follow-up to his Mercury debut. Among his recent albums, the highest charting of them teamed Cash with others, whether it was the Highwaymen, his old Sun buddies (*Class of '55* and *The Survivors*), or simply him and Waylon Jennings. Perhaps in an attempt to recapture some lost chart ground, then, each of this new album's ten songs paired Cash with another artist.

Up first, daughter Rosanne, along with the Everly Brothers, joins him for a new take on "Ballad of a Teenage Queen." Emmylou Harris and Roy Acuff come out for "As Long as I Live," a song written by Acuff and taken to #3 by Red Foley and Kitty Wells in 1955. "Where Did We Go Right" finds Johnny at home with June and the Carter Sisters, and "The Last of the Drifters" teams him with Tom T. Hall. "Sweeter Than Flowers" is a sad old song sung with Waylon Jennings, with Emmylou Harris and Jessi Colter joining in on harmony.

In a Mercury Nashville promotional interview (included on the 2003 reissue of the album), Cash reveals that he had high hopes for the next track on the album, "a Scottish folk song that I really believe that the people in Scotland are going to like, a song I wrote called 'The Ballad of Rob MacDunn' or 'A Croft in Clachan,' Clachan a little town in Scotland. It's a 17th-century war ballad about Scotland, and Glen Campbell sings with me on that. He flew in to Nashville to be on this session."

The most surprising collaboration on the album pairs Cash with former Beatle Paul McCartney on "New Moon over Jamaica," a song co-written by McCartney, Cash, and Tom T. Hall. Cash recalled how it came about:

> Over the years, from time to time, June and I have entertained the McCartneys, either at our home here in Nashville, when they'd come to Nashville, or more frequently in Jamaica when we were on vacation down there in the winter time. We have our house there where we stay and Paul and Linda and their family stay at a place called Round Hill, which is about twenty miles away. Well, there's no secrets in Jamaica, as they say, so we hear that the McCartneys are on the island, so we give them a call, this last Christmas, and they came right on over and had dinner with us. Tom T. Hall and Dixie were there, so we sat up all night on the front porch singing. A musical session, a guitar pull or a swapping-songs session, with Paul McCartney is really a trip. He's the only singer I've ever sat with across a porch from who plays a guitar left-handed and upside down. And he had the only guitar on the porch this night. To get it to sound all right to Tom and I, we had to tune it to an open tuning and use a bar to chord it with, but Paul did most of the guitar

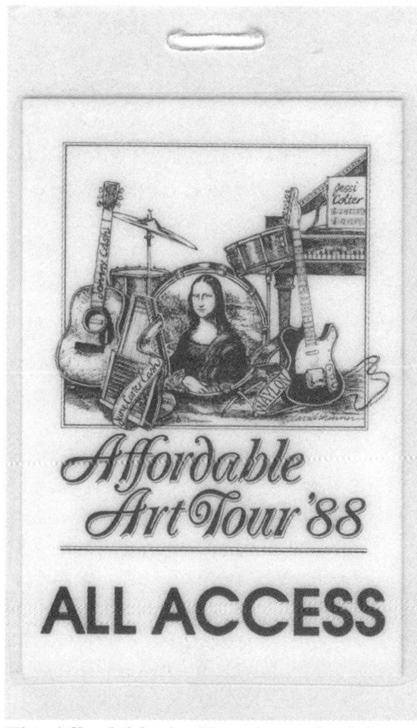

The Affordable Art Tour brought Johnny and June together with Waylon Jennings and Jessi Colter for a three-city tour of college towns. Ticket prices were kept low to accommodate the younger audiences. The tour was a test run for a longer run that never materialized.

Author's collection

> playing. Along about 2:00 or 2:30, the moon came on over the porch, and this sounds like a drummed up story, but it's true, the full moon—it wasn't a new moon, but a full moon—the full moon came on over the porch and Tom T. Hall looked up, and he said, "There's a new moon over Jamaica, that'd make a good song title." I said, "It's a full moon over Jamaica, Tom T.," and he said, "Yeah, but a new moon sounds like a better song title." So Tom T. and Paul started writing the song, and I came in on the chorus and wrote the third verse.

Another old friend who made the recording sessions was Hank Williams Jr. "I worked with Hank Jr. when he was fifteen, sixteen years old," Cash said. "He was part of my show, and he was stealing the show from me. I always wanted to have him on one of my records and we finally found a song." Williams had even recorded an entire album of his songs in 1970, titled *Hank Williams, Jr. Singing My Songs (Johnny Cash)*. It didn't hurt that Williams was a hot property at the time, though that was barely reflected in the single's chart performance.

With the exception of McCartney, who added his part in England, everyone on the album came to Nashville to record. "Every one of them who are singing on it only had to be asked one time and they were here," Cash said. "Rosanne came in pregnant and did her vocal on 'Ballad of a Teenage Queen,' and the Everly Brothers came in together, and one of them came back in to do his part over and the other one came back in. Everybody has worked really hard on this project, as I said, for a period of nine months."

One participant who didn't have to travel far was son John Carter, who joined his father for two songs, J. J. Cale's "Call Me the Breeze" and the title song, which father and son wrote together:

> The title came about just about a year ago this time. One day we were packing up to leave home and get on our bus, June and John Carter and I. We passed by the water fountain there by the door and I said, just a minute, before we go on this long run I want one more drink of the water from the wells of home. As we were walking to the bus, John Carter said that would be a good song title. So we get on the bus and sit down in my room. Got two guitars and sit there and in about thirty minutes we had the song all wrapped up. We came back in about the time, well actually, it was the first time we started this project, and John Carter and I came in together and put it down. Since that time we've gone through probably trying and recording and really actually finishing between twenty-five and thirty songs, but we've always gone back to this one song as kind of the anchor and as a theme for the songs that are in the album.
>
> It was a joy working with John Carter, too. To kind of feed off of that youth and that energy and that fire and that happiness and that joy in the studio. Sometimes with all the years that go by and the sessions we have we can get a little jaded and stilted, but every once in a while a spark like Paul McCartney will come, or John Carter to work with in the studio, will really inspire me and make me want to get up on my feet and sing it standing on my feet.

For all of the excitement, the album fared worse than its predecessor, striking only #48. The first single, "That Old Wheel" with Hank Williams Jr., reached only #21, making it Cash's highest-charting single since "The Baron" in 1981 but Williams' lowest in over a year. The second single, Cash's duet with daughter Rosanne, who was topping the charts as a solo performer on a regular basis, made it only to #45. And the final single, "Last of the Drifters" b/w "Water from the Wells of Home," didn't get to the charts at all.

Cash was right back where he had been when he left Columbia, feeling that no one was listening and that the record label wasn't backing him. Other changes were afoot, too. Marty Stuart, who had been playing in Cash's band for eight years, and been part of the family for six, left the band after his divorce from Cash's daughter Cindy. Stuart had been a driving force in trying to right the Cash ship but was now striking out on his own with the blessing of his mentor.

Around the same time, Cash discovered that he needed heart bypass surgery. The pain medication he was prescribed brought his addiction back to the surface, and he was checked into a drug program in late 1989—just as he was getting started on his next recording project.

Boom Chicka Boom (1989)

Cash's third album for Mercury reflects his drift into apathy, although he was still able to serve up a few gems along the way. To produce the album, Cash brought in Bob Moore, the one-time bass player in the Nashville A-Team of studio musicians. For *Boom Chicka Boom,* Moore returned Cash to just that: the sound he had leaned on for a career. Despite his mounting health problems, Cash's voice sounded as good as it had in recent years, though it lacks much of the energy that crackled through the Highwaymen sessions. That in itself didn't help as *Boom Chicka Boom* and *Highwaymen 2* were released very close together.

There were also problems with the material. Cash contributed four originals to the album—more than on any album since 1980's *Rockabilly Blues.* Anyone who scratches their head and wonders how Cash could have been talked into recording "Chicken in Black" need only listen to "A Backstage Pass" and "Farmer's Almanac." While neither is quite as absurd as "Chicken," both show his penchant for quirky, maybe even weird, songs—and both of these were written by Cash himself! "A Backstage Pass" is a good-natured jab at being backstage at a show by Willie Nelson, whom Cash was just getting ready to go out on the road with as part of the first Highwaymen tour. "Farmer's Almanac" is a talking blues that wouldn't have been out of place on *Everybody Loves a Nut.* One interesting thing to note about the song is the line about a shoeshine man. In the song, Cash sits down "at a real slow" shoeshine stand and comments that the man doesn't pop the rag like other shoeshiners. "The trouble with the world today is there's too much popping and not enough shining," the man replies, adding that he got the information from the *Farmer's Almanac.* Cash would later incorporate this episode (in interviews and from the stage) into the story of how he came to write "Get Rhythm."

Originally included on 1974's *Ragged Old Flag*, "Don't Go Near the Water" gets a reprise here, and the passage of time is telling. The new version includes a second verse, one that tells about a time when "the air was clear and you could see forever 'cross the plains," long before anyone had heard of acid rain. But now, after we've tortured the earth and poured "every kind of evil" into the sea, we know "our children have to pay the penalty." The problem here isn't the sentiment—in fact, this new version makes a bolder statement—but the arrangement and delivery. Where a rolling acoustic guitar introduced and accompanied

Our Kinda Cash was the long-running newsletter of the Johnny Cash fan club. Members of the club were spread all over the world. *Author's collection*

the song in 1974, the 1990 version replaces it with a bouncy boom-chicka-boom, which doesn't gel with the song's grounded message.

Cash's delivery of the spoken middle section brings further problems. The Cash of 1974, in the throes of being a fairly new father again, sounds regretful as he tells his son that it's no longer safe to eat the fish they catch, his voice stamped with fear of the future. The Cash of 1990 comes across simply as an old man sitting on the bank, thinking back to the good old days.

The lack of regret in Cash's voice also causes Harry Chapin's "Cat's in the Cradle" to suffer a bit, which is a shame, since he certainly lived the paternal regret of which the song speaks. It's also lacking in "Hidden Shame," written by Elvis Costello, though that didn't stop one critic from calling the song "one of the high points of [Cash's] amazing career." Both songs *could* have been high points, but not as they are presented here, where Cash's apathy and boredom are clear to see. Standing alone in the spotlight, he is revealed as what he is—a man standing at the crossroads, wondering whether to soldier on or rest on a laurel or two.

Reaching out to other songwriters couldn't mask it, either. "Harley," the story of a workingman with continual bad luck, written by Chick Rains and the cosmic cowboy Michael Martin Murphey, could have been much stronger than it turned out here.

"That's One You Owe Me," written by Jim Elliott and Mark D. Sanders, is the story of two old friends, and marks one instance where Cash seems to have come out of his fog enough to relay the feeling of the song. Another such moment is his version of "Family Bible"—ironically, one of the songs Cash alludes to in "A Backstage Pass," where he mentions Willie selling a song for $50. The two factors that drive "Family Bible" are the fact that it is a gospel song (a genre Cash always poured a little something extra into), and the presence of his mother, Carrie Cash, singing with him (though you'll need to strap on the headphones to hear her).

"Monteagle Mountain" is by Richard McGibony, whom Cash had met in the mid-1960s through Bob Johnson, who played acoustic guitar on the recordings McGibony was making at that time. The two hit it off, and McGibony was there for him during his dark periods, even picking him up from an overnight jail stay in Lafayette, Georgia, in October 1967. Though they had been friends for years, and McGibony's songs had been recorded by a few other artists (including Esquerita), Cash had never recorded one—until now. In a letter to his friend, Cash writes, "Well, Richard, perseverance does pay off. My record company loves 'Monteagle Mountain' as I do. First single is 'Farmers Almanac,' and it'll be up to the DJs what the second one will be. I hope it's your song."

The first single, backed with the non-album track "I Shall Be Free," met chart competition in the form of the Highwaymen's "Silver Stallion," which proved to be a stronger song, though its chart performance wasn't anything spectacular. Still, it did more than Cash's solo singles of the time. The follow-up, "Cat's in the Cradle," also failed to reach the charts. Maybe due to the close

The first multi-artist Cash tribute came from England in 1988. It is filled with punk-rock refugees like Michelle Shocked and the Mekons.
Author's collection

proximity of the second Highwaymen album, *Boom Chicka Boom*, stayed off of the charts as well.

The Mystery of Life (1991)

In the fall of 1990, between dates on the long-awaited Highwaymen tour and his own solo engagements, Cash found time to make it into the studio to begin work on a new album. *The Mystery of Life* marked the return of Cowboy Jack Clement to the fold, as well as the return on guitar of Marty Stuart, who was taking a break from his fledgling solo career. It could have been their return or residual energy from the continuing Highwaymen shows that helped bring back a more energetic Cash; either way, whatever the reasoning, he was there.

Although the album starts on a clumsy lyrical footing, presenting Jesus Christ as "The Greatest Cowboy of Them All," musically, the song's driving guitar and propulsive drums get the toe tapping right out of the gate. That continues with another Cash-penned tune, "I'm an Easy Rider," a road song featuring Kerry Marx's hard-edged and doubled-up baritone guitar. "The Mystery of Life," a truck-driving song by Joe Nixon, softens the sonic landscape with mandolins and Clements' Dobro, before "Hey Porter" cranks it back up, bringing back both Stuart and Marx's baritone guitar. "Beans for Breakfast" is another quirky Cash original about a man whose wife has left him, and who finally gives up, jacking up on pills and burning the house down.

Nineteen ninety saw the beginning of the first Gulf War, and in response, Cash pulled out a song that he had recorded four years earlier, "Goin' by the Book," which ties current events to biblical prophecy. It was released as a single at the end of the year, accompanied by a video assembled from news footage and shots of Cash standing, accompanied by a lone guitarist, in a darkened room. Nonetheless, the song spent only four weeks on the chart, peaking at #69.

Cash returns to familiar territory on "Wanted Man," the song he co-wrote with Dylan and debuted at Folsom Prison. Continuing on his visit to the past, he is joined by Tom T. Hall for a pedal-steel-soaked ode to doing your own thing on "I'll Go Somewhere and Sing My Songs Again." While he's there, Cash pulls out John Prine's 1978 composition "The Hobo Song" and gives it a good reading, while "Angel and the Badman" was a song Cash wrote in 1988.

The Mystery of Life was released to mixed reviews. In what had become the usual state of business for Cash, the album failed to chart, as did the second single, "The Mystery of Life." And with that, as the album died on the vine, Cash and Mercury quietly parted ways.

40

I Went Out Walking Under an Atomic Sky

Back to Youth, 1991–93

The 1990s had gotten off to a roller coaster–like start for Johnny Cash. His face was swollen and in constant pain, as a result of complications following dental surgery, and his weakened jaw broke soon after that, causing the pain to increase greatly. But he soldiered on, as he always had, making all of the dates on the Highwaymen's tour that year.

Nineteen ninety-one started with highs and lows, too. Even as his fifth and final album for Mercury was failing, the Grammys were honoring him with a Living Legend Award. Looking at the other recipients—Aretha Franklin, Billy Joel, and Quincy Jones—Cash wondered where he stood in the world of music. The others were still making charting singles, while his solo albums, though generally critically praised, were not selling or making any type of impact.

"The Man in Black"—One Bad Pig

As Cash was contemplating his place in the music world and plotting a course toward entertaining the middle-aged and older tourists of Branson, Missouri, his management received a call asking about the possibility of his guesting on a song by a young band. The band was a Christian punk outfit called One Bad Pig that had been moving in the contemporary Christian music scene for several years and had made its national debut in 1990. For its second album, the band decided to record "The Man in Black," Cash's self-mythologizing call for social justice, as lead singer Paul Q-Pek explained to *Cross Rhythms* in 1991:

> We wanted to do Johnny's "Man in Black," and Myrrh's A&R guy Mark Maxwell had the idea of asking him to sing on the track. So we made some calls. They asked us to send them a tape and some write-ups. We thought, once they hear the music, we'll have no chance! But then the word came back that Johnny had read the stuff we sent and said, "I want to be on their record." What really impressed him was that we were what he called "a gospel band." Also, he had a son who's twenty-one and who's really into metal. So Johnny came into the studio the last day of the sessions. It was a blast, Johnny doing his song. Johnny is an OLD guy. But he really

> seemed to get into it. We had a chance to talk with him and pray with him. He was just great. When the record came out, some people thought we'd sampled Johnny or used a Johnny Cash imitator. But it was the real Man in Black in person on *I Scream Sunday*.

It wasn't the first time in recent history that performers from across the musical spectrum had taken notice of Cash. *'Til Things Are Brighter*, a Cash tribute album featuring artists like the Mekons and Michelle Shocked, was released in 1988. Mekons leader Jon Langford had co-organized the album as a way to raise money for AIDS research. At the time, he was producing a band called the Creepers, featuring guitarist Marc Riley. Riley talked to Langford about how much Cash he was listening to at the time, and asked Langford if he liked him.

Langford picked up the story in an interview for Otis Gibbs' podcast *Thanks for Giving a Damn* in 2013:

> I loved Johnny Cash, you know, I've always liked Johnny Cash because he was quite visible in England. I didn't like country and western music, and I was just at that time getting into what I thought was country and western music, like Jerry Lee Lewis' stuff, and then Merle Haggard, Ernest Tubb, George Jones—I had never heard any of that stuff, I was getting into that. Johnny Cash, I thought he was like Elvis, kind of a rockabilly guy, you know, I didn't equate him with the honky-tonk thing at all. Marc said, "Oh no, you should really listen to some of these albums, they're really good. I've been listening to them driving my car. We should do an album of just us singing Johnny Cash."
>
> I was going, wow, that'd be weird, and people might not like it very much. I listened to it and was like, oh my God, this would be perfect! It just figured right in with what we were doing at the time. I suggested we get in some other people so it wasn't just me and him singing all the songs. Then it turned into, "Why would we do this?" Let's turn it into a benefit album or something. We both wanted to do it for AIDS research, which was a huge issue at the time, and we had a lot of friends who were affected directly by that.

Just after the album's release, Cash returned to the UK to play a show.

> He played Albert Hall, and Nick Lowe and Elvis Costello were up onstage with him, and we got in free. He did a little interview with the BBC and he named all the people on the album, which was really funny, because he said, "And Mary Mary from the Gay Bikers on Acid." My brilliant idea was to get Mary Mary from the Gay Bikers on Acid—who was a bloke—to do "A Boy Named Sue." Cash saw the humor in that, and also said the words Gay Bikers on Acid on British TV in the 1980s, which was fantastic! He says to me, "So when's the record out?" I said officially next week, but we're going to have a record release party on Saturday night, and this was the previous Sunday, or something. He said, "I wish I'd known. June and I would have stayed over for that." I'm like, "Oh my God, are you serious?" Missed opportunity.

"Cash to me was like Elvis," Langford added, in an interview for Graeme Thomson's book *The Resurrection of Johnny Cash.* "I had no perception in my head that he might have ups and downs in his career and that this might be a really bad time for him. He wasn't unfashionable to us but he was to everyone else." As Thomson writes, "It placed Cash's music into an entirely new, slightly subversive, and wholly contemporary context."

Now, Cash was being approached by a similar type of band in the US. He had courted the contemporary Christian audience before, releasing music on Christian labels. And what did he have to lose if he failed? Like *'Til Things Are Brighter*, "The Man in Black" recast his music by changing up the style—only this time it included Cash in the process. Even though the record was aimed only at a subculture (maybe even a subculture of a subculture), it was still one geared toward youth—an audience Cash hadn't had many dealings with in the past several years. In any event, the song went to #1 on the Christian Rock chart.

Life Moves On

Chart placement and audience acceptance were the furthest things from Cash's mind when, on March 11, 1991, his beloved mother, Carrie, passed away. Carrie had been his first and biggest booster, constantly encouraging him to use "The Gift," as she called his voice. She did this often in direct opposition of her husband, Ray, who thought J. R. was wasting his time and energy dreaming of being on the radio.

The time for grieving was short, however—the show had to go on. By May, Cash was out on tour, both solo and with the Highwaymen, on a trek through Australia and New Zealand. By now, with his increasing list of health problems, Cash was growing tired of the constant touring, but he felt he couldn't stop because he had several family members—and others who felt like family members—on the payroll. The increasing movement of older country stars to the tourist-trap attractions of Branson, Missouri, seemed like a solution that would alleviate one problem without collapsing the other. Some saw Branson as a career-saver, others as a sign of giving up and settling into the life of an oldies performer. For Cash it proved to be neither.

When a developer came to him proposing Cash Country—a 2,500-seat, $35-million entertainment complex—Cash listened. David Green, the California-based investor, laid out a no-money proposition that asked only that Cash lend his name to the project and commit to a given number of performances per year. While Cash might have had his misgivings about playing in Branson, this new proposal would get him off the road while still allowing him to keep up his income—which, in turn, allowed him to cover payroll for a staff that stretched from thirty to forty people at any given time. Green formally announced the project at a press conference on April 30, 1991, while Cash was on tour. Development soon began—and soon ended. Green wasn't able to come up with the funds to continue, and one year after he had made his initial announcement, the project's closure was confirmed.

Just prior to the second announcement, Cash was given another honor: induction into the Rock and Roll Hall of Fame, based on his early work at Sun. After a speech by Lyle Lovett, Cash looked humbled as he talked about his early influences and the types of music he listened to back then, focusing heavily on blues and gospel. "Maybe I was trying to make sure I belonged here tonight, in the Rock and Roll Hall of Fame," he told an Associated Press reporter after the ceremony. "Whether I belong in it or not, I am exceedingly proud of it." At the end of the show, Cash participated in the customary jam session, leading a group that included Steve Cropper, John Fogerty, and Keith Richards through "Big River."

The sudden halting of the Cash Country project left Cash angry and a little embarrassed, since people wouldn't know he hadn't actually put any money into the scheme. Though he had come to see that the move didn't necessarily speak highly of his career, he was still intrigued with the possibility of getting off

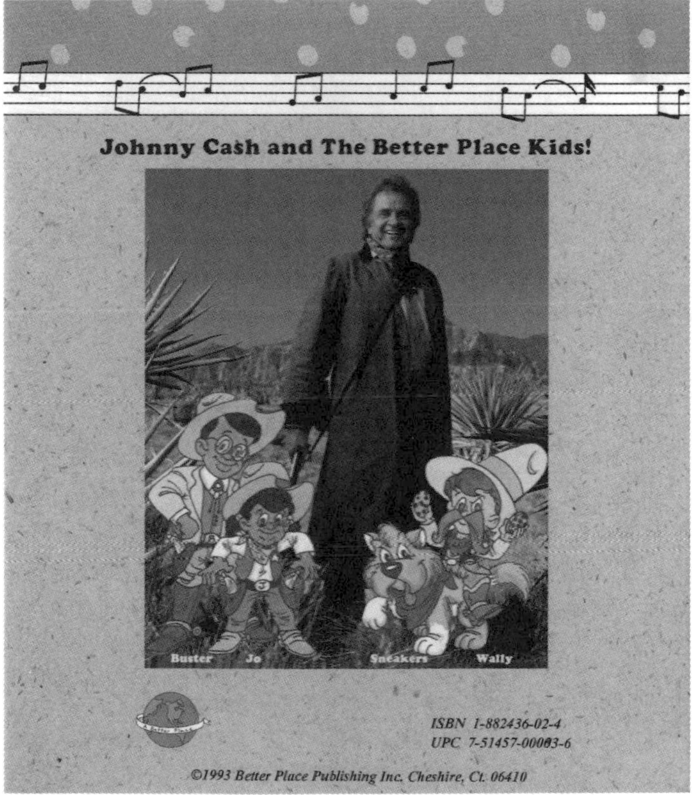

While Cash's dark persona was being pushed by America, he was still appearing in episodes of the family-friendly *Dr. Quinn, Medicine Woman* and starring in kids' books. *Author's collection*

the road yet still making money. With that in mind, and perhaps to save a little face, Cash signed up to do a series of shows at the Wayne Newton Theatre, the building that was to become Cash Country (subsequently sold off after Green filed for bankruptcy).

"The Wanderer"—U2

Collaborating with One Bad Pig on a punkish take on one of his signature songs had given Cash a little hope that he wasn't sliding completely into irrelevancy. His hopes were further bolstered when he got a call from another contemporary band keen to collaborate with him.

Cash had first met Bono and Adam Clayton of U2 a few years earlier, while they had worked with Jack Clement during the recording and filming of *Rattle and Hum.* During sessions for their new record, *Zooropa*, Bono had written a song he called "The Pilgrim," but he felt it was missing something. When he found out that Cash would be performing a concert in Scotland in February, he decided that Cash was what the track needed. He reworked some of the lyrics with Cash in mind and reached out to see about the possibility of having him record with them.

Sonically, the song was very different from Cash's other recent collaboration, with U2's atmospheric swells replacing the in-your-face assault of One Bad Pig. And instead of being a duet, Cash is the primary voice on the song, with Bono joining in only at the end, with a series of "ohhhs." Lyrically, the song was right in Cash's wheelhouse, with its talk of temptation and wandering, spirituality and sin. The song, now named "The Wanderer," shows Cash both out of his element and in his element at the same time.

At the time of the recording, Cash wasn't sure whether the song would make it onto U2's new album. But the band ended up deciding to include it, and the album hit #1 in ten countries, including the US, where it went double platinum.

What the One Bad Pig single had done for Cash in a subsection of a subculture, the U2 single did on a worldwide basis. Suddenly, here was Johnny Cash featured on the new album by the biggest band on the planet. Fans of both U2 and Cash alike took notice. And so did Cash. This new association with younger bands made him think about what he was doing, and who he was doing it for.

Shortly after the U2 collaboration, Cash canceled his remaining shows in Branson. "I have no plans to come back at all," he told a reporter. "I don't think I'm doing myself or my fans a favor by being here."

41

I'm Gonna Break My Rusty Cage and Run

American 1993–95

At the time he recorded "The Wanderer" with U2 in February 1993, Johnny Cash was a man adrift. He had ended his association with Polygram/Mercury, citing a lack of promotion and claiming the label had pressed less than 500 copies of his records. This was surely an exaggeration, but the sentiment was clear. In the years just prior, he had recorded only two full-length projects—a Christmas album and a gospel project—plus a few guest vocals on songs by Charlie Daniels, John Schneider, and Marty Stuart.

His touring was suffering, too. By 1993, country shows by Garth Brooks and Reba McEntire, among others, had evolved into elaborate productions that filled arenas. Cash had moved to playing much smaller venues, some of them seating fewer than 1,000 people. His camp tried to spin it as a way for Cash to visit smaller towns he hadn't been able to get to for several years, but the truth was, he needed the money.

This wasn't a new problem. Cash was generous to a fault. Producer Larry Butler recalled a time when Cash's management decided to hide his mail, because he would often get requests for monetary help from fans, and he would generally oblige. As Butler recalled to Kevin Sport, Cash had asked him, in complete sincerity, "Larry, you reckon they don't like me anymore? I don't get any mail." Cash soon figured out what was happening, although Butler and the rest of the team didn't know it until they received a letter from a fan that said, "Johnny, I want to thank you for that $20 you sent me."

Cash was also supporting a number of people on what had become a bloated payroll. And when his medical problems grew more frequent, beginning with his stay at the Betty Ford Clinic in 1984, these two money pits began to eat away at his finances. Later that year, House of Cash was forced into a foreclosure due to unpaid debt. In order to cover that debt, it was decided that the company would put a portion of its song catalogue on the auction block in 1986. Included in the sale were songs by Billy Joe Shaver, Rosanne Cash, the Statler Brothers, and Cash classics like "I Walk the Line" and "Folsom Prison Blues." Years later, he would eventually manage to get them back, but it was things like this that drove decisions like playing in Branson or recording "Chicken in Black."

Even hardcore fans would be hard pressed to find the Cash they loved in the two projects he recorded in 1991 and '92. Of the two, his latest gospel project, *Return to the Promised Land* (discussed elsewhere), was also to be a television event on the Nashville Network—not on the level of *The Gospel Road*, but an amendment of sorts. The network eventually decided against it, however, and the film went instead to Billy Graham's World Wide Pictures. Cash was floundering, creatively, without an idea of how to get back on track.

Enter Rick Rubin

Rick Rubin got his start producing hip-hop tracks in New York City, one of which was "It's Yours" by rapper T. La Rock and DJ Jazzy Jay. At a party, Russell Simmons, brother of Run DMC's Reverend Run (a.k.a. Joseph Simmons) and the group's manager, asked Jazzy who produced the record. Ronin Ro, author of the Run DMC biography *Raising Hell*, picks up the story: "Jazzy introduced him to its producer, Rick Rubin, a chubby white twenty-one-year-old New York University film student. Russell couldn't believe that this long-haired fan of Run DMC and rock music had created the compelling bass-heavy single, but once they started talking, he learned that Rick liked the same records and understood that rap music had to sound hard."

Rubin had grown up on Lido Beach, Long Island, and was a fan of punk, hard rock, and early rap. He attended NYU with a vague plan to somehow go into the music business—or, if all else failed, become a lawyer. Enamored with DJ scratching, Rubin sought to learn how to DJ himself, and ended up working with a new group of three white boys going by the name Beastie Boys. While he was working with the Beasties, Rubin also fronted a punk band of his own, Hose, and put out an album in the punk DIY fashion, which included making personal visits to record stores to restock product and talk about the album.

Simmons eventually signed up to manage both Rubin and the Beasties with the intention of finding them a home on a major label. Rubin's DIY instinct kicked in, and he convinced Simmons they could do it on their own and make more money that way. The pair then started Def Jam Recordings.

After five years of producing rap tracks, Rubin returned to another of his early loves, pairing Run DMC with Aerosmith to record a new take on "Walk This Way," which went to #4 on the Pop chart in 1986, revitalizing Aerosmith's career. That same year, he produced the thrash-metal band Slayer's third album, *Reign in Blood*. By 1988, Rubin was moving more toward rock, while Simmons was focusing on R&B. Rubin left for California to start Def American.

In the Cash narrative, Rubin is often characterized as simply a rap and metal producer, which he certainly was, but by 1990 he was doing much more than that, working as well with artists like the Black Crowes, Tom Petty, Dan Baird of the Georgia Satellites, and Raging Slab. One idea that Rubin was increasingly interested in, as a challenge to himself, was to take a big name—maybe someone a little down on their luck—and see what he could do with them. In one such example, he had entered the studio with Mick Jagger in 1992, then between Rolling Stones projects, to make the album *Wandering Spirit.*

Shortly after that, Rubin decided to get in touch with Johnny Cash. He placed a call to Lou Robin, Cash's longtime manager, and explained that he would like to discuss the possibility of recording an album together. Arrangements were made for them to meet at a Cash gig at the Rhythm Cafe, a 550-seat venue in Santa Ana, California. Rubin watched the show—a typical Cash production of the hits—and afterward went backstage to meet him.

After the two men had sized each other up, Cash had one question. "I said, 'So what makes you think you could—you would—do something with me that nobody else has tried or nobody else wants to do?'" Cash explained to *Billboard.* "He said, 'I just want you to take your guitar and sing me some songs, and those are the songs I want to put down on record. Sing me what you love and what you feel good about, and let's record those.'"

American Recordings (1994)

The answer satisfied—or at least intrigued—Cash, and in May, he flew to L.A. to sit down with Rubin. Rubin had set up recording equipment in his living room, and for the next four days, from May 17th to 20th, he instructed Cash to just play songs that he loved—songs of his own that he loved and had recorded, songs he had never recorded, songs by others that he loved, anything. They recorded over thirty songs, the majority spanning Cash's career, plus a few that Rubin brought in, including a couple by ZZ Top's Billy Gibbons. This process continued in two other sessions, held on June 30th, July 1st–2nd, and July 21st–23rd.

When Cash returned to L.A., in September, they tried tracking sixteen songs with Flea and Chad Smith of the Red Hot Chili Peppers on bass and drums, respectively, and Mike Campbell of Tom Petty's Heartbreakers on guitar. A few days later, Cash was joined for three songs by the L.A. blues band the Red Devils, who had previously played with Jagger, but the following day he was back on Rubin's couch, recording demos. He continued to make similar recordings back home in Hendersonville, and again back in California with Rubin, until they had amassed more than seventy songs to choose from. After listening through them, Rubin decided the best approach would be to release the songs they had recorded when they thought they were just demoing.

"There was just such a purity of hearing him in that light," Rubin told Wes Orshoski of *Billboard* in 2002. "For all the records he'd made over the years, he'd never really made one like that before. Without that being the plan in advance, it just kind of evolved into, 'Wow, ya know, this really kind of sounds like the record I wish I could get. Ya know, as a fan, this is the one I wish I could go buy.' But, again, it was completely by accident."

"It's just Cash doing exactly what he wants to do," Marty Stuart told Jim Patterson, for an Associated Press article. "They're done with a living room atmosphere, catching an American icon in his natural habitat and seeing what's on his mind. It's very earthy, very organic, very down to earth. It holds on to every tradition that he ever helped create, but it also busts down the walls of his future, as only he can do, to kind of help give us a different place to go."

Prior to finishing the album, Rubin encouraged Cash to perform—solo, with only his guitar—at the Viper Room, the trendy L.A. nightspot owned by Johnny Depp. It was an invitation-only crowd of tastemakers and celebrities, and Cash was nervous about performing in such a vulnerable way. But the crowd was receptive, and Cash wowed them.

"It was an incredible night," Rubin told Adam D. Miller of beingtheremag .com.

> Dead silent. You could hear a pin drop. People couldn't believe that it was Johnny Cash there in the Viper Room. He started playing, and I could see how nervous he was, but by the middle of the first song, or the beginning of the second song, all of the fear was gone. He was in the music and it was beautiful. People who were there that night still talk about it as one of the greatest things they've ever seen. And we recorded that night and I think one of those songs ended up on our first album.

That album, *American Recordings*, was released on April 26, 1994. Its thirteen songs included several from Cash's back catalogue, such as "Delia's Gone," which he had recorded in 1962 for *The Sound of Johnny Cash*, and "Oh, Bury Me Not," recorded for 1965's *Ballads of the True West.* There were also old songs he loved, like Jimmy Driftwood's "Tennessee Stud," a Top 5 hit for Eddy Arnold in 1959, and one of the live tracks taken from the Viper Room gig.

Cash also recorded three songs written specifically for him at the sessions. The first was "The Beast in Me," written by his ex-son-in-law, Nick Lowe. The lyrics speak to his battles with temptation, and the changes that occur in him when he gives in. "Thirteen," written by Glenn Danzig, highlights, as one might expect, the darker side of Cash's persona—something later marketing would also do. And Tom Waits' "Down There by the Train" is a song in which a rich cast of characters, including Judas Iscariot and John Wilkes Booth, move toward their salvation.

Returning to more familiar territory, Cash cut Kris Kristofferson's "Why Me, Lord?" and Leonard Cohen's "Bird on a Wire," a song he had talked about recording since 1974. There's also Loudon Wainwright's quirky "The Man Who Couldn't Cry," as recorded at the Viper Room show.

Cash also finds time to offer his point of view with four songs of his own. The first, "Let the Train Blow the Whistle," is a tuneful song about leaving this earth, but with a bouncy melody that shows Cash's liveliness. "I am not obsessed with death," he told Neil Strauss, in a 1994 *New York Times* interview.

> I'm obsessed with living. The battle against the dark one and the clinging to the right one is what my life is about. In '88, when I had bypass surgery, I was as close to death as you could get. The doctors were saying they

> were losing me. I was going, and there was that wonderful light that I was going into. It was awesome, indescribable—beauty and peace, love and joy—and then all of a sudden, there I was again, all in pain and awake. I was so disappointed. But when I realized a day or so later what point I had been to, I started thanking God for life and thinking only of life.

That didn't mean Cash's life was without trouble, as the song "Drive On" reminds us. Written after he read John Del Vecchio's *The 13th Valley* and other novels based on soldiers' experiences in Vietnam, the song talks about the frame of mind a soldier has to have in combat. If a fellow soldier is felled by a bullet, there is no time to stop, so they have to tell themselves to "drive on." But Cash also adopted the phrase as a personal mantra, telling Steve Pond, "If it isn't life-threatening, don't worry about it. Since I had my sixtieth birthday, I've been using that expression a lot. I'm trying to learn that I can't sweat the little things the way I used to do. So what if I've got a broken jaw? It could be worse. Could be a broken back. Screw it. It don't mean nothing. Drive on."

What Cash was driving on to culminated in "Redemption," a song he considered his personal testimony. That idea of pressing on, making choices, denying the flesh, permeated his thoughts on the album, right down to the artwork, which has him standing, hair windblown and eyes piercing, with a dog on either side of him. The dogs belonged to the owner of the land where the photos were taken, and made their way over to the photo shoot. One of the dogs was black with a white stripe, the other white with a mix of black. Cash decided to name them Sin and Redemption. "That's kind of the theme of that album," he explained to Jancee Dunn, in a 1994 *Rolling Stone* interview, "and I think it says it for me, too. When I was really bad, I was not all bad. When I was really trying to be good, I could never be all good. There would be that black streak going through."

The final Cash composition on the album is "Like a Soldier," in which he compares his journey in life to that of a soldier. With lines about somebody reaching down and touching him, and lifting "me up with you," it's left to the listener to decide whether he's talking about God or June (or both).

For years, Cash had said that he had wanted to make a stark album, even committing to tape the blueprint that eventually became *Personal File.* He had envisioned an album of intimate songs to a woman, with the prospective title *Johnny Cash: Late and Alone,* but the idea never found a supporter with his various labels. "I always wanted to do that," he told reporter Michael Hochanadel, "but never thought I could do it. They'd say, 'You got to be crazy! You gotta have electric instruments on your albums!' But I always thought that if ever I could do it, it would be one of my best records."

For many, *American Recordings* was just that. While some among the Cash faithful may have missed the boom-chicka-boom, they couldn't deny the honesty of his performance or the intimacy of hearing Cash alone. And that missing boom-chicka-boom cast Cash in a different light for casual, or even new, fans. *Dallas Morning News* reviewer Michael Corcoran, for example, described the new record as "the result of a producer and an artist tuned in to the same frequency and creating the best possible album. Fans of real music, rejoice!"

The same sentiment was echoed in newspapers and magazines across the country. Thanks in part to the marketing focus on the darker side of Cash—as seen in the video for "Delia's Gone," which co-starred the model Kate Moss and aired on MTV—the album also attracted a younger crowd, much as the stark sound of *At Folsom Prison* had done, decades before.

American Recordings entered the Top Country Albums chart at #29 and the *Billboard* 200 at #128 on May 14, 1994, and would go on to peak at #23 and #110, respectively. That was higher than any Cash album had managed in years, so the duo of legend and producer counted it as a victory. The accolades slowly poured in, and in 1995 Cash won a Grammy for Best Contemporary Folk Album.

While the marketing machine portrayed Cash as a dark, brooding figure, he went about his life the way he always had, making appearances on family-oriented shows like *Dr. Quinn: Medicine Woman*, and touring nearly nonstop, both solo and with the Highwaymen, with whom he had recently completed a new album.

One of those solo tour stops was at the Glastonbury Festival in England, where Cash played alongside artists like Elvis Costello, Blind Melon, and Peter Gabriel. "I booked Johnny Cash to play at Glastonbury in 1994," festival organizer Michael Eavis later told the *NME*. "He was spellbinding, bloody brilliant. That was one of my best bookings of all time. This was when Johnny wasn't nearly as fashionable as he was after 'Hurt.' Some of the youngsters thought I'd gone crazy, as they believed I should be booking new stuff all the time. They thought he was just a daft old country singer. But he was so good."

42

Through Glasses Dark as These

American 1996–99

In *Johnny Cash: The Life*, Robert Hilburn states that until Rick Rubin, no producer had understood what to do with Cash—including Sam Phillips. Speaking with Henry Carrigan at musictomes.com he elaborated: "[Cash] didn't really have his vision fully developed at Sun Records, which made it hard for Sam to understand the full scope of John's talent. By the time Rick entered the picture, Cash had defined his vision and that gave Rick an enormous advantage. He saw the great things John did at Sun and Columbia Records and he found a way to get John to trust him, which in turn enabled John to recapture that early greatness and, even, move beyond it."

The pairing of Rick Rubin and Johnny Cash was proving to be a successful one, and new fans—younger fans—were coming to the artist like they hadn't in years. At the same time, a similar thing was happening to crooner Tony Bennett. His take, as he told *Newsweek* in 1995, was that the younger fans liked him because of what he was not doing. "I'm not trying to sing rock music to them," he explained. "I'm not trying to 'connect' with them. I'm just doing what I've always done, and they see someone who's never given in—like a fighter who never took a dive."

Cash echoed that sentiment in an interview with Fred Shuster. "I look out at the audience now and see nose rings, shaved heads, punk rockers, as well as folks in cowboy boots and hats with that middle-aged spread. I guess it's pretty much everyone nowadays. I'm just doing what I've always done."

What Cash had always done was concentrate on finding great songs. He and Rubin planned to go back into the studio to make a follow-up, and while they wanted to continue that tradition, they planned to do something musically different than the spare guitar/vocal arrangements of their first outing together. Rubin was also working with Tom Petty at the time, so he invited Petty to bring in the Heartbreakers, though they often didn't perform in their usual band roles.

"It was great fun," Petty told Nick Hasted of *Uncut*. "I think about those sessions, and they were just some of the best times I ever had in the studio. Just very charmed sessions. Everyone was so at ease but really into the project at the same time, and really, really enjoying playing. You weren't even nailed down to your particular instrument. I might wind up playing the organ, and the bass quite a bit. . . . We didn't do a lot of takes of anything. And we'd come in, and it would sound really glorious, when Rick would play it back."

Unchained (1996)

Unlike *American Recordings*, the song selection for Cash's new album was more of a collaborative effort. He and Rubin would pick songs and present them to the other for discussion, though Cash had the final say on whether to record the song—or, at least, whether to include it. In the end, they recorded fifty songs before paring them down to the final fourteen featured on the album.

The opener came from a newer artist, Beck, who had opened a show for Cash a few months before he started work on *Unchained*. "I just loved his show, mainly because he did a lot of Appalachian-style folk songs," Cash told Paul Gorman of *Music Week*. "When Rick suggested I do 'Rowboat,' I just knew it was right." "Rowboat," from Beck's 1994 LP *Stereopathetic Soulmanure*, was one of the songs that Cash immediately identified with. "Beck's been reading my mail," he writes in the liner notes.

From the new to the old, the album's second song, "Sea of Heartbreak," was a #2 Country hit (#21 Pop) for Don Gibson in 1961, before being taken back to the charts by Kenny Price in 1972, Lynn Anderson in 1979, and Ronnie McDowell in 1989. To augment the band, Rubin brought in Fleetwood Mac's Lindsay Buckingham on guitar and Mick Fleetwood on percussion.

Swinging back to the new, "Rusty Cage," originally performed by the Seattle grunge band Soundgarden, was Rubin's first pick for the album. It was a song that Cash initially turned away. "I just couldn't see me doing it—didn't think it would work at all," Cash told Gorman.

"That was one where I had to rerecord the song to present it to him, because when he heard the original recording of the song it really terrified him," Rubin told *Performing Songwriter*'s Russell Hall. "He thought it was unrealistic and that I was crazy for suggesting it. But then when I recorded it more the way I imagined him doing it, just as a demo, he really liked it."

The process of Rubin breaking the song down and rebuilding it around Cash was one that would be revisited many times by the pair. It was a way for Rubin to communicate his vision to Cash in a shared language. It also provided Cash with a blueprint to navigate a song he might not be familiar with, making it less of a challenge to get through. "It's fascinating because that was actually the easiest song to record on the whole album," he told Gorman. "We went straight through it."

The original version of the song, with singer Chris Cornell's multi-octave range pushing the song over a rumbling, heavy musical backdrop, couldn't have been farther from Cash's element. But where Cornell pushes his voice higher to make a point, Cash comes to the mic more relaxed. Where Cornell unleashes a howl, Cash brings defiance. For the first verse, acoustic guitar

Cash's ex-son-in-law brought Cash into the studio to record a part on his song "I Walk the Line Revisited." The song recounted Crowell's feelings the first time he heard Cash sing the song.

Private collection

pulsates behind him, punctuated by piano. As he approaches the chorus for the second time, he sings, "I'm going to break my rusty cage"—elongating the word "cage" as if he's winding up his arm for the final blow, stretching it out until you can see the smirk creep across his face as he releases—"and run." At that point, electric guitars replace the acoustic, and by now Cash has taken the song from the novelty of "Hey, this old guy's singin' Soundgarden," to "Whoa, shit just got real." Cornell's pseudo-poetry—"rainin' icepicks on your steel shores"—is transformed from whatever it was originally supposed to mean to a post-apocalyptic vision, with Cash standing front and center. It doesn't matter what the words means: Cash seems to know, and that's all that matters.

The vision quickly returns from the future to the past as Cash turns to Jimmie Rodgers and "The One Rose (That's in My Heart)." From there, the album moves on to Cash's own "Country Boy," which here, in the hands of a crack band augmented by Cash's friend Marty Stuart, becomes a rockabilly rave-up in a way it wasn't even during the Sun in the late 1950s. Then Cash flips the tables again, swinging, literally, into Dean Martin territory, and "Memories Are Made of This."

By the halfway point of the album, Cash has been rocking and rolling and having fun, but at track seven, he decides it is time to give an offering of a different kind with "Spiritual." Written by Josh Haden, son of jazz bassist Charlie

Haden, the song is a prime example of Cash inhabiting somebody else's song to such an extent that it is hard to believe he didn't write it himself. It begins softly, with Cash telling his Savior, "Jesus, I don't want to die alone." It would be easy to add a retroactive meaning to the lyric, as Cash indeed did die shortly after the love of his life passed away, but that would be doing an injustice to the performance as it was presented at the time of the album's release. The original lyric is the familiar lament of someone who has had their heart broken by a lover who has proved untrue, followed by a jump from the breakup to dying alone. It's something everyone can relate to, but here, with a man in his sixties wrapping his battered voice around the lyric, it comes with a more immediate gravitas. This is a man who could very well die alone, even if he's surrounded by people, just as his friend Elvis did.

Cash's statement becomes a prayer as he asks Jesus not to leave him behind, pleading, "I know I've sinned, but, Lord, I'm suffering." As he continues his petition, his voice is supplanted by Mike Campbell's mandolin, which takes up the plea on Cash's behalf, as if he can't find the strength to finish the thought. When Cash returns, to repeat the first verse, there is a stronger urgency to his voice. The feeling of death is closer to him now, but again the mandolin takes over, giving Cash the time to gather his thoughts, his regrets, his pain, before he returns, singing higher, of how "all my troubles, all my pain, it's going to leave me once again." He's resigned to the fact, and has in fact gathered a form of strength in resignation. God has delivered him—or at least provided the road out—just as he asked.

These weren't idle words for Cash. The jaw problem that had caused him so much pain in the early '90s was flaring up again. Bouts of life-threatening pneumonia were becoming more frequent. But Cash was resolute in his decision to continue his recording career, as Tom Petty later told Nick Hasted for *Uncut*:

> Well, his jaw was bothering him at the time. And John had this incredible way of walking through extreme pain. At one point, I think he had his knee replaced, and he acted like that was nothing. That was around that time. I was saying, "Well, how do you deal with that?" He was on the road, and he called me from it. And he said, "Well, I go onstage and nothing hurts." But yeah, his health wasn't great. He wasn't as fragile as he would be some years later. He would work for a while and then he would rest for a while, you know. So with the sessions, we might work for an hour and then rest for half an hour, and then come back and work for a while longer. It just depended on how he was that day. But he was pretty sturdy. He was still hitting the road really hard then.

"It's a matter of mood and emotion for me," Cash told Paul Gorman. "Early in the day, I can tackle something real energetic, and as the day gets on everyone gets that mellow spirit." Outtakes from the sessions bear evidence to the fact that Cash's voice could get very rough during some recordings, to the point where it is sometimes hard to make out.

One prayer leads to another, and Cash decided to record "The Kneeling Drunkard's Plea," a song written by June, Anita, and Helen Carter, and cut decades earlier by Cash's early heroes, the Louvin Brothers. For Petty, this song was an example of the looseness of the sessions. "I didn't know it," he recalled, "and we started to play it, and John said, 'Ah, we need a Hammond organ on this. Tom why don't you play it, it just needs kind of a churchy intro.' I'm standing there going, 'Oh, OK . . .' and I just played some chords. And he seemed very pleased with it."

The teaming of Petty and Cash produced another song Cash was easily able to inhabit: Petty's 1985 composition "Southern Accents." It was the first of two Petty songs Cash would record. He also recorded Lucinda Williams' "Change the Locks," which Petty likewise cut a version of for the Rubin-produced soundtrack to *She's the One*, released around the time of the *Unchained* sessions. Ultimately, Cash's gruff voice kept the song off the final album.

As with "Country Boy," Cash revisits his past on "Mean Eyed Cat," a song he first recorded in 1955. And again, as with "Country Boy," the band pushes Cash deep into the rockabilly territory that the original version merely skirts. Cash also changes up the lyrics, switching to a happy ending of the girl returning.

Digging deeper into memory—deeper still than those Sun sessions—Cash brings out "Meet Me in Heaven," its title taken from the inscription on his brother Jack's gravestone. It isn't as powerful a meditation as "Spiritual," and Cash's delivery is not as strong, but it is a very personal statement from him to his brother, whom he loved dearly. It feels as though the audience is eavesdropping on a snippet of a conversation between the two brothers, as Cash longs to meet his long-lost sibling "out there beyond the stars."

Cash's memories of Jack would surely include plenty of time out in the cotton fields, but he suppresses them to slip into the character of "I Never Picked Cotton," perhaps the only misstep on an otherwise fine album. Roy Clark had taken the song to #5 in 1970, but here Cash barely gets the song off the ground. Its only purpose on the album seems to be to provide separation—and perhaps some levity—between "Meet Me in Heaven" and "Unchained."

Whereas "Meet Me in Heaven" has Cash in conversation with his brother about life on the other side, "Unchained" finds him searching himself to see if he thinks himself worthy to make the journey. "Where is that Rock of Ages when I need it most?" he asks, searching, yearning for something to lean on, to help him loose himself from the shackles that bind him to his earthly desires and toil, the chains that prevent him from going up to meet his dear brother in Heaven.

In what feels now like a sequencing misstep, though was presumably intended to end the album on an up note, *Unchained* closes with Cash's cover of Hank Snow's 1962 #2 hit "I've Been Everywhere." Cash's version wouldn't eclipse Snow's (or even Lynn Anderson's 1970 #16 version), but this jovial, bubbling take knocks some of the edge from what precedes it.

Unchained was released on November 5, 1996, and entered the charts two weeks later. Sales of some 7,000 copies placed it at #26 on the Top Country

Albums chart and #170 on the *Billboard* 200. In one of the first reviews to appear, veteran country music critic Alanna Nash wrote in *Entertainment Weekly* that the range of songs—from country to gospel to rock—seems "like an uneasy mix, until you realize it's really a travelogue of Johnny Cash's sticky psyche."

While the album sold steadily, it found very little action on radio. Kenny DiDia, then American's national sales manager, told *Billboard* that mainstream country radio was "a tough nut to crack," but that there had been interest from college, triple-AAA, and alternative stations. The only real action for the singles on country-related radio, DiDia noted, had been on the Real Country network, which was operated by Buck Owens. On the alternative side, *CMJ*, in March of 1997, listed *Unchained* at #2 on its Top 75 Radio Airplay survey, right between the Jon Spencer Blues Explosion and Wilco.

An additional benefit of the success of the two American albums was the bump it provided in Cash's back catalogue sales. *Johnny Cash Super Hits*, at the time one of the only available single-disc, moderately priced collections of Cash's music, reached the Top 25 on *Billboard*'s Catalog Sales chart, and would remain there for a stretch of years.

VH1 Storytellers: Johnny Cash and Willie Nelson

In November 1989, MTV aired the first episode of its new series, *Unplugged*, which featured artists performing their hits and new material in an acoustic setting. Over the next few years, artists including Paul McCartney, LL Cool J, John Mellencamp, Mariah Carey, and Eric Clapton appeared on the popular show. In 1996, MTV's sister station, VH1, premiered its new show *Storytellers*, which largely took the premise of *Unplugged*—musicians fronting acoustic versions of their bands—but added the extra element of having the artists tell stories from their careers as they relate to the songs.

VH1 was created to cater to a slightly older demographic than MTV, and the artists selected for *Storytellers* reflect that. By the end of 1996, the show had featured Ray Davies, Jackson Browne, Elvis Costello, and the Black Crowes, among others. Of the ten episodes that aired in 1996, two featured country artists Lyle Lovett and Garth Brooks, who was one of the hottest-selling acts of any genre at the time.

On May 12, 1997, two more country artists were added to the list when Johnny Cash and his old friend Willie Nelson performed together in front of a small audience for the show. Sitting alone onstage with their guitars, the veteran showmen come across as two old buddies sitting in a living room, rolling down memory lane. The mood is light, and their banter offers a window into their personalities—Cash's not as dark as his reputation might suggest, and Nelson's not as aloof.

Early on, Cash offers Nelson some water. "We've got water, coffee, and hot chocolate," Nelson notes. "What's going to happen to our image?" "Long as we keep wearing black, I think we might be all right," Cash replies, to the howling approval of the audience.

The two then run through their respective catalogues, with Cash bringing out the classics "(Ghost) Riders in the Sky," "Don't Take Your Guns to Town," "Flesh and Blood," "I Still Miss Someone," and "Folsom Prison Blues." He also plays the lesser-known "I'm a Worried Man," from 1974's *Ragged Old Flag*, which is introduced by Nelson, who had just recorded a version of it for his reggae album *Countryman* (which would not be released until 2005). The American recordings are represented by one song from each album, "Unchained" and "Drive On."

The Show Can't Go On

The show aired on June 15, 1997, at which point no one in the audience, whether in the auditorium or watching at home, could have known that it would have been one of the last times they'd be able to see Cash perform live. Quietly, away from the public eye, Cash's health had been slipping. The jaw problem and other surgeries were beginning to hamper his enjoyment of the road. Performing was still a possibility, but the long hours of travel were not. On September 16, 1997, he made the decision to retire from the road, performing his final concert on October 25 in Flint, Michigan.

That night, Cash had nearly toppled from the stage while bending down to pick up a guitar pick. He then told the crowd he had been diagnosed with Parkinson's disease. Some in the audience chuckled, thinking this was another example of his often-odd sense of humor, but he immediately set them straight. "Johnny feels confident that once the Parkinson's is medically stabilized, he can resume his normal work schedule," his manager told *Rolling Stone*. But it wasn't to be. Though Cash kept up a strong front, repeatedly telling people that he refused to give the disease any quarter, the truth was it prevented him from working the road. In case he had forgotten about his own mortality, he was given an

Twenty-three days after this appearance, Cash ended his touring and performing career, only playing live a handful of times between 1997 and 2003. *Author's collection*

The Johnny Cash Story is a six-episode radio show featuring Cash telling his life story. In 1999, it was released in six-disc and single-disc versions.
Author's collection

unwelcome reminder in January 1998, when his ex-Sun labelmate, touring partner-in-crime, and old friend Carl Perkins died of throat cancer at age sixty-five.

In February, *Unchained* won the Grammy for Best Country Album, beating Alan Jackson, George Strait, Dwight Yoakam, and Patty Loveless. The win gave birth to an infamous *Billboard* ad, placed by Rubin with Cash's consent, which showed a Jim Marshall photo of Cash flipping off the camera, accompanied by the words, "American Recordings and Johnny Cash would like to acknowledge the Nashville music establishment and country radio for your support."

To many in the Nashville music community, this was a polarizing move, but these things are often forgiven quickly. A couple of months later, on June 24th, the Ryman Auditorium hosted "Witness to History II: The Outlaw Years," a salute to Cash, Waylon Jennings, and Owen Bradley, who had passed away in January. The event was part of Chet Atkins' Musician Days, a celebration of the musicians whom Atkins called the backbone of the industry and the city of Nashville. Marty Stuart served as master of ceremonies, with artists including Travis Tritt and Mark Knopfler performing. Kris Kristofferson came to the stage to perform "Sunday Morning Coming Down" and recount the story of the first time he heard Cash perform the song, which was at the Ryman. It had been eight months since Cash had performed publicly, so when he strolled out unannounced—even to Kristofferson—mid-song to join his friend, it was a shock to all. As Chet Flippo noted in *Billboard*, there was "scarcely a dry eye in sight."

That same month, the *Storytellers* recording was released on CD, coming in at #27 on the Top Country Albums chart and #179 on the *Billboard* 200, selling a respectable 7,500 copies in its first week.

An All-Star Tribute to Johnny Cash

Cash took some time off from preparing for his next album to assist June with her album *Press On*. But the honors kept coming, and in February 1999 he was given a Lifetime Achievement award at the Grammys, though he didn't attend the ceremony, leading to speculation that he was too ill to do so.

He proved that speculation wrong on April 6, 1999, by traveling to New York for the taping of *An All-Star Tribute to Johnny Cash* at the Hammerstein Ballroom. Artists streamed across the stage to pay tribute to Cash, among them Chris Isaak, Willie Nelson, Sheryl Crow, Marty Stuart, and others. Videotaped performances were sent in by Bruce Springsteen, U2, and Bob Dylan. The night culminated with Cash making a rare onstage appearance, alongside the Tennessee Three—including Marshall Grant—to perform "Folsom Prison Blues" and "I Walk the Line." The show aired on TNT on April 18th, and was a huge ratings smash for the network, proving, once again, the Man in Black's potency with television audiences.

43

There Were Songs Before There Was Radio

American 2000–01

Just weeks after the All-Star Tribute to his career, Cash was back working on his next album with Rick Rubin. Though his touring days had been ended by a diagnosis of the Parkinson's-like Shy-Drager syndrome (a misdiagnosis later changed to autonomic neuropathy), Cash was able to see the bright side of things, telling Anthony DeCurtis that since he had come off the road, he was now able to pour his energy into studio work.

> The most pitiful thing that happened to me in my recording career is squeezing an album in between tours when you've got no reserve. So now that I've decided that I don't have to go on the road, I take that energy and creativity and put it into the songs and into recording. I'm much happier that way. I'm enjoying my life very, very much. I'm enjoying it a whole lot more than I did when I was on the road. I don't have any plans to go back and do concerts. I want to channel that energy into writing and recording.

Another side benefit of the enforced time at home was that his relationship with June had deepened and strengthened. As he shrank from the spotlight, he encouraged her to take it, and she did so with the release of her second solo album, *Press On* (covered in more detail in chapter 8). He had always encouraged her to sing—something she was never confident in her ability to do—and though he enjoyed sharing the spotlight with her, he was just as happy to see her stand in it alone, particularly after the death of her sister Anita in the summer of 1999. In many ways, June's step into the limelight took pressure off of Johnny, particularly at a time when his stays in the hospital were becoming more frequent.

American III: Solitary Man

In many ways, *Solitary Man* was the turning point in Cash's *American* series. Even on a surface level, the addition of the words "American III" to the title singled that this was now a continuing, growing, living document of the third act of his recording career. While the credits still read "Produced by Rick Rubin," Cash's limited traveling capacity meant that more of the album was recorded in Cash's cabin studio in Hendersonville, where it was produced, as such, by son John Carter Cash.

The song-selection process continued as it always had, and the album contained more songs brought by Cash than by Rubin. His voice is noticeably gruffer, more worn, than on the previous album, evidence of the toll his health problems were beginning to extract from his body. Those same health problems throw the words of the album opener into stark relief as he sings Tom Petty's "I Won't Back Down," from his 1989 LP *Full Moon Fever*. Cash felt an affinity for the song as soon as he heard it. "The first time I heard it, I thought, 'This song's for me,' but I forgot about it," he explained, in a promotional interview with Tim Robbins. "But then when I got into picking songs, I was planning on doing part of the album in California. Tom Petty & the Heartbreakers had been with me on the last album, and I talked to Tom and he wanted to come down and see what was going on, so I knew if he did I'd get him to sing on that song."

"I was really impressed when he cut a couple of my songs," Petty told Anthony DeCurtis. "The first time, I just went, 'Wow, I'm a songwriter.' But when he did 'I Won't Back Down,' I told him, 'This is much more the definitive version than mine. This is the first time the song really came to life for me. It sounds like God singing my song.'"

"That song says a lot of things that I wanted to say," Cash told DeCurtis. "It probably means different things to me than it did to Tom, which is great. . . . To me, [it] means I'll stand up to adversity and disease, to illness. I stand up on my faith in God. That is my power, and I won't back down from that."

Cash expanded on that thought in his conversation with Robbins. "I believe in God, that he is my power and my healer," he said, "and that's why I'm here today, because I'm healed of a physical affliction that had me down, had me at death's door. But I won't back down from my faith, and that power that keeps me alive."

Following "I Won't Back Down" is Neil Diamond's "Solitary Man," a song of lost love. The next track, the classic "That Lucky Old Sun (Just Rolls Around Heaven All Day)," was a song Cash had known since childhood—he even won a school talent competition singing it—but the recording of it didn't come as smoothly as the memory. "It took a while to get that done. I was kind of struggling with that back in Tennessee," Cash told Robbins. "It was only when I got with Benmont Tench, one of the Heartbreakers, in the studio out in California, he and Mike Campbell, that we did 'Lucky Old Sun.' It felt right."

Moving on from the 1940s, Cash then tackles a more contemporary song, U2's "One" from 1991. In his hands, the song became a testimony of his relationship with his wife:

> I was thinking about my wife June and I, when I head "One" the first time, and how we share everything. When one of us is cut, we both bleed. When one of us is hit, we both hurt. And we share all that. June and I have been married thirty-two years, and there were times that this and that pulled at either one of us from different directions and we came back together, clashing, and we got over that. We learned to carry each other, as the song says, and pull together as one. And it's the only way it would work, is for me to remember the simplicity of the marriage vows, that you were two, but when you're married, you're one. Whether that's a soul mate marriage or holy matrimony in the church, it's all the same, you know? You're bonded together with someone that you love then you pull together as one.

After these meditations on unconditional love and survival, Cash's humor resurfaces on the vaudeville song "Nobody," written by Egbert Williams around one hundred years before Cash recorded it. "It's so simple," Cash said. "It's like a country song—'I ain't never done nothing to nobody, I ain't never got nothing from nobody, no time, and until I get something from somebody sometime, I don't intend to do nothing for nobody, no time.' Those were tricky words that I liked very much, that I couldn't get out of my head."

Another of the songs brought in by Rubin that would figure prominently on the album, and in the slant of the marketing, was Will Oldham's "I See a Darkness." After Cash started working on the song, he called Oldham in to help with the recording. "He would ask me questions about the song: a couple of grammatical questions he wanted to clear up," Oldham told Sylvie Simmons. "Rick Rubin, the producer, had Will come to the studio and sing the chorus with me," Cash told Robbins. "I felt really comfortable in doing that."

When asked by Simmons if it felt odd to hear the song coming from someone in declining health, Oldham replied, "No, it didn't, because the song is about seeing a darkness and asking for friendship and support . . . it seemed good he was singing the song . . . at that time [it seemed like] an essential statement."

Cash had the same read on the song. "For me it's a song about bonding, friendships, or a song of lovers, or of marriage," he said. "But there's a darkness ahead, and I need you to help pull me through it. It's that kind of song to me." It wouldn't be reading too much into it to say that the darkness in Cash's vision of the song is death, although perhaps not his own. In the last two years, one of his oldest and best friends, as well as also a sister-in-law with whom he had traveled for years, had passed away. His best friend Waylon Jennings was fighting the effects of diabetes, which had forced him off the road. The two men had even shared a hospital room when no one was sure whether either of them would be making it out of there. As Cash sings, maybe he is offering friendship, rather than seeking it.

Sticking with contemporary songwriters, Rubin also brought Nick Cave's "The Mercy Seat" to Cash for consideration. Certainly, the subject matter—the final testimony of a man on death row—wasn't foreign to him. "My son John Carter, who's associate producer on the record, knew the song," Cash told Robbins. "When I told him that I was going to record it—that Rick Rubin wanted me to record it—he said, 'You should. It's exactly what you need to do right now.' And I believed it."

"The Mercy Seat" tells of a death-row inmate who defiantly swears his innocence—right up to the time of his execution, where he admits that maybe he lied. Cash latched onto its impactful anti-death-penalty message in a very personal way. He had long been an advocate for prisoners' rights, and at the time of recording he was being struck by their plight again.

> During the time that I recorded . . . all of that thing was going on in Texas about some guy was up for lethal injection and the governor of Texas, Governor Bush, wouldn't really hear his case. He made a statement that he believed that if anybody was sentenced to death, on death row, he needed to die. I thought about all the other things coming along, like DNA proof testing. . . . Anyway, during that time all that hassle was going on, I was all wrapped up in doing "The Mercy Seat," and there was a lot of anger there, too, when I was recording that song, and I didn't really know where to strike out. If I should strike out at the government or Texas or what, you know? But I thought, what a horrible thing it is that we have to kill our own—even the elephants don't do that—that we have to kill our own in order to stop the killing. It's a terrible thing. I don't know what the answer is, but it's a terrible thing.

"Would You Lay with Me (in a Field of Stone)" came from the pen of David Allan Coe, and had been a #1 hit for Tanya Tucker in 1974. Coe had written the song for his brother's wedding, but many listeners and radio programmers gave the lyrics a sexual overtone that simply isn't there (particularly as sung by Tucker, who was fifteen years old at the time). Here, with the song performed by a sixty-eight-year-old man, such nonsense is stripped away, and it can be heard only as Coe intended: as a dedication of love.

Listening to great songwriters like Coe, Cave, and Oldham got Cash's songcrafting juices flowing, and at the time of his interview with Anthony DeCurtis he indicated that he had three or four songs in various stages of completion. "It's the first time I've ever had them bombard my brain like that," he said. "I hadn't written for more than a year since I got sick, but when I started recording, the ideas started coming. I'll finish them as we work." Of the fourteen songs included on the album, though, only four came from his pen, and only one of them was a new composition.

"Field of Diamonds" was a co-write with ex-son-in-law Jack Routh that Cash had recorded first in 1977, again in 1980, and once again in 1985 for *Heroes*, his duet album with Waylon Jennings. "Country Trash," meanwhile, had been included on 1972's *Any Old Wind That Blows*. "I'm Leavin' Now" had been included on 1985's *Rainbow*, also with Jennings, but this new recording pairs Cash with another friend and country superstar, Merle Haggard, who had stopped by the studio on his way to a show in Chattanooga. "I got to spend a whole day with John," Haggard told *Billboard*. "We were just sort of like out there by ourself. It was a unique deal—like Cash always does—out in the middle of nowhere in a cabin. He had his son and an engineer, and we had the board layin' on the floor."

Cash cut two very old songs on the recording, "Mary of the Wild Moor" and "Wayfaring Stranger," both of which inspired the new song he wrote for it, "Before My Time."

> Going over all these old songs like "Nobody" and "Mary of the Wild Moor," which is an old, old country song that I love, I was thinking, I'm saying things that they were saying then, even in Stephen Foster's time, except I'm saying it differently. But I'm saying the same thing. I recorded a Stephen Foster song, it's not on this album, it's going to be on my next one, called "Hard Times," that is a plain, country, simple song written in 1847, by Stephen Foster. That's what I'm saying in "Before My Time"; he said things that all of a sudden I find myself saying now, but differently.

American III: Solitary Man was released in the fall of 2000 and debuted at #11 on the Top Country Albums chart (earning it "Hot Shot Debut" honors) and #88 on the *Billboard* 200. It was the highest debut of any of the American recordings to date, and with sales of around 16,000 units, it had outpaced both of Cash's previous albums combined. It was also his highest chart peak since 1976's *One Piece at a Time* made it to #2.

The critical response to this third outing was overwhelmingly positive. *Country Music* devoted its first two review slots to *Solitary Man* and Merle Haggard's *If I Could Only Fly*, his debut for the Anti- label, touted by many as an attempt at a Cash-like revival. In February 2001, Cash won the Grammy for Best Male Country Vocal Performance, beating out Vince Gill, Dwight Yoakam, Billy Gilman, and Tim McGraw.

44

Voices Callin', Voices Cryin'

American 2002–03

At age sixty-eight and with mounting health problems, Johnny Cash was still excited about making records, and as 2001 came to a close, he was looking forward to his next project with Rick Rubin. They had moved on from the solo guitar recordings of *American Recordings* to a full band on *Unchained* and *Solitary Man*. Now, on their fourth outing, Cash felt there were no limits to what they could do.

"For instance, I may record a real classic spiritual, and I might use an orchestra on it," he told Jim Patterson. "There are some things that Rick and I are finding that call for a little bigger sound . . . I said, 'Let's go for it. I am a rockabilly.' If nothing else, I am a rockabilly."

To celebrate Cash's upcoming seventieth birthday, Columbia, his former label, was set to release a round of reissues of his older work, with bonus tracks and additional liner notes, some of them by Cash himself. "What this says is that Johnny Cash is more than just a musician, more than just an artist," Adam Block, Columbia/Legacy's general manager and vice president of marketing, told *Billboard*. "In our minds, Johnny Cash is an American icon whose career has touched us in so many ways over such a wonderful, extended period of time. I think this really testifies to the cultural and creative artistic impact he's had on all of us."

As honored as he felt by the reissue program, Cash preferred to look toward the future. "We're not into stopping and polishing milestones," he said, of himself and June, in a promotional interview. "We look forward to the next year. We look forward to the work that needs to be done in that year."

The celebration was timed to coincide with his birthday, February 26th, but for Cash, it was a bittersweet affair. Just thirteen days earlier, Waylon Jennings had died in his Arizona home following complications relating to his diabetes, which had required him to have a foot amputated in December 2001. Waylon joined the growing list of Cash's friends who were gone: Carl Perkins, Elvis Presley, Roy Orbison, Anita Carter, Helen Carter, Mother Maybelle and Pop Carter, plus his mother and father.

Cash's own health was beginning to fade, and his hospital stays were increasing in frequency. He had been in a coma for eight days in October of 2001; glaucoma was stealing his sight while asthma took his breath. It was sheer force of will that kept him moving forward, and kept his mind off of the inevitable. "To tell you the truth," he told *Rolling Stone*'s Jason Fine, "I don't think about death at all. What's to think about? I enjoy my life now."

American IV: The Man Comes Around

Cash had been looking for songs for the fourth *American* album ever since he finished recording the third. The process for picking songs varied little from the previous albums, with Cash, Rubin, and even John Carter Cash putting in their two cents as to what should be recorded. An additional variable was Cash's diminished ability to travel. His illnesses had left him too weak to travel to California for extended periods to record with Rubin. Instead, the cabin sanctuary on his property was converted into a small studio, where he could work on songs whenever he felt able. But Rubin remained an integral part of the process, as Cash explained in a promotional interview:

> I would send him the songs to listen to and he would critique the songs for me and some of them he would tell me he liked and some he didn't really care that much for. I always knew the ones that he didn't like because he was very kind about that. He would say, "I don't care too much about that song, as I do some of the others"—[that] was the way he would put it to me.
>
> I would get the songs and get them honed down the way that I wanted to record them and send them out to him again. He'd shoot 'em back to me, and I go into the studio in Tennessee and go to work and record tracks. A couple of times we got some finished product. Usually, for the most part, like the other albums, I would go to California and do the bulk of the recording with Rick in his studio.

The album opener, "The Man Comes Around," was the only new Cash original to be included. The beat recalls the boom-chicka-boom of old, and the lyrics are some of Cash's most explicitly evangelical. He had written twelve pages of verses for the song before paring them down to the six included on the final cut. "I spent more time on this song than any I ever wrote," he said.

The song was inspired by a dream Cash had while staying in England. In it, he met Queen Elizabeth, who was sitting on the floor with someone else, knitting and talking. When she noticed Cash enter the room, the queen told him he was like "a thorn tree in a whirlwind." When he awoke, that phrase stayed with him, and it finally drove him to the Bible to look for an answer. In his study, Cash found that a whirlwind often referred to God, and a thorn tree stood for the stubborn will of God's people. From there, he combed the book of Revelations and constructed the song. "The Man" is Jesus, returning for the final judgment, and when he gets there, Cash says, "Everybody won't be treated all the same."

To celebrate Cash's seventieth birthday in 2002, Columbia reissued several albums with bonus tracks and new mastering. *Private collection*

The song opens with a portion of Revelation 6, Cash's voice processed to sound as if it is coming from an old record as he reads the scripture, before the guitar chimes in with that familiar loping rhythm. His voice sounds noticeably more constricted than it was on his previous album, the struggles of the past year readily evident. But for Cash, this was the centerpiece of the album, and one of the songs in his catalogue of which he was most proud.

Even so, the song that generated the most attention for the record was "Hurt," written by Nine Inch Nails' Trent Reznor. "I think that 'Hurt' is the best anti-drug song I ever heard," Cash said, in a promotional interview. "I think if it doesn't scare you away from taking drugs, nothing will. Also it's a song about a man's pain, about what we are capable of doing to ourselves and the possibility that we don't have to do that to ourself anymore."

At first, Cash didn't think he could adapt the song to his style, but as with "Rusty Cage" on *Unchained*, Rubin put together a rough demo to help him get a handle on it. His arrangement stripped down Reznor's version, slightly changing a chord here or there, removing some of the noisy elements from the background, and chopping the last two minutes from the song. The electronic instrumentation of the original is replaced by the guitars of Mike Campbell and Smokey Hormel, who play essentially the same parts, augmented by Benmont

Tench's percussive piano and swirling organ. But it is Cash's voice, weighted by time and experience, that gives the recording its immediate impact.

The gravity his voice brought was pushed front and center in the video shot for the song by director Mark Romanek. Cash stands before the world as the aged man he had become, but he stands proudly. "This is me," he seems to say. "Take it or leave it." He shakes at times, his frailty and vulnerability on display, juxtaposed elsewhere in the video with archival footage of him in his prime. For some, the video was a masterpiece, for others a farewell. Cash's own family watched it through tears, seeing it as both. (The video won the 2003 Country Music Association Music Video of the Year, the 2003 MTV Video Music Award for Best Cinematography, and the 2004 Grammy for Best Short Form Video.)

Returning to his own catalogue, Cash chose to record "Give My Love to Rose," a song he had originally released in 1957 (when it went to #7). It was, he said, "one that came up in the session at the spur of the moment. It was one of those things that all of a sudden it just felt like it needed to be recorded and I recorded it. I feel good about the performance on it this time, better than the original recording even."

The performance, if not better, is at least different. In the 1957 reading, with a young Cash encountering a dying ex-con, the songs comes off as a cautionary tale. But now, with Cash at age seventy, it sounds almost like a remembrance—still a cautionary tale, but one told in retrospect—and we, the listener, are given to decide whether he heeded that tale.

As on their previous American recordings, Cash and Rubin brought several contemporary songs into the mix. But though it had worked well in the past—particularly on songs Cash could fully inhabit, like "The Mercy Seat" or "I See a Darkness"—the clutch of material recorded for this album drew more divided opinions, with some fearing that Cash might be being exploited in his declining health.

"I think what meant the most to him was to create to the very end: create, create, create, because he was a true artist," Marty Stuart told Michael Streissguth. "And when I heard 'First Time Ever I Saw Your Face' and some of those kinds of songs, I'm going, 'Oh, what are we up to here, guys? What are we up to?' I didn't know if we were just trying to pile up a bunch of songs to sell later or what."

The idea that Rubin propped Cash up behind a microphone and fed him songs to sing was a criticism that was bandied about often. But that gives Cash short shrift, placing the "blame" on Rubin, and giving Cash a free pass on material that might not stack up in the eyes of fans. It was a continuation of the numerous reviews throughout the 1970s and '80s that had taken the position, almost as a mantra, that "Cash can't make a bad record." Furthermore, Cash was heavily involved in selecting the songs for *American IV*, and as always, he had the final say on what was included.

The criticisms were strongest in relation to the songs that had been recorded definitively by the artists they were most closely associated with, such as "Bridge over Trouble Water" and "First Time Ever I Saw Your Face." But Cash cared little about that.

> If I had tried to sing "First Time Ever I Saw Your Face" like Roberta Flack does, I would have had to head for the back door, because I can't touch that vocal. The way I approach a song like that—love the song up front, first, and "Bridge over Troubled Water." I knew that I could not sing either one of those songs the way that they were recorded, and I didn't *want* to record either one of them in the way they were recorded by the originals. I didn't *want* to sing them that way; I wanted to sing them *my* way. I had to make them my songs. I wanted to feel like I had made that song mine when I put it down in the studio. And it began to feel that way as I worked on these songs. If it doesn't begin to feel that way with me after I work on it awhile, I throw it out. But I didn't throw those out because they worked and I've begun to feel like these were my songs. It doesn't matter what anyone else has done with them, this is the way I do it.

Regardless, once they are ingrained into an audience's memory, the sounds of the original recordings echo behind most all others if the new versions do not significantly add to them. Both Roberta Flack and Simon & Garfunkel—and the Eagles and the Beatles, for that matter—had brought an expressiveness to these songs that Cash never had the ability to summon. His voice always brought authority, believability, and sincerity, but rarely, if ever, did it bring tenderness. These songs, by their nature, require such a reading. So, measured against their better-remembered versions, Cash's renditions fall flat, bringing nothing to the songs' history other than a footnote to say that they were once recorded by the great Johnny Cash.

Taken for what they are, and measured against his own catalogue, these songs are not among his greatest work. Where the combination of their two voices helped Simon & Garfunkel elevate "Bridge over Troubled Water" into an anthem of friendship, Cash's version suffers from the addition of Fiona Apple, who sounds simply as though she has been tacked on to the song. The age that Cash brought to songs like "Hurt" works against him here in a way that makes it hard to believe he truly has the strength to be leaned on. Likewise, "First Time Ever I Saw Your Face" is taken from sultry song of love to dirge-like remembrance.

For the Eagles' "Desperado," Rubin brought in the song's co-writer and original vocalist, Don Henley, but even his addition can't lift the song to a place where it might outshine the original recording. Depeche Mode's "Personal Jesus" receives a similar makeover to "Hurt," leaving behind the original's thick irony and replacing it with Cash's notion of the song as an evangelical anthem. "I was surprised that the song came out of the part of the music world it came from," Cash said. "It's probably the most evangelical gospel song I ever recorded, and I'm sure it wasn't meant to be that. Maybe it was. Maybe the writer meant for it to be. It's certainly a good song, it certainly speaks true of me and my faith." The arrangement is lose, and Billy Preston's always-great piano playing is nearly lost in the mix.

For his first-ever Beatles cover, Cash chose "In My Life." It was another case of him forcing the original out of mind and taking the same tact he did with the others, as he explained in a promotional interview.

> From the very first rehearsals, I didn't have any trouble getting away from the original vocal. I mean, you can imagine how silly I would have felt trying to sound like the Beatles or Paul McCartney or John Lennon, either. But I didn't try to; I heard that song for what it was to me, for what it meant to me. I identified with it. I saw all those people, all those old friends, all those old lovers, those old sweethearts, all those old times, hard times, and I identified with that immediately before I sang that song for the first time. So the first time I sang that song, it was my song.

Cash's comments on the song illustrate the divide that often arises between artist and audience. Of course there are those who love everything Cash put on tape, and others who are more critical of his recordings of well-known songs like "In My Life," but in the end, Cash recorded what he liked, what he felt, regardless of how it might be accepted. This is a common thread in his career, going back to the quirky, against-the-grain sound of "I Walk the Line" or the horns on "Ring of Fire." Those who dismiss these recordings forget that Cash had spent his career doing it his way, always.

In any case, those weaker songs only make up a portion of the record. Between "Bridge over Troubled Water" and "First Time Ever I Saw Your Face" sits Sting's "I Hung My Head." It was a song Cash's son had brought to him, and he felt the lyrics fit perfectly into the songs of "his people, country music people." They tell of a young boy playing with a gun and accidentally killing his older brother, and the guilt and shame associated with it. It could have fit anywhere in Cash's catalogue, and is an example of how Cash could inhabit a song and make it his own in a way he was unable to with some of the other songs on the album.

"I Hung My Head" could have even fit on Cash's 1965 LP *Ballads of the True West*, the album that included "Sam Hall" and "Streets of Laredo," both of which he revisited on *American IV*. "Sam Hall" shows him in a playful mood in the role of an obstinate prisoner, while "Streets of Laredo" gave him a second run at a song he had never been fully satisfied by.

"'Streets of Laredo' is a song that I recorded the first time in the '60s," he said, "but I wasn't happy with my recording of the song. Not at all; I hadn't been since I had recorded it. I came up with some new verses that made the song make more sense to me and made it stronger, made it a better song. Also, while I was taking the winter off way down south [in Jamaica], I worked on 'Streets of Laredo' and made it the song I wanted to record."

While revisiting that time period, Cash also took another pass at "Danny Boy," a song he had originally recorded for 1965's *Orange Blossom Special*. This time, he recorded it in a Los Angeles cathedral, accompanied only by Benmont Tench's pipe organ. Slightly earlier in that period, Cash had recorded Hank Williams' "I'm So Lonesome I Could Cry" for *Now There Was a Song*, which here becomes a duet with Nick Cave. Both songs are decent versions, though they add little to his original recordings. To follow them, moving forward in time, Cash brought out "Tear Stained Letter" from 1972's *A Thing Called Love.*

The album closer is for all intents and purposes a goodbye. "When we finished *American IV: The Man Comes Around*, Johnny insisted on the last song being 'We'll Meet Again,' and he wanted everyone who worked on the album, his family and me, to all sing the chorus, which we all did," Rick Rubin told Sylvie Simmons. "I think Johnny thought that was going to be his final recording."

The album was released on November 5, 2002, and debuted at #14 on the Top Country Albums chart and #70 on the *Billboard* 200. Reviews were mixed, but generally pleasant, focusing mainly on the contemporary songs chosen for the album, again echoing the sentiments of reviews from his musical "down" periods.

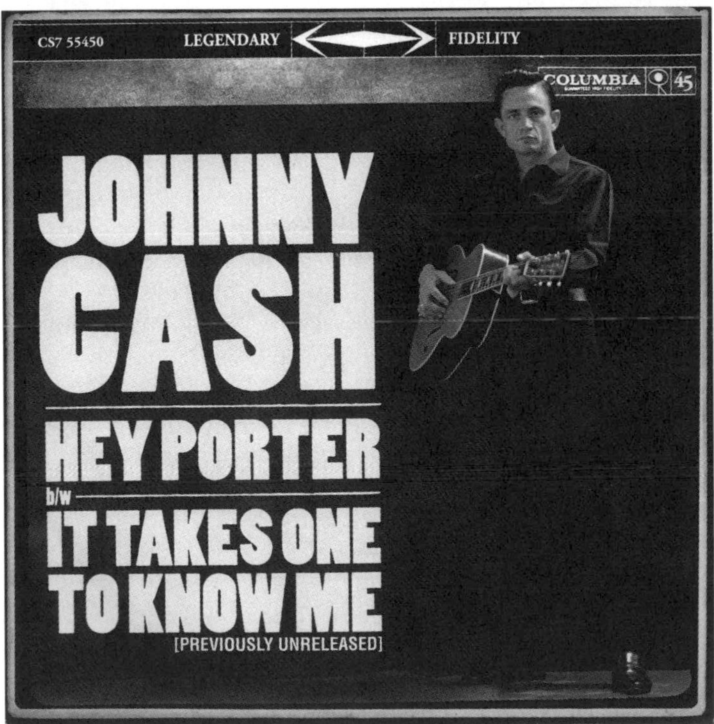

For the anniversary of Cash's fifty years of recording, Columbia released this promo single in 2005 to promote the release of *The Legend* box set.
Private collection

The Death of Johnny Cash

The album's chart history tells an interesting story of how music buyers respond to various cues. After its debut, the album began to move down the charts, slipping over thirty spots on the *Billboard* 200. With *American IV*, sales would spike when Cash was in the news, but, unfortunately, by the spring of 2003, what Cash was in the news for most often was his failing health. Between January and April, he had three lengthy stays in the hospital, by which time the album had risen to a peak of #4 on the Country charts and #51 on the *Billboard* 200.

Record sales were the last thing on Cash's mind by April, though, as his bride of nearly thirty-six years was hospitalized and required heart surgery. On May 15th, the world was shocked to hear that Valerie June Carter Cash had died.

It was a devastating time for the family, and especially so for Cash. After less than two weeks of grieving, he was ready to return to the studio, to keep busy. Working took his mind off of June's death and his own deteriorating condition. Doctors had loaded him down with drugs for all of his various ailments, and some of them didn't interact well with others, leaving him in a lifeless state at times. On September 10th, while working through a physical therapy session with sports physician Phil Maffetone, whom Rick Rubin had brought in, Cash turned and simply said, "It's time." An ambulance transported Cash to the hospital, and soon after that his family was gathering around his bedside, this time for the last time. On September 12, 2003, Cash joined his wife on the Far Side Banks of Jordan.

Unearthed

As could be expected, sales of Cash's records surged after his death. Within a couple of weeks, *American IV* had shot from #16 to #2 on the Country chart (and from #94 to #22 on the *Billboard* 200) and brought along with it four greatest-hits packages and a newly released live disc, *Johnny Cash at Madison Square Garden.* Cash product was seemingly everywhere, but one of the best was a new boxed set compiled by Rubin.

Unearthed, which had been in the works for months prior to Cash's passing, draws together five discs of music from his American years. The first three discs consist of outtakes taken from sessions for the first four albums, but though they are outtakes, they are not throwaways. The first disc, subtitled *Who's Gonna Cry*, contains excellent versions of sixteen Cash classics like "Long Black Veil," "Flesh and Blood," "Understand Your Man," and "Old Chunk of Coal," all taken from the session for *American Recordings* and featuring only Cash and his guitar. The disc also includes an alternate take of a song that was included on the original album, Tom Waits' "Down There by the Train."

Disc two, *Trouble in Mind*, is made up largely of other people's songs that were recorded during the *Unchained* sessions. There are several fantastic nuggets here, including Neil Young's "Heart of Gold," Merle Haggard's "Running Kind" (sung here as a duet with Tom Petty), and two songs, "Everybody's Trying to Be My Baby" and "Brown Eyed Handsome Man," performed with Carl Perkins.

Disc three, *Redemption Songs*, includes several alternate takes of songs included on *American III* and *IV*. A few of them, such as "Gentle on My Mind" with Glen Campbell and "He Stopped Loving Her Today," are mainly curiosities, but help to give a fascinating look at the whole of the American Recordings era.

Disc four offers a whole new album, *My Mother's Hymn Book* (discussed in chapter 49) and disc five a "best of" collection. Included with the set is a fantastic 104-page book featuring interviews with Cash, Rubin, Petty, and others about their time producing the music, plus a track-by-track breakdown of all the songs included in the package. It was a perfect commemoration of Cash's later work. "I can see future installments of *Unearthed*," Rubin told Sylvie Simmons in a 2013 article for *Mojo*. "Maybe this discussion will spark that process."

The American Recordings period proved to be a personal highlight of Cash's career, as he explained to *Billboard* in 2002:

> These records have meant everything to me. The last ten years I've been working with Rick—it's been like a new lease on life. I would be satisfied, so far as accomplishments, if it all ended now. But, boy, I sure wish I could live another few years and take it one, two, three years at a time, and do some more things like these records. That's what I really wanna do, some more of these records. It's all about being happy in my work, and knowing that I've done a good job—that I've done the best job that I could do with what I had to go with at the time.

You Are a Shining Path

American: 2004–10

Listening to *American IV: The Man Comes Around*, the final album released while he was alive, one could easily get the message that Johnny Cash was ending his recording career. But as Rubin, who was there with him, step for step, explained to Michael D. Ayers, that was not the case.

> In his mind, the series was done. Not because he wanted it to end, but I think he felt that he wasn't in great shape and thought that it was going to be it. But I could tell it was really breaking his heart that it was it. I remember, we were at my house and he shook my hand and said, "I want to thank you for this, it was so great that we could do this together." It was the goodbye conversation—we'd done our work. But I could tell it wasn't a happy conversation, it was more like, "I guess I'm done," and I said, "Well now that *IV* is done and it came out so great, why don't we start on *V* tomorrow?" And he lit up and said, "You really want to do another one?" And that's when it turned into recording every day. It went from this feeling of "I can't do it anymore" to "this is my reason to be."

First, Cash went to work on an album of gospel songs that had been recorded by groups such as the Golden Gate Quartet and the Five Blind Boys of Alabama—the music he listened to the most. "I've always wanted to do black gospel," he told Jason Fine, "and I know I'm a little tight-ass saying 'black'—I'm a honky—but I feel like I need to do it. I feel like it's going to be all right." Up next, he told Fine, would be an album he planned to call *Grass Roots*, a collection of country and folk songs from as far back as Stephen Foster.

"During the last months of his life, Johnny was recording a lot," Cash's Nashville-based engineer David Ferguson told Paul Tingen. "It was almost an every-day thing. Johnny got sick, and then he got a little better, and it seemed as if playing and singing was the only thing that took his mind off his health problems."

Between hospital stays at the end of 2002 and into 2003, Cash was in the studio whenever he could be, and when he couldn't, the studio was often brought to him, as Ferguson explained:

> It was hard for John to get around, so we took the recording equipment to him. He might decide that it was easier to record in the round room in his house overlooking the lake, or we worked at his mother's house across the street, where we recorded "Aloha Oe," or we recorded at John Carter Cash's Cash Cabin Studios. Everything was within a few hundred yards from each other. I would set up the equipment, and John or I would call his favorite musicians and we'd record. Rick came in for one of those sessions, and that really lightened Johnny's spirit. There was a great mutual respect between them.

The songs Cash recorded during that time lay dormant for nearly two years, until Rubin decided to come to them again to finish the work they had started together. He assembled a team that included musicians who had worked on other Cash recordings, including Mike Campbell, Benmont Tench, Smokey Hormel, and Randy Scruggs, along with engineers and mixers Ferguson, Greg Fidelman, and Dan Leffler. That team would work with the vocals Cash had recorded in Nashville with Ferguson, and overdub new music.

"At first it made me feel really bad," Rubin told Ayers.

> Like, just starting to hear him sing, I got really sad. It just felt like this was going to be a bummer, but then when we started to work on the music, that all changed. We didn't have a set direction to what it was supposed to sound like. It felt like he guided the proceedings and it turned into what it turned into. I was very pleasantly surprised by the creative unfoldment, in coming out of the sadness. It ended up feeling healing, where at first it seemed like, "Oh my God." It made me miss him at first, and I didn't even realize it was going to have that effect, I have to tell you. I think both *American V* and *American VI* are different from the rest of the series, and I feel like Johnny's presence did it, in a supernatural way. I don't know how to explain it, but it felt like a mystical thing happened.

Cash's health was failing, his longing to be reunited with his wife ever-mounting. He often sang just above a whisper, hampered by his asthma, but he always wanted to record with the musicians who were playing with him in Nashville (and whose parts were replaced later). Due to his lack of breath, his vocal performances were often assembled from two or three different takes.

American V: A Hundred Highways (2006)

Though he denied it in interviews, the theme of *American IV* could easily be summed up as Cash's testament to the end of his life, and many would say that theme continues on *American V*. While it is true that death and loneliness are major themes, it isn't a preoccupation with his own death, but rather, for the most part, the journal of a husband grieving his bride.

"Help Me," the song that starts *American V: A Hundred Highways*, was first recorded by Cash (with Kris Kristofferson and Rita Coolidge) on the 1973 soundtrack to his film *The Gospel Road*. In that version, Cash sang out to the

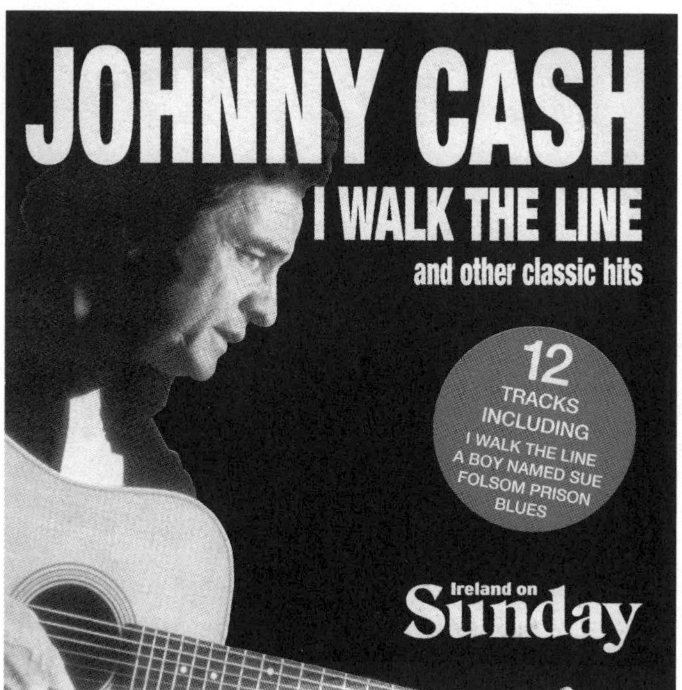

The newspaper *Ireland on Sunday* included this CD to coincide with the release of *I Walk the Line* in 2006. *Author's collection*

Lord, in character, asking for a miracle. But now, in the time just shortly after June's death, it becomes something much more personal. When Kristofferson recorded the song for his 1972 album *Jesus Was a Capricorn*, he chose it because he heard the songwriter, Larry Gatlin, perform it at a church service he and Coolidge had attended, and it struck a very personal chord in him. Here, that chord is struck in Cash, and the words are vivid reminders of both his spirituality and his humanity. "Oh come down from your golden throne," he sings, "I need to feel the touch of your tender hand," just as Thomas the Apostle had requested to feel the nail scar in order to fully believe and be comforted.

Cash continues to ask for help in "God's Gonna Cut You Down," but this time, he doesn't seek only comfort but also vengeance against Satan and those that do his work for trying to steal his joy and life. The song itself is an adaptation of a traditional that had been recorded under the title "God's Gonna Cut You Down" (by Odetta in 1957, and others even earlier) and "Run On" (by the Five Blind Boys of Alabama in 2001). Cash's take on the song is more ominous, with foot stomps and handclaps that sound as if he is marching on the gates of Hell, while the guitars, both acoustic and electric, swirl around his head.

"Like the 309" is one of the last songs Cash wrote, though few hear the humor he intended when they listen to it for the first time. By this time, asthma was taking his breath, making it hard for him to sing, so instead of completely hiding it—though it was certainly well hidden on the other recordings—Cash turned it into a point of humor. When the song starts, he sounds as if he is completely out of breath, and between lines he can be heard wheezing loudly. Hearing him in this condition would take many listeners by surprise, but this is Cash the showman, playing up his condition for levity, as he sings "asthma coming down like the 309" until they load on his box for his final train ride. Dark humor, maybe, but humor nonetheless.

The remainder of the album picks up the grief journal Cash began with "Help Me." Gordon Lightfoot's "If You Could Read My Mind" is a breakup song, but not for Cash at this time. For him, it is simply a conversation, one-sided as it is, with his wife on the other side. When he sings of the chains around his feet for the second time, it sounds as if he regrets that their weight won't let him to float to where she is. His voice is rough and breaking, but it matches his heart as he sings of how he is "just trying to understand," his voice falling, almost in a silent prayer—not to her, but to the God he cried out to in the first two songs. The way the words break, it is a small wonder that Cash was able to make it completely through Hank Williams' "On the Evening Train." He even manages to keep it together as his "tears fell like rain" while he watches them "place that long white casket in the baggage coach of the evening train," though his emotions are barely covered. "It's hard to know she'll be gone forever," he sings, as his voice drops slowly.

"I Came to Believe" was originally written and recorded by Cash in 1984 during sessions with producer Billy Sherrill for an album that was shelved at the time but later released in 2014 as *Out Among the Stars*. In it, Cash describes how he "called out for help and felt a warm Comforter there," and how "he came to believe he needed help to get by." With this song, he turns his attention from his wife to the listener, explaining how it is that he finds his daily strength—the strength to continue working, to continue living.

Rod McKuen's "Love's Been Good to Me" and Don Gibson's "A Legend in My Time" speak about past love affairs and the emptiness that comes after they've ended—simple remembrances of a life well lived. With those remembered fondly, Cash returns to the love of his life on "Rose of My Heart," where he recalls the one who really mattered, "the love of my life, a flower not faded."

Not all of the songs were about June's passing. Others were preparations for Cash's own upcoming trip. "Further on (up the Road)" returned him to the Bruce Springsteen songbook, this time with a track from the Boss' 2002 release *The Rising*. "Four Strong Winds" by Ian Tyson had been recorded by Ian & Sylvia and Neil Young before Cash took a swing at it. As on previous albums, he also returns to his own back catalogue, drawing on 1962's *The Sound of Johnny Cash* for "I'm Free from the Chain Gang Now."

Released on July 4, 2006, the album—spurred in part by the Johnny and June biopic *Walk the Line*, starring Joaquin Phoenix and Reese Witherspoon, that premiered on November 18, 2005—sold 88,336 copies in its first week and debuted at #1 on both the Country and Pop charts—a first for Cash, and the first time he had reached the top of the *Billboard* 200 since *At San Quentin* in 1969. "We can't get enough Johnny Cash," a music retailer told *Billboard* in January 2006. "We never learn, neither us or the labels. When a movie hits, you don't think it will more than double sales, but it always does." Sales of the recently released boxed set *The Legend* were similarly brisk over the holidays, and a single-disc collection, *The Legend of Johnny Cash*, made its way to #2 on the Country chart and #15 on the *Billboard* 200 (where it would eventually peak at #5).

As with Cash's previous album—and perhaps more so with this one—reviews were mixed. In his review for *Blender*, critic Robert Christgau pointed out a few strong parts but said the rest "bear the strain of sentimentality, denial, even exploitation." Stephen M. Deusner, writing for Pitchfork.com, called the album "a satisfying and often moving final chapter to Cash's life and career, one that rejects self-pity and remorse in favor of hopefulness and even celebration."

American VI: Ain't No Grave (2010)

Released to coincide with Cash's seventy-eighth birthday, *American VI* picks up where *V* left off, though it's a little more uneven. With the exception of two, most of the songs were recorded during the same timeframe, and because of that, the quality of Cash's vocals varies wildly.

On the opener, the traditional "Ain't No Grave"—a spiritual cousin to the last album's "God's Gonna Cut You Down"—Cash's voice is a gravelly whisper, straining at times to hit notes that he had once reached easily. Scott and Seth Avett of the Avett Brothers, on banjo and foot stomps, respectively, weave an atmospheric covering on the song, providing Cash a platform for his sermon.

For David Ferguson, working on the album years after Cash's passing was a strange experience. "John was gone, and here he was singing 'Ain't No Grave' to us," he told Paul Tingen, in an interview for *Sound on Sound* magazine. "When we started mixing that song, everybody on the project literally got goose bumps on their arms. It was really kind of spooky."

Sheryl Crow, who had made an appearance on *American III*, contributed a song from her self-titled 1996 album called "Redemption Day." The song calls on the leaders of the world to step out and take action to make a difference in the world. "At the time we recorded it, he said he would give up all the other songs just for this one," Rubin told Andrew Romano. Later on the album, Cash revisits a similar theme on Ed McCurdy's anti-war song "Last Night I Had the Strangest Dream," which he had performed live during the early 1970s.

Returning to the work of his dear friend Kris Kristofferson, Cash takes a stab at "For the Good Times," a song the great Ray Price took to #1 and won Song of the Year with in 1970. But with Cash never as emotive as Price to begin with, this version seems just to be a song he felt like recording.

"I Corinthians 15:55" is Cash's attempt at writing a hymn, using the scripture as part of his lyrics. In light of his impending death, the song sounds almost like a taunt, particularly when followed by Tom Paxton's "Can't Help but Wonder

Where I'm Bound." But Cash's vocal performance is one of his roughest, followed closely by his performance of "I Don't Hurt Anymore." The fact that "Satisfied Mind," which is sandwiched between the two, and "Cool Water," which follows "I Don't Hurt Anymore," were recorded during the *American III* sessions, offers a clear demonstration of his declining vocal ability. Rather than relying on the listener's memory, with this sequence, it was immediately obvious how greatly Cash's instrument had declined.

"Rick felt that they were really special, and he waited for the right time to release them," Ferguson said. "He's a great record producer, and he only releases things when he feels the time is right. In fact, when *American V* came out, I was surprised at his track choices, because I thought that 'Ain't No Grave' and 'Redemption Day' would be on there."

The final song on the album—and of Cash's original recording career—is the Hawaiian song "Aloha Oe." It features guitar playing by his old friend Cowboy Jack Clement, as tracked in Cash's Nashville studio; while all of the other musicians' parts were subsequently replaced, Clement's was retained. "The original playing was really intimate," Ferguson said, "and you don't take Jack Clement's playing off anything!"

Though it lay outside what most would consider Cash's usual repertoire, the song proved to be the perfect ending to the *American* series—a quirky song choice from an artist always full of surprises, with a deep sense of music history, and one that captures him playing with one of the friends who was with him at Sun Studios, back near the beginning of his long career.

Released on February 23, 2010, three days before Cash's birthday, *American VI: Ain't No Grave* debuted at #2 on the Country chart and #3 on the *Billboard* 200. With its release, Rubin made clear that the *American Recordings* had ended: "*VI* was the proper final album in the series."

Though some questioned the need for another *American* album, most critics were positive about the release. Steve Leftridge, for *PopMatters*, called the album "mined gold." Andy Gill called it "a cause for rejoicing." Keith Phipps concluded, "Cash is gone now. Aloha means goodbye. But it also means love, mercy, and compassion, all values he treasured. And in this context, it has another meaning found in the last words on the album, and delivered with all the conviction he could summon: 'Until we meet again.'"

Christmas Times A-Comin'

Christmas in Cash-land

While Johnny Cash always went his own way when it came to making records, even he wasn't immune to the Christmas album. Over the course of his career, he made four Christmas albums and hosted ten Christmas television specials, four of which were released on DVD through a partnership with the Country Music Hall of Fame in 2007 and 2008.

The Christmas Spirit (1963)

Cash's first Christmas album came during one of his most prolific runs in the '60s. The song selection includes Christmas classics ("I Heard the Bells on Christmas Day," "Silent Night"), contemporary favorites ("Blue Christmas," "Here Was a Man"), and a few originals. Two of the originals, "Christmas as I Knew It" and "Ringing the Bells for Jim" were written by June Carter and Jan Howard, and Cash contributed four of his own: "The Christmas Spirit," "The Gifts They Gave," "We Are the Shepherds," and "Who Kept the Sheep," which he co-wrote with his future father-in-law, Ezra J. Carter. The album also includes "The Little Drummer Boy," which Cash had released as a single in 1959, when it reached #63 on *Billboard*'s Hot 100 and peaked at #17 on the Country Singles chart in January 1960. He also recorded a recitation of the poem "The Ballad of the Harp Weaver" by Edna St. Vincent Millay, which he would perform occasionally on his live shows and later on his television series.

Bear Family's *The Man in Black: 1963–69* includes "It Came upon a Midnight Clear," which was recorded during these sessions but not included on the album.

The Johnny Cash Family Christmas (1972)

Recorded on July 27–28, 1972, during the period of his life when he was completely sober and drug-free, this album serves as a farewell sendoff for the Johnny Cash Roadshow as it existed since the mid-1960s—the Carter Family,

Carl Perkins, and the Statler Brothers. In November, just as the record was being released, Cash disbanded the Roadshow in favor of a smaller production that expanded his own role. This was also a period when he would become more involved with Billy Graham's Crusades and other religious causes that would limit his ability to tour his own fully self-contained show. But here all of them, and producer Larry Butler, join Cash for an album made up of songs performed by each of them. Between each song, Cash and the Family remember Christmases of years past. Of the four Christmas albums, this one has the most intimate feel and shows the tightness of the crew, displaying a happiness that they had probably not thought they would see during some of the darker days of the Roadshow.

Classic Christmas (1980)

As the title suggests, this album is made up entirely of Christmas carols. Unlike any other Cash release, it features no members of his band. Instead, he is backed by a full orchestra, led by Bill Walker, the musical director for Cash's television show and subsequent television specials.

Country Christmas (1991)

As Cash's time with Mercury was drawing to a close, he was approached by the German music company LaserLight to record a Christmas album. The resulting album is certainly a mixed affair. The songs are mainly carols, with the exception of "Blue Christmas" and "Here Was a Man," both of which Cash recorded superior versions of in 1963. The album was produced by Cash's trumpet player, Jack Hale Jr., who also did all of the arrangements. It is packed with strong players: famed Elvis drummer Ronnie Tutt, Nashville session ace Glenn Worf on bass, Cash guitarists James Horn and Kerry Marx, Paul Hollowell on piano and keyboards, and Stuart Duncan on mandolin and fiddle. Steel guitarist Bucky Baxter, who played with everyone from Steve Earle to Jim Lauderdale to Bob Dylan, steals the show, particularly on "Silent Night."

In one of their final recordings, the Carter Sisters—June, Anita, and Helen—perform four songs alone: "The First Noel," "O Christmas Tree," "It Came upon a Midnight Clear," and a fourth which, though listed as "Figgy Pudding," is actually "We Wish You a Merry Christmas." June takes the opportunity to flex her comedic muscle, shouting asides and one-liners and sounding a little like Granny Clampett.

On most of his songs, Cash sounds as if he's just going through the motions, adding little to material he had recorded better versions of in the past. There are, of course, a couple of exceptions, notably "Silent Night" and "What Child Is This," which he is able to turn into Christian worship songs, fully investing in the lyrics and turning in excellent performances.

The Johnny Cash Christmas Specials

The Johnny Cash Show was canceled in 1971. Cash told the media that he was relieved, and that the pressure of a weekly show and all the red tape that went with it had been too frustrating. But that didn't mean he was finished with television, or that television was done with him.

Producers continued to call asking for appearances. In late 1971, Cash hosted *Ballad of the West*, a show that highlighted the singing cowboy and featured Kirk Douglas, his co-star in *A Gunfight*, as a guest. He wouldn't return to TV, other than in guest appearances on various talk shows, until 1974, as the host of *Ridin' the Rails*. But in 1976, Cash signed a deal with CBS to produce a four-week variety show. *Johnny Cash and Friends* ran from August 29th through September 19th and featured regulars June Carter Cash, Steve Martin, and Jim Varney, with more of a focus on comedy. Guests for the show included Roy Clark, Waylon Jennings, and Tammy Wynette.

The Johnny Cash Christmas Special 1976

Aired on December 6, 1976, featuring guests Tony Orlando, Roy Clark, Barbara Mandrell, Merle Travis, Tommy Cash, Billy Graham

The success of that four-week stint led CBS to sign Cash up for a Christmas special, which was duly rushed into production. The show was filmed partly at Cash's Hendersonville home and partly at the Grand Ole Opry House in Nashville. The main guests for the first half of show were Tony Orlando and Roy Clark, both of whom sang songs with Cash. The first song has Cash singing the traditional "Wandering," which James Taylor had recorded and released the year before. It was a song Cash never recorded, and can only be heard here. The second half of the show was filmed with Cash's family and friends gathered around, among them Carrie Cash and friends Merle Travis and Barbara Mandrell, who each perform a song, plus Billy Graham, who provides "A Story of Christmas" to end the show.

Soon after the show aired, Cash was supposedly quoted by the Associated Press as saying that he would no longer be doing television, labeling his Christmas Special "the worst in the history of television" and adding that it wasn't a true representation of himself. A few days later, he refuted those quotes and said he was happy with the show. "We were the number-one show in our time slot Monday night," he added of the show, which aired on Monday, December 6th. Sister Reba Hancock told the Associated Press that Nielson estimated that the show captured a 35 percent share of the audience that night, and that "we'll be doing television as long as there is television. When it's time to move to something else, that's what we'll do."

The Johnny Cash Christmas Special 1977

Aired on November 30, 1977, featuring guests Roy Clark, Roy Orbison, Carl Perkins, Jerry Lee Lewis

In May 1977, CBS announced that it had signed Cash to a three-year contract to produce two musical specials a year, and would also be seeking acting roles for him. The first show of the new contract was a second Christmas special, recorded on October 17th in Nashville and featuring Cash's old Sun cohorts. The theme for the special was reliving Cash's past, starting with his being stationed in Germany with the Air Force. The Statler Brothers and the Tennessee Three (plus Earl Poole Ball and Jerry Hensley) join Cash in a barracks set to sing "This Ole House" and "Blue Christmas."

Roy Clark makes his second appearance on a Cash Christmas special, and he and Cash run through some festive hits by Gene Autry before the Sun boys make their way out. The show wraps up with a reunion of the Johnny Cash Roadshow, plus Roy Orbison and Jerry Lee Lewis, as they run through a couple of carols. To end the show, Cash brings out the Roadshows old closer, "Children Go Where I Send Thee," though it doesn't pack the punch of versions like the one on *Live in Denmark.*

The show followed Bing Crosby's Christmas special, *Bing Crosby's Merrie Olde Christmas,* which featured an infamous appearance by David Bowie, along with Twiggy, Ron Moody, British comedian Stanley Baxter, and London's Trinity Boys Choir. Cash's special landed him at #8 in the weekly ratings. Crosby came in at #3.

The Johnny Cash Christmas Special 1978

Aired on December 6, 1978, featuring guests Steve Martin, Rita Coolidge, Kris Kristofferson

Cash's first TV show of 1978 was the first of two spring specials, *Johnny Cash: Spring Fever.* In November, he took the show to Los Angeles to record another Christmas Special, with Steve Martin returning to the Cash fold, along with guests Rita Coolidge and Kris Kristofferson.

The only Cash solo song not available anywhere else is "Christmas Can't Be Far Away" written by Boudleaux Bryant and recorded by artists including Burl Ives and Eddy Arnold. Cash also debuts "The Greatest Cowboy of Them All," a song he had recorded earlier that year for *A Believer Sings the Truth,* and would record again on 1991's *Mystery of Life.* To end the show, he brings out daughters and stepdaughters Carlene, Tara, Rosanne, Cindy, Kathy, and Rosey, plus wife June, to join him on "Silent Night."

The Johnny Cash Christmas Special 1979

Aired on December 13, 1979, featuring guests Tom T. Hall, Anne Murray, Andy Kaufman
Cash returned to Nashville to record the 1979 special, which featured an eclectic guest list. Returning to one of the themes from the first special, Cash intersperses footage of his father Ray and brother Roy at the old homestead, talking about the flood they had to run from, with Johnny performing "Five Feet High and Rising" in the studio. The oddest part of the whole show is that Andy Kaufman is a guest, but in the Latka character from *Taxi*, though everyone still refers to him as Andy. He only breaks character to do his Elvis Presley impersonation, performing "That's When Your Heartaches Begin."

The highlight of the show is the last segment, featuring classmates of John Carter's from the B. C. Goodpasture Christian School while Tom T. Hall, Anne Murray, June, and Johnny each take a song. June does the bluegrass song "Back Up and Push," backed by the legendary Vasser Clements on fiddle, plus Marty Stuart on mandolin, Marshall Grant on stand-up bass, W. S. Holland on snare, and Jerry Hensley on acoustic guitar.

The show ends with Cash, surrounded by the children, singing "Let There Be Peace on Earth," written by Jill Jackson Miller and Sy Miller, a song only available on the special.

Continued Christmas

Cash's Christmas specials ran for ten years, though the first four are the only ones available on DVD at this time. Below is a bit of information on the others that hopefully, over time, will also be released.

The Johnny Cash Christmas Special 1980

Aired on December 3, 1980, featuring guests Larry Gatlin, Jeannie C. Riley, Mac Davis

Johnny Cash: Christmas in Scotland (1981)

Aired on December 10, 1981, featuring guests Andy Williams, Carlene Carter

Johnny Cash: Merry Memphis Christmas (1982)

Aired on December 7, 1982, featuring guests Crystal Gayle, Eddie Rabbitt, The Mighty Clouds of Joy, Rosanne Cash

Johnny Cash's Christmas 1983

Aired on December 16, 1983, featuring guests Merle Haggard, Ricky Skaggs
Portions of this show were recorded in Maces Springs, Virginia, home of the Carter Family.

Christmas on the Road (1984)

Aired on December 7, 1984, featuring guests Waylon Jennings, Willie Nelson, Kris Kristofferson

This is the special that launched the Highwaymen, and an overview of the show is given in chapter 35.

10th Anniversary Johnny Cash Christmas Show (1985)

Aired on December 10, 1985, featuring guests Jerry Lee Lewis, Carl Perkins, Larry Gatlin, Rosanne Cash

I'll Go Somewhere and Sing My Songs Again

Posthumous Releases

The period from Cash's death on September 12, 2003, to the time of this writing has been filled with multiple "greatest hits" packages and other compilations. What follows is a listing of some of the best officially released collections, boxed sets, and series. With the exception of the first entry, these are presented in chronological order of release.

Bear Family Boxed Sets

It should be said right up front: if you are a Cash completist, this is your first stop. Bear Family Records, Germany's venerable reissue label, started releasing Cash-related albums in 1978, beginning with *The Unissued Johnny Cash*, which features several of Cash's out-of-print Columbia singles as well as two songs he had recorded in German ("Viel Zu Spat" ["I Got Stripes"] and "Wo Ist Zu Hause, Mama" ["Five Feet High and Rising"]). It was followed the next year by *Johnny and June*, containing the duo's Columbia singles and B-sides, plus out-of-print singles by June Carter, and a few months later by *Tall Man*, a further collection of Cash's singles.

Bear Family's first Cash CD release was a single-disc collection of Cash's Sun years entitled *Johnny Cash—1955–57: Up Through the Years*. As good a set as it was, the label went one further in 1990 with the boxed set *The Man in Black: 1954–58*, which collects every false start, alternate or incomplete take, and master version of the period, and is *the* set for the deep fan of Cash's Sun Records period. Also covered in the set are the first set of sessions Cash recorded for Columbia, including a complete session from August 13, 1958, as Cash and crew record "Don't Take Your Guns to Town" and "I Still Miss Someone."

In 1991, Bear Family released two more sets, *The Man in Black: 1959–62* and *Come Along and Ride This Train*. *The Man in Black: 1959–62* covers his first eight Columbia albums (with the exception of *Fabulous Johnny Cash* and *Ride*

This Train) and also includes a complete session from May 9, 1960, featuring recordings by Roy Cash Jr. and Ray Liberto Jr. *Come Along and Ride This Train* gathers together five Cash concept albums (*Ride This Train, Sings the Ballads of the True West, America, From Sea to Shining Sea,* and *The Rambler*).

The final entry in the series, so far, came in 1995 with *The Man in Black: 1963–69.* Though it doesn't include the two prison albums from that period, it does feature *Keep on the Sunnyside,* an album by the Carter Family featuring Cash as a guest star, and Cash's full performance at the 1964 Newport Folk Festival.

All of these sets are imports, and are generally much more expensive than what can be purchased now in the States. But when they were first released, they offered a revelation of uncovered treasures. Today, nearly everything on them can be found on Stateside releases.

For the ultra-hardcore Cash fan, *Johnny Cash: The Outtakes* was released in 2007. This three-disc set assembles even more outtakes, incomplete takes, and false starts from the Sun sessions. It's not something that bears repeated listening, unless you really like hearing eleven swings at "Don't Make Me Go," for example. For those fans, there is also *Unseen Cash,* a small booklet of unseen photos of Cash that is accompanied by a CD with two early Cash performances on Armed Forces Radio shows.

The Complete Sun Recordings 1955–58 (2005)

The year 2005 was the kickoff for Cash-related posthumous releases, starting with this three-disc Time-Life collection that brings together all of Cash's Sun output, including a few false starts. For fans of Cash's time at Sun, this is the best way to go. There are enough false starts included to give the listener a sense of the newness of recording for Cash and the Tennessee Two, but not so many that it dulls the listening experience. Liner notes are provided by Sun Records expert Colin Escott (though they are largely a repeat of his notes for the first Bear Family boxed set).

The Legend (2005)

Compiled by reissue producer Gregg Geller, this four-disc collection contains material from both the Sun and Columbia days. Instead of a chronological song listing, Geller opts for dividing the discs by theme. *Win, Place, and Show—The Hits* covers just what the title states; *Old Favorites and New* has songs that weren't hits but are many of the first that come to mind when people recall their favorite Cash tunes. *The Great American Songbook* doesn't go for the standards most think of when that phrase is used, but rather the deeper, older songbook Cash liked to draw from, the one that includes Jimmie Rodgers, Hank Williams, and A. P. Carter. *Family and Friends* includes twenty-four duets with everyone from June Carter and Billy Joe Shaver, on the previously unreleased "You Can't Beat Jesus

Christ," to U2 and daughter Rosanne Cash. Of the 104 tracks included in the set, seven were previously unreleased.

If you are looking for a good, all-encompassing set that covers the breadth of Cash's Sun and Columbia work, this is the one to pick up. If you are looking to drop quite a bit more money, a deluxe version of the set was also released, with a fifth CD containing the earliest known Cash work—an episode of his fifteen-minute radio show on KWEM, later released in the *Bootleg* series—and a DVD of selections from the 1980 CBS special *Johnny Cash: The First 25 Years.* All six discs of the deluxe set are housed in a large hardcover coffee-table book filled with outstanding photos, some of which are rare. But at more than six times the cost of the four-disc set, this is another one for the hardcore fan only.

At San Quentin (Legacy Edition) (2006)

The "complete concert" that was released in 2000 turned out to be not so complete in 2006, when the Legacy Edition was released. Rather than the Cash-only ten cuts on the original album, or the eighteen tracks included on the 2000 reissue, the 2006 boxed set includes thirty-one cuts over two discs, encompassing performances by Carl Perkins, the Statler Brothers, and the Carter Family. As good as the original release is, this set gives a complete picture of Cash's roadshow as the '60s came to a close. Also included on DVD for the first time is the Granada TV documentary recorded at the event. Interspersed with the music are often-chilling interviews with inmates as they recount what put them behind bars in the first place. (For more on this show and Folsom recordings, see chapter 16.)

The *Bootleg* Series

The *Bootleg* series is also highly recommended, and does an excellent job of releasing hard-to-find and previously unissued material.

When *Personal File* was released in 2006, the series had yet to be named, and had maybe not even been conceived. The two-disc set includes forty-nine songs featuring only Cash and his guitar. Some of them were just songs Cash liked, or had grown up with, and several include spoken introductions with stories about when he first heard them, or how he found out about the original performers. Also included are several songs Cash wrote but had yet to record. The album first came in a double digipak with an acetate slipcover superimposing an image of Cash over the image of a tape box from the House of Cash recording studio, and there was no designation of it being part of the *Bootleg* series.

Making up for lost time, two entries in the newly named *Bootleg* series were released in 2011. The first was *Bootleg Volume II: From Memphis to Hollywood.* The first disc of the set opens with a recording of Cash's 1955 KWEM radio show (the same one included in the deluxe edition of *The Legend*), followed by twelve rare

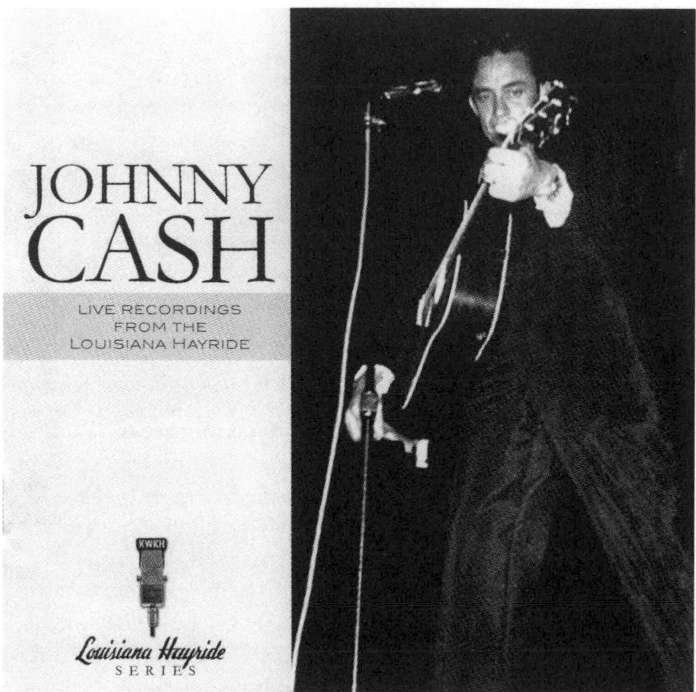

Part of a series that includes Johnny Horton and others, this CD includes some of Cash's earliest recorded live recordings. This version is out of print, but other compilations have since been released that include many of the songs on this CD along with a few that are not included in this original collection. *Author's collection*

late-'50s demos and a few Sun rarities. The second disc draws from hard-to-find 1960s Columbia outtakes, singles, and B-sides.

Bootleg Volume III: Live Around the World offers fifty-three tracks captured during ten different live performances, here spread across two discs. Performance settings range from the Big "D" Jamboree in Dallas, Texas, to Long Binh, Vietnam, to the White House. Each of the recordings shows just what a great performer Cash was, no matter what walk of life the audience came from.

To date, the latest release in the series is 2012's *Bootleg Volume IV: Soul of Truth.* Gospel music was one of Cash's greatest loves and influences, and the fourth volume in the series pulls together some of his best gospel performances. Disc one finally makes available the hard-to-find Cachet Records double album *A Believer Sings the Truth,* while disc two contains the similarly sought-after Word Records album *Believe in Him.* Also included on the second disc are nine previously unreleased gospel songs that Cash recorded with the Oak Ridge Boys in 1975.

The Great Lost Performance (2007)

One of the very few posthumous Cash releases by Mercury, this concert recording was made just as his time at the label was ending, and a few years before his resurgence with American. Taped on July 28, 1990, at the Paramount Theatre in Asbury Park, New Jersey, this is another snapshot of a legend between phases as he runs through his hits, backed by a solid band. Cash sounds as if he is having fun onstage, despite his recent health problems and a downturn in record sales. This is not an essential release, but it is interesting to Cash collectors for its historical value.

At Folsom Prison (Legacy Edition) (2008)

After the success of its expanded *At San Quentin*, Columbia decided to do the same with *At Folsom Prison* a couple of years later. Much like that release, this one contains nearly fifty tracks, including performances by Carl Perkins and the Statler Brothers. Cash performed two shows that day, to ensure that enough usable tracks were recorded, and both shows are included here.

At Folsom Prison was the album that pushed Cash to superstar level, and this expanded edition only solidifies why it was so. The set also includes a two-hour documentary called *Johnny Cash at Folsom Prison*, written by Cash biographer Michael Streissguth and based on his excellent book *Johnny Cash at Folsom Prison: The Making of a Masterpiece.* Like the Legacy Edition of the San Quentin album, this is a wonderful set.

Johnny Cash's America (2008)

Fourteen of this collection's eighteen songs were previously released at various points in Cash's career, but presented together here, each follows along a theme, evoking the structure of *Ride This Train* or *From Sea to Shining Sea* but without the narrations. Of the four previously unissued recordings, "Come Along and Ride This Train" starts the album, and is a hitherto unheard version of the song Cash used on the titular segment of his television show, originally recorded on July 24, 1969. "Children, Go Where I Send Thee" was recorded live in Denmark in 1971, the live version of Woody Guthrie's "This Land Is Your Land" was taken from *The Johnny Cash Show*, and the recitation "I Am the Nation" was recorded in 1974 during sessions for *The Junkie and the Juicehead Minus Me.*

While the album offers a good selection of Cash songs, the bigger draw here is the DVD documentary included alongside it. The ninety-minute film, written and directed by Morgan Neville and Robert Gordon, originally debuted on the Biography Channel. It sets Cash's life against the backdrop of interviews with artists like John Mellencamp, Al Gore, Snoop Dogg, Bob Dylan, and several others as they tell what he meant to them.

The Greatest

Released in 2012, the four parts of *The Greatest* are essentially a beginner's series, each covering a different aspect of Cash's career: *The Country Classics*, *The Duets*, *The Gospel Songs*, and *The Number Ones*. Chances are, if you're reading this book, you've got at least a small collection of Cash albums. If not—or if you're looking to buy something to get someone else started—these aren't a bad place to look. Each of the four discs in the series includes both Sun and Columbia material, with the songs assembled to fit the topic of each release.

Even Cash fans who have it all will be interested in picking up the deluxe edition of *The Number Ones*, which includes a DVD containing ten of the songs as performed live on *The Johnny Cash Show*. Each clip has been digitally restored, making these performances a real treat to see.

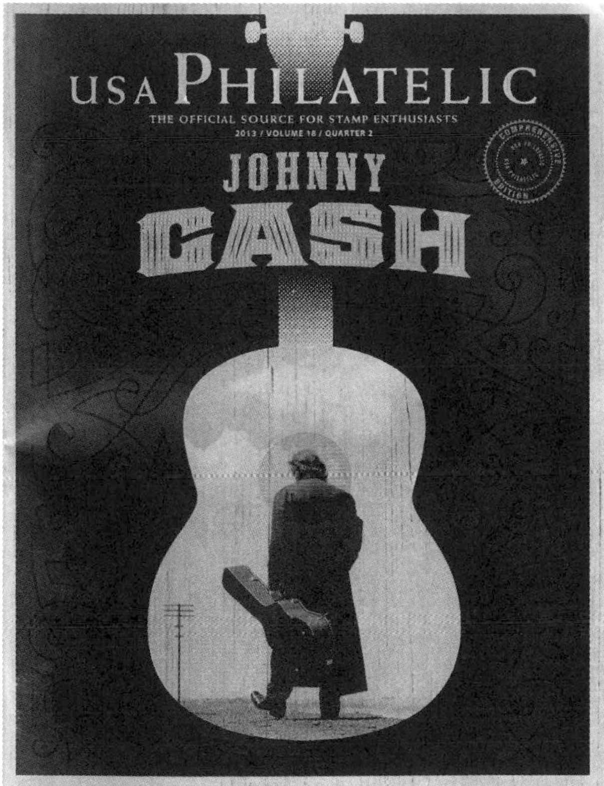

The Johnny Cash postage stamp was released in 2013. The release was celebrated with an event at the Ryman Auditorium that featured John Carter Cash, Marty Stuart, the Oak Ridge Boys, Randy Travis, and Jamey Johnson. *Author's collection*

Love God Murder (2000)

Though not a posthumous release, this set is worth mentioning alongside *The Greatest.* This collection was initially made available as a three-disc set or as three single discs; later, in 2008, a fourth disc, *Life*, was added. These are great starter discs, and the only discs on the list that cover Cash's career from Sun right through to American Recordings.

Johnny Cash: Life Unheard

This single-disc collection was released in 2013 as a companion to the book *Johnny Cash: Life Unseen*, a collection of rare Cash photos assembled by *Life* magazine. It essentially amounts to a sampler of the *Bootleg* series. Of the twelve selections included, six are live cuts from *Bootleg III*, two are from *Bootleg I* (originally released as *Personal File*), one is from *Bootleg II*, and one is from *Bootleg IV.* The two remaining tracks are previously unreleased songs from the '80s. "Movin' Up" was used in Cash's 1980 made-for-TV-movie *The Pride of Jesse Hallam*, and "Ben Dewberry's Final Run" comes from a session on February 4, 1982.

The Complete Columbia Collection (2012)

If you are tired of digging for old vinyl copies of some of Cash's harder-to-get material, or if you are just looking to pick up the whole collection in one fell swoop, this is your set. Made up of all fifty-nine Columbia albums—all remastered, and many available here for the first time on CD—*The Complete Columbia Collection* also includes a two-disc set of songs that were originally singles and not available on albums, and another disc containing Cash's Sun album *Johnny Cash with His Hot and Blue Guitar.* While the set might seem pricey, it breaks down to a pretty cheap price per disc. And for the completist, it's a no-brainer.

48

Up Front There Ought to Be a Man in Black

Concert Videos

ver the years, Johnny Cash concentrated as much on his live shows as he did his recording career, and at least a sampling from each period of his live career has been released on DVD.

Town Hall Party (1958/1959)

Co-hosted by Jay Stewart and singing cowboy Tex Ritter, *Town Hall Party* was a three-hour radio broadcast originating from the Los Angles suburb of Compton. The show started in 1952, and was soon picked up by television station KTTV, allowing the audience to not only hear but see program regulars like the Collins Kids, Merle Travis, Wanda Jackson, Freddie Hart, Carl Perkins, and Patsy Cline.

This release from Bear Family Records presents two of Cash's appearances. The first is from November 15, 1958, and has him leaning heavily on his Sun recordings, with only two songs from his recent first Columbia album included, "Don't Take Your Guns to Town" and "Frankie's Man Johnny." The second set presented comes from August 8, 1959, and has Cash varying the set list a bit by adding a few more songs from his Columbia output.

To date, few videos of early Cash performances have been released, so this one gives us about as good a look as we are likely to get of what his late-1950s and early 1960s shows were like. Though he is often recalled as a dark figure, his early shows—from before he began to wear black on a consistent basis—featured regular bursts of humor and even a comedy bit, where Cash would impersonate the stars of the day. One of his funniest and most popular impersonations was of Elvis Presley (or, as Cash says, "a rock 'n' roll singer").

Some of what is included on this release can also be found on discount-bin releases that don't give an indication of where the clips come from (some of which also include clips from other Cash appearances), but this is the best looking of the bunch, presenting his sets as they originally appeared.

Rainbow Quest with Pete Seeger (Recorded 1966)

In 1957, Pete Seeger was indicted by the Committee on Un-American Activities of the House of Representatives, and he was formally convicted of contempt of Congress in early 1961. On May 18, 1962, he was acquitted, and resumed his role as a prominent folksinger, working to bring his message and his love of the music to audiences.

Shown predominately in the New York area, on UHF channel 47, *Rainbow Quest* was a do-it-yourself-type affair; the networks and potential sponsors were hesitant to showcase Seeger because of the stigma that was still attached to him even after his acquittal. Seeger's guests showcased the best in folk, bluegrass, and blues, including the Stanley Brothers, Mississippi John Hurt, Richard & Mimi Farina, and Sonny Terry, among others.

On this episode, June Carter acts as a link between the modern country-music world and one of the primary sources of its beginnings in the Carter Family (one of Seeger's early influences). Accompanying her, and representing the modern country-music performer with ties to the folk world, was Cash. The show's set is dressed like a minimalist dining area, outfitted with a table, three chairs, and a refrigerator.

Seeger plays the congenial host, intently interested in hearing June's account of her famous family's history, and June is affable with her folksy charm, talking softly while cradling a banjo or guitar. Then there's Cash, fidgeting constantly, and occasionally talking over them both. Seeger and Carter both give him space, like two sober friends not wanting to upset their drunk buddy. He begins the show in a vest and low boots, and by the end of the hour has removed them both, leaning back in his chair to the point of nearly tipping over, his sock-covered foot dangling over his knee.

Seeger opens the show with a medley before introducing his guests. Cash begins his segment with the standard "I Am a Pilgrim." The only evidence of his drug use is his gaunt appearance; his voice is strong, and his presentation of the song solid. It is a fascinating glimpse at Cash at his drug-addled best, and a look at how he would pull himself together to present his concerts. When it comes time for him to present his songs here, the result is the same. The fidgeting stops and the music takes over. As well as talking about the Carter Family, Seeger and Cash take the opportunity to discuss their mutual friend Peter LaFarge and Cash's album *Bitter Tears.*

As with the 1950s, there is very little video available of Cash in performance in the mid-1960s, making this perhaps the only way to get a glimpse of him during that time.

The Best of the Johnny Cash TV Show (1969–71)

While not strictly a collection of Cash performances, this is a must-have for Cash fans. *The Johnny Cash Show* featured a wide variety of performers, from Pete Seeger to Merle Haggard, O. C. Smith to Creedence Clearwater Revival. This collection is available in single-disc and two-disc versions. The single-disc version pulls together twenty-one performances, seven of which are by Cash solo, the rest featuring guests alone or with Cash. The two-disc version presents sixty-six performances from Cash, his guests, or both.

While the DVDs don't contain any full episodes—or enough of any one episode to give a good feeling of the whole show—the performances presented are a great overview of the fifty-eight episodes produced. A CD was also issued to coincide with the DVD release. There is also a second single-disc version available on the secondary market, originally available through a PBS pledge drive. This version subtracts four performances from the original single-disc release and replaces them with four from the two-disc version. Also included in this package is a CD containing seventeen tracks taken from the show, including a few that aren't on the original CD release.

Even taking into consideration the amount of red tape that would need to be cut through to secure the rights, it would be fantastic to see all fifty-eight episodes of the show released on DVD in the future.

Live in Denmark (1971)

Originally recorded for a Danish television show, this is the best example available of the Johnny Cash Roadshow as it was in the 1960s and early 1970s. In 1971, with *The Johnny Cash Show* entering its third and final season, the troupe was in peak form. Though this show is shorter than a standard Cash show, clocking in at sixty minutes, it is an excellent representation of the type of ensemble show Cash was known for.

The set list is an abbreviated version of Cash's *På Österåker* album, ranging from classic Sun hits ("I Walk the Line," "Folsom Prison Blues") to recent releases ("Man in Black"). It also includes duets with June ("Darlin' Companion," "If I Were a Carpenter," "Help Me Make It Through the Night") and songs by Carl Perkins ("Blue Suede Shoes," "Matchbox"), the Statler Brothers ("Bed of Roses," "Flowers on the Wall"), and the Carter Family ("A Song for Mama," "No Need to Worry," "Rock of Ages").

Taken from an African American spiritual, "Children, Go Where I Send Thee" served as the roadshows concert closer for a stretch of time, and would bring the whole troupe together. The version presented here is an enthusiastic one, proving the group to be at the top of its game at the time of the recording.

At the time of this writing, this is the only commercially available video outside of the *Johnny Cash at San Quentin* documentary to showcase the Johnny Cash Roadshow as it existed from the mid-1960s through to 1973. But it's readily available, and well worth picking up.

Live in Austin, TX (1987)

Austin City Limits premiered on PBS in 1975, and the show eventually grew beyond geographical and genre borders to become a showcase for country, blues, folk, rock, and world music. In 2004, PBS launched the DVD and CD series *Live in Austin, TX*, expanding the artists' thirty-minute segments to full performances.

Cash's episode was given over to his whole roadshow, including brother Tommy Cash and the Carter Sisters (here represented by June, Anita, Helen, and Carlene, who sang with the group between her roots-rock and country careers).

It starts with seven of his best-known songs, including "Ring of Fire," "Folsom Prison Blues," "I Walk the Line," and " Long Black Veil," and showcases the late-1980s version of the band, which included Bob Wootton and Jim Soldi on guitar, W. S. Holland on drums, Earl Poole Ball on piano, Joe Allen on bass, and Jack Hale Jr. and Bob Lewen on trumpets.

The middle section of the show is given over to four songs from Cash's soon-to-be-released Mercury debut, with the show having been shot on January 3, 1987, four months before the album's release. Included among them is a song called "Sam Stone," written by John Prine, that was recorded for the album but ultimately left off. Cash follows it with "(Ghost) Riders in the Sky," his hit from a few years earlier. Neither song was included in the original broadcast.

There is certainly enough material to reissue the show in an expanded format, including a solo performance by Tommy Cash and a duet between the brothers on "That Silver-Haired Daddy of Mine." There's also "Heavy Metal (Don't Mean Rock and Roll to Me)" and "The Big Light" (both from *Johnny Cash Is Coming to Town*), and "Gospel Boogie (a Wonderful Time up There)," with the latter pair of songs including the Carter Sisters.

Cash comes across as rejuvenated and energetic. He was about to begin a second leg of his career, and was hopeful about what the new label would bring about. At the time, he had pared back the roadshow to simply the band and the Carter Sisters, and this snapshot gives a good look at how those shows were structured.

Cash for Kenya (Recorded 1991; Released 2006)

Recorded live in Johnstown, Pennsylvania, on September 17, 1991, this concert was a benefit put on by Cash's longtime friend Jack Shaw, a minister who often traveled with Cash and wanted to raise money to build a hospital and education center in Nakuru, Kenya, to help in the fight against AIDS. Cash volunteered to headline a concert to help raise money for the cause.

The concert, which took place at the Greater Johnstown Christian Fellowship Church, leans, as one might expect, given the setting, a little more toward the gospel-tinged songs in Cash's catalogue. The show is divided into

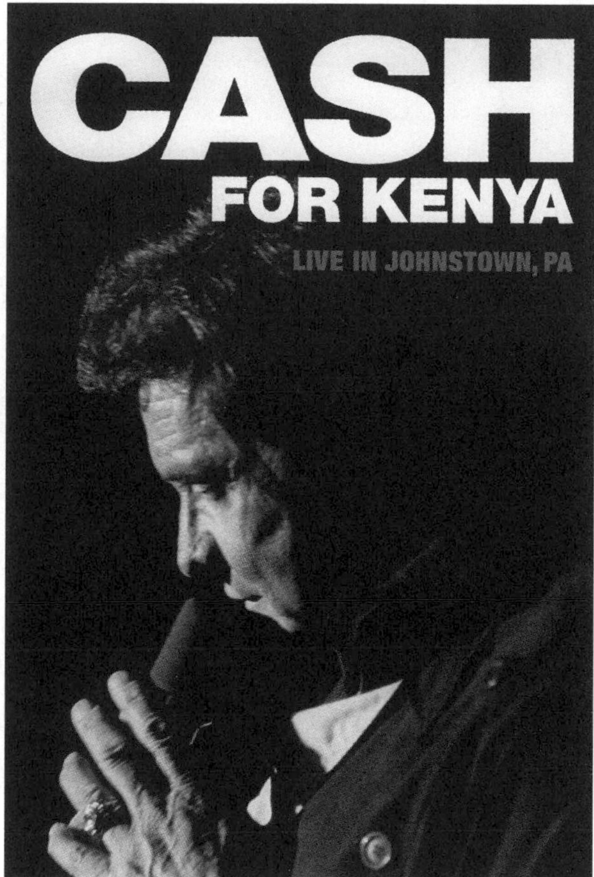

This one flew somewhat under the radar when it was released, but the video shows a Cash show as it was in 1991. The show was a benefit for AIDS relief in Kenya.
Author's collection

three sections. In the first, Cash is joined by the June, Helen, and Anita Carter as he runs through a few venue-appropriate selections, including "A Thing Called Love," "Peace in the Valley," and "The Greatest Cowboy of Them All." He also sings "Man in White," a song he suggests he had never performed live before. It had been written and released as a single in 1986, around the release of Cash's novelization of the life of the Apostle Paul, *Man in White.*

At the conclusion of "Man in White," and with the Carter Family leaving the stage, Cash notes that he generally starts a show with the words "Hello, I'm Johnny Cash," and with that the band launches into "Folsom Prison Blues." The band runs through a funky version of "Get Rhythm" before Cash tells a story to lead into "Five Feet High and Rising," which in turn segues into "Pickin'

Time." He is then joined by June for "Beautiful Life," "Jackson," and "If I Were a Carpenter."

For the next section, Cash turns the stage over to the Carter Family, who run through several family classics, ending with "Will the Circle Be Unbroken," for which they are joined by John Carter Cash. The finale comes as the crew runs through "Angel Band."

It is interesting to watch Cash in the period of transition between his last Mercury album and his "rediscovery" following the release of his critically acclaimed *American Recordings* LP. But even with the business pressures he must have felt at the time, he appears in good spirits, joking with the band and June throughout the show. One poignant moment comes as he switches from "Five Feet High and Rising" to "Pickin' Time" by relating a piece advice given to him by his mother, Carrie. A constant source of encouragement and moral guidance, she had passed away only a few months earlier, in May 1991. With the loss fresh on his mind and heart, you can tell there is a void left in his life just from the fondness in his speech.

Johnny Cash in Ireland (1993)

On February 11, 1993, Cash brought his show to the Olympia Theatre in Dublin, Ireland, and the show was filmed for a television special called *Country at the Olympia*. What is presented is essentially the Cash Family Revue, with Cash joined onstage and in song by John Carter and the Carter Family (this time consisting of June, Helen, and June's daughter Rosey).

The set list is made up entirely of Cash classics, with nothing any newer than 1979's "(Ghost) Riders in the Sky." The Carter Family joins Cash on the opener, "Daddy Sang Bass," and then runs through "Keep on the Sunny Side" before John Carter makes his way through Billy Joe Shaver's "Georgia on a Fast Train." At times, the family's performance makes the watching a little rough. Rosey seems a little too excited at times, and John Carter had yet to reach any maturity as an artist. Still, it shows the world as it was for Cash at the time.

The show picks up when Cash launches into "Long Black Veil" and Kris Kristofferson surprises the audience by walking onstage with guitar in hand to join him. He stays on for a duet of "Big River," much to the delight of the audience. June then joins Johnny onstage for "Jackson" before the Carter Family returns for "Wabash Cannonball" and "Will the Circle Be Unbroken." The finale features the Carter Family, Kristofferson, and Irish country singer Sandy Kelly on "Forty Shades of Green." The song never made any waves in the States, but had remained popular in Ireland since its release there in 1960.

Despite this being one of Cash's lowest points, both commercially and in terms of his health, he looks well and trim, his black hair now a heavy salt-and-pepper. This period was not one of commercial viability, and Cash had resigned himself to traveling the world—or at least the States—with his Revue in tow, giving the people the hits they wanted. Overall, though, the Cash performances on this DVD are fun and tight, and well worth having in the library.

Johnny Cash Live at Montreux (1994)

What a difference a year makes. A couple of weeks after the Irish show detailed above, Cash met with Rick Rubin, and began the journey that would make up the third and final leg of his career. By May, he was in Rubin's Hollywood Hills home, recording his first album for American. Nearly a year later, in April 1994, *American Recordings* was released. Coming off of a successful appearance at the Glastonbury Festival in England in late June, Cash rolled into Montreux, Switzerland, on July 5th, for the annual Montreux Jazz Festival.

By now, his group had been whittled down to Wootton and Holland, with Dave Roe on bass and John Carter on rhythm acoustic, removing the piano and second electric guitar. The performance is more energetic than it was in Ireland, and the sound closer to the stripped-down sound of Cash's most popular recordings. The song selections lean in that direction, too, with Cash running through fine versions of many of the same classics he played at the Irish show, but throwing in "Guess Things Happen That Way," a hit from his Sun days that he didn't play live often.

Nearly halfway through the set, the band leaves the stage and Cash pulls up a stool—a new addition to his shows since the release of *American Recordings*. With just his voice and guitar, he introduces the next segment by saying, "I've got a new album out. It's called *American Recordings*. It was for the American recording company, and it was recorded in America," he adds, breaking out into a smile as the audience chuckles. Within the first two words of "Delia," the crowd responds with whistles and applause. The mini-set also includes "Tennessee Stud," "Bird on a Wire," "Let the Train Blow the Whistle," "The Beast in Me," and "Redemption."

The band returns for a rousing version of "Big River" before Cash introduces June for "Jackson" and "Will the Circle Be Unbroken." To wrap up the show, Cash pulls out a couple of older crowd-pleasers, "Orange Blossom Special" and "San Quentin." He closes with a Mark Knopfler tune, "Next Time I'm in Town," that he recorded for *American Recordings*, but which didn't make the cut and remains officially unreleased.

If only for Cash's performances of the *American Recordings* songs, this DVD is certainly worth picking up. It captures Cash as he was regaining his confidence in himself and moving, every so slightly, out of the constraints of being a legacy touring act. At times, he seems genuinely humbled by the audience's response, and the energy the fans give him is reflected in his performances.

49

Till the Lord Comes and Calls Me Away

Gospel Recordings

The First Baptist Church in Dyess, Arkansas, of 1944 would have been considered large even by modern standards. The wooden building housed oak benches that seated 500 people, and its annual revival services ran for two weeks. On a Saturday night in 1944—February 26th, to be exact—Johnny Cash turned twelve years old. His older brother Jack was already a devout follower of God who planned to become a full-time minister. Johnny looked up to Jack and wanted to follow his example. Encouraged by his mother, he attended every night of the revival.

A number of religions consider thirteen to be the "age of accountability," when the difference between right and wrong is now fully within a child's grasp. At twelve, Cash knew he needed to make a decision soon. At the end of service, the congregation would rise and sing the invitation hymn, inviting those who wished to commit to a relationship with God to come to the front of the church and make that public profession of faith before being baptized. The sound of "Just as I Am" began to fill the auditorium: "Just as I am / without one plea / but that thy blood was shed for me / and that thou bidst me come to thee / O Lamb of God, I come, I come."

"As the people sang, I began to get miserable and twitchy and nervous," Cash later wrote, in *Man in Black*. "I wanted out of that church. As the song kept on flowing, I started thinking of all those songs I'd been hearing at home on the radio and how they were pointing out the direction for me to turn right then. It was time to make a move."

The congregation moved into the second verse of the song. "Just as I am, and waiting not / to rid my soul of one dark blot / to thee whose blood can cleanse each spot / O Lamb of God, I come, I come." Cash looked down the aisle and saw his brother standing at the end, holding his Bible to his heart and singing with conviction. It was enough to ease his mind, and he stepped out of the pew, walking with purpose to the altar to take the preacher's hand.

"It was something which happened so naturally for me that it was like a birthday rolling around," he writes. "It was a milestone in my life, something that was planned for me to do all along."

His first test of faith came just three months later, when Jack was killed in an accident in a woodshop. It simultaneously shook his young faith and strengthened it. On his deathbed, Jack was calm, describing visions of heaven and angels to those at his bedside. "We watched him die in such bliss and glory that it was like we were almost happy because of the way we saw him go. We saw in our mind's eye what he was seeing—a vision of heaven."

The boys' mother, Carrie, set another example. The death devastated her, but she leaned on her faith to get her through—and it did. She not only set an example through her faith, she also encouraged Johnny to pursue his dream, as she later explained to *Country Music.*

> He came in the back door, I was making biscuits, and he began singing "Everybody's Gonna Have Religion in Glory." He had such a deep voice. I looked around to see if it was him. And I said, "Was that you singing that?" He said, "Yes'm, it sure was." And I said, "Well, the Lord's got his hand on you, someday you'll be singing on the radio, and people will hear you all over the nation." He said later, he went out on the front porch and sat down in the swing, and he told me later that he wanted to tell me that he knew that.

The road to getting there is outlined in other sections of this book, but suffice it to say, he made it.

Hymns by Johnny Cash (Columbia Records, 1959)

Cash had told Sam Phillips he wanted to be a gospel singer in their very first meeting, but Phillips wasn't interested. Original gospel songs by an unknown artist were a hard sell, and Phillips told Cash he just didn't have the resources to break the records. Cash held on to that thought, though, and would occasionally record gospel-oriented songs like "Belshazzar" and "I Was There When It Happened." He even claimed later that "I Walk the Line" was as much about God as it was his then-wife Vivian.

Gospel music played a part in Cash's move to Columbia. "With Sam Phillips, the issue was gospel," he writes. "I wanted to record gospel music, and I wanted it badly. He refused to let me for purely financial reasons." When Don Law approached him in 1957 about the possibility of moving to Columbia, the first question Cash asked was whether he would be allowed to record gospel music. Law's answer was yes, and the move was sealed.

It wasn't just idle talk. When Cash entered the studios on July 24, 1958, to begin recording his first three-hour session for Columbia, he recorded six songs, two of which were gospel: "Suppertime," which would be included on his first Columbia LP, and "It Was Jesus," the opening track on his second Columbia LP, *Hymns by Johnny Cash.* "It Was Jesus" showed that he could write gospel music that was at once respectful in praise and in line with the quasi-rockabilly boom-chicka-boom he was becoming famous for, even when surrounded by the chorus of voices that would become another mainstay of his sound throughout the '60s.

At his third Columbia session, on August 13, 1958, Cash recorded one gospel song for the album among nine sides in total: another original, "Lead Me Father," which he had written three years earlier. Right after the release of his first Sun single, "Hey Porter" b/w "Cry, Cry, Cry," Cash stopped by WMPS, where he asked disc jockey and future manager Bob Neal to play the record, which he did, live over the air. Cash was overwhelmed and thanked God for his dream come true. "That night I went home and wrote a song, which concerned 'tithing' my music and called it 'My Prayer,'" he recalls, in *Man in Black*. "It was recorded three years later on Columbia records in my first hymn album and renamed 'Lead Me Father.' It was never a big seller, but every few days for the last twenty years I have sung this song over in my mind, if not aloud."

On January 13, 1959, Cash's dream of making a gospel album edged closer to becoming a reality when a whole session was devoted to recording the remainder of the songs to make up the LP. Joining the two previously recorded originals were two others he had penned: "I Call Him," co-written with his brother Roy, and "He'll Be a Friend."

For the remaining eight songs, Cash drew on a mix of contemporary and older gospel songs. Among the contemporary songs, "I Saw a Man" came from writer Arthur "Guitar Boogie" Smith, and the recitation "Are All the Children In" from Craig Starrett. "Snow in His Hair" came from the Southern gospel tradition, having been written by South Carolina native and gospel songwriter Marshall Pack, while Marijohn Wilkin and John D. Loudermilk co-wrote the album closer, "God Will."

Stuart Hamblen wrote "These Things Shall Pass," and he and Cash had a lot in common. Hamblen starred in many of the early singing-cowboy movies, but the pressures of stardom led him to the bottle. In 1949, he experienced a religious conversion at a Billy Graham Crusade and became a well-known gospel songwriter. His songs were recorded by artists including Cash, Tammy Wynette, Ray Price, and Eddy Arnold.

The depth of Cash's knowledge of gospel music is clear from his song choices. "The Old Account," though credited to Cash in the liner notes, was actually written by Frank Graham in 1902 and arranged by Cash for the album. Cash would return to the song a few times over the years, even rerecording it in 1977, though that version has not yet been released. "Lead Me Gently Home" was written in 1879 by Will Lamartine Thompson, while "Swing Low, Sweet Chariot" was a Negro spiritual written by Wallis Willis and first recorded in 1909.

Cash's voice carries a weight and a joy on the album. The weight was that of respect for the material and the meaning of the songs. The joy came from finally fulfilling a lifelong dream—one his mother would be even more proud of than his already skyrocketing career.

The performances on this album are that of a man in worship, and it is evident in the conviction that rings out from his bass voice. By now, he had already begun to take pills, but his drug use had not yet spun out of control, and he was able to justify it in his mind, freeing himself from any guilt or shame as he sang. This was not an album made to chase the success he was seeing with *The Fabulous Johnny Cash.* It was an album he wanted to make as part of his tithe to God, and sales numbers were not even a consideration.

Hymns from the Heart (Columbia Records, 1962)

By the time Cash entered the studio on February 27, 1961, to record the first song for his next gospel project, his world was anything but perfect. Drugs had taken deeper root in his life and were driving an increasingly large wedge between him and wife Vivian. What should have been bright spots in the year—like the birth of his fourth daughter, Tara, and the move to a larger home in Casitas Springs, California—were marred by the distance he put between himself and his family.

The February session produced two songs for the new album, "He'll Understand and Say Well Done" and "God Must Have My Fortune Laid Away." They laid the groundwork for the album, and provided the path Cash would follow for the rest of the project, which is to say that the album would be made up of the songs written by others, with Cash himself not contributing any originals.

For the April 26th and 27th sessions, Cash brought songs from other writers and a few from the public domain. He gave fine performances of all of them, but they lack the fire and passion of those on his first gospel album. Though he was going through hard times in his personal life, he resisted crying out to God, instead preferring to go through the motions.

Nickajack Cave

One of most famous stories about the life of Johnny Cash takes place in Nickajack Cave, near Chattanooga, Tennessee, in October of 1967. As he told it, at that point in his life he simply couldn't take it anymore. The drugs had shrunk his six-foot frame to 155 pounds. His marriage was a shambles, he was estranged from his daughters, and he had alienated much of his family and squandered the gift his mother had encouraged. "I had wasted my life," he writes, in *Cash.* "I had drifted so far away from God and every stabilizing force in my life that I felt there was no hope for me."

His solution was to go to Nickajack Cave and die. Armed with only a flashlight, he walked back through the caverns until they became so narrow that he was forced to crawl. When the batteries in his flashlight died, he lay down and resigned himself to death. In complete and total darkness, he felt as far away from God as he ever had before. But God hadn't given up on him. "I felt something very powerful start to happen to me, a sensation of utter peace, clarity, and sobriety," he adds. "I didn't believe it at first. I couldn't understand it."

In that darkness, Cash felt God leading him out of that cave, using a gentle breeze to guide him to the entrance. When he finally reached the opening of the cave, his body weak and ravaged, he saw June and his mother standing nearby, holding a basket of food. His mother had flown from California to Nashville to find June, to tell her something was wrong with Johnny, whom June had been looking for. It was then and there that Cash decided to give his life to God and do whatever he needed to kick the drugs.

Now, even if you are a staunch believer in miracles, several moments in this story require a leap of faith. How did June know to drive hundreds of miles to that exact spot? Would Mama Cash really have flown across the country on a motherly hunch? But the most telling fact was uncovered by Cash's close friend and personal historian Mark Stiepler: Nickajack Cave was already underwater by October of 1967, having been flooded by the building of a new dam. So, to put it bluntly, this never happened—or at least not in the way Cash said it did.

Cash was known as a spinner of tales, but this isn't just any tale. Whether it happened or not is of no matter—it is still a very important turning point in the life and faith of Cash. Where the story first crops up is a little fuzzy. In his 1973 book *The New Johnny Cash*, Charles Paul Conn focused on Cash's conversion, and the time just after it. He makes no mention of the Nickajack event, instead pinpointing as the catalyst of Cash's turnaround his arrest in Lafayette, Georgia. This is the same version of events given in the 1971 episode of *This Is Your Life* featuring Cash (for which the sheriff who made the arrest was even brought out).

In a 1980 interview with Don Cusic (published in his 1990 book *The Sound of Light: A History of Gospel Music*), Cash mentioned that the story features in the manuscript of his 1975 autobiography *Man in Black*, not realizing until Cusic told him that, in fact, the story doesn't appear in the book. Cash decided it must have been cut in the editing process.

The story would not resurface publicly until the mid-1990s. "It is also important, historically, though, to note that he did not mention this 'event' until years after November 1967, around the time he began to identify with St. Paul," Stiepler writes. "He may not have fully formed in his mind and his soul an understanding of the journey he was on until later."

And therein lies the crux of the story. It is fascinating how this construct that Cash uses to tell the world about his conversion coincides with the thoughts of the sixteenth-century saint, St. John of the Cross. In his poem 'Dark Night of the Soul,' St. John details an event many believers go through as they surrender their lives to Christ. In more recent years, the phrase "dark night of the soul" has come to refer to a period of doubt. But what St. John had in mind was something deeper, more existential—a point of total surrender, often caused by outside stimuli. Once a person has reached that point of total and complete surrender, nothing but the soul matters; the things that make you an individual—or that you would use to identify yourself—fall away and mean nothing. And in that total darkness of the night, the soul cries out to God for direction.

The final two stanzas of the poem read:

> The breeze blew from the turret as I parted his locks; with his gentle hand he wounded my neck and caused all my senses to be suspended.
>
> I remained, lost in oblivion; My face I reclined on the Beloved. All ceased and I abandoned myself, leaving my cares forgotten among the lilies.

Even though he would become quite the Bible scholar, it is not known whether Cash would have known of this poem and its meanings, particularly when he was first crafting the story. But the parallels are there to be seen. What Cash was able to do, using his creativity and storytelling abilities, was craft a conversion story that drew in the listeners; that created an atmosphere where they would be rooting for Cash to come out of that cave alive and healthier than when he entered. It was a story that allowed him to relay his conversation to the media in a way they would respond to more than if he simply said, "I found God and moved on," thus furthering the reach of his testimony. The ethics of making up one's Christian testimony . . . well, that's for someone else to figure out.

The Holy Land (Columbia Records, 1969)

At the close of the 1960s, Cash was in the process of taking control of his pill addiction and turning his life around. He had married June Carter, climbed to the top of the charts with *At Folsom Prison* (the live album he had wanted to make for so long), and was recommitting his life to God.

After their wedding, on March 1, 1968, Johnny and June postponed their honeymoon to keep up with concert appearances. In May, they were scheduled to begin a British tour, so they decided to plan a trip to Israel after completing those shows. They had been to Israel once before, in 1966, and for Cash, the excitement of returning to see where his Savior lived began to bubble up in the form of an idea for an album. He took a tape recorder on the trip, and as they toured the historic sites, he and June recorded their thoughts on what they were seeing and feeling. Bob Johnston then took the tapes into the studio in July, and he and Cash began to craft a narrative, with the tape-recorded spots serving as narration between the songs.

Throughout the '60s, Cash experienced a prolonged dry spell in his songwriting. But now, as with *From Sea to Shining Sea*, he was inspired to write on a particular subject matter. Of the eight songs on the album, five were his own. "Land of Israel," "Nazarene," and "Come to the Wailing Wall" simply expand on the history of where he and June had visited, describing some of the sites and giving a little history. "Beautiful Words" was performed on the site of the Sermon of the Mount, and includes a simple chorus bookending Cash's recitation of the Beatitudes.

"God Is Not Dead" is Cash's definitive statement on his faith, starting with a simple guitar accompaniment and then moving into a strings- and chorus-backed reading of scripture. It was a statement that he would later make, joined by June, on an episode of *The Johnny Cash Show*.

The best song Cash wrote for the project was inspired by the miracle of Christ turning water into wine at a wedding feast. "He Turned the Water into Wine" came to him as he stood in the spot were it was claimed to have happened. The song stands as a powerful testimony to the power of belief, and Cash would return to it often over the next few years in concert, including the shows he recorded at Madison Square Garden and San Quentin.

Cash also chose three songs that he didn't write to express the feelings he wanted to convey with the album. The first was "The Ten Commandments," written by Statler Brother Lew DeWitt. In a syndicated review column, music critic Forester called the song the album's "strongest track in thought and voice." Cash also recorded "The Fourth Man," written by Arthur Smith, and here featuring some great guitar work by Carl Perkins. He would go on to include it in his live sets throughout his life, even recording a version for Rick Rubin during those first American sessions, as later included in the *Unearthed* boxed set.

The album's only single was the Carl Perkins–penned "Daddy Sang Bass," which went to #1 on the Country Singles chart (and is covered in chapter 18). In *Johnny Cash: A Life*, Robert Hilburn states that Johnston knew this wasn't the type of album Columbia wanted to follow *At Folsom*, and that label even considered not releasing a single from it. But Columbia was smart enough to realize that it could sell well just on the merits of the previous album. The LP was gussied up with a lenticular cover that showed a 3D Cash in front of a building in Israel. It spent twenty-three weeks on the Country chart—eleven of them in the Top 10—peaking at #6, and rose to #54 on the Pop chart.

The Johnny Cash Show and a Public Profession of Faith

Coming off the popularity of *At San Quentin*, Cash signed up for a weekly variety show on the ABC network. On each show, he included a hymn or gospel song, while during an episode in the first season, on September 20, 1969, he showcased an appearance by the Staple Singers. "The songs and hymns I'd been singing since I was a kid were brought into the format of the weekly TV show," he writes, in *Man in Black*. "I sang all the ones I loved. The Carter Family, the Statler Brothers, and Carl Perkins joined in on them, as did June."

Limiting his message to a song or two a week was fine with the network, but the executives bristled when Cash began to back up that message elsewhere on the show. "It wasn't something I was driven to do by an urge to convert anybody or spread the word of the Lord," he adds, in *Cash: The Autobiography*. "I did it because people kept asking me where I stood, in interviews and letters to the network, and I thought I ought to make it clear that yes, I was a Christian."

It wasn't the first time Cash had talked about such things on air. He had discussed his trip to the Holy Land in at least one segment on the show. But this time he wasn't talking about his vacation—he was essentially making a stand. "When I actually came out and said the words 'I am a Christian' on TV, that was the context: introducing a gospel song," he continues. A producer decided to tell Cash his opinion on the matter, that he shouldn't be discussing the matters of faith on his show. "I didn't like *that,*" he adds. He then proceeded to tell the executive that perhaps he was producing the wrong man, because this was a part of who Cash was. He didn't intend to use the show as a soapbox, but he wasn't about to back down based on one man's opinion. "If you don't like it, you can edit it," he said. They didn't.

On April 19, 1969, Bob Churovia, a columnist for the *Beaver County Times,* wrote about Cash's emotional Holy Land recollections on the television show *Kraft Music Hall,* which carried the subtitle "Johnny Cash . . . On the Road." "Millions of television viewers Wednesday watched and listened as the firm, smooth voice of the western guitarist retold the story of miracles Jesus had performed," Churovia wrote. "Millions were at peace while Johnny Cash expressed himself."

Nonetheless, following the incident, the writing was on the wall for *The Johnny Cash Show.* But Cash remained steadfast, continuing to include gospel songs in the show, and during the final season, when each episode carried a theme, he put together a gospel-themed edition entitled "Make a Joyful Noise." Broadcast on February 24, 1971, it boasted appearances by Mahalia Jackson, the returning Staple Singers, the Edwin Hawkins Singers, the Blackwood Brothers, the Oak Ridge Boys (at the time a Southern gospel quintet), and Stuart Hamblen.

Grand Ole Gospel Time

On February 11, 1972, a new show premiered live after *Friday Night Opry*: *Grand Ole Gospel Time.* The host of the show was Cash's pastor at Evangel Temple, Jimmie Snow, the son of Cash's boyhood musical hero, Hank Snow (and named after their mutual musical hero, Jimmie Rodgers). To help build the audience, attendees of the *Friday Night Opry* were encouraged to stay on for the service. The show was free, so anyone who wanted to could attend.

Johnny and June signed up to appear on the first show along with the twenty-eight-person Evangel Temple Choir and a seven-piece band. Other guests scheduled to appear over the next few weeks included Pat Boone, Connie Smith, and Wilma Lee & Stoney Cooper, Snow's mother- and father-in-law (he was married at the time to Carolee Cooper, who went on to serve as part of the *Grand Ole Opry*'s house vocal group with the Carolee Singers).

"I'm glad to be with you tonight," Cash told the crowd. "I particularly appreciate the opportunity of being on *Grand Ole Gospel Time* for our second time since it started ten weeks ago. We're happy to be able to sing you some gospel songs. It's not something we just started doing recently. Actually, the first thing we recorded seventeen years ago was a gospel-type song, and we've always done gospel songs on our shows. It's just that in the past year we've begun to feel it the way we should have been feeling it all along."

After ten weeks' worth of shows—two of which featured appearances by Cash—Opry manager Bud Wendell announced that the response to *Grand Ole Gospel Time* had been so good that they planned to move the program to the new Opry building once it opened.

At the time, the *Grand Ole Opry* was taking place in its home of thirty-one years, the Ryman Auditorium, in downtown Nashville. Back then, Nashville wasn't the tourist attraction it would become in the 1990s. The seedy clubs and attractions of downtown encouraged the *Opry* management to plan to move to a new state-of-the-art facility at Opryland USA. That move took place on March 16, 1974, with the final shows of the Ryman run taped on March 15. As had been the case for the past two years, *Grand Ole Gospel Time* followed the *Opry*. For the finale, Reverend Jimmie Snow was joined by his father, Hank, Carl Perkins, Johnny Cash, and June Carter to sing "Will the Circle Be Unbroken"—the last song sung on the Ryman stage until 1992. The show continued to be a success, remaining on the air for twenty-three more years and a total of 1,184 episodes.

The Billy Graham Crusades and Explo '72

Two months after the last episode of *The Johnny Cash Show* aired, Cash, with a year-old son at home and now completely clean for the first time in over ten years, replayed the scene that opens this chapter in his head. This time, it was in a small Pentecostal church near his home in Hendersonville that he rededicated his life to God. He then made the mistake countless other celebrities have made, before and since (including Bob Dylan). "I don't have a career anymore," he declared. "What I have now is a ministry."

While the sentiment might have been admirable, cooler heads prevailed—the coolest among them belonging to the Reverend Billy Graham. Graham had been in ministry since 1943, and he knew what that phrase really meant—one thing being intense public scrutiny. Cash and Graham had met in 1970, and now Graham told Cash that instead of giving up his career, he should find ways to serve God with the talents and platform he had.

In keeping with that, Graham invited Cash to appear at a Crusade in Knoxville, Tennessee, so Cash packed up the whole roadshow and made an appearance. "Billy Graham and Johnny Cash were a great combination," Marshall Grant later wrote. "They were so compatible in so many ways. Both had tremendous charisma, and when they were onstage together, it was an event."

One of the most important events Cash played with Graham was in Dallas, Texas, in 1972. Billed as Explo '72, this was a production of Campus Crusade for Christ International, a college-oriented youth-evangelism organization led by Bill Bright. The event was held from June 13th through 17th and drew "delegates" from every state to learn about better ways to spread God's word on their campus. The culmination of Explo was a huge concert held at the Cotton Bowl in downtown Dallas. The Jesus Music Festival was billed as "the Christian Woodstock," and it was expected they would draw 100,000 fans. Contemporary

Christian music (CCM) was in its infancy back then, and the bill was made up of acts that would form the foundation of the Jesus music movement: Larry Norman, Andrea Crouch, the Second Chapter of Acts, Love Song, Randy Matthews, and Barry McGuire, who had had a #1 pop hit in 1965 with "Eve of Destruction."

Topping the bill was Johnny Cash and his roadshow. Cash also brought along Kris Kristofferson—still reeling from the positive religious experience he had had at Cash's church—and Rita Coolidge. The promoter's estimates weren't far off, with 70,462 teens and young adults attending the event, which was recorded for an album release and television special. It was even covered by *Life* magazine in a full-color six-page photo spread. "This is the most important place I've ever performed," Cash told the crowd. "It's my biggest thrill. I hope you won't lose your enthusiasm when you get back home, but carry it throughout your life."

The Gospel Road (Columbia Records, 1973)

The germ of an idea for a movie about the life of Christ was planted in Johnny and June's first trip to the Holy Land in 1966. One morning, June came to Johnny and said she had dreamed of him standing on a mountaintop in Israel, with a Bible or some other book in his hands, talking to millions of people. "That scared me a little," Cash writes, in *Man in Black*, "because I wasn't physically and spiritually able for such a role."

Indeed, he was still a year away from his dark night of the soul, and his platform hadn't been lifted high enough to reach the millions with the message that June envisioned. Instead, he decided she must have been dreaming about a new record. He hadn't made a gospel album since 1962, so they began to plan for a new one. But when they passed a mountain in Galilee, June pointed it out as the one in her dream. "Well, it must be something else besides a record," Cash said.

The idea grew until Cash decided to write a screenplay for the film. (In the meantime, they did return, in 1968, to make an album, *The Holy Land.*) Cash called in writer Larry Murray, who had helped write the "Ride This Train" segments for *The Johnny Cash Show*, to go over the outline he had created. By November 1971, he was ready to go to Israel to begin shooting the movie.

As he writes in *Man in Black*, the movie was "designed to be entertaining, carrying the identification mark of my music, but a movie that is an expression of our faith: our witness and testimony and overshadowing power in it to be the words of Jesus." Or, as he put it more succinctly to an AP reporter in 1971, "I've never seen a movie about Jesus that I really liked, so I thought I'd make one myself."

The initial idea was to shoot the film in a documentary style, using only shots of "Jesus'" hands and feet, with Cash providing the narration. But as the script grew, so did the production. Robert Elfstrom, who had produced a Cash documentary called *Johnny Cash: The Man, His World, His Music* in 1968, was brought in as director.

The goal was to show Christ as a real person, or as Cash put it, "the man, as a real man, very human, and as a divinity—very divine." The ultimate goal of the movie, according to Cash, was "that you worship God, and that you love your neighbor."

Eventually, the production grew beyond the "hands and feet" idea to bringing in a cast to play the parts of Jesus and other figures from the Bible stories. Director Elfstrom became Jesus, while June played the part of Mary Magdalene. Others in Cash's circle—including Larry Lee, who helped run the House of Cash, sister Reba Hancock, Reverend Jimmie Snow, and manager Saul Holiff—also had roles in the film.

Cash served as narrator, providing the voices of the characters that don't speak. The soundtrack that was subsequently released is quite literally the soundtrack to the film—all of the music, the voices, and Cash's narration. The majority of the songs were written by Cash and serve to illustrate the story or further the narrative. There were also songs by John Denver, Joe South, Kris Kristofferson, and Christopher Wren, a journalist who had recently completed a biography on Cash.

Kristofferson is also heard on the soundtrack, along with his wife Rita Coolidge, on a song by a young writer June had discovered, Larry Gatlin. Gatlin's song "Help Me" (listed simply as "Help" on the album) is performed by the trio in the film. It is a powerful song of surrender, and one that Cash would return to during the last recording sessions of his life, as eventually included on *American V: A Hundred Highways.* (Kristofferson was also so taken with the song when he heard Gatlin perform it at Evangel Temple that he included it on his 1972 album *Jesus Was a Capricorn.* The song also inspired his own "Why Me, Lord?" which became the biggest seller of his career and a huge award winner.)

In his autobiography, *Just as I Am,* Billy Graham states that the Holiday Inn chain had "expressed interest in sponsoring it as a TV special, but the corporation wanted artistic as well as financial control. The Cashes said no; they wanted to tell the story their way. That meant they had to finance it themselves."

Cash spent $500,000 of his own money on the film and shot it in Israel in somewhere between five weeks and two months (depending on the source). For Cash, the price was worth it, as it meant he was able to tell the story as he saw fit. "I've made a lot of big money, and I think God let that happen for a purpose," he told Charles Paul Conn. "It's God's money anyway—he's just letting me use it to make a film about Jesus."

The film premiered in various locations to enthusiastic crowds of fans and believers. At the Nashville premiere, Cash told Harry Haun of *Country Music*:

> This film is my life's work. It's the reason I'm on this earth. . . . It was an unbelievable undertaking now that I sit down and think about it. Anybody in his right mind would have said it would be impossible to film the story of Jesus in a month's time. But there we were, waking up at 3:30 every morning, getting to location before sun-up, shooting straight through until ten or eleven at night. That went on for a month. Thank

goodness it rained a day and a half or we would have worked ourselves into a frenzy.

"We didn't set out to stimulate the intellect," director Elfstrom told Haun. "Everyone knows the story of Christ and draws their own conclusions. What we wanted to do was stimulate the soul, and I think Johnny can do that better than any performer around."

Cash's vision of the Christ story is richly told—particularly for the time, and considering he had no real background or history in filmmaking, other than his few starring roles. To his credit, the film doesn't come off as a vanity piece but a serious attempt to create something to spread the message that he held so dear. To drive that message home, Cash utilizes the crucifixion scene, where the image of Christ on the cross moves from Golgotha to a modern city, and then to another, symbolizing the universal nature of the message.

A few months after its release, Bill Littleton reviewed the album for *Country Music.* "I can easily understand why John is proud of this project," he wrote. "With the soundtrack of his movie *The Gospel Road,* he has created a piece of religious art in the truest tradition of Michelangelo and the countless others who have felt a binding compulsion to proclaim the glories of God through their creative endeavors."

The following month, the magazine published a letter from a fan that summed up the success of Cash's mission. "*The Gospel Road* hasn't come to our area yet," the fan explained, "but we do have the soundtrack. John does a very beautiful and effective job of breathing new life and meaning into the words and life of Jesus. If there is anyone who can make a person think about living by those words, it's him. After all, it doesn't seem logical that a big, long-legged guitar picker could know all that much about God. He does though, and I'm thankful that he has been blessed with his unique gift for expressing it."

Hoping to get the film shown in as many places as possible, Cash sold the distribution rights to 20th Century Fox. Fox, though, had trouble marketing it. "The film is specialized," Hal Sherman, the company's coordinator of national promotions, told George Vecsey for a 1973 *New York Times* article. "It's good quality, but it has a very strong fundamentalist opinion. In the South, people take the Bible more literally than in New York, Chicago, or Los Angeles. Theater owners resist this kind of picture because traditionally people go to church on Sunday and they want entertainment from the movies. We'll schedule it where we get requests."

Disappointed, Cash resigned himself to the fact that he had still fulfilled most of his dream. Graham called one day and asked how the film was doing, and after hearing Cash's disappointment, he said he'd just buy the film back and have his companies, BGEA and World Wide Pictures, distribute it.

"The studio wanted to get its money back, of course, but eventually they came down," Graham writes. "As I recall, they sold it to us for about $250,000. Since then, it has been one of the best evangelistic film tools that the BGEA has had, with hundreds of prints in circulation. Missionaries are using it in video vans in Africa, India and elsewhere."

The double-disc soundtrack album spent fourteen weeks on the Country chart, peaking at #12.

Johnny Cash Sings Precious Memories (Columbia Records, 1975)

Cash followed *The Gospel Road* with a less ambitious—but no less heartfelt—album of strictly gospel hymns. This album, recorded on June 17 and 18, 1974, utilized the backing of the Bill Walker Orchestra, which had accompanied Cash on his TV show and subsequent television specials.

Cash dedicated the album to his brother Jack, noting that some of the same songs had been sung at his funeral. In the liner notes, David Allen Coe takes the opportunity to thank Cash for always being a strong example of a good Christian.

Johnny Cash Sings Precious Memories was nominated for a Grammy for Best Gospel Performance in 1976, for which it competed against Connie Smith, the Happy Goodman Family, his old friends the Statler Brothers, and the eventual winners, the Imperials.

A Believer Sings the Truth (Cachet/Columbia Records, 1979)

Throughout 1977–78, Cash's albums were charting lower and lower, and as he had in the past, he began to retreat to the things that comforted him. In part, this meant a slow but increasing return to his old drug habit, but he also found two more creative outlets: gospel music and Jack Clement. The idea for another gospel album had been percolating for a bit, and Cash had enlisted son-in-law Jack Routh to help out.

> We were doing the *Silver* album at the same time, so it was pretty nuts there for about a year, year and a half, all the time before recording, getting the songs together and arranging them. John and I spent a lot of time going through songs at the cabin—he didn't have a studio there then, just a little cabin, but later in life he did build a studio at the cabin. John also had a place down in Florida, New Port Richey, about a half a mile in from the Gulf, on the river, that used to be Mother Maybelle and Pop Carter's. John and I used to go down there a lot and fish and work on this project.

On January 15, 1979, Cash went into Columbia Studios in Nashville with Routh and Clement to begin work on the new gospel project, which would be based on old favorites and new songs Cash had written. "The whole project was really, really important to him," Routh says, "because he grew up with those songs and then throughout his musical career, the majority of those songs he'd heard, and several new ones too."

To kick things off, Cash started with songs he had sung all his life, and that had first introduced "the gift" to his mother, including "Gospel Boogie (a Wonderful Time up There)." Others included "That's Enough," a song he had originally recorded in 1958 for his Columbia debut, "Children Go Where I Send Thee," a staple of the Johnny Cash Roadshow since the 1960s, and the traditional "Oh Come Angel Band."

Marshall Grant made an appearance—as he had over the years—on a new recording of "I Was There When It Happened." The recording came at a time when their relationship was being strained to its limits by Cash's relapse into drug use, and it would be the last time the two sang the song together.

Cash also drew four songs from the catalogue of Sister Rosetta Tharpe, turning in spirited versions of "Strange Things Happening Every Day," "Don't Take Everybody to Be Your Friend," "This Train Is Bound for Glory," and "Didn't It Rain."

"He's Alive" is a vivid story song of the resurrection of Christ from the perspective of the disciple Peter. It was written by Don Francisco, whose version of it spent fourteen weeks at #1 on the newly established CCM charts in 1978. In 1980, the song won him two Dove awards, for Song of the Year and Songwriter of the Year. Dolly Parton would later reach #39 on the Country chart with the song in 1990.

"I'm Just an Old Chunk of Coal" came from outlaw songwriter Billy Joe Shaver, and would become a staple of Cash's live shows. In 1981, John Anderson took the song to #4, making it his highest-charting single at the time.

Eight songs came from Cash, including a few that he had previously attempted. He had recorded "Over the Next Hill (We'll Be Home)" in 1974, but not released it, while a live version of "I'm Gonna Try to Be That Way" was released in 1970 as the flip side to "Sunday Morning Coming Down." "What on Earth Will You Do (for Heaven's Sake)" was included on 1974's *Ragged Old Flag*, and Cash and Waylon Jennings had recorded a version of "Greatest Cowboy of Them All" together in 1978. The version on *A Believer* instead features Routh.

Cash's Cajun friend Jo-El Sonnier co-wrote two songs on the album, one of them being "I've Got Jesus in My Soul," a collaboration with Tom Ross. The second was "Lay Me Down in Dixie" with Judy Ball. Of all the songs on the album, this one had the least to do with gospel music, but it would nevertheless be the one Peter Stampfel singled out as a "remarkably beautiful" highlight of the record in his *Country Music* review. "This song pays to the South the love and respect the other songs here pay to heaven," he wrote. "There are religious references here, but the emphasis is on Dixie. The result is a piece of heaven brought to earth. Cindy Cash adds a harmony of heartbreakingly gentle beauty."

"Wings of the Morning" was one of the new songs Cash recorded for the album. It served as the only single, but failed to chart. "I'm a New Born Man" was credited to Cash and his nine-year-old son John, with daughter Rosanne joining him on "When He Comes." Her husband at the time, Rodney Crowell, joins Cash for "You'll Get Yours and I'll Get Mine."

Cash had entered the studio with Brian Ahern on February 12th to begin work on *Silver*, the album Columbia wanted to release to commemorate his twenty-fifth anniversary in the music business. By now, he had recorded the bulk of the gospel tracks, but he and his crew continued to spend a lot of time fixing, overdubbing, and rerecording parts of them, as Jack Routh recalls:

> He was really into making it really good and we spent a lot of time . . . . We'd be in the studio three or four days at a time. We'd do day sessions on *Silver* and then night sessions on the gospel—they were overlapping. That's probably when it got the most intense, working on both of those projects at the same time. He was real, real proud of that album, and so were Cowboy and I. We just had a great time. I was talking to Cowboy [one time], and we said, "Well, we didn't make much money off of it, but we sure had a good time hanging out."

Even with the amount of work going into both albums, it is obvious from the recordings released as *A Believer Sings the Truth* that Cash was serious in his desire both to put his all into this gospel album and to have a lot of fun doing it. But not everyone was into the idea of having fun, particularly Columbia Records, which was ready for *Silver* but didn't want anything to do with *A Believer*.

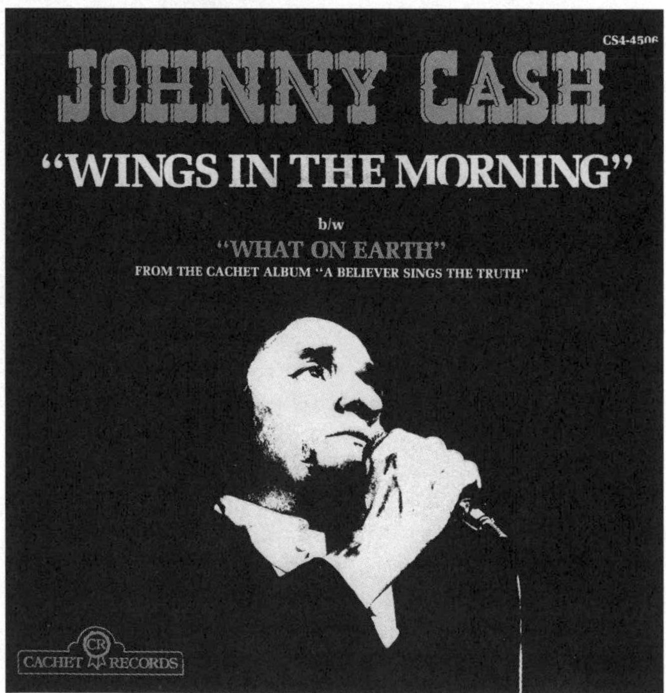

"Wings in the Morning," the lead single from Cash's Cachet Records debut, failed to chart, and the album failed to gain traction with fans. *Private collection*

Lou Robin, Cash's manager, asked the label for permission to place the album elsewhere, and Columbia granted it.

Ed LaBuick was a Canadian who had made a name for himself in the record business by creating Tee Vee Records. The label assembled hits by musicians like Charley Pride, Loretta Lynn, and Conway Twitty and sold them on television, and within a couple of years had become the primary competitor to K-Tel, another mail-order repackaging label. By the late 1970s, LaBuick had started Cachet Records with the intention to release original records, the first of which was by Greek vocalist Nana Mouskouri. The next was an Ernest Tubb collection that included duets with, among others, Merle Haggard, Willie Nelson, and Johnny Cash.

LaBuick had met Cash during his visits to Nashville, and after becoming the producer of the country-music variety show *Country Music Celebration.*

> I had always followed his career. Lou Robin told me about [the record] and I went to Nashville when they were recording it and rather enjoyed what he was doing. He put a lot of time and effort into that album and I was quite enthused. I thought the album would do extremely well.
>
> The reason Johnny went with me on the album was he knew the success I had had with Charley Pride and with Loretta Lynn and Conway Twitty. What I was trying to do with him was to break him as an artist, again, rather than just a TV album, so I serviced radio nationally, hired some people to try to make it happen, but it didn't happen.

They soon made a deal for Cachet Records to release the double album. The album had a faux-leather look, with a gold-embossed image of Cash singing. A TV commercial was produced and aired in the US and Canada, while a single, with a picture sleeve, was released to radio. With each record sent to radio, there was also an offer for the station to broadcast (for free) a two-hour radio special, *The Johnny Cash Radio Special: A Believer Sings the Truth.*

"I think it was one of the finest albums he did, but just didn't go anywhere," LaBuick says. "It wasn't for lack of trying. I tried, and I spent a lot of money on it. But that's the business. I was involved with Colonel Parker and Elvis; I was involved with a lot of the big boys. I thought I had the magic touch and could make it happen, but it didn't."

Part of the problem LaBuick faced—as 20th Century Fox and Columbia had found before him—was that marketing a decidedly Christian product to the fans wasn't always a sure thing. "The Christian market just did not grab on to it, and the mass market didn't," he says, "so it was one of those situations that we tried, but it didn't work. My opinion of Johnny—I think his Christian side, I think the country consumer took it serious, but they [also] didn't. In other words, they really didn't buy into him on the whole Christian thing that he was. They wanted this Johnny Cash the bad boy, so therefore, it didn't happen. That album was more Christian than it was country."

It had also so happened that a year before signing Cash, LaBuick had sold his label to a much larger company, Global Television. He soon found that he was having more financial problems with Global than he had beforehand, and a year after Cash's record was released, he quit the company.

Despite all of this, the album did spend six weeks on the Country chart, peaking at #43, which was within the same range as *Silver*, released around the same time. But with LaBuick no longer around, Cachet lost interest in the project. Cash and Robin eventually took back the rights for the album, and in 1982 talked Columbia into rereleasing it. Columbia agreed to issue a ten-song, single-record version on its new Christian music subsidiary, Priority Records. As luck, or fate, would have it, Priority then closed its doors, after only two years of operation, in July 1983.

Sings with the B. C. Goodpasture Christian School (1980)

If you've ever wondered what Johnny Cash would sound like backed by a high-school band, this is your chance. In early 1979, he was approached to help with an album that was being assembled to benefit the school John Carter attended, B. C. Goodpasture Christian School, and agreed to lend his voice to the project. The resulting album was made up primarily of hymns, with the school's band and choir providing the music, over which Cash overdubbed his vocals. Included among the hymns were "An American Trilogy," "Daddy Sang Bass" (listed as "Will the Circle Be Unbroken/Daddy Sang Bass"), and Ray Stevens' "Everything Is Beautiful." The album was only sold through the school and the House of Cash, and as such is difficult to find these days.

I Believe (Arrival, 1984)

The single-record version of *A Believer Sings the Truth* contained only half of the songs from the two-disc version, so Cash struck a deal with Arrival Records to salvage the other half. K-Tel had formed Arrival around 1982–83 to market products to the burgeoning Christian music market. For this release, the remaining ten songs from *Believer* are joined by four previously unissued songs recorded at the same sessions: "I'll Have a New Life," written by Luther G. Presley (writer of "When the Saints Go Marching In"), "Didn't It Rain" (the H. T. Burleigh song often performed by Sister Rosetta Tharpe), Bill Gaither's "He Touched Me," and A. P. Carter's "Wayworn Traveler."

Believe in Him (Word Records, 1986)

While Cash was in the studio with Jack Clement in 1982, working on what would become *The Adventures of Johnny Cash*, he was also working on a gospel album produced by his then-sideman and son-in-law Marty Stuart. Stuart stripped down the musical backdrop to the basic sound of the Tennessee Three and then built on it sparsely with occasional mandolin, fiddle, Dobro, piano, and steel guitar.

The title track was written by another guitar-picking son-in-law, Jimmy Tittle, and set the tone for the album nicely. "Another Wide River to Cross" was written by Cash, and is in the Southern gospel tradition, gaining in that feeling with the accompaniment of vocal quartet the Cathedrals. "God Ain't No Stained Glass Window," by singer/songwriter Mark Germino, turns up the schmaltz a bit, but Cash's conviction keeps it from going over the top. The Cathedrals return for an excellent version of Ray Pennington's "Over There," with Cash sounding right at home as he takes it straight to church. To bring the album to its halfway point, Jessi Colter joins Cash for a duet on the hymn "Old Rugged Cross."

Drawing on a sentiment close to the heart of many religious parents, Cash wrote "My Children Walk in Truth," a song he sings here as a prayer. Here, Stuart strips the instruments down to the core, before bringing the Cathedrals back in for Bill Monroe's song to the backsliders, "You're Driftin' Away." Cash and crew then take it back to the Sun days to revisit "Belshazzar," though this version is somewhat marred by some strangely placed electric guitar and piano. Cash, again backed by the Cathedrals, then brings out a traditional-sounding "Half Mile a Day," advising the listener to just keep on keeping on. The album ends with the last of the Cash-penned tunes, the swinging "One of These Days I'm Gonna Sit Down and Talk to Paul."

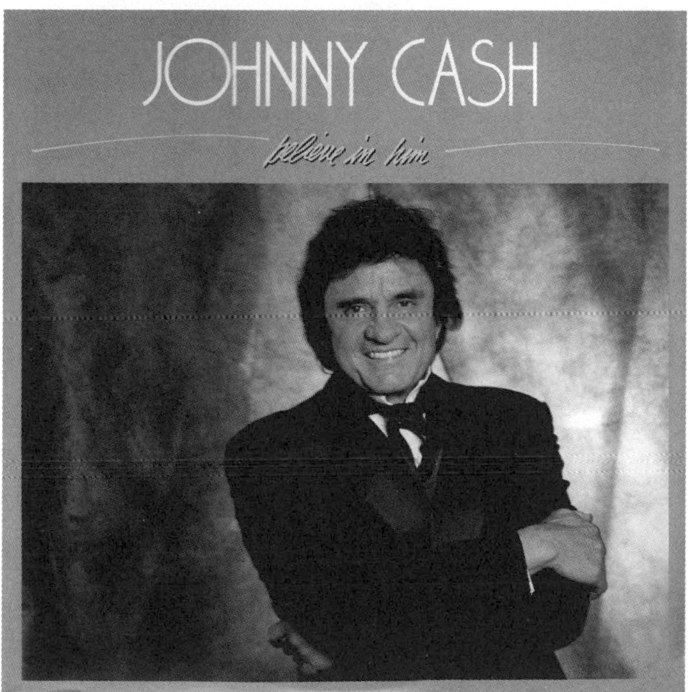

Believe in Him was the second gospel album that Columbia didn't want, so Cash took it to the Christian label Word. Produced by Marty Stuart, the album captured some of Cash's best performances of the time.
Author's collection

The album was finally released in 1986, just as Cash was being released from his Columbia contract. In fact, in press articles announcing his release from Columbia, Lou Robin pointed out that Cash had a project coming out on the Christian record label. It was released to little fanfare, which is a shame, because it is, with the few minor blemishes, one of his best. Cash was clearly inspired by the addition of the Cathedrals, and Stuart knew exactly how to present him.

Around the same time, Cash also released his first novel, based on the life of the Apostle Paul. *Man in White* was a labor of love that took him ten years to complete.

Return to the Promised Land (Renaissance Records, 1992)

Between the end of recording for *Highwayman 2* and the start of work of *Boom-Chicka-Boom,* Cash went into the studio on March 16, 1989, to record an audio version of the New Testament. Through the end of his time with Mercury Records, gospel music was never far from his thoughts.

In 1991, the twentieth anniversary of *The Gospel Road* was approaching, and Cash began to think about ways to commemorate it and work on a new project. He approached the Nashville Network with the idea of either a Christmas or an Easter special. Assuming this would mean Cash being joined onstage

Cash put out "Man in White," a song which was self-released by Cash on the label named after his father-in-law. The release was planned to coincide with the publishing of *Man in White,* Cash's novelization of the life of the Apostle Paul. *Private collection*

by up-and-comers like Garth Brooks, the Network agreed. But special guests weren't what Cash had in mind. Instead, he, June, and their son John went to Israel and hired a local production company to follow them around various sites of interest.

The result was something more akin to *The Holy Land* than *The Gospel Road*, with the three of them reminiscing and talking about the sites they were seeing. When they returned the tapes to the Nashville Network, however, they found that the Israeli production company hadn't been as good as they had hoped, and the footage was not up to the network's broadcast standards. This presented Cash with a small problem. In planning to do the special, Lou Robin had negotiated airfare and boarding in exchange for promotional consideration, and without the special, they'd be on the hook for the costs.

Cash turned to longtime family friend and now personal assistant Hugh Waddell, who had produced a local television show where he interviewed artists like B. B. King and James Brown. Cash asked Waddell to look over the tapes and see if anything could be salvaged. "At the time, John was going to do the Johnny Cash Theater in Branson," he recalls. "So I took the tapes to Branson and took a little VHS player and a little portable TV and stayed up all night for a couple of weeks in Branson just looking through it."

After reshooting some of the close-ups, and having Johnny or June rerecord the audio, Waddell was able to salvage enough footage to create an hour-long show that was then released by Billy Graham's World Wide Pictures on VHS in 1993. It has yet to be rereleased in any other format.

In 2000, Renaissance Records, a small label out of Brentwood, Tennessee, set up a deal to release the audio. The resulting CD consisted of the twelve songs on the video, as well as the narration between them. The songs included a few that were new to Cash, like "When I Look" and "Let Me Help You Carry the Weight." Others songs drew from his past recordings, ranging from *Hymns from the Heart* to *A Believer Sings the Truth*. To round out the CD, four demo recordings were added: "Hello out There," "Like a Soldier Getting Over the War," "Poor Valley Girl" (a tribute to June), and "Soldier Boy." "Like a Soldier" had also been recorded for *American Recordings*, but this take includes a full band in the vein of Cash's Mercury recordings.

Only 1,000 copies of the CD were pressed, with the intention that they would go to advance reviewers, but the company filed for bankruptcy before that could happen. Its inventory was sold off in bankruptcy court and ended up in truck stops and budget stores across the country. Because of this, the album is now extremely hard to find, and generally sells for $75–$200.

The album also includes a hidden track featuring Cash's mother, Carrie, which grew out of the idea of trying to come up with a birthday present for him, as Waddell recalls.

> What do you get John Cash that he can't get for himself or he doesn't already own or have? He was always talking about, on the road, how he missed his mother, and he'd always call her. . . . I thought, I'm going to

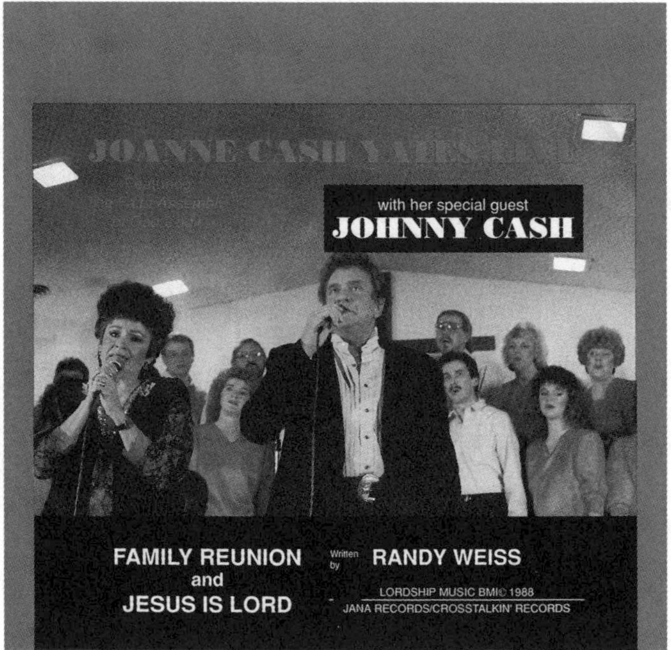

Joanne Cash Yates is Cash's little sister and a gospel singer in her own right. In 1988, Cash recorded this single with her live.

Private collection

give him something that he can take with him and have his mother anywhere he goes. So I actually spent two hours and recorded her doing a bunch of songs, and telling a bunch of stories, knowing that they were for John, knowing that he would be the only one to hear it. I went through and took some of the best of that and cut it, and made like a fifteen-minute bonus track, just as something obscure. Of course, John was still alive and he loved it. I thought it was really cool, because John's mother had already passed away [in the interim] and it was a way to pay homage to her.

My Mother's Hymn Book (American, 2004)

Originally included in the *Unearthed* boxed set, this album is made up entirely of songs taken from the hymnal that Cash's mother used to sing from. "The songs in that old book mean more to me than I can tell you," Cash told Sylvie Simmons, who wrote the liner notes, "so I'll just sing 'em, me and my guitar, simple, no adornment, knowing that God loves music and that music brings hope for a better tomorrow. You asked me to pick my favorite album I've ever made, and this is it, *My Mother's Hymn Book*."

Cash chose fifteen songs from the hymnal, all classic gospel gems like "Do Lord," "I Shall Not Be Moved," and "When the Roll Is Called Up Yonder." Recorded in October 1993, at the same time as he was working on *American Recordings*, Cash sounds strong and convicted as he goes through the songs. When the boxed set was released, many reviews highlighted the disc. For Steve Morse of the *Boston Globe*, "This may be the best of the bunch, given the accumulating emotion it represents." For Chet Flippo, "It's the true heart and soul of this work."

The album was released as a stand-alone CD in April 2004, entering the Country chart at #28, the *Billboard* 200 at #194, and the Top Christian Albums chart at #11—the first time Cash had hit that chart. It peaked at #27 on the Country chart and #9 on the Top Christian Albums listing.

Selected Bibliography

Books

Cash, Johnny, with Patrick Carr. *Cash: The Autobiography.* New York: HarperCollins, 2003.

Cash, Johnny. *Man in Black.* Grand Rapids, Michigan: Zondervan, 1975.

Cash, John Carter. *Anchored in Love: An Intimate Portrait of June Carter Cash.* Nashville, Tennessee: Thomas Nelson, 2007.

Cash, John Carter. *House of Cash: The Legacies of My Father, Johnny Cash.* San Rafael, California: Insight Editions, 2012.

Cash, June Carter. *Among My Klediments.* Grand Rapids, Michigan: Zondervan, 1979.

Cash, June Carter. *From the Heart.* New York: Prentice Hall Trade, 1987.

Cash, Vivian, with Ann Sharpsteen. *I Walked the Line: My Life with Johnny.* New York: Simon and Schuster, 2007.

Conn, Charles Paul. *The New Johnny Cash.* Grand Rapids, Michigan: Fleming H. Revell Co., 1973.

Cusic, Don. *Johnny Cash: The Songs.* New York: Da Capo Press, 2004.

D'Ambrosio, Antonino. *A Heartbeat and a Guitar: Johnny Cash and the Making of Bitter Tears.* New York: Nation Books, 2009.

Escott, Colin, with Martin Hawkins. *Good Rockin' Tonight: Sun Records and the Birth of Rock 'N' Roll.* New York: St. Martin's Press, 1991.

Grant, Marshall, with Chris Zar. *I Was There When It Happened: My Life with Johnny Cash.* Nashville, Tennessee: Cumberland House Publishing, 2006.

Hilburn, Robert. *Johnny Cash: The Life.* Boston, Massachusetts: Little & Brown Company, 2013.

Lewry, Peter. *Johnny Cash: I've Been Everywhere.* London, England: Self Published, 2010.

Malone, Bill C. *Country Music, USA* (Second Revised Edition). Austin, Texas: University of Texas Press, 2002.

Millard, Bob. *Country Music: 75 Years of America's Favorite Music.* New York: Da Capo Press, 1999.

Miller, Bill. *Cash: An American Man.* New York: Simon and Schuster, 2004.

Perkins, Carl, and David McGee. *Go, Cat, Go: The Life and Times of Carl Perkins, the King of Rockabilly.* New York: Hyperion, 1996.

Prial, Dunstan. *The Producer: John Hammond and the Soul of American Music.* New York: Farrar, Straus, and Giroux, 2006.

Rolling Stone Magazine. *Cash.* New York: Crown Archetype, 2004.

Smith, John L. *Another Song to Sing: The Recorded Repertoire of Johnny Cash.* Lanham, Maryland: Scarecrow Press, 1999.

Smith, John L. *The Johnny Cash Discography.* Westport, Connecticut: Greenwood Press, 1985.

Smith, John L. *The Johnny Cash Discography, 1984-1993.* Westport, Connecticut: Greenwood Press, 1985.

Smith, John L. *The Johnny Cash Record Catalog.* Westport, Connecticut: Greenwood Publishing Group, 1994.

Streissguth, Michael. *Johnny Cash at Folsom Prison: The Making of a Masterpiece.* New York: Da Capo Press, 2004.

Streissguth, Michael. *Johnny Cash: The Biography.* New York: Da Capo Press, 2006.

Streissguth, Michael, ed. *Ring of Fire: The Johnny Cash Reader.* New York: Da Capo Press, 2003.

Thomson, Graeme. *The Resurrection of Johnny Cash: Hurt, Redemption, and American Recordings.* London, England: Jawbone Press, 2011.

Tost, Tony. *Johnny Cash's American Recordings* (33⅓ Series). New York: Continuum, 2011.

Turner, Steve. *The Man Called Cash: The Life, Love, and Faith of an American Legend.* Nashville, Tennessee: W. Publishing Group, 2004.

Urbanski, Dave. *The Man Comes Around: The Spiritual Journey of Johnny Cash.* Lake Mary, Florida: Relevant Media Group, 2003.

Wren, Christopher S. *Winners Got Scars Too: The Life of Johnny Cash.* New York: Dial Press, 1971.

Zwonitzer, Mark, with Charles Hirshberg. *Will You Miss Me When I'm Gone: The Carter Family and Their Legacy in American Music.* New York: Simon and Schuster, 2002.

Additional Sources

For all things Johnny Cash related, I would highly recommend *Man in Black: The Johnny Cash Fanzine.* It can be found at www.johnnycashfanzine.com.

The official Johnny Cash website has all of the up-to-date news on Cash-related events and merchandise, as well as information on the Cashes' history and recordings. www.johnnycash.com.

Also be sure to visit www.johnnycashmuseum.com for more information on the highly rated Johnny Cash Museum.

Billboard
Country Music
Country Song Roundup
Mojo
Musician
Performing Songwriter
Rolling Stone
Uncut

Index